ENGLISH BATTLES
AND
SIEGES

IN THE PENINSULA

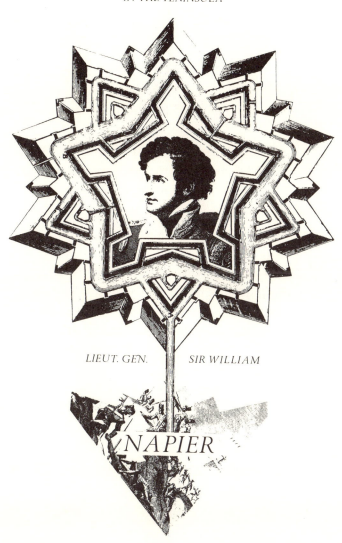

LIEUT. GEN. SIR WILLIAM

NAPIER

This edition published by
R.J. LEACH & Co.
38 Inglemere Road
Forest Hill
London
SE23 2BE

R.J. LEACH & Co. © 1990

First published by John Murray
Albermarle Street
in 1855.

ISBN 1-873050-00-3

Printed by Harlequin Press
Oban, Argyll. 0631 65299

CONTENTS

BOOK I.

BOOK II.

BOOK III.

BOOK IV.

BOOK V.

CONTENTS.

BOOK VI.

BOOK VII

BOOK VIII

BOOK IX

BOOK X

BOOK XI

CONTENTS.

BOOK XII.

Page

BOOK XIII.

BOOK XIV

BOOK XV

BOOK XVI

NOTICE

IN this publication, the combats of Rioriça, Vimiero and Coruna, and the character of Sir John Moore, have been entirely recomposed. The other battles and seiges are, with more or less compression of details, transcripts from the History of the Peninsula War. Thus arranged they will perhaps most effectually exhibit the constant energy of the British soldier, and draw attention in their neighbourhoods to the veterans who still survive. Few of those brave men have more than scanty provision, many have none; and nearly all, oppressed with wounds, disease and poverty, sure attendants on an old soldier's services, feel life a burthen, so heavy as to make them envy the lot of comrades who threw it off early on the field of battle.

For the authenticity of the events the reader has this guarantee. The author was either an eye-witness of what he relates, or acquired his knowledge from those that were. Persons of no mean authority. Commanders-in-chief, generals, and other officers on both sides; private official correspondence of the English envoys; military journals and reports of the French leaders; the correspondence of the intrusive King Joseph, and his ministers, and the private military notes and instructions of the Emperor Napoleon, have all contributed to establish the truth of the facts and motives of action.

For the great Captain who led the British troops so

NOTICE.

triumphantly, this record gives no measure of ability. To win victories was the least of his labours. Those who desire to know what an enormous political, financial, and military pressure he sustained, what wiles he circumvented, what opposing skill he baffled, what a powerful enemy he dealt with and overcame, must seek the story in the original History from which this work has been extracted. For the soldiers it is no measure of their fortitude and endurance: it records only their active courage. But what they were, their successors now are—witness the wreck of the Birkenhead, where four hundred men, at the call of their heroic officers,*Captain Wright and Lieutenant Girardot, calmly and without a murmur, accepted death in a horrible form rather than endanger the women and children already saved in the boats. The records of the world furnish no parallel to this self-devotion !

*After the above notice was published the author was informed that *Lieut.Col. Alexander Seton* was the officer in command of the troops on board the Birkenhead, that he called to the men not to swim to the boats, and continued in the active discharge of his duty until the vessel sank. He then perished; but the following extract of a letter from the Secretary at War to
his brother, Mr. D. Seton, dated War Office, 24th May, 1852, bears testimony to the conduct of Lieut.-Col. Seton:—

" The first Official Report, as well as all the accounts which have been given in all private letters, bear a concurring testimony to the noble and self-devoted conduct of Lieut-Col. Seton, who, being the commanding officer on board the Birkenhead, must be considered by all military men to have originated by the authority which he had acquired, and to have stimulated by the example which he set, that display of discipline and self-devotion which the troops, without exception, exhibited on that melancholy occasion.

(Signed)   " Wm. BERESFORD."

BATTLES AND SIEGES

OF THE

PENINSULA

BOOK 1

Combat of Roriça —Battle of Vimiero—Coruna—Battle of Coruna.

IN the year 1808 Sir Arthur Wellesley marched from the Mondego river with twelve thousand three hundred men, and eighteen guns, to attack General Junot who was in military possession of Portugal. The French troops were scattered, but General Laborde had been detached with a division to cover their concentration, and watch the English movements. This led to the first fight between the French and English in the Peninsula.

COMBAT OF RORIÇA.

Fourteen hundred Portuguese, under Colonel Trant, a military agent, joined the British on the march, and the French were felt the 15th of August at Brilos, in front of Obidos, where some men fell in a skirmish. Sir A. Wellesley then entered the Valley of Obidos, in the middle of which Laborde occupied isolated ground of moderate elevation, near the village of Roriça; he had only five thousand men and six guns, little more than one-third of the English numbers, but he had five hundred cavalry, had chosen his position well, and could handle troops with dexterity.

On his right was a lofty mountain ridge, on his left lower but very rough ground, and the valley behind him was closed, not only by the commingling of the hills in a mountainous knot, but by a rocky projection called the Zambugeira or Columbeira heights, which, at less than a mile, stood like a citadel in his rear, and was so covered with copses, wild evergreens and forest trees, and so rugged that only by paths leading up deep clefts and hollows could it be ascended.

The British general marched from the town of Obidos on the 17th with fourteen thousand men and eighteen guns in order of battle. His light, composed of Trant's Portugese, returned the French left; his centre, nine thousand infantry with twelve guns, moved against their front; his left, one division with six guns, having gained the crest of the mountain ridge by a wide movement from Obidos, turned the French right, and was to oppose any counter attack from General Loison, who had been heard of on that side, andmight come up during, the action with a division six thousand strong of all arms. Such an order of battle, with such superior numbers, forbade Laborde to maintain his ground at Roriça, and after a cannonade, during which his skirmishers vigorously disputed the approaches, he, with a nice calculation of time and distance, retreated under the protection of his cavalry to the rocks of Zambugeira, and then turned to fight, still hoping to be joined by Loison.

This masterly movement compelled Sir Arthur Wellesley to show all his forces, and imposed a change in disposition.His left was then reinforced on the mountain, because each passing hour rendered Loison's arrival more likely; Trant was more closely to menace the French heights on the right, and the centre was to break in on the front when the strength of the position should be shaken by the progress of the wings.

In war, however, error is the rule not the exception.Some mistake caused the left to move directly against the French right instead of passing the flank to take them inrear, and as Trant was distant and too feeble to give uneasiness, the centre dashed prematurely against the crags of Zambugeira on a front of less than a mile. The advantage of superior numbers was thus lost, and that of ground was entirely with the enemy. Only four thousand British could be thrust into the fight, and though the remainder were at hand, the foremost combatants had to win their way against an equal force of brave and active troops, defending rocks which vigorous men only could scale unopposed. Very crowded also were the assailing columns in the narrow paths, which only admitted a few men abreast, and hence no positive connection could be maintained between the different attacks, nor could any unity of. power be insured: but the skirmishers soon covered the face of the ascent, and the noise and flashing of their musketry, with the smoke bursting up through the foliage, enabled the English general to mark the progress of the battle and govern his masses: it was soon manifest that the position would be finally forced, but within that flame-shooting, smoking labyrinth, rough work was being done and various turns of fortune had place.

Laborde, unable to hold his ground alone against the great force opposed, sought to gain time for Loison's .junction by clinging tenaciously to the side from whence that general was expected, and gradually drawing off his troops from the left as the battle approached. While thus operating, two English regiments, the 9th and 29th, were by a false movement suddenly thrown into his hands. Forming with the 5th regiment one column of attack;, they were to have united with Trant on the left of the French, but with a fierce neglect of orders had taken a path leading more directly to the enemy: the head of the 29th thus reached the table-land above at a point where Laborde was concentrating his left wing on his centre, and as some of the former were still coming in, the regiment was assailed in front and flank. Colonel Lake fell, many men went down with him,and the French on the English right, few in number and thinking they should be cut off, furiously broke through the disordered mass, carrying with them a major and many other prisoners.

Then, dropping below the brow of the hill, the oppressed troops rallied on their left wing and on the 9th Regiment, and all rushing up together, regained the table-land, presenting a confused front, which Laborde vainly endeavoured to destroy: yet many brave men he struck down, and mortally wounded Colonel Stewart of the 9th, fighting with great vehemence. Soon the 9th Regiment, which had not deviated from the true path, appeared on his left, while the skirmishers of theother attacks emerged thickly from the crags and copses of the ascent: the left flanking column had now also turned his right, had cut off the line of communication with Loison, and was so rapidly advancing, as to render a retreat imperative and difficult. His situation was indeed critical in the extreme, and he was wounded, but with unyielding resolution he made the movement along a narrow table-land leading from his position to the knot of mountains behind, checking pursuit by partial charges of cavalry, until he reached the village of Zambugeira: there the ground opened, and the danger from the flanking force being fended off by deep ravines, he turned and made another stand, but was finally forced to seek refuge in the higher mountains, having lost three guns and six hundred men killed and wounded: the British loss being nearly five hundred.

BATTLE OF VIMIERO.

Laborde was not pursued, his retreat was inland, and to keep near the coast was essential to the English general, because he expected reinforcements by sea, and desired to insure their disembarkation and receive provisions from the ships. In this view he designed to march by his right on Torres Vedras, which would bring him near the ocean, give command of the great road to Lisbon, and throw off Loisonand Laborde from that capital; but in the night came intelligence that a large fleet, conveying two brigades of infantry, was on the coast, and to protect their landing he made for Vimiero, a village near the sea, nine miles from Torres Vedras: there the brigades from the ocean augmented his force to sixteen thousand British soldiers. Junot, meanwhile, having rallied Laborde's and Loison's troops, had fore-stalled him at Torres Vedras, with fourteen thousand good soldiers and twenty-three guns of small calibre; and while his powerful cavalry prevented the scouts from making observations, he prepared to march in the night of the 20th and attack on the 21st. Sir Arthur had also projected a march for the night of the 20th, to turn Junot's left and gain Mafra in his rear, without assailing Torres Vedras, which, though shrouded by the horsemen, was known as a strong position. The armies would thus have changed places without encountering, if the English ministers had not appointed three generals senior to Sir Arthur to act in Portugal, one of whom, Sir Harry Burrard, had arrived. He did not land and assume command, but he forbade the projected march, and thus deprived the: English army of the initiatory movement, giving it to the French: moreover, as the ground at Vimiero had been taken temporarily and for ease, the troops were not in fighting order, thus violating the maxim which prescribes constant readiness for battle when near an enemy. It was thus posted.

On the right a mountain ridge, trending from the sea inland, ended abruptly on a small plain in which the village of Vimiero was situated, and the greater part of the army was heaped on the summit.

On the other side of the plain the same line was continued by a ridge of less elevation, narrow, yet protected by a ravine almost impassable, and being without water had only one regiment and some picquets posted there.

In front of the break between these heights and within cannon-shot, was an isolated hill of inferior elevation, yet of good strength, masking the village and plain of Vimiero, and leaving only narrow egress from the latter on the right. On this hill six guns and two brigades of infantry, Fane's and Anstruther's, were posted, the former on the left: behind them in the plain the commissariat and artillery stores were parked.

All the cavalry with the army—a single squadron under Col. Taylor—was placed at the egress from the plain, on the direct road to Torres Vedras; but from the counter hills, facing the position, another road, running from Torres Vedras to Lourinham, led at the distance of two miles round the left, and by it an enemy could gain the ridge where the picquets were posted, seize the artillery and commissariats stores in the plain, and take the central hill and right-hand mountain in reverse.

In the night of the 20th a German officer of cavalry aroused Sir Arthur Wellesley, saying the French army, twenty thousand strong, was within an hour's march. Incredulous of this tale, the bearer of which was in evident consternation, he merely took some additional precautions; and at sunrise all eyes were turned southward, seeking an enemy who wasnnot to be seen. Nevertheless the German's report was only an exaggeration. * Junot had been in march all night with

* The Chaplain-General Gleig has in one of his publications contradicted this fact, on the authority of a German Chelsea-pensioner, who affirms, according to Mr. Gleig, that it was he who awakened Sir Arthur, and that he was cool and collected. My authority is the Duke of Wellington, who assured me that it was not only a German officer, but a titled one; a Baron; and that he was anything but cool or collected. The name had escaped his memory at the time, but he made

fourteen, not twenty, thousand men, designing to fall on at daybreak; but the rugged ways had retarded his progress, and his vanguard of cavalry did not crown the hills facing the English position before eight o'clock —the dust of its march having been discovered an hour before. Had he arrived by daybreak this dust could not have been observed,and an hour of preparation would have been lost to the English general, which, with a good plan of battle, would have enabled the French to gain the left-hand ridge, by the Lourinham road, before the troops on the right could cross to occupy that part of the position.

Junot employed little time to note his adversary's ground and dispositions, and entirely neglected the mountain on the English right, as being refused to his line of march; but as the left-hand ridge appeared naked of troops, he resolved to seize it by a detachment, and take the English central hill in reverse while he attacked it in front with his main body, thinking he should find the bulk of the army there. In this view he directed General Brennier with a brigade across the ravine covering the ridge, and Laborde with another against the central hill, supporting the latter with Loison's division, a reserve of grenadiers under Kellermann, and the cavalry, thirteen hundred strong, under Margaron.

To act on conjecture is dangerous in war. Junot conjectured falsely, and his entire disregard of the English right was a great error; for when his cavalry crowned the counter hills, Sir A. Wellesley, seeing the movements did not menace that part of his position, retained there one brigade under General Hill to serve as a support to the centre, while four other brigades were sent across the plain to occupy the left-hand ridge, and a fifth, reinforced with Trant's Portugese, moved to a parallel ridge in rear, where they could watch the Lourinham road.

All these movements were hidden from Junot by the central hill, and two brigades reached their ground before the action commenced; yet, knowing the ravine in front to be impracticable, they looked for an attack from the left, and formed two lines across the ridge, trusting to a chain of

---

frequent attempts to recover it, and said several times that he was a Baron. The two authorities may be weighed by those who are fastidious.

skirmishers to protect their right. The two other brigades were to have furnished a third line, but while they were passing the plain below the battle was begun in the centre with great fury.

In front of the English position the ground was so broken and wooded that the movements of the French, after they passed the counter hills, could not be discerned until they burst upon the centre in attack; and though their artillery was most numerous, the tormented ground impeded its action, while the English,,guns, of heavier metal, had freeplay: their infantry, inferior in number, would therefore have fought at great disadvantage, even if Junot's combinations had not failed; but soon that general discovered the mischief of over-haste in war. Brennier found the bottom of the ravine impracticable, and floundering amidst rocks and the beds of torrents was unable to co-operate with Laborde; hence Junot had to reinforce the latter with Loison's infantry, and detach another column of all arms under General Solignac to turn the English flank by the Lourinham road. But he did not perceive that Sir Arthur, anticipating such an effort, had there, not a flank but a front, three lines deep, while the fifth brigade and Trant's Portuguese were so disposed, that Solignac, whose movement was isolated, could be cut off and placed between two fires.

Laborde and Loison opened three attacks, one principal, with minor bodies on the flanks. The first, being well led and covered by skirmishers, forced its way up with great vehemence and power, but with great loss also; for General Fane had called up the reserve artillery under Colonel Robe to reinforce the six guns already on the platform, and while they smote the column in front, another battery, belonging to one of the brigades then ascending the left-hand ridge, smote it in the right flank, and under this conjoint fire of artillery and a wasting musketry the French reached the summit, there to sustain a murderous volley, to be charged by the 50th Regiment, overturned, and driven down again.

Of the other two columns, the one assailing Anstruther's brigade was beaten quickly, and that general had time to reinforce Fane's left with the second battalion of the 43rd in opposition to Kellermann's grenadiers, half of whom now reinforced the third column on that side. This regiment, posted in a churchyard on the edge of the declivity, had one or two companies in advance amongst some trees, and from thence the first burst of the grenadiers drove them upon the main body; but then Robe's battery so smote the left of the French that they dipped into the ravine on their right, where the battery from the ridge caught them on the other flank; the moment was happily seized by the 43rd to pour down in a solid mass, and with ringing shouts it dashed against the column, driving it back with irrecoverable disorder: yet not without the fiercest fighting. The loss of the regiment was a hundred and twenty, and when the charge was over, a French soldier and the Sergeant Armourer, Patrick, were found grimly confronting each other in death as they had done in life, their hands still clutching their muskets, and their bayonets plunged to the sockets in each manly breast ! It is by such men that thousands are animated and battles won.

Broken by these rough shocks, the French, to whom defeat was amazement, retired in confused masses and in a slanting direction towards the Lourinham road, and while thus disordered Colonel Taylor rode out upon them doing great execution; but as suddenly Margaron came down with his strong cavalry, and the gallant Englishman fell with most of his horsemen. However, half of Junot's army was now beaten with the loss of seven guns, and though Margaron's powerful cavalry, and that moiety of Kellerman's grenadiers which had not been engaged, interposed to prevent pursuit, the line of retreat left the shortest road to Torres Vedras uncovered—a great fault which did not escape the English general's rapid comprehension.

Brennier, unable to emerge from the rocks and hollows where he was entangled. had been of no weight in this action, but Solignac, having turned the ravine, appeared on the left about the time Taylor's charge terminated the fight in the centre, and his division, strongly constituted with all arms, was advancing impetuously along the narrow ground, when General Ferguson, who was there in opposition, met him with a counter attack, so fierce, so rapid and sustained, that the French, though fighting stubbornly, bent to the strong pressure. Solignac was wounded, his cavalry, artillery and infantry, heaped together and out-flanked, were cut off from their line of retreat and forced into low ground on their right with a loss of six guns. These pieces, placed under guard of the 71st and 82nd while Ferguson continued his course, were again lost by one of those events which make battles the property of fortune; for Brennier, after long struggling, having worked up the ravine by his light to an accessible place, had ascended the ridge, and, unexpectedly falling upon the two regiments in charge of the captured guns, beat them back. He thus got behind Ferguson, and had time been given to reform his troops and assail that general's rear mischief would have ensued; but the English regiments were disordered only for a moment; they rallied on higher ground, poured in their fire, broke the French brigade with a charge and made Brennier, who was wounded, a prisoner. Solignac's division was then without resource, when suddenly another and more decisive change came over this fitful battle.

Junot's left wing and centre had been so discomfited, that only half of Kellerman's grenadiers and Margaron's cavalry remained unbroken, and the road of Torres Vedras, the shortest to Lisbon, was uncovered; Brennier's column was entirely broken; Solignac's division was in confusion on low ground, cut off from Junot, and menaced front and rear. But of the English army, Hill's brigade had not fired a shot; neither had the brigade conjoined with Trant's Portuguese, and it was then marching to take Solignac's division in rear. The two brigades of Ferguson's third line had lost only a few men, and those on the central hill had not been hardly handled; there was therefore a powerful force in hand for further operations. Now Brennier, when first taken, eagerly asked if the reserve had attacked, and the other prisoner being questioned on this point replied in the affirmative*, wherefore the English general, judging the French power exhausted, and the moment come for rendering victory decisive, with the genius of a great captain resolved to make it not only decisive on the field but of the fate of Portugal.

Expecting, Solignac's division to lay down its arms, he

---

* General Brennier published a denial of this fact; but it may well be imagined that a short sentence uttered at such a moment by a prisoner wounded and highly excited, would escape his recollection. My authority is the Duke of Wellington, who not only caught the words at the time, and questioned the other prisoners as to their value, but drew from them a conclusion on which to rest a great counter movement.

designed to push his own right wing and centre, under Hill, on Torres Vedras, to which they were two miles nearer than any part of the French army; that stroke was sure, and Junot would have been cut off from Lisbon. Meanwhile Sir Arthur meaned in person vigorously to drive him across the Baragueda mountain on to the Tagus, by which he would lose his remaining artillery, and have with disorganised and dispirited troops to seek refuge under the guns of one of the frontier fortresses. This great project was stifled as soon as conceived. General Burrard had arrived on the field of battle, he could not comprehend such a stroke of war, and not only stopped the execution but ordered Ferguson to halt. Then Solignac's division, with the alacrity which distinguished Napoleon's soldiers, instantly rejoined Junot, who as promptly recovered his original ground, and being joined by twelve hundred fresh men from Lisbon regained Torres Vedras. The battle of Vimiero thus terminated impotently. Nevertheless, Burrard's decision, with exception of the unaccountable order to arrest Ferguson's career, was not without a military justification, admitted to be of weight by Sir Arthur, but it was that of an ordinary general in opposition to a great captain.

CORUNA.

The battle of Vimiero, in which the French lost thirteen guns and about two thousand killed or wounded, the British eight hundred, was followed by a convention which relieved Portugal, and the English Government then sent an army into Spain under Sir John Moore. Great success was looked for by the ministers, yet they took no measures to render it even probable; and the incredible absurdity of the Spaniards, who were overthrown in every quarter before the English could reach them, made that which was improbable impossible. Moore found himself alone in the midst of a French arm;y commanded by Napoleon, of which the cavalry alone counted twelve thousand more than the whole British force ! Compelled to retreat, he was pursued by the Emperor, who made a prodigious march to cut him off at Astorga, and failing of that, launched Marshal Soult on his traces with one army, supported by another under Marshal Ney. Through the mountains of Gallicia the three arms passed like a tempest, yet Moore, with unflinching resolution, amidst winter rains and appalling difficulties, and without one gleam of good fortune to nourish energy, reached Coruna with a gain of two marches on his pursuers. His retreat was one of suffering, of privation and fatigue, but he met with no disaster in arms, and in many combats taught the enemy to beware of his sword. At Rueda his cavalry, under C. Stewart,* surprised a French post and made eighty prisoners. Near Valladolid Major Otway † in a sharp action took a colonel, and more prisoners than he had men to guard them with. At Sahagun Lord Paget†† overthrew six hundred dragoons, killed twenty, and took thirteen officers and one hundred and fifty men. At Mayorga the same nobleman killed as many, and took a hundred prisoners; and at Benevente defeated the light cavalry of the Imperial Guard, capturing General Lefebre and seventy men. At Calcavallos Moore, in person, repulsed a serious attack in which the French general Colbert was killed. At Constantino he repulsed another attack, and at Lugo checked the enemy with a loss of four hundred men.

At Coruna his design was to embark without fighting, but the ships did not arrive in time, and he had to accept battle in a bad position. The ground he desired to take was a rocky range abutting on the Mero, a tidal river, but it being too extensive for his troops, he was compelled to adopt a similar yet lower range, likewise abutting on the Mero, yet inclosed on two sides by the greater heights, which were left for the enemy. Neither of these ranges were crested, and on the inferior one Moore had to display a front in opposition to the superior range, from whence the French not only commanded most of the English line in front within cannon-shot, but could flank it also on the right. Soult's ground was indeed in every way advantageous. His left rested on a clump of rocks overlooking both ranges, and all the country immediately about; and in the night of the 15th he placed there eleven heavy guns which, from their elevation, could oppress the right of the English line and send their bullets raking even to the centre.

Between the two positions the ground was comparatively easy of passage, though broken and laced with stone inclo-

---

* Now Marquis of Londonderry.   † Lieut.-General Sir Loftus Otway.
†† Marquis of Anglesey

sures; and as both ridges ended abruptly on a narrow valley running perpendicular to their range, there was a seeming facility from their proximity at that flank for the French to envelop the British right with superior numbers. On the far side of this valley also was a mountainous chain of hills on which all Soult's cavalry were posted, his light horsemen being pushed far behind the British rear, while his heavy dragoons dismounted to act as infantry. Thus the French army seemed to be surrounding the English, but Moore, comprehending all the defects of his position, had adopted a counteracting order of battle, evincing his own martial vigour, and the confidence a long career of glorious and successful service had given him in the stern valour of the British soldier.

To receive battle on the inferior ridge was of necessity, but to extend his line athwart the narrow valley on his right to the height occupied by the French cavalry would only have placed more men under the rock battery, and his flank would still be exposed to the dismounted French dragoons. Therefore he merely stretched a thin line of skirmishers across, and placed a battalion on the lower falls of the hills on their right, to check the horsemen on the summit. This disposition, and a scanty manning of the main ridge, where he posted only two divisions, Hope's and Baird's, the latter on the right, gave him two divisions of reserve, Paget's and McKenzie Frazer's. The last he placed on rising ground closely covering Coruna, to watch a road leading round the heights where the French cavalry were, and which Soult, whose movements could not be seen, might use to turn the British and cut them off from the town and harbour. Paget's division, the best in the army, remained, and with it Moore resolved to strike for victory. He kept it in mass behind the right of his main line, on a moderate elevation, from whence it commanded a full view of the narrow valley, and could support the screen of light troops without being exposed to the fire of the eleven-gun battery. Thus, while the main ridge, strong in itself though ill presented to the enemy, was offered in defence, with protected flanks, two other divisions remained in hand to meet the changes of battle—a fine result to obtain for an inferior army occupying unfavourable ground. But Moore meaned more than defence.

Confident that Baird and Hope would repel every attack on the ridge.
he designed, when time should be ripe, if the French did not join
infantry to their cavalry on the other side of the valley, to pour down
the latter with Paget's division, reinforcing it with Frazer's, and thus
carry   in one course the rock battery; then changing from the
defensive to the offensive with all his troops, to drive the enemy into
the Mero: it was the conception of a daring man and a great
commander, and only with such potent soldiers as the British could
a like stroke be made. And only a general who had proved their
quality in many a desperate fight could have expected this effort from
his men, after a distressing winter retreat, with a strong enemy in front
and the sea behind ! But general and soldiers were of England's best.
No suffering, no danger could quell their courage, or shake his confidence in them: and it was so proved in that hour, for many of the
principal officers, appalled at the superior force of the enemy, the disadvantage of ground, and the difficulty of embarkation, proposed
negotiations, which Moore rejected vith cold disdain, trusting as he
had ever done to his gallant troops.

Belonging to the French position, and occupied by them in force,
were two villages, Palavia Abajo in front of their right, Portosa in
front of their centre.

Belonging to the English position, though rather too much advanced, the village of Elvina covered the right flank, and was
occupied by the picquets of the 50th Regiment.

These features dictated Soult's order of attack. Forming three columns of infantry, which he supported with all his light artillery, he
directed two by Palavia and Portosa against the left and centre of
Moore's line—-those villages serving as intermediate supports in
case of disaster—while the third and strongest column was destined
to carry Elvina and then lap round Baird's right.

BATTLE OF CORUNA.

On the 16th of January, 1809, at two o'clock in the
afternoon, twenty thousand French veterans opened this
battle against fourteen thousand British, who, having but
nine six-pounders to oppose to a numerous light artillery, were also

galled by eleven heavy guns on the rocks: and soon that formidable battery opened the fight with a slaughtering fire, sending its bullets crashing through the English ranks from right to centre. Then the columns of infantry, throwing out clouds of skirmishers, descended from their strong ridge to the fight. Those coming from Palavia and Portosa, having some distance to march, did not immediately engage, but the third dashed at once against Elvina, and there was the stress of battle; the picquets were driven in heaps out of the village, and when that was passed the French mass divided, one portion advancing against Baird's front, the other turning his right by the valley, where it was only opposed by the screen of light troops.

Sir John Moore sent the 42nd and 50th Regiments against the half column at Elvina, and wheeling back the 4th Regiment on the extremity of his right, poured a fire into the flank of the mass penetrating by the valley, where it was also stoutly opposed by the light troops, and soon abated of its vehemence in attack. Then the English general knew that his adversary's whole force and order of battle was unfolded. No infantry menaced the valley from where the French cavalry stood, and the number in front showed that no body of strength for mischief was behind those heights: it was evident that Soult offered a close rough trial of arms, without subtlety, trusting to the valour of his veterans. Eagerly the gallant Moore accepted the challenge. The moment for his counter-stroke had arrived, and at once he called up Frazer's division in support of Paget, giving the latter, who was previously well instructed, the signal to descend into the valley: the French column on his flank being thus provided with opponents, he turned to observe the progress of the fight at Elvina, for as yet the battle had but slightly touched his centre and left.

The 42nd and 50th had driven the enemy back into the village, and the last-named regiment, entering the streets with the repulsed disordered mass and giving no respite, forced it through and broke out, still fighting, on the other side. To support this advance the general now sent a battalion of the Guards down, whereupon the 42nd, thinking it a relief and not a reinforcement, retired, with exception of the grenadier company. Some confusion thus occurred, the village was not occupied, and the 50th, still accompanied by the 42nd Grenadiers, were engaged without support beyond the houses, their array being quite broken by stone inclosures and the disorder of the street fight. At that critical moment the French were strongly reinforced, retook the offensive and forced the regiment back into Elvina, having killed beyond it the second Major, Stanhope, a nephew of Mr. Pitt, and made prisoner the commanding officer, Major Napier, known since as the conqueror of Scinde; encompassed by enemies, and denied quarter, he received five wounds, but he still fought and struggled for life until a French drummer with a generous heat and indignation forcibly rescued him from his barbarous assailants. :Meanwhile Sir John Moore, observing the error of the 42nd, had galloped down and with a fiery exhortation sent it back to the village, where the 50th not withstanding the loss of their commander was successfully sustaining a very violent conflict: then with heroic anticipations from the development of his counter-combination, he returned to the ridge from whence he could view the whole action.

Elvina was now his centre of battle and pivot of movements, for on his left the battle had then become general and furious, yet the French made no progress against Hope's division; and on the right, in the valley, the attacking column was at bay, wavering under a double fire in front and flank: everywhere the signs of coming victory were bright, when the gallant man, the consummate commander, who had brought the battle to this crisis, was dashed from his horse to the earth. A cannon-shot from the rock battery had torn away all the flesh from his left breast and shoulder, and broken the ribs over a heart undaunted even by this terrible this ghastly mortal hurt; for with incredible energy he rose to a sitting posture, and with fixed look and unchanged countenance continued to regard the fight at Elvina until the Frenchmen's backward steps assured him the British were victorious: then sinking down he accepted succour.

Being placed in a blanket for removal, an entanglement of his belts caused the hilt to enter the wound and Captain Hardinge* attempted to take away the weapon altogether;

* The present Lord Hardinge.

but with martial pride the stricken man forbade the alleviation—*he would not part with his sword in the field !* Epaminondas, mortally wounded at Mantinea, was anxious for the recovery of his shield. Moore, mortally wounded at Coruna, sustained additional torture rather than part with his sword !

The Theban hero's fall dismayed and paralyzed his victorious troops. It was not so with the British at Coruna. They saw Baird, second in command, carried from the field as the General-in-Chief had been, and they would have seen all their generals fall one after another without abating their battle; hence it was not long before the French were entirely driven from Elvina, while on the left, they were not only repulsed from the ridge, but pursued and assailed in their own villages; that of Palavia, defended by the since celebrated General Foy, was taken. Meanwhile Paget, pouring into the valley with conquering violence, overthrew everything in his front, and driving off the dismounted French dragoons who had descended to the lower falls on his right, màde for the great rock battery, which he would certainly have stormed if the counter-attack had been continued, and Frazer's division been thrown, as Moore designed, into the fight. The French would thus have been wrecked; for their ammunition of which the rapid marches through Gallicia had only allowed them to bring up a small supply, was exhausted, the river Mero was in full tide behind them, and only one bridge remained for retreat. but this want of ammunition was unknown to the English general Hope, on whom the command had devolved, and he, judging a night action, for it was then dark, too hazardous, profited from the confusion of the French to embark the army without loss and sailed for England. The heroic spirit of Moore went with the troops, his body rested with the enemy.

For some hours after receiving his hurt that great man had lived painfully, but with a calm fortitude that excited the admiration of those about him. several times he expressed his satisfaction at having won the battle, and his last words were to express a hope *"that his country would do him justice !"*

Full justice has not been done, because malignant faction has strived hard to sully his reputation as a general—but thus he died, and the record of his worth will be as a beacon to posterity so long as heroic virtue combined with great capacity is reverenced, for in any age, any nation, any conjuncture, Sir John Moore would have been a leading man. Tall he was and vigorous of person, and of a very comely noble aspect, indicating penetration which no subtlety could deceive, valour which no danger could appal, and withal a dignity of mind which awed while it attracted admiration and confidence. With him indeed, all commanding qualities seemed to be united to and inseparable from estimable sentiments. Integrity, honour, generosity, patriotism, adorned the whole course of his existence, and his death furnished an irrefragable test of the sincerity of his life: for both he may claim a place with the greatest men of antiquity.

BOOK II.

Passage of the Douro—Talavera—Combat of Salinas
—First Combat of Talavera—Second Combat of Talavera
—Battle of Talavera.

NAPOLEON having failed to cut off the English army, returned to France, leaving precise instructions with his lieutenants for the invasion of Portugal. Marshal Ney, who reached Coruna three days after the battle, was to hold Gallicia. Soult was to march by Oporto upon Lisbon. General Lapisse, previously directed on Ciudad Rodrigo with twelve thousand men, was to connect Soult's invasion with another, to be conducted south of the Tagus by Marshal Victor, who had thirty thousand troops. Soult had twenty-five thousand, and, after several battles with the Portuguese of the northern provinces, stormed Oporto in March; but he could hear nothing of Lapisse or Victor, and, his own progressive strength being then exshausted, he endeavoured to establish himself solidly until new combinations could be formed.

Lapisse took no pains to open a communication with Soult, and after several weeks of inactivity suddenly made for Alcantara, crossed the Tagus there and joined Victor. The Portuguese and Spaniards, thinking he was flying, rose along his line of march on both sides of the frontier and cut off all communication between Victor and Soult. The former was however little disposed to act. He had defeated the Spanish general Cuesta in a great battle at Medellin, and only accidentally failed to obtain Badajos by treason; but then he took quarters at Merida, sullenly resistant of his orders to enter Portugal. This enabled Cuesta, who had all the resources of Andalusia, to reappear in Estramadura with an army of thirty thousand infantry and six thousand cavalry —and at the same time a new force sprung up in Portugal.

Previous to this period the English ministers, without resolution or capacity to adopt any judicious course, at one time looking, to Portugal, at another negotiating for the occupation of Cadiz, had during these events displayed only infirmity of purpose and ignorance of the real state of affairs; but after four months of vacillation, subsequent to the battle of Coruna, they decided to act in Portugal, where the Regency had accepted General Beresford as their field marshal. The British troops in that country were then largely reinforced, and Sir Arthur Wellesley, assuming the supreme military command of both nations, commenced that series of victories which has placed him amongst the truly great generals of the world—and they are few, though the vanity of nations would make them many.

Soult was then in Oporto, Victor at Merida, but the frontier insurrection debarred all intercourse between them; and Sir Arthur, after making arrangements to cover Lisbon from Victor, marched against Soult, in whose army there was a conspiracy of officers to deliver him to the English. One D'Argenton twice secretly visited head-quarters on this subject, yet the treason, though of weight as an accessory, was not permitted to affect the British preparations or movements, which were carefully concealed.

On the 7th of May Beresfold was detached with a mixed force, six thousand being Pc;rtuguese, to operate on the sideof Lamego.

On the 8th, sixteen thousand British troops, fifteen hundred being cavalry, with twenty-four guns, moved from Coimbra under Sir A. Wellesley's personal command towards the Vouga river.

Up to this time Soult was ignorant that such a force had been assembled, but hearing nothing of Lapisse or Victor he had decided to make a flank march into the Salamanca country, and had pushed his light cavalry under Franceschi to the Vouga, supporting it with Mermet's division of infantry. Loison's division, six thousand strong, was then beyond the Tamega at Pezo de Ragoa, and Lorge's heavy cavalry was on the Lima, watching the Portuguese insurgents.

In this scattered state the French on the Vouga were surprised and driven fighting upon the Douro, which they crossed in the night of the 11th and destroyed the boat bridge. Soult, who had discovered the conspiracy on the 9th, was thus suddenly beset with perils. Treason in his army which he could not probe, a powerful enemy suddenly springing up in front, an active insurrection on his rear; his troops parcelled frcm the Vouga to the Lima and Tamega, and under officers neccssarily suspected while the extent of the conspiracy was unknown ! He did not quail. Directing Lorge to abandon the Lima and make for the Tamega, he ordered Loison to hold Amarante on that river, as the only means of concentration and safety for the army; he sent his stores and most of the heavy guns towards that place on the 10th and night of the llth; and when the troops from the Vorga came pouring in, the remaining heavy guns and the baggage were also put in movement, Mermet's division following them as far as Vallonga, with orders to secure the boats on the Doulo and vigilantly patrol up the bank. All the craft from Oporto to the mouth of the river was then drawn to the right bank, guards were set, and Soult, thinking his position secure, decided to hold Oporto another day, to give Lorge's dragoons and other detachments time to reach Amarante: he was however curiously misled. In the recent operations, an English column, moving in boats up the Lake of Ovar, which runs parallel with the coast, had disembarked on Melmet's flank, who thought it had landed from the ocean; hence Soult, expecting the empty vessels would enter the Douro to effect a passage, directed his attention entirely to the lower river, while on the upper his orders were neglected and false reports made of their execution, for the conspirators were many and busy.

PASSAGE OF THE DOURO.

Before eight o'clock on the morning of the 12th the British army was secretly concentrated behind a rocky height, on which stood a convent immecliately facing Oporto. The Douro rolled in front, and the French on the other side could with two marches gain the Tamega, secure their retreat, and defeat Beresford in passing; for that general had been sent over the Douro, above the confluence of the Tamega, merely to infest Soult's line of march towards the Salamanca country, and thus induce him to take the rugged Chaves road leading to Gallicia, and that could not be risked unless the main army under Sir Arthur was closely pressing the French rear; hence his safety, and the forcing Soult into Gallicia, alike called for an immediate passage of the Douro. Yet how pass a river, deep, swift, more than three hundred yards wide, and in the face of ten thousand veterans guarding the opposite bank. The Macedonian hero might have turned from it without shame.

The stream came with an elbow round the convent height, which barred sight of the upper water from the place where Soult was watching for ships which did not exist; and he knew not that the British army was behind the frowning rock above, nor that a great captain was on its summit, searching with an eagle glance the river, the city, and the country around. Horses and baggage that captain saw on the Vallonga road, and the dust of distant columns as in retreat, but no large force near the river; the guards also were few and widely spread, the patrols not vigilant—an auspicious negligence seeming to prevail. Suddenly a large unfinished building called the Seminary caught his eye; it was isolated, had an easy access from the water, and was surrounded by a high wall which extended to the river bank on each side, inclosing space enough for two battalions, the only egress being an iron gate opening on the Vallonga road. This structure commanded everything around, except one mound, within cannon-shot, but too pointed to hold guns; there were no French posts near the building, and as the direct line across the water was entirely hidden from the city by the rock, Sir Arthur, with a marvellous hardihood, instantly resolved to force a passage there in face of a veteran army and a renowned general, his means being as scanty as his resolution was great, yet with his genius they sufficed.

Colonel Waters, an officer on his staff, a quick-witted, daring, man, discovered a poor barber, who had come over the river the night before in a small skiff and readily agreed to go back; he was accompanied by the Prior of Amarante, who gallantly offered his services: thus Waters crossed unperceived and returned with three large barges. Meanwhile eighteen guns had been placed in battery on the convent rock, and General John Murray was detached with a brigade of German infantry, the 14th Dragoons, and two guns, to seek a passage at the Barca de Avintas, three miles up the river: he was reinforced with other troops when the barges were secured, and then also the head of the army cautiously approached the water.

At 10 o'clock, the French being tranquil and unsuspicious, the British wondering and expectant, Sir Arthur was told that one boat was ready. *Well! Let the men cross* was the reply, and a quarter of an hour afterwards an officer and twenty-five British soldiers were silently placed on the other side of the Douro in the midst of the French army ! The Seminary was thus gained, all remained quiet, and a second boat passed. No hostile stir succeeded, no sound of war was heard; but when the third boat passed, tumultuous noises rolled through Oporto, the drums beat to arms, shouts arose, the citizens, vehemently gesticulating, made signals from their houses, and confused masses of troops rushing out from the higher streets threw forward swarms of skirmishers, and came furiously down on the Seminary.

Secrecy was then no longer valuable and the army crowded to the river bank. Paget's and Hill's divisions pressed to the point of passage, Sherbrooke's to where the bridge had been cut away the night before. Paget himself passed with the thirdboat, but on the roof of the Seminary was deeply wounded. Hill took his place, and the musketry, sharp and voluble from the first, augmented as the forces accumulated on each side; yet the French attack was eager and constant, their fire increased more rapidly than that of the English, and their guns soon opened against the building. The English battery on the convent rock swept the inclosure on each side and confined the attack to the front; but Murray did not come down the right bank, and the struggle was such that Sir Arthur was only restrained from crossing by the remonstrances of those about him, and the confidence he had in Hill. Soon, however, some citizens were seen bringing over several great boats to Sherbrooke, while a prolonged shout from the streets, and the waving of handkerchiefs from the windows, gave notice that the enemy had abandoned the lower town: Murray also was then descried on the right bank.

Three battalions were now in the Seminary, the attack slackened, and the French began to hurry across the front of the inclosure by the Vallonga rcad, and Hill, advancing to the inclosure wall, was pouring a heavy fire into the disordered masses as they passed his front, when suddenly five guns galloped out of the city on his left, but appalled at the terrible stream of musketry pulled up: while thus hesitating a volley from behind stretched most of the artillerymen in the dust, and the rest dispersing left the guns on the road. It was from Sherbrooke, who had passed through the streets this volley came, and he now pressed the French rear while Hill sent his damaging fire into their flank, and the guns from the rock deeply searched their masses. The passage was thus won, the allies were on the right bank of the Douro, and if Murray had fallen on the disordered crowd, approaching him, the discomfiture would have been complete. He however suffered column after column to pass, and seemed to fear they would step aside to push him into the river. General C. Stewart and Major Harvey, impatient of this timidity, took two squadrons of the 14th Dragoons, and riding over the French rear in a narrow way unhorsed General Laborde and wounded General Foy; but having no support from Murray fought their way back with loss, and Harvey lost his arm. Of the English twenty were killed, one general and nearly a hundred men wounded on the day; the French lost a general and five hundred men killed or wounded, and they left several hundreds in hospital. Five guns were taken in the fight; and stores of ammunition with fifty pieces of artillery, the carriages of which had been burned, were found in the arsenal. The overthrow was great, but Napoleon's veterans were so inured to war that no troops so readily recovered from a surprise. Before they reached Vallonga their order was restored, a rear-guard was formed, and in the night was rejoined by a detachment from the mouth of the Douro, which had been guided by some friendly Portuguese: then Soult, believing Loison held Amarante, thought himself well out of his difficulties. He was soon undeceived.

Sir Arthur Wellesley now brought his baggage, stores, and artillery over the Douro; but this was not effected until the evening of the 13th, and though Murray's Germans were sent in pursuit on the morning of that day, they did not advance more than ten miles. " *An enemy once surprised should never be allowed time to recover,*" *is* a great maxim, and so proved on this occasion: yet there were sound reasons for the halt. Part of the troops were still on the left bank of the Douro, and the whole had outmarched provisions, baggage and spare ammunition, having made more than eighty miles of rough ground in four days, besides fighting. Men and animals required rest, and nothing was known of Beresford, whose proceedings had been of far greater importance than either he or Sir Arthur knew at the time.*

Loison had fallen back from Pezo de Ragoa on the Douro the 10th when Beresford crossed that river. The latter was then in the position required for turning Soult on to the Chaves road; but Loison again retreated on the 11th, and Beresford, finding him timid, followed briskly, while a Portuguese insurgent force under General Sylveira closed on his flank. The 12th his outposts were driven into Amarante, and next day he abandoned that place.

These events were unknown to Sir Arthur on the 13th, but he heard Soult had destroyed guns and ammunition near Penafiel, and judging that to be a result of Beresford's operations, reinforced Murray with cavalry, ordering him to push on to Penafiel, and if Loison lingered near Amarante to open a communication with Beresford— the latter was then to ascend the Tamega and intercept the French at Chaves.

On the 14th Sir Arthur had moved forward himself, and the 15th reached Braga; Beresford was then near Chaves, Sylveira marching towards Salamonde, and Soult's capture seemed inevitable to his pursuers; he was however beyond their toils, having by a surprising; effort extricated himself from perils as fearful as ever beset a general.

While retreating towards Amarante he was between the Douro and the Sierra de Catalina, both said to be impassable, and the road was very narrow and very rugged. His design was to pass the Tamega and march on Braganza; failing in that, he could from Amarante and Guimaraens reach Braga by a good road leading behind the Catalina ridge; in either case however Amarante was to be first gained, and his safety

---

* A writer, or rather writers in the *Quarterly Review*, for there were two of them, indulging in the graceless effrontery of assertion so common with anonymous critics, treated these reasons for halting with ridicule, calling them imaginary, and affirming that they were unknown to the General-inChief ! My authority however was that very Generaal-in-Chief. The Duke of Wellington not only gave me verbally a description of his motives and proceedings on this occasion, but supplied me with written notes, from which and from a memoir received from Marshal Soult, and information derived from Colonel Waters and other officers engaged, my narrative was composed

depended on Loison holding that place. But that general had relinquished it to Beresford on the 13th, and marched on Guimaraens, though a staff officer, sent by Soult on the 12th, was in his camp protesting against the movement: the r retreat from Oporto being also known to him. He thus deliberately abandoned his general and two-thirds of the army to what appeared certain destruction; for Beresford could not be forced, and if Murray only had come up on the French rear, and he was not far off, Soult must have laid down his arms.

This calamity was made known to that marshal as he was passing the rugged bed of the Souza, a cross torrent falling into the Douro. The weather was boisterous, the troops worn with fatigue and recently defeated were dismayed, voices were heard calling for capitulation, and all things tended to ruin: but in that hour of peril the Duke of Dalmatia justified fortune for having raised him to such dignity. He had fallen from his horse and severely injured his hip, broken before by a shot at the siege of Genoa, yet neither pain nor bodily weakness nor danger could abate his resolution. A Spanish pedlar told him of a path leading up that bank of the Souza which he had just left, by which he could scale the Catalina ridge and reach the Guimaraens road to Braga: whereupon, with a haughty commandment he silenced the murmurs of treacherous officers and fearful soldiers, destroyed his guns, abandoned his military chest and baggage, loaded the animals which had carried them with sick men and ammunition, and repassed the Souza to follow his Spanish guide. Torrents of rain descended and the path was wild and rough as the desolate region it threaded, y et with a fierce domination he forced his troops over the mountain, and descending on Guimaraens, refound Loison: Lorge's dragoons came in at the same time from Braga, and thus almost beyond hope the whole army was concentrated Soult's energy had been great, his sagacity was now as conspicuous. The slackness of pursuit, after passing Vallonga, made him judge Sir Arthur was pushing for Braga and would reach it first; a fighting retreat and the loss of guns and baggage would then ensue, and perhaps fatally depress the soldiers' spirit; it would also favour the malcontents, and already one general, apparently Loison, was urging a convention. Soult replied by destroying the guns, ammunition, and baggage of the divisions he found at Guimaraens, and again taking to the mountains crossed them to Carvalho d'Este, thus gaining a day's march and baffling the combination to surround him. Next morning he drew up his twenty thousand men on the position they had occupied two months before at the battle of Braga, an imposing spectacle, and on the scene of a recent victory, by which he aroused the sinking pride of the French soldier. It was a happy reach of generalship !

Now he reorganized his army, giving Loison the advanced guard and taking the rear himself; at which, says the French historian of this expedition, "the whole army was astonished." As if it were not consummate policy to oppose the British pursuit with men under the General-in-Chief, while the van, having to fight insurgents, was led by an officer whose very name called forth execrations from the natives— *Maneta, the one-handed*, as Loison was called, however willing, dared not surrender to a Portuguese force.

From Carvalho the French made for Salamonde, whence there were two lines of retreat; the one by Ruivaens to Chaves, the other, shorter and more rugged, by the Ponte Nova to Montelegre. The scouts said the bridge at Ruivaens was broken, the passage defended by twelve hundred insurgents with artillery; moreover, that men had been all the morning working to destroy the Ponte Nova. The breaking of the first blocked the road to Chaves, the breaking of the second would, if completed, cut the army off from Montelegre.

Night was setting in the soldiers were harassed, barefooted, and starving, the ammunition was injured by rain, which had never ceased since the 13th, and was now accompanied by storms of wind, with the morning the British army would be on the rear, and if the Ponte ~Tova could not be secured the hour of surrender was come ! In this extremity, Major Dulong, justly reputed as one of the most daring men in the French ranks, was thus addressed by Soult: " I *have chosen you from the whole army to seize the Ponte Nova, which has b een cut by the enemy. Take a hundred grenadiers and twentyfive horsemen, surprise the guards and secure the passage. If you succeed, say so, but send no other report; your silence will suffice."*

Dulong, favoured by the storm, reached the bridge, killed the sentinel without any alarm being given, and being followed by twelve grenadiers, crawled along a narrow slip of masonry which had not been destroyed. The Cavado river was flooded and roaring in its deep rocky channel below, and one of the grenadiers fell into the gulf, but the waters were much louder than his cry, and the others surprised the nearest guards; then the main body rushed on, and some crossing the broken bridge while others ascended the heights, shouting and firing, scared the insurgents away.

At four o'clock the bridge was repaired and the troops filed slowly over; but the road beyond was only a narrow cut in the side of a mountain, an unfenced precipice yawned on the left for several miles, and the way was finally crossed by the Misarella torrent, rolling in a deep chasm and only to be passed by the Saltador or *leaper*, a bridge so called because it was a single arch, high and boldly thrown, which admitted only three persons abreast: it was not cut, but was intrenched, and the rocks on the further side were occupied by some hundred armed insurgents. Here the good soldier Dulong again saved the army. For when two assaults had been repulsed he won the passage with a third, in which he fell deeply wounded; yet his admiring soldiers carried him forward in their arms, and then the head of the long French column poured over the Saltador. It was full time, for the English guns were thundering on the rear and the restored Ponte Nova was choked with the dead.

Sir Arthur Wellesley, quitting Braga in the morning of the 16th, overtook Soult's rear-guard in the evening, at Salamonde, before it could cross the Ponte Nova; it was in a strong position, but men momentarily expecting an order to retire seldom stand firmly. Some light troops turned their left, Sherbrooke assailed their front, and after one discharge they fled by their right to the Ponte Nova. It was dusk, the way to the bridge was not that of apparent retreat, and for a while the French were lost to view; they thus gained time to form a rear-guard, but ere their cavalry could pass the bridge the English guns opened, sending men and horses crushed together into the gulf, and the bridge and the rocks and the defile beyond were strewed with mangled carcasses.

This was the last infliction by the sword in a retreat signalized by many horrid and many glorious actions; for the peasants in their fury tortured and mutilated the sick and straggling soldiers who fell into their hands, the troops in revenge shot the peasants, and the marches could be traced from afar by the smoke of burning houses.

TALAVERA.

When Soult saved himself in Gallicia Sir Arthur Wellesley marche 1 to Abrantes on the Tagus, from whence, thinking the French marshal's army so ruined it could be of no weight in the war for several months, he designed to make a great movement against Madrid, in concert with the Spanish generals Cuesta and Venegas. He was at the time incredulous.s of the Spaniards' failings, thinking Sir John Moore had misrepresented them as apathetic and perverse; but this expedition taught him to respect that great man's judgment, both as to the people and the nature of their warfare.

His plan of operations, as might be expected from so great a general, was bold, comprehensive, and military, according to the data presented: but he accepted false data. He undercalculated the French in the Peninsula by more than a hundred thousand men, he overrated the injury inflicted on Soult; and while slighting the personal energy and resources of that marshal, relied on Spanish politicians, Spanish generals, Spanish troops, and Spanish promises. The time was indeed one of riotous boasting and ill-founded anticipations with the Spanish, Portugese, and British governments. Their agents and partisans were incredibly noisy, their newspapers teemed with idle stories of the weakness, misery, fear and despondency of the French armies, and of the successtul fury of the Spaniards; the most inflated notions of easy triumph pervaded councils and camps, and the English general's judgment was not entirely proof against the pernicious influence.

Victor, relinquishing the south side of the Tagus, was then in position at Talavera, and behind him King Joseph had his own guards, a great body of horsemen, and Sebastiani's army corps. Thus more than fifty thousand men, seven thousand being cavalry, covered Madrid.

Cuesta, following Victor's movements, had taken post at Almaraz, with thirty thousand infantry, seven thousand cavalry, and seventy pieces of artillery.

Venegas was in La Mancha with twenty-five thousand men.

Sir Arthur Wellesley had eighteen thousand infantry, and three thousand cavalry, with thirty guns; eight thousand men, recently landed from England, were on the march to join him, and both the Spanish government and generals gave him the strongest assurances of co-operation and support. He had made contracts with the alcaldes in the valley of the Tagus for a supply of provisions, and, confiding in those promises and contracts, entered Spain the latter end of June, with scanty means of transport and without magazines, to find every Spanish promise broken, every contract a failure. When he remonstrated, all the Spaniards concerned, political or military, vehemently denied that any breach of engagements had taken place, and as vehemently offered to make new ones, without the slightest intention to fulfil them.

A junction with Cuesta was effected the 18th of July.

He was sullen, obstinate, and absurdly prompt to display contempt for the English general; he marched with him, yet rejected his counsels, and after reaching Talavera, from whence Victor had retired, pushed on alone, thinking in his foolish pride to enter Madrid. But King Joseph, who had concentrated fifty thousand men and ninety guns on the Guadarama stream, drove him back the 26th with the loss of four thousand men, and his army would have dispersed, if Sherbrooke, who was in advance of the English forces, had not interposed his division between the scared troops and the enemy.

Sir Arthur Wellesley, whose soldiers were starving, from the failures of the Spanish authorities, had not passed the Alberche, and was intent to retire from Spain; yet now, seeing the disorder beyond that river, judged that a great battle was at hand, and being convinced that in a strong position only would the Spaniards stand, besought their general to withdraw to Talavera, where there was ground suited for defence. Cuesta's uncouth nature then broke out. His troops, beaten, dispirited, fatigued, and bewildered, were clustering in fear on a low narrow slip of land, between the Alberche, the Tagus, and the heights of Salinas. The first shot must have been the signal for dispersion; yet when entreated to avoid the fall of the rock thus trembling overhead, he replied, that his army would be disheartened by further retreat—he would fight where he stood: had the French advanced his ruin would have ensued. At day break Sir Arthur renewed his solicitations, but they were fruitless, until the enemies cavalry came in sight and Sherbrooke prepared to retire: then indeed the sullen old man yeilded yet with frantic pride told his staff, " He had first made the Englishman go down on his knees." Having vented this stupid folly, he retired to a lumbering coach which attended his headquarters, while the Englishman, by virtue of an imperious genius, assumed command of both armies, and leaving one division with a brigade of cavalry under General McKenzie on the Alberche to mask his movements, retired six miles to Talavera; having before chosen a field of battle there, and strengthened it with some field-works on a line perpendicular to the Tagus.

The country in front was a plain, open near this position, but beyond it covered with olive and cork trees up to the Alberche. A series of unconnected hills, steep, yet of moderate height, and running parallel with the Tagus at a distance of two miles, bounded this plain on the left, and half a mile beyond them was a mountain-ridge, from which they were separated by a rugged valley:

Sir Arthur posted the Spanish infantry in two lines on the right, having their flank resting on the town of Talavera, which touched the river.

Their left was closed by a mound crowned with a large field redoubt, behind which a brigade of British cavalry was posted.

Their front was protected by a convent, by ditches, mud walls, breastworks, and felled trees; their cavalry was behind their line, and in rear of all, nearly touching on the town, was a wood with a large house, well placed for and designed by the English general to cover a retreat on the main roads leading from Talavera to Arzobispo and Oropesa.

From the large redoubt, on the mound closing the Spanish left, the line was prolonged by the British army. Campbell's division, in two lines, touched the Spaniards; Sherbrooke's touched Campbell's, but arrayed in one line only, McKenzies division, then on the Alberche, being to form the second. Hill's division should have closed the left, by taking post on the highest of the isolated heights which bounded the plain, but from some error only the flat ground was occupied, and the height was left naked, an error afterwards felt. The English left wing was covered in front by a watercourse, which, shallow at first, went deepening and widening as it passed the round hill, and became a formidable chasm in the valley. The cavalry, originally placed along the front, was destined to take post, partly behind the British left wing, partly behind the redoubt on the Spanish left, and the whole front of battle was two miles long. The Spaniards, reduced by their recent action to thirty-four thousand combatants, but still having seventy guns, occupied one-third of it, and were nearly inattackable from the nature of the ground. The British and Germans held the remainder of the position, and the weakest part, although they were but nineteen thousand sabres and bayonets with thirty guns. The combined armies therefore, with forty-four thousand infantry, ten thousand cavalry, and one hundred pieces of artillery, offered battle to the king, who was coming on with eightyguns and fifty thousand men, seven thousand being cavalry.

Before daylight the French were in march to attack, and at one o'clock Victor reached the heights of Salinas overhanging the Alberche, from whence he could see the dust raised by taking up the position, though the forest masked the dispositions. The ground was however known to him, and the king, at his instance, sent Sebastiani at once against the allies' right, the cavalry against the centre, and Victor himself against the left—supporting the two first with his guards and the reserve.

COMBAT OF SALINAS.

Victor first marched on the *Caza de Salinas,* a house situated in the plain below . To reach it he had to ford the Alberche and penetrate two miles through the forest, yet the position of McKenzie's division was indicated by the dust, and as the British cavalry had sent no patrols, tho post was surprised. England was then like to have lost her great commander, for Sir Arthur, who was in the house for observation, very hardly escaped capture; for the French charged so hotly that the English brigades were separated, fired on each other, and were driven in disorder through the forest into the open plain. In the midst of this confusion the 45th, a stubborn cld regiment, accompanied by some companies of the 60th Riflemen, kept good array, and on them Sir Arthur rallied the others and checked the enemy, covering his retreat with cavalry; yet he lost four hundred men, and the retrograde movement was hastily made in face of both armies.

McKenzie with one brigade now took post behind the Guards in the centre, but Colonel Donkin, seeing the hill on the extreme left unoccupied, crowned it with the other brigade, and thus accidentally filled the position. meanwhile Victor, issuing from the forest in fine martial order, rapidly crossed the plain, seized another isolated hill, opposite to that held by Donkin, and opened a heavy cannonade: at the same time Sebastiani approached the Spanish line, and pushed forward his light cavalry to make Cuesta show his order of battle; whereupon happened one of those events which show what a chance-medley thing a battle is, even in the hands of a great captain. The French horsemen, riding boldly up, commenced a pistol skirmish, to which the Spaniards replied with one general discharge of musketry, and then ten thousand infantry, with all the artillerymen, as if deprived of their senses, broke and fled away in confused heaps; the gunners carried away their horses, the footmen threw away their arms, the Adjutant-General O'Donoghue was foremost in flight, and even Cuesta went off some distance in his coach: the panic was spreading wide, and the elated horsemen charged down the Royal road, but Sir Arthur instantly flanked them with some English squadrons, the ditches on the opposite side were impracticable, the Spaniards who stood fast began to use their firearms, and those daring troopers had to retreat.

Most of the Spanish runaways made for Oropesa, saying the allies were defeated, the French in hot pursuit. Incredible disorder followed. The English commissaries went off with their animals, the paymasters carried away their moneychests, the baggage was scattered, and the alarm spread along the rear even to the frontier of Portugal. Cuesta indeed, having recovered his presence of mind, sent several thousand horsemen to head the fugitives and drive them back, and some of the artillerymen and horses were thus recovered; many of the infantry also, but in the next days battle the Spanish army was less by six thousand fighting men than it should have been, and the great redoubt in the centre was silent for want of guns.

While this disgraceful flight was being perpetrated on the right, the left of the English line displayed the greatest intrepidity. The round hill at the extremity was of easy ascent in rear, but steep and rugged towards the French, and was also protected there by the deep watercourse at the bottom. Nevertheless Victor, seeing Donkin's brigade was not numerous, and the summit of the hill still naked of troops, thought to seize the latter by a sudden assault.

FIRST COMBAT OF TALAVERA.

The sun was sinking, but the twilight and the confusion amongst the Spaniards appeared so favourable to the French marshal, that, without informing the king, he directed Ruffin's division to attack, Villatte's to follow in support, and Lapisse to assail the German Legion as a diversion for Ruffin, without engaging seriously. The assault was vigorous, and though Donkin beat back the French in his front, many of them turned his left and won the height in his rear. General Hill had been previously ordered to reinforce him, and it was not quite dark when that officer, while giving orders below, was shot at by men on the highest point; thinking they were English stragglers firing at the enemy, he rode up, followed by his brigade-major Fordyce, and in a moment found himself in the midst of the French. Fordyce was killed, Hill's horse was wounded, and a grenadier seized his bridle, but spurring hard he broke the man's hold and galloping down met the 29th Regiment, which he led up with so strong a charge the enemy could not sustain the shock.

When the summit was thus happily recovered, the 48th Regiment and a battalion of detachments were brought forward, and in conjunction with the 29th and Donkin's brigade presented a formidable front and in good time; for the troops beaten back were but part of a regiment forming the van of Ruffin's division, the two other regiments having lost their way in the watercourse; the attack had therefore only sub ~ sided, Lapisse soon opened fire against the Germans, and Ruffin's regiment in one mass again assailed the hill. The fighting then became vehement, and in the darkness the opposing flashes of musketry showed how resolutely the struggle was maintained, for the combatants were scarcely twenty yards asunder, and the event seemed doubtful; but the charging shout of the British soldier was at last heard above the din of arms, and the enemy's broken troops went down once more into the ravine below: Lapisse, who had made some impression on the Germans, then abandoned his false attack and the fighting of the 27th ceased. The British lost eight hundred men, the French a thousand.

Now the bivouac fires blazed up and the French and British soldiers were quiet, but at midnight the Spaniards opened a prodigious peal of musketry and artillery without cause or object; and during the remainder of the night, the line was frequently disturbed with desultory firing, which killed several men and officers.

From the prisoners Victor ascertained the exact position of the Spaniards, until then unknown, and when reporting his own failure proposed a second attack for next morning on the hill. Marshal Jourdan, chief of the king's staff, opposed this as a partial enterprise leading to no great result; yet Victor was so earnest for a trial, urging his intimate knowledge of the ground, that he won Joseph's assent. Then he placed all his guns in one mass on the height to the English left, from whence they could plunge into the great valley on their own right, range the summit of the hill in their front, and obliquely search the whole British line as far as the great redoubt between the allied armies. Ruffin was in front of the guns, Villatte in rear, yet having one regiment close to the watercourse; Lapisse occupied low table-land, opposite Sherbrooke; Latour Maubourg's cavalry formed a reserve for Lapisse; Beaumont's cavalry a reserve for Ruffin.

On the English side, Hill's division was concentrated on the disputed height; the cavalry was massed in a plain behind; the park of artillery and the hospitals were between the cavalry and Hill.

SECOND COMBAT OF TALAVERA.

About daybreak Ruffin's troops again menaced the English hill, moving against the front and by the great valley on their own right, thus embracing two sides. Their march was rapid and steady; they were followed by Villatte's men, and the assault was preceded with a burst of artillery that rattled round the height and swept away the English ranks by sections; the sharp chattering of musketry succeeded, and then the French guns were pointed towards the British centre and right. Soon their grenadiers. closed, the height sparkled with fire, and, as the inequalities of ground broke the formation, on both sides small bodies were seen, here and there, struggling for the mastery with all the virulence of a single combat. In some places the French were overthrown at once, in others they would not be denied and reached the summit, yet the English reserves always vindicated their ground and no permanent footing was obtained. Still the conflict was maintained with singular obstinacy. Hill himself was wounded and his men were falling fast, but the enemy suffered more and gave way, step by step at first and slowly to cover the retreat of their wounded, yet finally, unable to sustain the increasing fury of their opponents and having lost above fifteen hundred men in the space of forty minutes, the whole mass broke away in disorder, sheltered by the renewed play of their powerful artillery. To this destructive fire no adequate answer could be made, for the English guns were few and of small calibre, and when a reinforcement was demanded from Cuesta he sent two pieces ! useful however they were, and the Spanish gunners fought them gallantly.

Most of the repulsed troops had gone off by the great valley, and a favourable opportunity for a charge of horse occurred, but the English cavalry, having retired during the night for water and forage, were too distant to be of service. However, these repeated efforts of the French against the hill, and the appearance of their light troops on the mountain beyond the valley, taught the English general that he should prolong his flank on that side; wherefore he now posted a mass of cavalry with the leading squadrons looking into the valley, and sent a Spanish division of infantry to the mountain itself. At this time also, the Duke of Albuquerque, discontented with Cuesta's arrangements, came with his cavalry to the left and was placed behind the British: a formidable array of horsemen, six lines in depth, was thus presented.

Joseph, after examining the position from left to right, demanded of Jourdan and Victor if he should deliver a general battle. The former replied that when the great valley and the mountain were unoccupied on the 27th, Sir Arthur Wellesley's attention should have been drawn to the right by a feint on the Spaniards: that during the night the whole army should have been silently placed in column at the entrance of the great valley, ready at daybreak to form line of battle to its left on a new front, and so have attacked. Such a movement would have compelled the allies to change their front also, and during the operation they might have been assailed with success. This project could not then be executed. The English, aware of their mistake, had occupied the valley and the mountain, and were, front and flank alike, inattackable. *Hence, the only prudent line was to take up a position on the Alberche, and await the effect of Soult's operations on the English rear.*

Victor opposed this counsel. He engaged to carry the hill on the English left notwithstanding his former failures, provided Sebastiani would attack the right and centre at the same moment, finishing his argument thus: " *If such a combination failed, it was time to renounce making war.*" *

The king was embarrassed. His own opinion coincided with Jourdan's, yet he feared Victor would make the emperor think a great opportunity had been lost, and while thus wavering a despatch arrived from Soult, saying his forces could only reach Placencia between the 2nd and 5th of August; intelligence also came that a detachment from the army of Venegas had appeared near Toledo, and his van

---

* My authority for this colloquy is a written communication from Marshal Jourdan.

was approaching Aranjuez. This made the king tremble for Madrid. The stores, reserve artillery, and general hospitals of all the armies in Spain were there, and the tolls received at the gates formed almost the only pecuniary resource of his court: so narrowly did Napoleon reduce the expenditure of the war. These considerations overpowered his judgment; rejecting the better counsel, he resolved to succour the capital, yet first to try the chance of battle.

While the French chiefs were thus engaged in council, the wounded were carried to the rear on both sides; but the English soldiers were suffering from hunger, regular service of provisions had ceased for several days, and a few ounces of wheat in the grain formed the subsistence of men who had fought and were yet to fight so hardly. The Spanish camp was full of confusion and distrust. Cuesta inspired terror by his ferocity, but no confidence; and Albuquerque, from conviction or momentary anger, just as the French were coming on to the final attack, sent one of his staff to inform the English commander that Cuesta was betraying him. This message was first delivered to Colonel Donkin, who carried it to Sir Arthur, then seated on the hill intently watching the movements of the advancing enemy; he listened without turning his head, and drily answering—*Very well, you may return to your brigade*—continued his survey of the French. Such was his imperturbable resolution and quick penetration, and his conduct throughout the day was such as became a general upon whose vigilance and intrepidity the fate of fifty thousand men depended.

The dispositions of the French were soon completed. Ruffin's division, on the extreme right, was destined to cross the valley and move by the foot of the mountain to turn the British left

Villatte was to menace the key hill with one brigade, and guard the valley with another, thus connecting Ruffin's movement with the main attack.

Lapisse, supported by Latour Maubourg's dragoons and the king's reserve, was to fall with half his infantry upon Sherbrooke; the other half, connecting its attack with Villatte's brigade, was to make a third effort to master the twice-contested hill.

Milhaud's dragoons were placed in front of Talavera to

keep Cuesta in check; the rest of the heavy cavalry was brought into the centre behind Sebastiani, who was to assail the right of the British army.

Part of the French light cavalry supported Villatte's brigade in the valley, part remained in reserve, and many guns were distributed among the divisions; but the principal mass remained on Victor's hill with the reserve of light cavalry, where also the Duke of Belluno took post to direct the movements of his corps.

BATTLE OF TALAVERA.

From nine o'clock in the morning until mid-day there was no appearance of hostility, the weather was intensely hot, and the troops on both sides descended and mingled without fear or suspicion to quench their thirst at a brook separating the positions; but at one o'clock the French soldiers were seen to gather round their eagles, and the roll of drums was heard along their whole line. Half an hour later, Joseph's guards, the reserve, and Sebastiani's corps were descried in movement to join Victor's corps, and at two o'clock, the table-land and the height on the French right, even to the great valley, were covered with dark lowering masses of men.

At this moment, some hundreds of English soldiers employed to carry the wounded to the rear returned in one body, and were by the French supposed to be a detached corps rejoining the army; nevertheless, the Duke of Belluno gave the signal for battle, and eighty pieces of artillery sent a tempest of bullets before the light troops, who came on with the swiftness and violence of a hail-storm, and were closely followed by the broad black columns in all the majesty of war.

Sir Arthur Wellesley had from the summit of the hill a clear view of the whole field of battle. First he saw Sebastiani's troops rushing forwards with the usual impetuosity of French soldiers, clearing the intersected ground in their front and falling upon Campbell's division with infinite fury; yet that general, assisted by Mackenzie's brigade and two Spanish battalions, withstood their utmost efforts; for the English regiments, putting the French skirmishers aside, met the advancing columns with loud shouts, broke their front, lapped their flanks with fire, and giving no respite pushed them back with a terrible carnage. Ten guns were taken, but as Campbell would not break his line by a pursuit, the French, rallying on their supports, made head for another attack; yet the British guns and musketry played so vehemently on their masses while a Spanish cavalry regiment charged their flank, that they again retired in disorder and the victory was secured in that quarter.

During this fight Villatte, preceded by chosen grenadiers and supported by two regiments of light cavalry, advanced up the great valley, and Ruffin was discovered marching towards the mountain, whereupon Sir Arthur directed Anson's cavalry, composed of the 23rd Light Dragoons and 1st German hussars, to charge the head of Villatte's column. Going off at a canter and increasing their speed as they advanced, these regiments rode against the enemy, but soon came upon the brink of the water-course, which, descending from the hill, was there a chasm though not perceptible at a distance; the French, throwing themselves into squares behind it, opened their fire, and then the German Colonel Arentschildt, an officer whom forty years' service had made a master in his art, reined up at the brink, exclaiming, in his broken phrase, *I will not kill my young men !* Higher up however, facing the 23rd, the chasm was more practicable, and that regiment plunged down, men and horses rolling over each other in horrible confusion, the survivors ascending the opposite bank by twos and threes; their colonel, Seymour, was wounded, but Frederick Ponsonby, a hardy soldier, rallied all who came up, passed through Villatte's columns, which poured fire from each side, and fell with inexpressible violence upon a brigade of French *chasseurs* in the rear. The combat was fierce yet short, for Victor had before detached his Polish lancers and Westphalian light horse to support Villatte, and these fresh troops coming on when the 23rd, already over-matched, could scarcely stand against the *chasseurs,* entirely broke them: those who were not killed or taken made for the Spanish division on the mountain, leaving behind more than two hundred men and officers.

During this time the hill, the key of the position, was

again attacked, while Lapisse, having crossed the watercourse, pressed hard upon the English centre, where his artillery, aided by the great battery on Victor's hill, opened large gaps in Sherbrooke's ranks, and his columns went close up in the resolution to win. They were vigorously encountered and yielded in disorder, but the English Guards, quitting the line and following with inconsiderate ardour, were met by the French supporting columns and dragoons, whereupon the beaten troops turned, while heavy batteries pounded the flank and front of the Guards, who, thus maltreated, drew back, and coincidently, the German Legion being sorely pressed, got into confusion.

At this time Hill's and Campbell's divisions stood fast on each extremity of the line, yet the centre of the British was absolutely broken, and victory inclined towards the French, when suddenly Colonel Donellan was seen advancing with the 48th through the midst of the disordered masses. It seemed as if this regiment must be carried away with the retiring crowds, but wheeling back by companies it let them pass through the intervals, and then resuming its proud and beautiful line struck against the right of the pursuing enemy, plying such a destructive musketry and closing with such a firm countenance that his forward movement was checked. The Guards and Germans then rallied, a brigade of light cavalry came up from the second line at a trot, the artillery battered the flanks without intermission, the French wavered, and the battle was restored.

In all actions there is one critical and decisive moment which offers victory to the general who can seize it. When the Guards made their rash charge, Sir Arthur, foreseeing the issue, had sent the 48th down from the hill, although a rough battle was going on there, and at the same time directed the light cavalry to advance. This made the British strongest at the decisive point, the French relaxed their fighting while the English fire grew hotter, and their ringing shouts— sure augury of success—were heard along the whole line. In the hands of a great general, Joseph's guards and the reserve might have restored the combat, but combination was over with the French. Sebastiani's corps, beaten on the left with the loss of ten guns, was in confusion; the troops in the great valley on the right, amazed at the furious charge of the 23rd, and awed by four distinct lines of cavalry still in reserve, remained stationary, and no impression had been made on the hill; Lapisse was mortally wounded, his division had given way, and the king retired to his original position.

This retrograde movement was covered by skirmishers and an increasing fire of artillery; the British, exhausted by toil and want of food, and reduced to less than fourteen thousand sabres and bayonets, could not pursue, and the Spanish army was incapable of any evolution: at six o'clock hostilities ceased, yet the battle was scarcely over when the dry grass and shrubs took fire, and a volume of flames passing with inconceivable rapidity across a part of the field, scorched in its course both the dead and the wounded !

Two British generals, Mackenzie and Langworth, thirty one officers of inferior rank, seven hundred and sixty-seven sergeants and soldiers were killed. Three generals, a hundred and ninety two officers, three thousand seven hundred and eighteen sergeants and privates were wounded; nine officers, six hundred and forty-three sergeants and soldiers were missing: making a total loss of six thousand two hundred and sixty-eight in the two days' fighting, of which five thousand four hundred and twenty-two fell on the 28th.

On the French side, nine hundred and forty-four, including two generals, were killed. Six thousand two hundred and ninety-four were wounded, one hundred and fifty-six made prisoners; giving a total of seven thousand three hundred and eighty-nine men and officers, of which four thousand were of Victor's corps: ten guns were taken and seven left in the woods by the French. The Spaniards returned twelve hundred men killed and wounded, but the correctness of their report was very much doubted.

Early on the 29th the French quitted their position for the heights of Salinas behind the Alberche; and that day, General Robert Craufurd reached the English camp with the 43rd, 52nd and 95th regiments, and immediately took charge of the outposts. These troops, after a march of twenty miles, were in *bivouac* near Malpartida de Placencia when the alarm caused by the Spanish fugitives spread to that part. Craufurd, fearing the army was pressed, allowed his men to rest

for a few hours, and then withdrawing fifty of the weakest marched
with a resolution not to halt until he reached the field of battle. As the
brigade advanced it met crowds of the runaways, not all Spaniards,
but all propagating the vilest falsehoods: *the army was defeated—Sir
Arthur Wellesley was killed—the French were only a few miles
distant:* some, blinded by their fears, pretended even to point out the
enemy's posts on the nearest hills ! Indignant at this shameful scene
the troops pressed on with impetuous speed, and leaving only seventeen stragglers behind, in twenty-six hours crossed the field of battle,
a strong compact body, having during that time marched sixty-two
English miles in the hottest season of the year, each man carrying
from fifty to sixty pounds weight. Had the historian Gibbon known
of such an effort, he would have spared his sneer about the delicacy
of modern soldiers !*

The desperate fighting of the English soldier, responding to his
general's genius, had now saved the army from the clanger imposed
by Cuesta's perverseness and the infirmity of the Spanish troops; but
Sir A. Wellesley had still to expiate his own errors as to Spanish
character, Spanish warfare, and the French power and resources.
Soult, after his retreat, had so promptly reorganized his force as to be
co-operating with Ney against the Gallician insurgents, when in the
British camp he was supposed to be wandering, distressed, and
shirking every foe. Meanwhile Napoleon, foreseeing with intuitive
sagacity that the English general would operate by the valley
of the Tagus, and Gallicia consequently be abandoned, gave
Soult authority to unite in Leon the troops of Mortier, Ney
and Kellermann to his own, above fifty thousand fighting men
in all. With them he was to fall on the British communications,
by crossing the Gredos mountains and entering the valley of

---

* In a recent work upon the war in Algeria, written by General Yusuf, a French
Zoave, evidently a man of great military talent, a march of sixty miles in twenty-si~
hours by a French detachment is recorded, and by an English writer has been compared
with this of the light division. But the French soldier does not carry more than two-
thirds of the weight an English soldier carries,and Yusuf does not say how many
stragglers there were; moreover the lightdivision had previously made a march of
twenty miles with only a few hours to rest, or rather to wash and cook: their real march
was therefore eighty-two miles.

the Tagus; but Ney, discontented at being under Soult's command, was dilatory, and the latter only passed the Gredos the 31st instead of the 29th as he designed; the allies thus escaped being inclosed between two French armies, each an overmatch for them in numbers and power of movement.

Sir A. Wellesley had heard on the 30th that Soult was likely to cross the mountains, yet, thinking him weak, only desired Cuesta to reinforce some Spanish troops previously posted at the pass of Banos, which had however been already forced by the French; but on the 2nd of August it became known that Soult had descended upon Placencia and taken all the English stores there; news which aroused both generals; then they agreed that Sir Arthur should march against him, while Cuesta remained at Talavera to watch the king— promising to bring off the men in the British hospitals if forced to retreat. Sir Arthur, relying on this, marched the 3rd, still thinking Soult had only fifteen thousand men, the remnant-of his former army; but he had fifty-three thousand, and on the morning of the 4th the English general found himself with seventeen thousand half-starved soldiers at Oropesa, Soult being in his front, Victor menacing his rear, and Cuesta' false to his word, close at hand, having left fifteen hundred British sick and wounded to the enemy. The fate of the Peninsula was then hanging by a thread which could not support the weight for twelve hours, and only one resource remained: the bridge of Arzobispo was near, and the army crossed the Tagus, leaving the French with all the credit of the campaign.

On the mountains beyond that river, the English general maintained a defensive position until the 20th against the enemy; but against the evil proceedings of the Spanish government and Spanish generals he could not hold his ground, and therefore retired into Portugal; having during his short campaign lost by sickness and in battle, or abandoned,- three thousand five hundred gallant soldiers and nearly two thousand horses, fifteen hundred of which died of want.

BOOK III.

Combats on the Coa and Agueda—Barba de Puerco—Combat of
Almeida—Anecdotes of British Soldiers—Battle of Busaco.

COMBATS ON THE COA AND AGUEDA.

" *I have fished in many troubled waters, but Spanish troubled
waters I will never try again.*"

Thus said Sir A. Wellesley after the campaign of Talavera, by
which he had acquired the title of Viscount Wellington, and a
thorough knowledge of the Spanish character. Looking then to
Portugal as his base for future operations, he conceived and commenced the gigantic lines of Torres Vedras as a depository for the
independence of the Peninsula —a grand project, conceived and
enforced with all the might of genius. But while preparing this
stronghold he did not resign the frontier, and when Massena, Prince
of Essling, menaced Portugal in 1810 with sixty-five thousand
fighting men in line, besides garrisons and reserves, he found a
mingled British and Portuguese army ready to oppose him.

This defensive force was disposed in two distinct masses. One
under General Hill opposed invasion by the line of the Tagus, the
other under Lord Wellington opposed it by the line of the Mondego;
they were however separated by the great Estrella mountain and its
offshoots, and Massena, when he took Ciudad Rodrigo, could concentrate his whole army on either line, moving in front of the Estrella
by a shorter and easier road than the English general could concentrate his troops behind that mountain. Lord Wellington opened
indeed a military road which shortened the line of co-operation with
Hill; yet this was only an alleviation, the advantage remained with the
French, and Wellington had to trust his own quickness and the
strength of intermediate positions for uniting his army in the lines of
Torres Vedras. Yield ground without force however he would not,
and therefore had, previous to the fall of Ciudad Rodrigo, detached
General Robert Craufurd with the light division, two regiments of

cavalry, and six pieces of horse-artillery, to the Agueda, in observation of the French army. On that advanced position they sustained several actions. The first at Barba de Puerco, a village, between which and the opposite French post of San Felices yawned a gloomy chasm, and at the bottom, foaming over huge rocks, the Agueda swept along beneath a high narrow bridge. This post, held by the English riflemen, was of singular strength, yet scarcely was the line of the Agueda taken when General Ferey, a bold officer, desirous to create a fear of French enterprise, attempted a surprise.

Secretly placing six hundred grenadiers below, at an hour when the moon, rising behind him, cast long shadows from the rocks deepening the darkness of the chasm, he silently passed the bridge, surprised and bayoneted the sentinels, ascended the opposite crags with incredible speed, and fell upon the picquets so fiercely that all went fighting into the village while the first shout was still echoing in the gulf behind. So sudden was the attack, so great the confusion, that no order could be maintained, and each soldier encountering the nearest enemy fought hand to hand, while their colonel, Sidney Beckwith, conspicuous from his lofty stature and daring action, a man capable of rallying a whole army in flight, exhorting, shouting, and personally fighting, urged all forward until the French were pushed down the ravine again in retreat.

After this combat Craufurd kept his dangerous position for four months, during which several skirmishes took place. The one of most note was at the village of Barquilla, where he surprised and captured some French horsemen, but afterwards rashly charging two hundred French infantry under Captain Gouache, was beaten off with the loss of the cavalry colonel, Talbot, and thirty-two troopers.

COMBAT OF ALMEIDA ON THE COA.

Soon after this skirmish Ciudad Rodrigo fell, and Ney advanced towards Almeida on the Coa. Craufurd's orders were to recross that river, yet from headstrong ambition he remained with four thousand British and Portuguese infantry, eleven hundred cavalry and six guns to fight thirty thousand French on bad ground; for though his left, resting on an unfinished tower eight hundred yards from Almeida, was protected by the guns of that fortress, his right was insecure; most of his cavalry was in an open plain in front, and in his rear was a deep ravine, at the bottom of which, more than a mile off, was the Coa with only one narrow bridge for a retreat.

A stormy night ushered in the 24th of July, and the troops, drenched with rain, were under arms before daylight expecting to retire when some pistol-shots in front, followed by an order for the cavalry reserves and guns to advance, gave notice of the enemy's approach; then the morning cleared, and twenty-four thousand :French infantry, five thousand cavalry, and thirty pieces of artillery, were observed in march beyond the Turones. The British line was immediately contracted and brought under the edge of the ravine, but Ney had seen Craufurd's false disposition, and came down with the stoop of an eagle—four thousand horsemen and a powerful artillery swept the English cavalry from the plain, and Loison's infantry, rushing on at a charging pace, made for the centre and left of the position.

While the French were thus pouring down, several illjudged changes were made on the English side; a part of the troops were advanced, others drawn back; the 43rd Regiment was placed within an inclosure of solid masonry ten feet high, near the road, about half-musket-shot down the ravine and having but one narrow outlet! The firing in front became heavy, the cavalry, the artillery and Portuguese caçadores successively passed this inclosure in retreat, the sharp clang of the rifles was heard along the edge of the plain above, and in a few moments the imprisoned regiment would have been without a hope of escape, if here, as in every other part of the field, the battalion officers had not remedied the faults of the general. The egress was so narrow that some large stones were loosened, a powerful simultaneous effort of the whole line then burst the wall, and the next instant the regiment was up with the riflemen. There was no room for array, no time for anything but battle, every captain carried off his company independently, joining as he could with the riflemen and 52nd, and a mass of skirmishers was thus presented, acting in small parties and under no regular command, yet each confident in the courage and discipline of those on his right and left, and all keeping together with surprising vigour.

It is unnecessary to describe the first burst of French soldiers, it is well known with what gallantry the officers lead, with what vehemence the troops follow, with what a storm of fire they waste a field of battle. At this moment, with the advantage of ground and numbers, they were breaking over the edge of the ravine, their guns, ranged along the summit, pouring down grape, while their hussars galloped over the glacis of Almeida and along the road to the bridge sabreing everything in their way. Ney, desirous that Montbrun should follow the hussars with the whole of the French cavalry, sent five officers in succession to urge him on, and so mixed were friends and enemies, that only a few guns of the fortress dared open, and no courage could have availed against such overwhelming numbers: but Montbrun enjoyed an independent command, and as the attack was made without Massena's knowledge he would not stir. Then the British regiments, with singular intelligence and discipline, extricated themselves from their perilous situation. Falling back slowly and stopping to fight whenever opportunity offered, they retired down the ravine, tangled as it was with crags and vineyards, in despite of their enemies; who were yet so fierce and eager that even their horsemen rode amongst the inclosures, striking at the soldiers as they mounted the walls or scrambled over the rocks.

Soon the retreating troops approached the river, and the ground became more open, but the left wing, hardest pressed and having the shortest distance, arrived while the bridge was crowded with artillery and cavalry, and the right was still distant! Major Macleod of the 43rd instantly rallied four companies of his regiment on a hill to cover the line of passage, he was joined by some riflemen, and at the same time the brigade-major Rowan* posted two companies on another hill to the left, flanking the road: these posts were maintained while the right wing was filing over the river, yet the French gathering in great numbers made a rush, forcing the British companies back before the bridge was

---

* Now Sir Charles Rowan, Metropolitan Police.

cleared, and when part of the 52nd was still distant from it. Very imminent was the danger, but McLeod, a young man endowed with a natural genius for war, turned his horse, called on the troops to follow, waved his cap, and rode with a shout towards the enemy, on whom the suddenness of the thing and the animating gesture of the man produced the effect designed, for the soldiers rushed after him, cheering and charging as if a whole army had been at their backs: the enemy's skirmishers not comprehending this stopped short, and before their surprise was over the 52nd passed the river, and McLeod followed at speed: it was a fine exploit !

As the infantry passed the bridge they planted themselves in loose order on the side of the mountain, the artillery went to the summit, and the cavalry observed the roads to the right; this disposition was made to watch some upper fords two miles off, and the bridge of Castello Bom; for it was to be apprehended that while Ney attacked in front, other troops might pass by those fords and bridge of Castello Bom and so cut off the division from the army: the river was however rising fast with the rain, and it was impossible to retreat farther until nightfall.

Soon the French skirmishers opened a biting fire across the water: it was returned as bitterly; the artillery on both sides played vigorously, the sounds were repeated by numberless echoes, and the smoke slowly rising, resolved itself into an immense arch, spanning the whole gulf and sparkling with the whirling fuzes of the flying shells. Fast and thickly the French gathered behind the high rocks, and a dragoon was seen to try the depth of the upper stream above, but two shots from the 52nd killed horse and man, and the carcasses floating down between the contending forces intimated that the river was impassable save by the bridge. Then the monotonous tones of a French drum were heard, the head of a noble column darkened the long narrow bridge, a drummer and an officer, the last in a splendid uniform leaped together to the front and the whole rushed on with loud cries. The depth of the ravine so deceived the English soldiers' aim at first, that two-thirds of the passage was won ere a shot had brought down an enemy; yet a few paces onwards the line of death was traced, and the whole of the leading French section fell as one man; the gallant column still pressed forward, but none could pass that terrible line, and the killed and wounded rolled together until the heap rose nearly even with the parapet, while the living mass behind them melted away rather than gave back.

The shouts of the British now rose loudly, yet they were confidently answered, and in half an hour another column, more numerous than the first, again crowded the bridge: this time the range was far better judged and ere half the passage was gained the multitude was again torn, shattered, dispersed or slain: only ten or twelve men crossed to take shelter under the rocks at the brink of the river. The skirmishing was then renewed, yet a French surgeon, coming to the very foot of the bridge, waved a handkerchief and commenced dressing the wounded under the hottest fire; nor was the brave man's touching appeal unheeded, every musket turned from him, although his still undaunted countrymen were preparing for a third attempt, a last effort, which was made indeed, yet with fewer numbers and less energy, for the impossibility of forcing the passage was become apparent. The combat was however continued. By the French as a point of honour, to cover the escape of those who had passed the bridge; by the English from ignorance of their object. One of the enemy's guns was dismantled, a field magazine exploded, and many continued to fall on both sides until about four o'clock, when torrents of rain caused a momentary cessation of fire, the men amongst the rocks then escaped to their own side, the fight ceased and Craufurd retired in the night behind the Pinhel river. Forty-four Portuguese, two hundred and seventy-two British, including twenty-eight officers, were killed, wounded, or taken; and it was at first supposed that half a company of the 52nd, posted in the unfinished tower, were captured; but their officer, keeping close until the night, had passed the enemy's posts, and crossed the Coa. The French lost above a thousand men, and the slaughter at the bridge was fearful to behold. During the combat General Picton came up from Pinhel alone, and Craufurd asked him for the support of the third divi sion; he refused, and they separated after a sharp altercation.*

* This altercation, though public and known to the whole division, has been
ridiculously denied by the writer of Picton's life.

Picton was wrong, for Craufurd's situation was one of extreme danger; he could not then retire, and Massena might, by the bridge of Castello Bom, have taken the division in flank and destroyed it between the Coa and Pinhel rivers. Picton and Craufurd were however not formed by nature to agree. The stern countenance, robust frame, saturnine complexion, caustic speech and austere demeanour of the first promised little sympathy with the short thick figure, dark flashing eyes, quick movements and fiery temper of the second: nor did they often meet without a quarrel. Nevertheless, they had many points of resemblance in their characters and fortunes. Both were harsh and rigid in command; both prone to disobedience, yet exacting entire submission from inferiors; alike ambitious and craving of glory, they were both enterprising, yet neither was expert in handling troops under fire. After distinguished services both perished in arms, and being celebrated as generals of division while living, have been, since their deaths, injudiciously spoken of as rivalling their great leader in war.

That they were officers of mark and pretension is unquestionable—Craufurd far more so than Picton, because the latter never had a separate command and his opportunities were more circumscribed— but to compare either to the Duke of Wellington displays ignorance of the men and of the art they professed. If they had even comprehended the profound military and political combinations he was then conducting, the one would have carefully avoided fighting on the Coa, and the other, far from refusing, would have eagerly proffered his support.

Here some illustrations of the intelligence and the lofty spirit of British soldiers will not be misplaced.

When the last of the retreating troops had passed thebridge, an Irishman of the 43rd, named Pigot, a bold turbulent fellow, leaned on his firelock, regarded the advancing enemy for some time, and then in the author's hearing thus delivered his opinion of the action.

" *General Craufurd wanted glory, so he stopped on the wrong side of the river, and now he is knocked over to the right side. The French general won't be content until his men try to get on the wrong*

side also, and then they will be knocked back. Well ! both will claim
a victory, which is neither here nor there, but just in the middle of the
river. That's glory !" Then firing his musket he fell into the ranks.
Even to the letter was his prediction verified, for General Craufurd
published a contradiction of Massena's dispatch.

This sarcasm was enforced by one of a tragic nature. There was
a fellow-soldier to Pigot, a north of Ireland man, named Stewart but
jocularly called the Boy because of his youth, being only nineteen,
and of his gigantic stature and strength. He had fought bravely and
displayed great intelligence beyond the river, and was one of the last
men who came down to the bridge, but he would not pass. Turning
round, he regarded the French with a grim look, and spoke aloud as
follows. *" So ! This is the end of our boasting. This is our first battle*
and we retreat! The boy Stewart will not live to hear that said." Then
striding forward in his giant might he fell furiously on the nearest
enemies with the bayonet, refused the quarter they seemed desirous
of granting, and died fighting in the midst of them !

Still more touching, more noble, more heroic was the death of
Sergeant Robert McQuade. During McLeod's rush this man, also
from the north of Ireland, saw two Frenchmen level their muskets on
rests against a high gap in a bank, awaiting the uprise of an enemy;
the present Sir George Brown, then a lad of sixteen, attempted to
ascend at the fatal point, but McQuade, himself only twenty-four
years of age, pulled him back, saying with a calm decided tone *"You*
are too young Sir to be killed," and then offering his own person to
the fire fell dead, pierced with both balls !

BATTLE OF BUSACO.

Soon after Craufurd's combat, Almeida was betrayed by some
Portuguese officers, and Massena, who had previously menaced both
lines of invasion, adopted that of the Mondego. This river, flowing
between the Estrella mountain and the Sierra de Caramula, is separated by the latter from the coast,along which the Royal road runs
from Oporto to Lisbon.The roads on each side of the river were very
rugged, and at the southern end of the valley crossed by two mountain

ridges, namely, the Sierra de Murcella on the left bank, the Sierra de Busaco on the right bank. Wellington had prepared the former for battle, and General Hill was coming to it by the military road, but Massena, aware of its strength, crossed to the right of the Mondego, and moved by Viseu, to turn Wellington's flank and surprise Coimbra; he however knew nothing of Busaco, which covered that city, and so fell into the worst road and lost two days waiting for his artillery. Meanwhile his adversary also passed the Mondego, and sending troops to the front broke the bridges on the Criz and Dao, mountain torrents crossing the French line of march.

Coimbra could not then be surprised, yet Massena could from Viseu gain the Royal coast-road and so reach Coimbra, turning the Busaco position; he could also repass the Mondego and assail the Murcella; wherefore the allied army was necessarily scattered. Hill had by forced marches reached the Murcella; Spencer was detached to watch the Royal coast-road; the light division, Pack's Portuguese, and the cavalry, were in observation on the Viseu road; the remainder of the army was in reserve at the fords of the Mondego, to act on either side. In this state of affairs happened a strange incident. The light division had established its bivouac towards evening in a pine-wood, but a peasant advised a removal, saving it was known as the Devil's wood, that an evil influence reigned, and no person who slept there had ever escaped it. He was laughed at, yet he did not fable. In the night all the troops, men and officers, seized as it were with sudden frenzy, started from sleep and dispersed in all directions: nor was their strange terror allayed until voices were heard crying out ·that the enemy's cavalry were amongst them, when the soldiers mechanically ran together and the illusion was dissipated.

After some delay Massena moved down the Mondego and Busaco was then occupied by the English general. His line was eight miles long, flanked on the right by the river, and on the left connected with the Caramula by ridges and ravines impervious to an army. A road along the crest furnished easy communication, and the ford of Pena Cova, behind the right, gave direct access to the Murcella ridge. Rugged and steep the face of Busaco was, yet the summit had space for the action of a few cavalry and salient points gave play to the artillery, while the counter-ridge offered no facility to the enemy's guns. When it was first adopted some generals expressed a fear that the Prince of Essling would not attack—*"But if he does I shall beat him"* was Wellington's reply: he knew his obstinate character.

Massena had three army corps, Ney's, Junot's, and Reynier's, with a division of heavy cavalry under Montbrun; and as he knew nothing of the Torres Vedras lines, and despised the Portuguese, he was convinced the English would retreat and embark. A great general in dangerous conjunctures, he was here, from age and satisfied ambition, negligent, dilatory, and misled by some Portuguese noblemen in his camp. Instead of marching with his whole army compact for battle he retained Junot and Montbrun in the rear, while Ney and Reynier, restoring the bridges over the Criz, drove the English cavalry into the hills, forced back the light division with a sharp fight, and crowned the counter-ridges in front of Busaco.

Ney seeing that Busaco was a crested mountain and could not hide strong reserves, that it was only half-occupied and the troops were moving about in the disorder of first taking up unknown ground, wished to attack at once; but Massena was ten miles in rear, and an officer sent to ask his assent was kept two hours without an audience and then sent back with an order to await the prince's arrival*. A great opportunity was thus lost, for Spencer had not then come in, Leith was only passing the Mondego, Hill was on the Murcella scarcely twenty-five thousand men were in line, and there was unavoidable confusion and great intervals between the divisions.

Ney and Reynier wrote in the night to Massena, advising an attack at daybreak, yet he did not come up until midday with Junot's corps and the cavalry, and then proceeded leisurely to examine the position. It was now completely manned. Hill had the extreme right, Leith was next in line, Picton next to Leith. Spencer's division and a regiment of dragoons were on the highest crest in reserve, having on their left the convent of Busaco. In front of Spencer a Por-

---

* For this anecdote my authority was Colonel D'Esmenard, Ney's first aide-de-camp, the officer employed. He said Massena was in bed, and spoke to him through the door.

tuguese division was posted half-way down the mountain, and on his left, in front of the convent, was the light division, supported by a German brigade and the 19th Portuguese Regiment. Cole's division closed the extreme left, on a line ,with the light division and covered, flank and front, by impassable ravines. There were long intervals in the line, but the spaces between were unassailable, artillery was disposed on all the salient points, skirmishers covered all the accessible ground, and so formidable did the position appear that Ney now strongly objected to an attack. Reynier however, a presumptuous man, advised one, and Massena made dispositions for the next morning.

His ground did not permit any broad front of attack, and two points were chosen. Reynier was to fall on Picton; Ney was to assail the light division. These attacks, governed by the roads, were about three miles asunder. and as Junot's corps and Montbrun's cavalry were held in reserve, only forty thousand men were employed to storm a mountain on which sixty thousand enemies were posted; yet the latter, from the extent of their ground and the impossibility of making any counter attack, were the weakest at the decisive points. The light division was on a spur, or rather brow of ground, overhanging a ravine so deep that the eye could scarcely discern troops at the bottom, yet so narrow that the French twelve-pounders ranged across. Into the lowest parts of this ravine their light troops towards dusk dropped by twos and threes, and endeavoured to steal up the wooded dells and hollows, close to the picquets of the division; they were vigorously checked, yet similar attempts at different points kept the troops watchful, and indeed none but veterans tired of war could have slept beneath that serene sky, glittering with stars above, while the dark mountains were crowned with innumerable fires, around which more than a hundred thousand brave men were gathered.

Before daybreak on the 27th, five columns of attack were in motion, and Reynier's troops, having comparatively easier ground, were in the midst of the picquets and skirmishers of Picton's division almost as soon as they could be perceived; the resistance was vigorous and six guns played along the ascent with grape, yet in half an hour the French were close to the summit of the mountain, with such astonishing power and resolution did they overthrow everything that opposed their progress ! The right of the third division was forced back, the 8th Portuguese Regiment broken, the highest part of the crest was gained between Picton and Leith, and the leading battalions established themselves amongst some crowning rocks, while a following mass wheeled to the right, designing to sweep the summit of the sierra. Lord Wellington immediately opened two guns loaded with grape upon their flank, a heavy musketry was poured into their front, and the 88th Regiment, joined by a wing of the 45th, charged furiously; fresh men could not have withstood that terrible shock; the French, exhausted by their efforts, opposed only a straggling fire, and both parties went mingling together down. the mountain side with a mighty clamour and confusion, their track strewed with the dead and dying even to the bottom of the valley.

Meanwhile the battalions which had first gained the crest formed to their left, resting their right on a precipice overhanging the reverse side of the sierra: the position was thus won if any reserve had been at hand; for the greatest part of Picton's troops were engaged elsewhere, and some of the French skirmishers actually descended the back of the ridge.A misty cloud capped the summit, and this hostile mass, ensconced amongst the rocks, could not be seen except by Leith; but that officer had put a brigade in motion when he first perceived the vigorous impression made on Picton, and though two miles of rugged ground were to be, passed on a narrow front before it could mingle in the fight, it was coming on rapidly; the Royals were in reserve, the 38th were seeking to turn the enemy's right, and the 9th, under Colonel Cameron, menaced his front: the precipice stopped the 38th, but Cameron, hearing from a staff-officer how critical was the affair, formed line under a violent fire, and without returning a shot run in upon the French grenadiers and drove them from the rocks with irresistible bravery; then he plied them with a destructive musketry as long as they could be reached, yet with excellent discipline refrained from pursuit lest the crest of the position should be again lost; for the mountain was rugged, and to judge the general state of the action difficult. Hill however now edged in towards the scene of action, Leith's second brigade joined the first, and a great mass of fresh troops was thus concentrated, while Reynier had neither reserves nor guns to restore the fight.

Ney's attack had as little success. From the mountainspur where the light division stood the bottom of the valley could be discerned, the ascent was much steeper than where Reynier had attacked, and Craufurd in a happy mood of command made masterly dispositions. The platform which he held was scooped so as to conceal the 43rd and 52nd Regiments, though in line, and hence the German infantry who were behind them, being on higher ground, appeared the only solid force for resistance. Some rocks overhanging the descent furnished natural embrasures, in which the divisional guns were placed, and the riflemen and Portuguese caçadores, planted as skirmishers, covered the slope of the mountain.

While it was still dark a straggling musketry was heard in the deep ravine, and when light broke, three heavy masses, entering the woods below, threw forward a swarm of light troops. One column, under General Marchand, on emerging from the dark chasm, turned to its left, and seemed intent to turn the right of the division; a second under Loison made straight up the face of the mountain by a road leading to the convent; the third remained in reserve. General Simon's brigade was at the head of Loison's attack, and it ascended with a wonderful alacrity; for though the skirmishers plied it unceasingly with musketry, and the artillery bullets swept through it from front to rear, its order was not disturbed, nor its speed abated. The English guns were worked with great rapidity, yet their range was contracted every round, the enemy's musket-balls came singing up in a sharper key, and soon the British skirmishers, breathless and begrimed with powder, rushed over the edge of the ascent—the artillery then drew back, and the victorious cries of the French were heard within a few yards of the summit.

Craufurd, standing alone on one of the rocks, had silently watched the attack, but now, with a quick shrill cry, called on the two regiments to charge ! Then a horrid shout startled the French column, and eighteen hundred British bayonets went sparkling over the brow of the hill: yet so sternly resolute, so hardy was the enemy, that each man of the first section raised his musket, and two officers with ten soldiers of the 52nd fell before them—not a Frenchman had missed his mark! They could do no more: the head of their column was violently thrown back upon the rear, both flanks were overlapped, three terrible discharges at five yards' distance shattered the wavering mass, and a long trail of broken arms and bleeding carcasses marked the line of flight. The main body of the British stood fast, but some companies followed down the mountain, whereupon Ney threw forward his reserved division, and opening his guns from the opposite heights, killed some of the pursuers: thus warned, they recovered their own ground, and the Germans were brought forward to skirmish: meanwhile a small flanking detachment had passed round the right, and rising near the convent, was defeated by the 19th Portuguese regiment under Colonel McBean.

Loison did not renew the fight, but Marchand, having gained a pine-wood half-way up the mountain, on the right of the light division, sent a cloud of skirmishers up from thence about the time General Simon was beaten: the ascent was however so steep that Pack's Portuguese sufficed to hold them in check, and higher up Spencer showed his line of foot-guards in support; Craufurd's artillery also smote Marchand's people in the pine-wood; and Ney, who was there in person, after sustaining this murderous cannonade for an hour relinquished that attack. The desultory fighting of light troops then ceased, and before two o'clock parties from both armies were, under a momentary truce, amicably mixed searching for wounded men.

Towards evening a French company with signal audacity seized a village half musket-shot from the light division, and refused to retire; whereupon Craufurd, turning twelve guns on the houses, overwhelmed them with bullets; but after paying the French captain this distinguished honour, recovering his temper, he sent a company of the 43rd down, which cleared the village in a few minutes. Meanwhile an affecting incident, contrasting strongly with the savage character of the preceding events, added to the interest of the day. A poor orphan Portuguese girl, seventeen years of age and very handsome, was seen coming down the mountain, driving an ass loaded with all her property through the midst of the French army. She had abandoned her dwelling; in obedience to the proclamation, and now passed over the field of battle with a childish simplicity, totally unconscious of her perilous situation, and scarcely understanding which were the hostile and which the friendly troops, for no man on either side was so brutal as to molest her.

This battle was fought unnecessarily by Massena, and by Wellington reluctantly, being forced thereto from the misconduct of the Portuguese government. It was however entirely to the disadvantage of the French, who had a general and eight hundred men killed, two generals wounded, and one, Simon, made prisoner. Their whole loss may be estimated at four thousand five hundred men, while that of the allies did not exceed thirteen hundred.

Massena now judged Busaco impregnable, and as it could not be turned by the Mondego, because the allies might pass that river on a shorter line, it was proposed in council to return to Spain; but at that moment a peasant told him of a road leading over the Caramula and he resolved to turn the allies' left. To mask this movement the skirmishing was renewed on the 28th so warmly that a general battle was expected; yet an ostentatious display of men, the disappearance of baggage, and the casting up of earth indicated some other design. In the evening, the French infantry were sensibly diminished, the cavalry was descried winding over the distant mountains towards the allies' left, and the project was then apparent. Wellington arrived from the right, and observed the distant columns for some time with great earnestness; he seemed uneasy, his countenance bore a fierce and angry expression, and suddenly mounting his horse he rode off without speaking—one hour later and the army was in movement to abandon Busaco, for Massena had threaded the defiles of the Caramula and was marching upon Coimbra.

Wellington's plan was to lay the country waste before the enemy, but only the richest inhabitants had quitted Coimbra; that city was still populous when the enemy's approach left no choice but to fly or risk the punishment of death and infamy announced for remaining: then a scene of distress ensued that the most hardened could not behold without emotion. Mothers with children of all ages, the sick, the old, the bedridden, and even lunatics, went or were carried forth, the most part with little hope and less help, to journey for days in company with contending armies. Fortunately for this unhappy multitude the weather was fine and the roads firm, or the greatest number must have perished in the most deplorable manner: but all this misery was of no avail, for though the people fled, the provisions were left and the mills were but partially and imperfectly ruined.

On the 1st of October, the allied outposts were driven from a hill north of Coimbra, and the French horsemen entered a plain, where they suffered some loss from a cannonade. The British cavalry were there drawn up on open ground in opposition, and as the disparity of numbers was not very great, the opportunity seemed fair for a good stroke; yet they withdrew across the Mondego, and so unskilfully that some of the hindmost were cut down in the middle of the river, and the French were only prevented from forcing the passage of the ford by a strong skirmish in which fifty or sixty men fell.

This untoward fight compelled the light division to march hastily through the city to gain the defile of Condeixa, which commenced at the end of the bridge; all the inhabitants who had not before quitted the place then rushed out with what could be caught up in hand, driving animals loaded with sick people and children on to the bridge where the press became so great the troops halted. This stoppage was close to the prison, from whence the jailer had fled with the keys, and the prisoners, crowding to the windows, strived to tear the bars off with their hands, and even with their teeth, bellowing in the most frantic manner. Then the bitter lamentations of the multitude increased, and the pistol-shots of the cavalry engaged at the ford below were distinctly heard; it was a shocking scene; but William Campbell, a staff officer of heroic strength and temper, broke the prison doors and freed the wretched inmates. The troops now forced a way over the bridge, yet at the other end, the defile was cut through high rocks, and so crowded that no passage could be made, and a troop of

French dragoons, having passed an unwatched ford, hovered close to the flank: one regiment of infantry could have destroyed the whole division, wedged as it was in a hollow way, unable to retreat, advance, or break out on either side.

Three days Massena halted at Coimbra, the fourth he advanced, leaving behind his sick and wounded with a garrison, in all five thousand men, who were suddenly captured four days later by a small militia force under Colonel Trant! This *" heavy blow and great discouragement "* * did not stop the French prince, and during his pursuit thirty-six French squadrons fell on ten British squadrons, but in a severe fight did not gain five miles in as many hours; yet a few days after his cavalry had the advantage in a greater action, and finally the allies entered the lines of Torres Vedras, the existence of which was first made known to Massena by the bar they offered ! Several skirmishes, in which the English general Harvey was wounded and the French general St. Croix killed, were necessary to convince him they could not be stormed; but though he was without magazines, he continued to hold his menacing position until the country behind him was a desert: then falling back two marches, he took a defensive position at Santarem, and was in turn blockaded by Lord Wellington.

---

* This forcible expression, now become common, is generally supposed to be an original saying of the late Lord Melbourne; but it is not so. It was first employed by the Spanish government in a manifesto, to characterise the battle of Baylen, and Lord Melbourne adopted it without acknowledging its source.

BOOK IV.

Matagorda—Battle of Barosa—Massena's Retreat—Combat of Redina
—Cazal Nova—Foz d' Aronce—Sabugal—Fuentes Onoro—Battle of
Fuente Orono—Evacuation of Almeida.

MATAGORDA.

Before Massena invaded Portugal king Joseph had subdued Andalusia, except the Isla de Leon where Cadiz stands. He left Soult in that
province with a large army, of which a part under Sebastiani held
Granada, while another part under Victor blockaded the Isla with
immense works; the remainder, under Soult in person, formed a field-
force to war against insurrections and the numerous Spanish troops,
which in separate bodies acted against him. The Spaniards, after long
demurring, admitted an auxiliary British and Portuguese force into
Cadiz, under General Graham,* whose arrival was signalized by
the cannonade of Matagorda. This small fort, without ditch or bomb-
proof, was held for fifty-four days by a garrison of seamen and
soldiers, under Captain McLean,† close to the French lines at the
Trocadero. A Spanish seventy-four, and a flotilla, had co-operated in
the resistance until daybreak on the 21st of March, but then a hissing
shower of heated shot made them cut their cables and run under the
works of Cadiz, while the fire of forty-eight guns and mortars of the
largest size, was turned upon the fort, whose feeble parapet vanished
before that crashing flight of metal, leaving only the naked rampart
and undaunted hearts of the garrison for defence. The men fell fast,
and the enemy shot so quick and close, that a staff bearing the Spanish
flag was broken six times in an hour; the colours were then fastened
to the angle of the work itself, but unwillingly by the men, especially
the sailors, all calling out to hoist the British ensign, and attributing
the slaughter to their fighting under a foreign flag !

Thirty hours this tempest lasted, and sixty-four men out of one
hundred and forty had fallen, when Graham, finding

* Lord Lynedoch.   †Now Lieut.-Gen. Sir A. McLean.

a diversion he had projected impracticable, sent boats to carry off the survivors With these boats went Major Lefebre, an engineer of great promise, but to fall there, the last man whose blood wetted the ruins thus abandoned: and here be recorded an action of which it is difficult to say whether it were most feminine or heroic. A sergeant's wife, named Retson, was in a casemate with wounded men, when a young drummer was ordered to fetch water from the well of the fort; seeing the child hesitate, she snatched the vessel from him, braved the terrible cannonade, and when a shot cut the bucket-cord from her hand, recovered it and fulfilled her mission.

BATTLE OF BAROSA.

After Matagorda was abandoned, the Spaniards in Cadiz became so apathetic that General Graham bitterly said of them *"They wished the English would drive away the French, that they might eat strawberries at Chiclana."* However, in December, Soult was ordered to co-operate with Massena, and when his departure was known in January;s~, 1811, Victor's force being then weak, Graham undertook, in concert with La Pena, captain-general at the Isla, to raise the blockade by a maritime expedition. Contrary winds baffled this project, and in February Victor was reinforced; nevertheless ten thousand infantry and six hundred cavalry were again embarked, being to land at Tarifa, march upon Chiclana, and take the French lines in reverse. Meanwhile General Zayas, who remained with the Spanish forces left in the Isla, was to cast a bridge near the sea-mouth of the Santi Petri, a ship-canal joining the harbour to the sea and cutting off the Isla from the continent; Ballesteros was to menace Seville; the Partidas were to keep Sebastiani in check, and insurrections were expected in all quarters.

The British troops, passing their port in a gale the 22nd, landed at Algesiras and marched to Tarifa, being there joined by the garrison. Somewhat more than four thousand men, including two companies of the 20th Portuguese, and one hundred and eighty German hussars, were thus assembled under Graham, good and hardy troops, and himself a daring old man of a ready temper for battle. La Pena arrived the 27th with the Spanish contingent, and Graham, to preserve unanimity, ceded the command, although contrary to his instructions. Next day the whole moved forward twelve miles, passing some ridges, which, descending from the Ronda to the sea, separate the plains of San Roque from those of Medina and Chiclana. The troops were then reorganized. General Lardizabal had the vanguard, the Prince of Anglona the centre; the reserve, of two Spanish regiments and the British troops, was confided to Graham, and the cavalry of both nations was given to Colonel Whittingham, an English officer in the Spanish service.

At this time a French covering division, under General Cassagne, was at Medina, with outposts at Vejer de la Frontera and Casa Vieja. La Pena stormed the last the 2nd of March, and then General Beguines, coming from San Roque, augmented his force to twelve thousand infantry, eight hundred horsemen, and twenty-four guns. The 3rd, hearing Medina was intrenched, he turned towards the coast and drove the French from Vejer de la Frontera. In the night of the 4th he continued his movement, and on the morning of the 5th, after a skirmish, in which his advanced guard of cavalry was routed by a French squadron, he reached the Cerro de Puerco, called by the English the heights of Barosa, four miles from the sea-mouth of the Santi Petri.

This Barosa ridge, creeping in from the coast for a mile and a half, overlooked a broken plain, which was bounded on the left by the coast cliffs, on the right by the forest of Chiclana, in front by a pine-wood, beyond which rose a long narrow height called the Bermeja, to be reached by moving through the pine-wood, or by the beach under the cliffs. Graham, foreseeing Victor would come out of his lines to fight, had previously obtained La Pena's promise to make short marches, and not approach the enemy except in a mass. In violation of this promise the march from Casa Vieja had been one of fifteen hours on bad roads, and the night march to Barosa was still more fatiguing. The troops therefore straggled, and before all had arrived, La Pena, as if in contempt of his colleague, neither disclosing his own plans nor communicating by signal or otherwise with Zayas, sent Lardizabal straight to the mouth of the Santi Petri. Zayas had there cast his bridge on the 2nd, but he was surprised in the night and driven into the Isla; Lardizabal had therefore to win his way with a sharp fight, in which three hundred Spaniards fell, yet he forced the French posts and effected a junction.

La Pena directed Graham to follow the vanguard, but the latter desired to hold Barosa, arguing justly that Victor could not attack Lardizabal and Zayas, as no general would lend his flank to an enemy by assailing the Bermeja while Barosa was occupied: Lascy, chief of the Spanish staff, controverted this, and La Pena peremptorily commanded Graham to march. With great temper he obeyed this discourteous order, leaving only the flank companies of the 9th and 82nd regiments under Major Brown to guard his baggage. He moved however in the persuasion that La Pena would remain at Barosa with Anglona's division and the cavalry, because a Spanish column was still behind near Medina: yet scarcely had he entered the pine-wood when La Pena carried off the corps of battle and the cavalry by the sea-road to Santi Petri, leaving Barosa crowded with baggage and protected only by a rearguard of four guns and five battalions.

During these events Victor kept close in the forest of Chiclana, the patrols could find no enemy, and Grahams march of only two miles seemed safe—but the French marshal was keenly watching, the movement. He had recalled Cassagne from Medina when La Pena first reached Barosa and hourly expected his arrival; yet he felt so sure of success, as to direct most of his cavalry, then at Medina and Arcos, upon Vejer and other points to cut off the fugitives after the battle. He had in hand fourteen pieces of artillery and nine thousand excellent soldiers, commanded by Laval, Ruffin, and Villatte. From this force he drafted three grenadier battalions as reserves, two of which and three squadrons of cavalry he attached to Ruffin, the other to Laval. Villatte with two thousand five hundred men, originally on the Bermeja, now covered the works of the camp against Zayas and Lardizabal; but Cassagne was still distant when Victor, seeing Graham in the pine-wood, Zayas and Lardizabal on the Bermeja, a third body and the baggage on the Barosa height, a fourth in movement by the coast, a fifth still on the march from Vejer, poured at once into the plain and began the battle. Laval confronted the British force, while Victor, leading Ruffin's men in person, ascended the rear of the

Barosa height, and having thus intercepted the Spanish column on the Medina road, drove the rear-guard off the hill towards the sea, dispersed the baggage and followers, and took three Spanish guns.

Major Brown, who had kept his troops in good order, being unable to stem the torrent, slowly retired into the plain and sent for orders to Graham, who was then near Bermeja. Fight ! was the laconic answer, and facing about himself he regained the open plain, expecting to find La Pena and the cavalry on the Barosa hill. But when the view opened, he beheld Ruffin's brigade, flanked by the two grenadier battalions, near the summit on the one side, the Spanish rear guard and the baggage flying towards the sea on the other, the French cavalry following the fugitives in good order, Laval close upon his own left flank, and La Pena nowhere !

In this desperate situation, feeling that a retreat upon Bermeja would bring the enemy pell-mell with the allies on to that narrow ridge and be disastrous, he resolved to make a counter-attack, although the key of the battle-field was already in the enemy's possession. Ten guns under Major Duncan instantly opened a terrific fire against Laval's column, and Colonel Andrew Barnard* running vehemently out with his riflemen and some Portuguese companies, commenced the fight; the rest of the troops, without attention to regiments or brigades, so sudden was the affair, formed two masses, with one of which General Dilkes marched against Ruffin while Colonel Wheatley led the other against Laval. Duncan's guns ravaged the French ranks, Laval's artillery replied vigorously, Ruffin's batteries took Wheatley's column in flank, and the infantry on both sides closed eagerly and with a pealing musketry; but soon a fierce, rapid and prolonged charge of the 87th Regiment overthrew the first line of the French, and though the latter fought roughly, they were dashed so violently upon the second line that both were broken by the shock and went off, their retreat being covered by the reserve battalion of grenadiers.

Meanwhile Graham's Spartan order had sent Brown headlong upon Ruffin, and though nearly half his detachment went down under the first fire, he maintained the fight until General Sir A. Barnard.

Dilkes' column, having crossed a deep hollow, came up, with little order indeed but in a fighting mood. Then the whole ran up towards the summit, and there was no slackness, for at the very edge of the ascent their gallant opponents met them and a dreadful and for some time a doubtful combat raged; but soon Ruffin, and Chaudron Rousseau who commanded the chosen grenadiers fell, both mortally wounded, the English bore strongly onward, and their incessant slaughtering fire forced the French from the hill with the loss of three guns and many brave soldiers. All the discomfited divisions then retired concentrically from their different points, and thus meeting, with infinite spirit endeavoured to renew the action, but the play of Duncan's guns, close, rapid and murderous, rendered the attempt vain: Victor quitted the field, and the British, who had been twenty-four hours under arms without food, were too exhausted to pursue.

While these terrible combats of infantry were being fought, La Pena looked idly on, giving no aid, not even menacing Villatte who was close to him and comparatively weak. The Spanish Walloon guards, the regiment of Ciudad Real, and some Guerilla cavalry, turning without orders, came up indeed just as the action ceased, and it was expected that Colonel Whittingham, an Englishman commanding a strong body of Spanish horse, would have done as much; yet no stroke of a Spanish sabre was that day given, though the French cavalry did not exceed two hundred and fifty men, and the eight hundred under Whittingham would have rendered the defeat ruinous. So certain was this, that Frederick Ponsonby, drawing off his hundred and eighty German hussars, reached the field of battle, charged the French squadrons in their retreat, overthrew them, took two guns, and even attempted though vainly to sabre Rousseau's chosen grenadiers. Such was the fight of Barosa. Short, for it lasted only one hour and a half; violent and bloody, for fifty officers, sixty sergeants, eleven hundred British soldiers, and more than two thousand French were killed and wounded; and six guns, an eagle, two generals, both mortally wounded, with four hundred other prisoners fell into the hands of the victors.

Graham remained several hours on the height, still hoping

La Pena would awake to the prospect of success and glory which the extreme valour of the British had opened. Four thousand fresh men and a powerful artillery had come over the Santi Petri; he had therefore twelve thousand infantry and eight hundred cavalry, while before him were only the remains of the French line of battle, retreating in the greatest disorder upon Chiclana; but military spirit was extinct with the Spaniard, Graham could no longer endure his command and leaving the dastard on the Bermeja filed the British troops into the Isla.

MASSENA'S RETREAT.

Soon after the Barosa fight, Wellington and Massena were again pitted in attack and defence. Massena had kept Santarem until the 6th of March expecting Soult's co-operation, yet retreated when that marshal after defeating twenty thousand Spaniards on the Gebora, and taking Olivenza, Badajos, Albuquerque and Campo Mayor, was coming to his aid; of this however he was ignorant, because Wellington's forces on the south bank of the Tagus had intercepted all communication. Hence when Soult was invading Portugal on one side of that river, Massena abandoned the other side and was pursued by the allied army. He left however a desert behind him, and soon a horrible spectacle disclosed all the previous misery of the inhabitants. In the hills was found a house where thirty women and children were lying dead from hunger, and sitting by the bodies fifteen or sixteen living beings—only one a man—so enfeebled by want they could not devour the food offered to them. All the children were dead; none were emaciated, but the muscles of their faces were invariably dragged transversely, as if laughing, and unimaginably ghastly. The man was most eager for life, the women patient and resigned, and they had carefully covered and laid out the dead ! A field of battle strewed with bloody carcasses would have been a solacing sight by comparison !

Strong positions crossed Massena's line of retreat, which was confined by mountains, every village being a defile;and Ney, governing the rear-guard, lost no advantage. Hewas driven by the light division with a sharp skirmish from

Pombal the 10th, but on the 11th he offered battle at Redinha with five
thousand infantry, some cavalry and guns; his wings were covered by
pine-woods which, hanging on the brow of the table-land he occupied, were filled with light troops; the deep bed of the Soure protected
his right, his left rested on the Redinha, which flowed also round his
rear; behind his centre the village of Redinha, lying in a hollow,
masked a narrow bridge, and on a rugged height beyond a reserve was
so posted as to seem a great force

COMBAT OF REDINHA

   The light division under Sir William Erskine soon won the wooded
slopes covering Ney's right, and the skirmishers pushed into the open
plain, but were there checked by a heavy rolling fire, and a squadron
of hussars, charging, took fourteen prisoners Erskine then formed his
line, which, outflanking the French right, was reinforced with two
regiments of dragoons Picton had also seized the wood covering the
French left, and Ney's position was laid bare; but he, observing that
Wellington, deceived by the reserve beyond the bridge, was bringing
all the allied troops into line, would not retire; he even charged
Picton's skirmishers and held his ground, though the third division
was nearer to the bridge than his right, and there were troops and
guns enough on the plain to overwhelm him In this posture both sides
remained an hour, but then three cannon-shots fired from the British
centre, gave the signal for a splendid spectacle of war The woods
seemed alive with troops, and suddenly thirty thousand men, presenting three gorgeous lines of battle, were stretched across the plain,
bending on a gentle curve and moving majestically onwards, while
horsemen and guns, springing simultaneously from the centre and
left, charged under a general volley from the French battalions, who
were thus covered with smoke, and when that cleared away none were
to be seen ! Ney, keenly watching the progress of this grand formation, had opposed Picton's skirmishers with his left, while he
withdrew the rest of his people so rapidly as to gain the village before
even the cavalry could touch him, the utmost efforts of the

light troops and horse-artillery only enabling them to gall the hind-most with fire.

One howitzer was dismounted, but the village of Redinha was in flames between it and the pursuers, and Ney in person carried off the injured piece; yet with a loss of fifteen or twenty men and great danger to himself; for the British guns were thundering on his rear, and the light troops, chasing like heated bloodhounds, almost passed the river with his men; his reserve beyond the bridge then opened a cannonade, but fresh dispositions soon made it fall back ten miles Twelve officers and two hundred men were killed and wounded in this combat Ney lost as many, but he might have been destroyed, Wellington paid him too much respect.

Condeixa, where the French now took position, commanded two roads, one behind their right leading to Coimbra; the other on their left, leading to the Sierra de Murcella The first offered the Mondego as a permanent line of defence, with the power of seizing Oporto by a detachment The second presented only a rugged narrow line of retreat up the left bank of the Mondego, and involved the evacuation of Portugal; for that river was not fordable at the season and the Portuguese militia were in force on the other side Massena first detached Montbrun to ascertain the state of Coimbra, which was really defenceless, yet Trant with a few militia-men made such show of resistance that it was reported inattackable; whereupon the French prince set fire to Condeixa and adopted the position of Cazal Nova on the Murcella road not however without a skirmish in which he narrowly escaped capture

No orders were given in the night to attack, nevertheless, next morning, although an impenetrable mist covered the French position and the dull sound of a stirring multitude came from its depths, Sir W Erskine, with astounding indifference, and against the opinion of all the officers about him, ordered the 52nd Regiment to plunge in column of sections, without even an advanced guard, into the sea of fog below him The road dipped suddenly and the regiment was instantly lost in the mist, which was so thick that, the troops, unconsciously passing the enemy s out-posts, nearly captured Ney, who slept with his pickets The rest of the division was about to descend into the same gulf, when the rattling of musketry and the booming of round shot were heard, the vapour rose slowly, and the 52nd was seen on the slopes of the opposite mountain, closely engaged in the midst of an army !

COMBAT OF CAZAL NOVA.

Wellington arrived. His design was to turn the French left, for their front was strong, and they held mountain ridges in succession to the Deuca river and the defiles of Miranda de Corvo He had sent Cole by a circuit towards the sources of the Deuca and Ceira, Picton more directly to menace the French flank, and the main body was coming up, when Erskine forced the light division prematurely into action. Ney's ground was extensive, his skirmishers so thick and well supported, that the light division offered only a thread of battle, closely engaged in every part, without any reserve; nor could it then present an equal front, until Picton sent some riflemen to prolong the line. Some advantages were indeed gained, but the main position was not shaken, until Picton near and Cole further off, had turned the left, and three divisions, with the heavy cavalry and artillery, came up in the centre Then Ney, covering his rear with guns and light troops, retired from ridge to ridge without confusion until midday, when the guns got within range of his masses and his retreat became more rapid and less orderly, yet he reached the strong pass of Miranda de Corvo, where Massena was in position The light division lost eleven officers and a hundred and fifty men; the French loss was greater, and a hundred prisoners were taken.

COMBAT OF FOZ D'ARONCE

Massena, fearing Cole would get in his rear, set fire to the town of Miranda, crossed the Ceira in the night, and being then crowded in a narrow way between the sierras and the Mondego, destroyed ammunition and baggage, and directed Ney to cover the movement with a few battalions, but charged him not to risk an action: Ney, however, little regarding his orders, kept the left bank with ten or twelve battalions, a brigade of cavalry and some guns, and thus provoked a combat. His right was on rugged ground, his left at the village of Foz d'Aronce; the weather was obscure and rainy, the allies did not come up until evening, and little expecting an action kindled their fires; but Wellington, suddenly directing the light division and Pack's brigade to hold the French right in check, sent the third division against their left, and the horse-artillery on the gallop to rising ground, whence it opened with a surprising effect

Ney's left wing was soon overthrown by the third division and fled in such confusion towards the river that many men rushed into the deeps and were drowned, while others madly crowding the bridge were crushed to death On the other flank the ground was so rough the action resolved itself into a skirmish, and Ney sent some battalions to stop the pursuit of his left; but then darkness fell and the French troops in their disorder fired on each other. Four officers and sixty men fell on the side of the British; the enemy lost above five hundred, one half drowned, and an eagle was afterwards found in the bed of the river Massena retired in the night behind the Alva Ney kept his post on the Ceira until every encumbrance had passed, and then blowing up seventy feet of the bridge, remained with a weak rear-guard. Wellington halted

Up to this point of the retreat the French prince had displayed infinite ability, with a ruthless spirit. The burning of some towns and villages protected his rear, but Leiria and the convent of Alcobaca were off the line yet given to the flames by express orders and in a spirit of vengeance But every horror that could make war hideous attended this retreat. Distress, conflagrations, death, in all modes from wounds, from fatigue, from water, from the flames,   from starvation! On all sides unlimited violence, unlimited vengeance. I myself saw a peasant hounding on his dog to devour the dead and dying, and the spirit of cruelty smote even the brute creation; for the French general, to lessen encumbrances, ordered beasts of burden to be destroyed, and the inhuman fellow charged with the execution hamstringed five hundred asses and left them to starve; they were so found by the British, and the mute, sad, deep expression of pain and grief visible in the poor creatures' looks, excited a strange fury in the soldiers. no quarter would have been given at that time: humane feelings would have thus led direct to cruelty . But all passions are akin to madness.

From this quarter, Lord Wellington, who had before detached troops with the same view, now sent Cole's division to join Beresford in the Alemtejo, where the latter had been left to oppose Soult's progress.

COMBAT OF SABUGAL.

The pursuit of Massena was soon resumed. He attempted to hold the Guarda mountain on the flank of the Estrella, and being driven from thence with the loss of three hundred prisoners descended the eastern slopes to take a position behind the Coa. There being reinforced, he disposed his troops on two sides of a triangle, the apex at Sabugal, where Reynier commanded. Both wings were covered by the river, which had a sharp bend at Sabugal, and the right had free communication with Almeida, on which side the craggy ravine of the Coa forbade an attack. Above Sabugal it was easier, and Wellington, after menacing the right for two days, suddenly, at daybreak on the 3rd of April, sent Slade's cavalry and the light division to pass the upper stream by a wide movement and penetrate between the left wing and centre of the French. The third division moved at the same time to cross the river by a closer movement, yet still above the bridge of Sabugal, which the fifth division and the artillery were to force. Two other divisions were in reserve, and it was hoped Reynier, whose main body was some distance above bridge, would be thus turned surrounded and crushed before the wings could succour him: one of those accidents so frequent in war marred this well-concerted scheme.

A thick fog prevented the troops gaining their points of attack simultaneously, and Erskine took no heed to put the light division in a right direction; his columns were not even held together, and he carried off the cavalry without communicating with Colonel Beckwith, who commanded his first brigade. That officer thus left without instructions halted at a ford, until one of the general staff came up and rudely asked why he did not attack; the thing appeared rash, yet with an enemy in front, Beckwith could only reply by passing the river, which was deep and rapid. A very steep wooded hill was on the other side and four companies of riflemen ascended, followed by the 43rd Regiment, but the caçadores of the brigade had joined another column which was passing the river higher up and moving independently to the right, on the true point of direction. At this time very heavy rain was falling, all was obscure, and none of the other divisions had yet reached their respective posts; Beckwith's attack was therefore premature, partial, dangerous, and at the wrong point; for Reynier's whole corps was in front, and one bayonet-regiment, with four companies of riflemen, were assailing more than twelve thousand infantry supported by cavalry and artillery !

Scarcely had the riflemen reached the top of the hill when a strong body of French drove them back upon the 43rd, the weather cleared at the instant, and Beckwith saw and felt all the danger, but his heart was too big to quail. With one fierce charge he beat back the enemy, and he gained, and kept the summit of the hill, although two French howitzers poured showers of grape into his ranks, while a fresh force came against his front, and considerable bodies advanced on either flank. Fortunately, Reynier, little expecting to be attacked, had for the convenience of water placed his main body in low ground behind the height on which the action commenced; his renewed attack was therefore up-hill, yet his musketry, heavy from the beginning, soon increased to a storm, and his men sprung up the acclivity with such a violence and clamour it was evident that desperate fighting only could save the British from destruction, and they fought accordingly. Captain Hopkins, commanding a flank company of the 43rd, running out to the right, with admirable presence of mind seized a small eminence, close to the French guns and commanding the ascent up which the French troops turning the light flank were approaching. His first fire threw them into confusion; they rallied and were again disordered by his volleys; a third time they made head; but a sudden charge shook them, and then two battalions of the 52nd regiment, attracted by the fire, entered the line. The centre and left of the 43rd were all this time furiously engaged, and wonderfully excited; for Beckwith, with the blood streaming from a wound in the head, rode amongst the skirmishers, praising and exhorting them in a loud cheerful tone as a man sure to win his battle; and though the bullets flew thicker and closer, and the fight became more perilous, the French fell fast and a second charge again cleared the hill. A howitzer was taken by the 43rd, and the skirmishers were descending in eager pursuit when small bodies of cavalry came galloping in from all parts and compelled them to take refuge with the main body, which had reformed behind a low stone wall; one French squadron however, with incredible daring; rode close to this wall, and were in the act of firing over it with pistols when a rolling volley laid nearly the whole lifeless on the ground. A very strong column of infantry then rushed up and endeavoured to retake the howitzer, which was on the edge of the descent, fifty yards from the wall, but no man could reach it and live, so deadly was the 43rd's fire. Two English guns now came into action, and the 52nd charging violently upon the flank of the enemy's infantry again vindicated the possession of the height; nevertheless fresh squadrons of cavalry, which had followed the infantry in the last attack, seeing the 52nd men scattered by this charge, flew upon them with great briskness and caused some disorder before they were repulsed.

Reynier, convinced at last that he should not use his troops piecemeal, then put all his reserves, six thousand infantry with artillery and cavalry, in motion, and outflanked the English left, resolute to storm the contested height. But at that moment the fifth division passed the bridge of Sabugal, the British cavalry appeared on the hills beyond the French left, and, emerging from the woods close on Reynier's right, the third division opened a fire which instantly decided the fate of the day. The French general, fearing to be surrounded, hastily retreated, and meeting the right wing of the army, which had also retired, both fell back, pursued by the English cavalry.

In this bloody encounter, which did not last quite an hour, nearly two hundred British were killed and wounded, and the enemy's loss was enormous: three hundred dead bodies were heaped together on the hill, the greatest part round the captured howitzer, and more than twelve hundred were wounded, so unwisely had Reynier handled his masses, and so true and constant was the English fire. It was no exaggeration of Lord Wellington to say, "this was one of the most glorious actions British troops were ever engaged in."

Massena retreated on Ciudad Rodrigo, and the 5th crossed the frontier of Portugal, when the vigour of French discipline was surprisingly manifested. Those men who had for months been living by rapine, whose retreat had been one continued course of violence and devastation, having passed a conventional line became the most orderly of soldiers. Not the slightest rudeness was offered to any Spaniard, and every thing was scrupulously paid for, although bread was sold at two shillings a pound! Massena himself also, fierce and terrible as he was in Portugal, always treated the Spaniards with gentleness and moderation.

During these events Trant crossed the Lower Coa with four thousand militia near Almeida, but the river flooded behind him, the bridges had been broken by Massena, and there was a French brigade close at hand; hence, constructing a temporary bridge with great difficulty, he was going to retire, but there came a letter from Wellington, desiring him to be vigilant in preventing communication with Almeida, and fearless, because next morning a British force would be up to his assistance. Boldly then he interposed between the fortress and the French brigade, yet the promised succour did not appear, and the advancing enemy was within half a mile. His destruction appeared inevitable, when suddenly two cannon-shots were heard to the southward, the French hastily formed squares to retire, and six squadrons of British cavalry with a troop of horse-artillery came up like a whirlwind in their rear; military order however marked their perilous retreat, and though the bullets fearfully ploughed through their masses while the horsemen flanked their line of march, they got over the Agueda by Barba de Puerco, with the loss of only three hundred men killed wounded and prisoners.

A few days after this, Colonel Waters, the boat-finder at Oporto, who had been taken prisoner, escaped by an effort of extraordinary daring. Confident in his own resources he refused parole, but having rashly mentioned his intention of escaping to the Spaniard in whose house he was lodged at Ciudad Rodrigo, the man betrayed counsel; his servant, detesting the treachery, secretly offered his own aid, but Waters only told him to get the rowels of his spurs sharpened, no more, for his design was one of open daring. Guarded by four *gens d'armes,* he was near Salamanca when the chief, who rode the only good horse of the party, alighted, whereupon Waters gave the spur to his own mare, a celebrated animal, and galloped off. They were on a wide plain, and for many miles the road was covered with the French columns, his hat fell off, and thus marked he rode along the flank of the troops, some encouraging him, others firing at him, the *gens d'armes* being always, sword in hand, close at his heels. Suddenly he broke at full speed between two of the columns, gained a wooded hollow, baffled his pursuers, and the third day reached head-quarters, where Lord Wellington had caused his baggage to be brought, observing that he would not be long absent !

FUENTES ONORO.

On the Agueda Massena could not subsist. He retired to Salamanca, where he was in communication with Marshal Bessieres, who commanded a great force called the Army of the North. Wellington then invested Almeida, thinking it was provisioned only for a fortnight, yet it was still resistant the latter end of April, when the Prince of Essling, having reorganized his army and obtained cavalry and guns from Bessieres, came down to raise the blockade. The English general, not expecting this interference, had gone southwards to superintend the operations of Marshal Beresford, but he returned rapidly when he heard of the French movement, and fixed on a field of battle between the Agueda and Coa. There the ground, though open and fit for cavalry, was traversed from east to west by three nearly parallel rivers, the Azava, Duas Casas, and Turones; the first considerable, and all having, in common with the Agueda and Coa, this peculiarity, their channels deepen as the water flows: mere streams with low banks in their upper courses, they soon become foaming torrents rushing along rocky gulfs.

Almeida, situated on high table-land between the Turones and Coa, was closely blockaded, the light division and the cavalry were on the Azava covering the investment, the rest of the army was cantoned in the villages behind them. Swollen and unfordable was the Azava, and two thousand French attempted to seize the bridge of Marialva on the 24th, but the ground was strong, and they were vigorously repulsed by Captain Dobbs of the 52nd, though he had but a single bayonet-company and some riflemen. Next day Massena reached Ciudad Rodrigo in person, and the 27th he felt the light division posts from Espeja to Marialva. On the 28th Wellington arrived, and took position behind the Duas Casas.

The Azava was still difficult to ford, and Massena continued to feel the outposts until the 2nd of May, when the waters subsided and his army came out of Ciudad Rodrigo. The light division, after a slight skirmish of horse at Gallegos, retired from that place and Espeja upon the Duas Casas, a delicate operation, for though the country behind those villages was a forest, an open plain between the woods offered the enemy's powerful cavalry an opportunity of cutting off the retreat; the French neglected the advantage and the separated brigades of the division remained in the woods until the middle of the night, and then safely crossed the Duas Casas at Fuentes Onoro, a beautiful village which had been uninjured during the previous warfare although occupied alternately for above a year by both sides. Every family was well known to the light division, and it was with deep regret and indignation they found the preceding troops had pillaged it, leaving shells of houses where three days before a friendly population had been living in comfort. This wanton act was felt indeed so much by the whole army, that eight thousand dollars were subscribed for the inhabitants, yet the injury sunk deeper than the atonement.

Wellington did not wish to risk much for the blockade, and he knew Massena could bring down superior numbers; for so culpably negligent was the Portuguese government that their troops were starving under arms, the infantry abandoning their colours or dropping from extenuation by thousands, the cavalry useless: it was even feared that a general dispersion would take place. Nevertheless, when the trial came, he would not retreat, although his troops, reduced to thirty-two thousand infantry, twelve hundred cavalry in bad condition, and forty-two guns, were unable to oppose the enemy's numerous horsemen in the plain. His position was on the table-land between the Turones and the Duas Casas, his left being at Fort Conception, his centre opposite the village of Alameda, his right at Fuentes Onoro. The whole distance was five miles, and the Duas Casas, here flowing in a deep ravine, protected the front of the line.

Massena dared not march by his own right upon Almeida, lest the allies, crossing the ravine at the villages of Alameda and Fuentes Onoro, should fall on his flank and drive him upon the Lower Agueda; hence, to cover the blockade, maintained by Pack's brigade and an English regiment, it was sufficient to leave the fifth division near Fort Conception, and the sixth division opposite Alameda, while the first and third concentrated on a gentle rise cannon-shot distance behind Fuentes Onoro, and where a steppe of land turned back on the Turones, becoming rocky as it approached that river.

COMBAT OF FUENTES ONORO.

On the 3rd of May the French came up in three columns abreast. The cavalry, the sixth corps, and Drouet's division, threatened Fuentes, while the eighth and second corps moved against Alameda and Fort Conception, menacing the allies' left, which caused the light division to reinforce the sixth. Loison, without orders, now fell upon Fuentes, in which were five battalions detached from the first and third divisions. Most of the houses were in the bottom of the ravine, but an old chapel and some buildings on a craggy eminence behind offered a prominent point for rallying, and all the low parts were vigorously defended; yet the attack was so violent and the cannonade so heavy the British abandoned the streets, and could scarcely maintain the upper ground about the chapel; the commanding officer fell badly wounded, and the fight was being lost, when the 24th, the 71st, and 79th regiments, coming down from the main position, charged the French and drove them quite over the

Duas Casas. During the night the detachments were withdrawn, the three succouring regiments keeping the village, where two hundred and sixty British and somewhat more of the French had fallen.

On the 4th Massena arrived, accompanied by Bessiares who brought up twelve hundred cavalry and a battery of the imperial guard. Designing to fight next morning he resolved to hold the left of the allies in check with the second corps, and turn their right with the remainder of the army. Forty thousand French infantry and five thousand horse, with thirty pieces of artillery, were under arms, and they had shown their courage was not abated; it was therefore a very daring act of the English general to receive battle; for though his position, as far as Fuentes Onoro, was strong and covered his communication across the Coa by the bridge of Castello Bom, the plain was continued on his right to Nava d'Aver, where a round hill, overlooking all the country, commanded the roads leading to the bridges of Seceiras and Sabugal. Massena could therefore have placed his army at once in battle-array across the right flank and attacked the army between the Duas Casas, the Turones, the Coa and the fortress of Almeida: the bridge of Castello Bom alone would then have been open for retreat. To prevent this, and cover his communications with Sabugal and Seceiras, Wellington, yielding to Spencer's suggestions, stretched his right wing out to the hill of Nava d'Aver, where he placed Julian Sanchez, supporting him with the seventh division under General Houstoun. This line of battle was above seven miles, besides the circuit of blockade; and above Fuentes Onoro the Duas Casas ravine became gradually obliterated, resolving itself into a swampy wood, which extended to Poco Velho, a village half-way between Fuentes and Nava d'Aver.

BATTLE OF FUENTES ONORO.

Massena's intention was to attack at daybreak, but a delay of two hours occurred and all his movements were plainly descried. The eighth corps, withdrawn from Alameda and supported by all the French cavalry, was seen marching to turn Poco Velho and the swampy wood, both occupied by Houstoun's left, his right being thrown back on the plain towards Nava d'Aver. The sixth corps and Drouet's division were likewise taking ground to their left, yet keeping a division to menace Fuentes Onoro. At this sight the light division and the cavalry hastened to the support of Houstoun, while the first and third divisions made a movement parallel to that of the sixth corps; the latter, however, drove the seventh division from Poco Velho, and was gaining ground in the wood also, when the riflemen of the light division arrived there and restored the fight.

The French cavalry, after passing Poco Velho, formed an order of battle on the plain between the wood and the hill of Nava d'Aver, whereupon Sanchez retired across the Turones, partly in fear, more in anger, because his lieutenant, having foolishly ridden close up to the enemy, making violent gestures, was mistaken for a French officer and shot by a soldier of the Guards before the action commenced. Montbrun lost an hour observing this *partida,* but when it disappeared he turned the right of the seventh division and charged the British cavalry; the combat was unequal; for by an abuse too common, so many men had been drawn from the ranks as orderlies to general officers, and other purposes, that not more than a thousand English troopers were in the field. The French therefore with one shock drove in all the outguards, cut off Norman Ramsay's battery of horse-artillery, and came sweeping in upon the reserves and the seventh division.

Their leading squadrons, approaching in a loose manner, were partially checked by the British, and then a great commotion was observed in their main body. Their troopers were seen closing with disorder and tumult towards one point, where a thick dust arose, and where loud cries and the sparkling of blades and flashing of pistols indicated some extraordinary occurrence. Suddenly the crowd became violently agitated, an English shout pealed high and clear, the mass was rent asunder, and Norman Ramsay burst forth sword in hand at the head of his battery, his horses, breathing fire, stretched like greyhounds along the plain, the guns bounded behind them like things of no weight, and the mounted gunners followed close, with heads bent low and pointed weapons in desperate career. At this sight Brotherton*

* Lieut.-General Brotherton.

of the 14th Dragoons, instantly galloping to his aid with a squadron, shocked the head of the pursuing troops, and General Charles, Stewart,* joining in the charge, took the French colonel Lamotte, fighting hand to hand. However the main body came forward rapidly, and the British cavalry retired behind the light division, which was thrown into squares; the seventh division, which was more advanced, endeavoured to do the same, but the horsemen were too quickly upon them, and some were cut down; the remainder stood firm, and the Chasseurs Britanniques, ranged behind a loose stone wall, poured such a fire that the French recoiled and seemed bewildered.

While these brilliant actions were passing, the enemy had made progress in the wood of Poco Velho, and as the English divisions were separated and the right wing turned, it was abundantly evident the battle would be lost if the original position above Fuentes Onoro was not quickly regained. To effect this Wellington ordered the seventh division to cross the Turones and move down the left bank to Frenada, while the light division and the cavalry retired over the plain; he also withdrew the first and third divisions, and the Portuguese, to the steppe of land before mentioned, as running perpendicularly from the ravine of Fuentes Onoro to the Turones.

Craufurd, who had now resumed command of the light division, covered the passage of the seventh over the Turones, and then retired slowly along the plain in squares. The French horsemen outflanked him and surprised a post of the Guards under Colonel Hill, taking that officer and fourteen men prisoners, but continuing their course against the 42nd regiment were repulsed. Many times, this strong cavalry made as if it would storm the light division squares, yet always found them too formidable, and happily so, for there was not during the war a more perilous hour. The whole of that vast plain was covered with a confused multitude of troops, amidst which the squares appeared as specks, and there was a great concourse of commissariat followers, servants, baggage, led horses, and peasants attracted by curiosity, and all mixed with broken picquets and parties coming, out of the woods: the seventh division was separated

* Lord Londonderry

by the Turones, while five thousand French horsemen, with fifteen pieces of artillery, were trampling, bounding, shouting, and impatient to charge; the infantry of the eighth corps being in order of battle behind them, and the wood on their right filled with the sixth corps. If that latter body, pivoting upon Fuentes, had come forth while Drouet's division fell on that village, if the eighth corps had attacked the light division and all the cavalry had charged, the loose crowd encumbering the plain, driven violently in upon the first division, would have intercepted the latter's fire and broken its ranks: the battle would have been lost.

No such effort was made. The French horsemen merely hovered about Craufurd's squares, the plain was soon cleared, the British cavalry took post behind the centre, and the light division formed a reserve to the first division, the riflemen occupying the rocks on its right and connecting it with the seventh division, which had arrived at Frenada and was again joined by Julian Sanchez. At sight of this new front, perpendicular to the original one and so deeply lined with troops, the French army stopped short and commenced a cannonade, which did great execution amongst the close masses of the allies; but twelve British guns replied with such vigour that the enemy's fire abated, their cavalry drew out of range, and a body of infantry attempting to glide down the ravine of the Turones was repulsed by the riflemen and the light companies of the Guards.

All this time a fierce battle was going on at Fuentes Onoro. Massena had directed Drouet to carry this village when Montbrun's cavalry first turned the right wing, it was however two hours later ere the attack commenced. The three British regiments made a desperate resistance, but, overmatched in number and unaccustomed to the desultory fighting of light troops, they were pierced and divided; two companies of the 79th were taken, their Colonel, Cameron, mortally wounded, and the lower part of the town was carried: the upper part was however stiffly held and the musketry was incessant.

Had the attack been made earlier, and all Drouet's division thrown frankly into the fight, while the sixth corps from the wood of Poco Velho closely turned Fuentes Onoro, the latter must have been forced and the new position falsified. But Wellington, having now all his reserves in hand, detached considerable masses to support the fight, and as the French reinforced their troops, the whole of the sixth corps and part of Drouet's were finally engaged. At one time the fighting was on the banks of the stream and the lower houses, at another on the heights and around the chapel, and some of the enemy's skirmishers even penetrated towards the main position; yet the village was never entirely abandoned by the defenders, and in one charge against a heavy mass on the chapel eminence a great number of French fell. Thus the fight lasted until evening, when the lower part of the town was abandoned by both parties, the British holding the chapel and crags, the French retiring about cannon-shot distance from the stream.

After the action a brigade of the light division relieved the regiments in the village, a slight demonstration by the second corps, near Fort Conception, was checked by a battalion of the Lusitanian legion, and both armies remained in observation. Fifteen hundred men and officers, of which three hundred were prisoners, constituted the loss of the allies. That of the enemy was estimated at the time to be near five thousand, but this was founded on the supposition that four hundred dead were lying about Fuentes Onoro. Having had charge to bury the carcasses at that point, I can affirm, that about the village not more than one hundred and thirty bodies were to be found, more than one-third of which were British.

EVACUATION OF ALMEIDA.

Massena retired on the 10th across the Agueda, and was relieved in his command by Marmont. The fate of Almeida was then decided, yet its brave governor, Brennier, who had been exchanged after the battle of Vimiero, carried off the garrison. He had fifteen hundred men and during the battle had skirmished boldly with the blockading force, while loud explosions, supposed to be signals, were frequent in the place. When all hope of succour vanished, a French soldier, named Tillet, penetrated in uniform through the posts of blockade, carrying an order to evacuate the fortress and rejoin the army by Barba de Puerco. Meanwhile the British general, placing the light division in its old position on the Azava with cavalry-posts on the Lower Agueda, had desired Sir William Erskine to send the 4th Regent to Barba de Puerco, and directed General Alexander Campbell to continue the blockade with the sixth division and Pack's brigade. Campbell's dispositions were negligently made and negligently executed. Erskine transmitted no orders to the 4th Regiment, and Brennier resolved to force his way through the blockading troops. An open country and a double line of posts greatly enhanced the difficulty of the enterprise, yet he was resolute not only to cut his own passage but to render the fortress useless. In this view he had mined the principal bastions, and destroyed his guns by a singular expedient, firing several at the same moment with heavy charges but placing the muzzles of all but one against the sides of the others; thus while some shots flew towards the besiegers others destroyed the pieces without attracting notice: these were the explosions supposed to be signals.

At midnight on the 10th he sprung his mines and in a compact column broke through the picquets, passing between the quarters of the reserves with a nicety proving his talent and his coolness. Pack, following with a few men collected on the instant, plied him with a constant fire, yet could not shake or retard his column, which in silence gained the rough country leading upon Barba de Puerco, where it halted just as daylight broke. Pack still pursued, and knowing some English dragoons were a short distance off sent an officer to bring them out upon the French flank, thus occasioning a slight skirmish and consequent delay. The other troops had paid little attention to the explosion of the mines, thinking them a repetition of Brennier's previous practice, but Pack's fire had roused them, the 36th Regiment was now close at hand, and the 4th also, having heard the firing, was rapidly gaining the right flank of the enemy. Brennier drove off the cavalry and was again in march, yet the infantry, throwing off their knapsacks, overtook him as he descended the deep chasm of Barba de Puerco and killed or wounded many, taking three hundred, but the 36th Regiment rashly passing the bridge was repulsed with a loss of forty men. Had Erskine given the 4th Regiment its orders, the French column would have been lost, and Lord Wellington, stung by this event, and irritated by previous examples of undisciplined valour, issued this strong rebuke. " *The officers of the army may depend upon it that the enemy to whom they are opposed is not less prudent than powerful. Not with standing what has been printed in gazettes and newspapers, we have never seen small bodies unsupported successfully opposed to large; nor has the experience of any officer realized the stories which all have read of whole armies being driven by a handful of light infantry and dragoons.*"

Book V.

Combat of Campo Mayor—First English Siege of Badajos—Battle of Albuera—Renewed Siege of Badajos—First Assault of Christoval —Second Assault on Christoval.

COMBAT OF CAMPO MAYOR.

It has been shown how Beresford was sent to oppose Soult beyond the Tagus, but the latter, disturbed by the battle of Barosa, which put all Andalusia in commotion, had returned to Seville, leaving Mortier to continue the operations. Campo Mayor surrendered the 21st of March, and four days after, Latour Maubourg, having to bring away the battering train and a convoy of provisions, issued from the gates with nine hundred cavalry, three battalions of infantry, some horse-artillery and sixteen heavy guns, all in column of march, just as Beresford emerged from an adjacent forest with twenty thousand infantry, two thousand cavalry and eighteen field-pieces. An astonishing apparition this was to the French, for so adroitly had Wellington, while seemingly absorbed in the pursuit of Massena, organized this army, that its existence was only made known by its presence.

All Beresford's cavalry, supported by a field battery and a detachment of infantry under Colonel Colborne*, were close up ere the enemy knew of their approach, and the horsemen, sweeping by their left round the town and moving along gentle slopes, gradually formed a crescent about the French, who were retreating along the road to Badajos. Colborne was then coming up at a run, a division was seen behind him, and the French infantry formed squares, supported by their cavalry, while their battering guns and baggage hurried on. General Long, holding back his heavy cavalry, directed some Portuguese squadrons, and the 18th Light Dragoons under Colonel Head, to charge. Head, galloping forward under a fire from the square, was

*Now Lord Seaton.

met half-way by the French hussars with loose reins, and fiercely they came together, and many went down on both sides, yet those who kept the saddle drove clean through each other, re-formed, and again charged in the same fearful manner ! Desperately all struggled for victory, but Head's troopers riding close and on better chargers overthrew horse and man, and the hussars dispersed, yet still fighting in small bodies with the Portuguese, while the British squadron, passing under the fire of the square without flinching, rode forward, hewing down the gunners of the battering train and seeking to head the long line of convoy.

They thought the heavy dragoons, the infantry and the artillery, marching behind them, would suffice to dispose of the enemies they passed, but Beresford took a different view. He stopped a charge of the heavy dragoons; he suffered only two guns to open when six were at hand; he even silenced those two after a few rounds, and let the French recover their battering train, rally their hussars, and retreat in safety. Meanwhile the 13th and some of the Portuguese dragoons reached the bridge of Badajos and there captured more guns, but were repulsed by the fire of the fortress, and being followed by Mortier and met by Latour Maubourg's retreating column lost some men, but passing by the flanks they escaped, to be publicly censured by Beresford! The admiration of the army consoled them. One hundred of the allies were killed, or hurt, and seventy taken; the French lost only three hundred and a howitzer, but the colonel of hussars, Chamorin, a distinguished officer, fell in single combat with a trooper of the 13th Dragoons, an Irishman of astonishing might, whose sword went through helmet and head with a single blow.

FIRST ENGLISH SIEGE OF BADAJOS.

Mortier now resigned the command to Latour Maubourg, who spread his foragers fifty miles abroad to gather provisions for Badajos, which General Phillipon, one of the best governors that ever defended a fortress, was with scanty means striving to prepare for a siege. Beresford, by adopting a wrong line of operations, lost time, his first bridge was swept away by floods, he passed the Guadiana with some difficulty at Jerumenha, and a squadron of the 13th

Dragoons was carried off bodily by the French at that place; but he reduced Olivenza, drove Latour Maubourg into the Morena, and defeated two regiments of cavalry near Usagre: he however neglected to restrain the garrison of Badajos, by which he gave Phillipon time and license to prepare for resistance—a great error and pregnant with terrible consequences. His field operations were inadequate to his means, for he was not only master of the open country with his own troops, but had been joined by the captain-general Castanos with the fifth Spanish army, and was in communication with Ballesteros and Blake, co-operating Spanish generals, at the head of considerable bodies. In this state he was first reinforced with a German brigade from Lisbon under General Alten, and then Wellington arrived from the north.

He came the 21st of April and immediately changed the direction of the warfare. Looking to Badajos, and feeling the value of time, he instantly forded the Guadiana and pushed close to it with the German troops and some Portuguese cavalry, to take a convoy going into the place, but the governor sallied, the convoy escaped, and the allies lost a hundred men. Beresford had been contemptuous of Soult's power and resolution to disturb the siege; but Wellington had learned to respect that marshal's energy and resources, and knowing well he would come with strength and danger, refused to invest the place until the Spanish generals consented to the following co-operation. Blake to bring his army from Ayamonte, and in concert with Ballesteros and the cavalry of Castanos to watch the passes of the Morena. Castanos, furnishing three battalions for the siege, to support the other Spanish generals. The British covering troops to be in second line having their point of concentration for battle at Albuera, a village centrically placed with respect to the roads leading from Andalusia to Badajos. While awaiting the Spaniards' consent he prepared the means of siege, yet under great difficulties.

The Portuguese government had reported that guns, provisions, boats, stores and means of carriage had been actually collected for the operation: this was false. The battering train and stores for the attack had therefore to be taken from Elvas, and as it was essential for the safety of the fortress to preserve its armament, and the Guadiana had again carried away the bridge at Jerumenha, that direct line of communication was given up for the circuitous one of Merida, where a stone bridge rendered all safe. But then political difficulties arose. The Portuguese government was on the point of declaring war against Spain, which made the Spanish generals delay assent to the plan of co-operation, and in the midst of this confusion Massena's advance recalled Wellington to fight the battle of Fuentes Onoro.

As Latour Maubourg still held on to Estremadura and foraged the fertile districts, Colonel Colborne, a man of singular talent for war, was sent with a brigade of infantry, some horsemen and guns to curb his inroads. In concert with Count Penne Villemur, a commander of Spanish cavalry, he intercepted several convoys, forced the French troops to quit many frontier towns, and acted with so much address, that Latour Maubourg went into the Morena, thinking a great force was at hand. Colborne then attempted to surprise the fortified post of Benelcazar. Riding on to the drawbridge in the grey of the morning, he summoned the commandant to surrender, as the only means of saving himself from a Spanish army which was coming up and would give no quarter; the French officer was amazed at the appearance of the party, yet hesitated, whereupon Colborne, perceiving he would not yield, galloped off under a few straggling shot and soon after rejoined the army without loss. During his absence, the Spanish generals had acceded to Wellington's proposition, Blake was in march, the Guadiana had subsided and the siege was undertaken.

General William Stewart invested Badajos the 5th of May, on the left bank of the Guadiana, where the principal features were an ancient castle and some out-works.

On the 8th General Lumley invested Christoval, an isolated fort or citadel, on the other bank of the Guadiana, which commanded the bridge; but this operation was not well combined, and sixty French dragoons, moving under the fire of the place, maintained a sharp skirmish beyond the walls.

Thus the first serious siege undertaken by the British army in the Peninsula was commenced, and, to the discredit of the English government, no army was ever worse provided for such an enterprise. The engineers were zealous, and some of them well versed in the theory of their business, but the ablest trembled at their utter destitution. Without sappers and miners, or a soldier who knew how to carry on an approach under fire, they were compelled to attack a fortress defended by the most practised and scientific troops of the age; hence the best officers and boldest soldiers were forced to sacrifice themselves in a lamentable manner, to compensate for the negligence and incapacity of a government *always* ready to plunge into war without the slightest care for what was necessary to obtain success. The sieges carried on by the British in Spain were a succession of butcheries, because the commonest materials and means necessary for their a were denied to the engineers.

To breach the castle, while batteries established on the right bank of the Guadiana took it in reverse, and false attacks were made against the out-works, was the plan adopted; but San Christoval was to be reduced before the batteries against the castle could be constructed; wherefore on the night of the 8th, the captain of engineers, Squire, was ordered to break ground there at a distance of four hundred yards. The moon shone bright, he was ill provided with tools, and exposed to a destructive fire of musketry from the fort, of shot and shells from the town; hence he worked with loss until the 10th, and then the French in a sally entered his battery; they were driven back, but the allies pursued too hotly, were caught with grape and lost four hundred men. Thus five engineers and seven hundred officers and soldiers of the line were already inscribed upon the bloody list of victims offered to this Moloch, and only one small battery against an outwork was completed ! On the 11th it opened, and before sunset the fire of the enemy had disabled four of its five guns and killed many soldiers. No other result could be expected. The concert essential to success in double operations had been neglected by Beresford. Squire was exposed to the undivided fire of the fortress before the approaches against the castle were even commenced, and the false attacks scarcely attracted the notice of the enemy.

To check future sallies a second battery was erected against the bridge-head, yet this was also overmatched, and Beresford, having received intelligence that the French army was again in movement, then arrested the progress of all the works. On the 12th, believing this information premature, he directed the trenches to be opened against the castle; but the intelligence was confirmed at twelve o'clock in the night, and measures were taken to raise the siege.

BATTLE OF ALBUERA.

Soult had resolved to succour Badajos the moment he heard that Beresford was in Estremadura, and the latter's tardiness gave him time to tranquillise his province and arrange a system of resistance to the allied army in the Isla during his absence. Beresford believed he was trembling for Andalusia. Nothing could be more fallacious. He had seventy thousand fighting men there, and Drouet, who had quitted Massena immediately after the battle of Fuentes Onoro, was in march for that province with eleven thousand, by the way of Toledo.

On the 10th of May Soult quitted Seville with three thousand heavy dragoons, thirty guns, and two strong brigades of infantry under the generals Werle and Godinot.

The 13th a junction was effected with Latour Maubourg, who assumed the command of the heavy cavalry, resigning the fifth corps to General Girard.

On the 14th, having reached Villa Franca, thirty miles from Badajos, Soult caused his heaviest guns to fire salvos in the night to notify his approach to the garrison. This expedient failed, but on the evening of the 15th the whole French army was concentrated at Santa Marta.

Beresford had raised the siege in the night of the 12th, against the wish of the chief engineer, who promised him the place in three days! This promise was nought, and had it been good Soult would yet have surprised him in his trenches: his firmness therefore saved the army, and his arrangements for carrying off the stores were well executed. By twelve o'clock on the 15th the guns and stores were on the left bank of the Guadiana, the gabions and fascines were burnt, the flying-bridge removed; all being so well masked by the fourth division, which in concert with the Spaniards continued to maintain the invest-ment, that a sally on the rearguard, in which some Portuguese picquets were roughly treated, first told the French the siege was raised— of the cause they were still ignorant.

Beresford held a conference with the Spanish generals at Valverde on the 13th, and the chief command was ceded to him by the management of Castanos, to the discontent of Blake,who soon showed his ill-will. It was agreed to receive battle at the village of Albuera. Ballesteros' and Blake's corps had then united, and Blake engaged to bring them into line before twelve o'clock on the 15th. Meanwhile, Badajos being the centre of an arc sweeping through Valverde, Albuera and Talavera Real, it was arranged that Blake should watch the roads on the right; the British and fifth Spanish army those leading upon the centre, and Madden's Portuguese cavalry those on the left. The main body of the British could thus reach Albuera by a half march, as no part of the arc was more than four leagues from Badajos, and the enemy was still eight leagues from Albuera: Beresford therefore, thinking he could not be forestalled on any point of importance, kept the fourth division in the trenches.

On the 14th Colborne rejoined the army, Madden took post at Talavera Real, Blake was in march and his dragoons had joined the Anglo-Portuguese cavalry under General Long, who was at Santa Marta.

In the morning of the 15th the Anglo-Portuguese army occupied the left half of the Albuera position, a ridge four miles long, having the stream of the Aroya Val de Sevilla in rear and the Albuera in front. The ascent from the last river was easy for cavalry and artillery, and in advance of the centre were the bridge and village of Albuera—the former commanded by a battery, the latter occupied by Alten's Germans. Behind Alten, the second division, under William Stewart, formed one line, the right on a commanding hill over which the Valverde road passed, the left on the road of Badajos, beyond which the array was continued on two lines by the Portuguese troops under Hamilton and Collins.

The right of the ground being roughest, highest, and broadest, was left open for Blake, because Beresford, thinking the hill on the Valverde road the key of the position as covering the only line of retreat, was desirous to secure it with his own troops. The fourth division and the infantry of the fifth Spanish army were still before Badajos, but had orders to march on the first signal.

About three o'clock on the evening of the 15th, Beresford being on the left, the whole mass of the allied cavalry, closely followed by the French light horsemen, came pouring in from Santa Malta, and finding no infantry beyond the Albuera to support them passed that river in retreat. The wooded heights on the right bank being thus abandoned to the enemy, his force and dispositions were effectually concealed and the strength of the position was already sapped. Beresford was disquieted, he formed a temporary right wing with his cavalry and artillery, stretched his picquets along the road by which Blake was expected, and sent officers to hasten his movements; that general had only a few miles of good road to march and promised to be in line at noon, yet did not even bring up his van before eleven at night, nor his rear before three in the morning.

Cole and Madden were now called up. The order failed to reach Madden; but Cole brought the infantry of the fifth army, two squadrons of Portuguese cavalry, and two brigades of his own division to Albuera between eight and nine o'clock on the morning of the 16th: his third brigade having invested San Christoval was unable to pass the Guadiana above Badajos, and was in march by Jerumenha. Cole's Spanish troops joined Blake on the right, the two brigades of the fourth division were drawn up in columns behind the second division, the Portuguese squadrons reinforced Colonel Otway, whose horsemen, of the same nation, were pushed forwards in front of the left wing: all the rest of the allied cavalry was concentrated behind the centre, and Beresford, dissatisfied with General Long, gave Lumley the chief command.

Thirty thousand infantry, more than two thousand cavalry, and thirty-eight pieces of artillery, eighteen being ninepounders, were now in line; but one brigade of the fourth division was still absent, the British infantry, the pith and strength of battle, did not exceed seven thousand, and already Blake's arrogance was shaking Beresford's authority. The French had forty guns, four thousand veteran cavalry and nineteen thousand chosen infantry: obedient to one discipline, animated by one national feeling, their composition compensated for the want of numbers, and their general's talent was immeasurably greater than his adversary's.

Soult examined Beresford's position without hindrance on the evening of the 15th. He knew the fourth division was then before Badajos, heard that Blake would not arrive before the 17th, and resolved to attack next morning, having detected all the weakness of the English order of battle. The hill in the centre, commanding the Valverde road, was undoubtedly the key of the position if an attack was made parallel to the front; but Soult saw that on the right, through broad heights trended back towards the Valerde road, looking into the rear of Beresford's line, and if he could suddenly place his masses there he might roll up the right on the centre and push it into the valley of the Aroya: the Valverde road could then be seized, the retreat cut, and his strong cavalry would complete the victory.

Beresford's right and Soult's left were only divided by a hill about cannon-shot from each. Seperated from the allies by the Albuera, from the French by a rivulet called the Feria, this height was neglected by Beresford: but Soult in the night placed behind it the greatest part of his artillery under General Ruty, the fifth corps under Girard, the heavy cavalry under Latour Maubourg; thus concentrating fifteen thousand men and thirty guns within ten minutes' march of Beresford's right wing: and yet that general could not see a man, or draw a sound conclusion as to the plan of attack. The light cavalry, the brigades of Godinot and Werle, and ten guns remained. These were placed in the woods which lined the banks of the Feria towards its confluence with the Albuera. Werle was in reserve, Godinot was to attack the village and bridge, bear strongly against Beresford's centre, attract his attention, separate his wings, and double up his right when the principal attack should be developed.

Blake and Cole brought up more than sixteen thousand men, the first joining in the night, the second at nine o'clock in the morning after the action was begun; yet so defectively had Beresford occupied his position that Soult, though he saw how the allied army had been reinforced, made no change of disposition. At nine o'clock Godinot emerged from the woods with his division in one heavy column, preceded by a battery of ten guns; he was flanked by the light cavalry, followed by Werle's division, and made straight for the bridge of Albuera, attempting with a sharp cannonade and musketry to force a passage. General Briche, being on his right, now led two hussar regiments down the river in observation of Otway's horsemen, while the French lancers passed the stream above bridge. The 3rd Dragoon Guards drove the lancers back, and Dickson's Portuguese guns from a rising ground above the village, ploughed through Godinot's column, which crowded towards the bridge although the water was fordable above and below.

These feints along the front did not deceive Beresford, he saw Werle did not follow Godinot closely, and felt the principal effort would be on the right; he therefore desired Blake to throw part of his first and all his second line across the broad part of the hills, at right angles to their actual front. Then drawing the Portuguese infantry of the left wing to the centre, he sent a brigade to support Alten at the bridge, and directed Hamilton to hold the others in hand as a general reserve. The 13th Dragoons he posted near the river above bridge, and sent the second English division to support Blake. The horse-artillery, and cavalry under Lumley, and Cole's division, took ground to their right, the two first on a small plain behind the Aroya stream, the last about half musket-shot behind them. This done, Beresford galloped to Blake, who had refused to change his front, and with great heat told Colonel Hardinge, the bearer of the order, the real attack was at the village and bridge; he was entreated to obey, but was obstinate until Beresford arrived in person, and then only assented because the enemy's columns were appearing on his flank, acting however with such pedantic slowness, that Beresford, impatient of his folly, took the direction in person.

Great was the confusion and delay thus occasioned, and ere the troops were formed the French were amongst them. For scarcely had Godinot engaged Alten's brigade, when Werle, leaving only a battalion of grenadiers to support the former, and some squadrons to watch the 13th Dragoons and connect the attacks, countermarched and gained the rear of the fifth corps as it was mounting the hill on the right of the allies. The light cavalry, also quitting Godinot, crossed the Albuera above bridge, ascended the left bank at a gallop, and sweeping round the rear of the fifth corps joined Latour Maubourg, who was already in face of Lumley's squadrons ! Half-an-hour had thus sufficed to render Beresford's position nearly desperate; for two-thirds of the French had been thrown in order of battle across his right, while his army, disordered and of different nations, was still in the act of changing its front. Vainly he strove to get the Spaniards forward and make room for Stewart's division, the French guns opened, their infantry threw out a heavy musketry fire, their cavalry menaced different points, and the Spaniards, falling fast, drew back. Soult thought the whole army was yielding, he pushed forward his columns, his reserves came up the hill, and General Ruty placed all the French batteries in position.

At this moment William Stewart reached the foot of the height with the brigade under Colborne, and that able officer, seeing the confusion above, desired to form in order of battle previous to mounting; but Stewart, whose boiling courage generally overlaid his judgment, heedlessly led up in column of companies, passed the Spanish right and attempted to open a line as the battalions arrived: he could not do it, for so galling was the French fire that the foremost troops impatiently charged, heavy rain obscured the view, and four regiments of hussars and lancers, which, unseen, had gained the right flank, immediately galloped upon the rear of the disordered brigade and slew or took two-thirds: the 31st only, being still in column, escaped this charge and maintained its ground, while the French horsemen, riding violently over everything else, penetrated to all parts and captured six guns. The tumult was great and a lancer fell upon Beresford, but he, a man of great strength, putting the spear aside, cast the trooper from his saddle, and then a shift of wind blowed aside the smoke and mist, whereupon Lumley, seeing the mischief from the plain below, sent four squadrons up against the straggling hussars and cut many off. Penne Villemur's Spanish cavalry was at the same time directed to charge some French horsemen in the plain, but when within a few yards of their foes they turned and shamefully fled.

Great was the disorder on the hill. The shrinking Spaniards

were in one part blindly firing, though the British troops were before them, and in another part, flying before the lancers, would have broken through the 29th, then advancing to the succour of Colborne; but, terribly resolute, that regiment smote friends and foes without distinction in their onward progress: meanwhile Beresford urging the main body of the Spaniards to advance in his heat seized an ensign by the breast and bore him and his colours by main force to the front, yet the troops did not follow, and the coward ran back when released from the marshal's iron grasp.

In this crisis, the weather, which had ruined Colborne's brigade, saved the day, for Soult could not see the whole field of battle and kept his troops halted in masses when the decisive blow might have been struck. His cavalry indeed, began to hem in that of the allies, yet the fire of the horse-artillery enabled Lumley, covered by the bed of the Aroya and supported by the fourth division, to check them; Colborne still kept the height with the 31st Regiment, and the British artillery, under Julius Hartman, was coming fast into action; William Stewart, also, having escaped the lancers, was again mounting the hill with Houghton's brigade, which he brought on with the same vehemence but in a juster order of battle. The day now cleared and a dreadful fire poured into the thickest of the French columns taught Soult the fight was yet to be won.

Houghton's regiments reached the height under a heavy cannonade, and the 29th, after breaking through the fugitive Spaniards, was charged in flank by the French lancers, but two companies, wheeling to the right, foiled this attack; and then the third brigade of Stewart's division came up on the left, and the Spaniards under Zayas and Ballesteros moved forward. Hartman's artillery had made the enemy's infantry recoil, yet, soon recovering, they renewed the battle with greater violence than before, and the cannon on both sides discharged showers of grape at half-range, while the play of musketry was incessant and often within pistol shot; but the crowded columns of the French embarrassed their battle, and the British line would not yield them an inch of ground or a moment of time to open their ranks. Their fighting was however fierce and dangerous. Stewart was twice wounded, Colonel Duckworth was slain, and the gallant Houghton, having received many wounds without shrinking, fell and died in the act of cheering on his men.

Still the struggle continued with unabated fury. Colonel Inglis, twenty-two officers, and more than four hundred men, out of five hundred and seventy, fell in the 57th alone, and the other regiments were scarcely better of, not one-third were standing in any; their ammunition failed, and as their fire slackened the enemy established a column in advance upon the right flank, which the play of the artillery could only check for a time, and in that dreadful crisis Beresford wavered ! Destruction stared him in the face, his personal resources were exhausted and the unhappy thought of a retreat rose in his agitated mind. He had before posted Hamilton's Portuguese with a view to a retrograde movement, and now sent Alten orders to abandon the bridge of Albuera, to rally the Portuguese artillery on his Germans, and take ground to cover a retreat by the Valverde road. But while the commander was thus preparing to resign the contest, Colonel Hardinge, using his name, had urged Cole to bring up the fourth division, and then riding to the third brigade of Stewart's division, which, under Colonel Abercrombie, had hitherto been only slightly engaged, directed it also to push forward. The die was thus cast, Beresford acquiesced, Alten received orders to retake the village, and this terrible battle was continued.

Two brigades of the fourth division were present, one of Portuguese under General Harvey, the other under Sir William Myers, composed of the 7th and 23rd Regiments, was called the fusileer brigade. Harvey, pushing between Lumley's cavalry and the hill, was charged by some French horse and beat them off, while Cole led the fusileers up the contested height. At this time six guns were in the enemy's possession, Werle's reserve was pressing forward to reinforce the French front, and the remnant of Houghton's brigade could no longer maintain its ground, the field was heaped with carcasses, the lancers were riding furiously about the captured artillery on the upper parts of the hill, and Hamilton's Portuguese and Alten's Germans, withdrawing from the bridge, seemed to be in full retreat. Soon however Cole's fusileers, flanked by a battalion of the Lusitanian legion under Colonel Hawkshawe, surmounted the hill, drove off the lancers, recovered five guns and one colour, and passed the right of Houghton's brigade, precisely as Abercrombie passed its left.

Such a gallant line, issuing from the midst of the smoke and rapidly separating itself from the confused and broken multitude, startled the enemy's masses, then augmenting and pressing onwards as to an assured victory; they wavered, hesitated, and vomiting forth a storm of fire hastily endeavoured to enlarge their front, while a fearful discharge of grape from all their artillery whistled through the British ranks. Myers was killed, Cole, the three colonels, Ellis, Blakeney and Hawkshawe fell wounded, and the fusileer battalions, struck by the iron tempest, reeled and staggered like sinking ships: but suddenly and sternly recovering they closed on their terrible enemies, and then was seen with what a strength and majesty the British soldier fights. In vain did Soult with voice and gesture animate his Frenchmen; in vain did the hardiest veterans, breaking from the crowded columns, sacrifice their lives to gain time for the mass to open out on such a fair field; in vain did the mass itself bear up, and fiercely striving fire indiscriminately upon friends and foes, while the horsemen hovering on the flank threatened to charge the advancing line. nothing could stop that astonishing infantry. No sudden burst of undisciplined valour, no nervous enthusiasm weakened the stability of their order, their flashing eyes were bent on the dark columns in their front, their measured tread shook the ground; their dreadful volleys swept away the head of every formation, their deafening shouts overpowered the dissonant cries that broke from all parts of the tumultuous crowd, as slowly and with a horrid carnage it was pushed by the incessant vigour of the attack to the farthest edge of the height. There the French reserve, mixing with the struggling multitude, endeavoured to restore the fight but only augmented the irremediable disorder, and the mighty mass giving way like a loosened cliff went headlong down the steep: the rain flowed after in streams discoloured with blood, and eighteen hundred unwounded men, the remnant of six thousand unconquerable British soldiers, stood triumphant on the fatal hill !

While the fusileers were battling above, the cavalry and Harvey's brigade advanced, and Latour Maubourg's dragoons, battered also by Lefebre's guns, retired before them, yet still threatening the fusileers with their right, and with their left preventing Lumley falling on the defeated infantry. The crisis was however past, and Beresford, seeking to profit from the circumstances of the moment, made Alten retake Albuera, supported him with Blake's first line, which had not been engaged, and quickly brought up Hamilton's and Collins's Portugese, ten thousand fresh men, to strengthen the fusileers and Abercrombie's brigade. But so rapid was the execution of the last, the enemy was never attained by these reserves, which yet suffered severely, for Ruty having set the French guns altogether, worked them with prodigious activity while the fifth corps was still making head, and when the day was irrevocably lost, he regained the other side of the Albuera and protected the passage of the broken infantry.

Beresford, too hardly handled to pursue, now formed a front with the Portuguese parallel to the heights where Soult's troops were rallying, and though the action continued a short time after at the bridge, all was terminated before three o'clock. The serious fighting had endured only four hours, and in that time seven thousand allies and above eight thousand of their adversaries were struck down. Three French generals were wounded, two slain, and eight hundred soldiers so badly hurt as to be left on the field. On Beresford's side only two thousand Spaniards and six hundred Germans and Portuguese were killed or wounded, and with what resolution the pure British fought was thus made manifest, for they had but eighteen hundred men left standing! The laurel is nobly won when the exhausted victor reels as he places it on his bleeding front. The French took five hundred unwounded prisoners, a howitzer and several stand of colours. The British had no trophy to boast of, but the horrid piles of carcasses within their lines told with dreadful eloquence who were the conquerors, and all that night the rain poured down, and the river and the hills and the woods resounded with the dismal clamour and groans of dying men.

Beresford was oppressed with the number of his wounded, far exceeding the sound amongst the British soldiers. When the picquets were posted few remained to help the sufferers, and in this cruel distress he sent Hardinge to demand assistance from Blake; but wrath and mortified pride were predominant with that general; he refused, saying, it was customary with allies for each to take care of their own men. Yet the British had fought for Spain.

Morning came and both armies remained in their respective situations, the wounded still covering the field of battle, the hostile lines still menacing and dangerous. The greater number had fallen with the French, the best soldiers with the allies, and Soult's dark masses of cavalry and artillery, covering all his front, seemed able alone to contend again for victory. The right of the French appeared also to threaten the Badajos road, and Beresford in gloom and doubt awaited another attack; soon however the third brigade of the fourth division came up from Jerumenha, and then the second division retook its old ground between the Valverde and Badajos roads: on the 18th Soult retreated.

He left to English generosity several hundred men too deeply wounded to be removed, but all those who could travel he had, in the night of the 17th, sent by the royal road of Monasterio to Seville; and now, protecting his movements with his horsemen and six battalions of infantry, he filed his right on to the road of Solano. When this flank march was completed, Latour Maubourg covered the rear with the heavy dragoons, while Briche protected the march of the wounded men by the royal road.

Beresford sent Hamilton to re-invest Badajos, and the whole of his cavalry, supported by Alten's Germans, after the French; but soon Wellington, hurrying from the north, reached the field of battle and directed him to follow the enemy cautiously in person, while the third and seventh divisions, just come down from the Coa, completed the reinvestment of the fortress.

Soult now took a permanent position at Llerena, to await the junction of Drouet's division and reinforcements from Andalusia, resolved to contend again for Badajos. Meanwhile his cavalry advanced to Usagre designing to scour the country beyond; but the only outlet from that place was a bridge over a river with steep banks, which the French general Bron passed rashly with two regiments and being charged by General Lumley lost two hundred men. This terminated Beresford's operations. The miserable state to which the Regency had reduced the Portuguese troops required his presence at Lisbon and General Hill succeeded to his command.

RENEWED SIEGE OF BADAJOS.

Lord Wellington had left General Spencer with an army to straiten Ciudad Rodrigo and watch Marmont, who had succeeded Massena; but Marmont could from the Salamanca country cross the mountains and join Soult to disturb the siege of Badajos, and in that case Spencer, who had a shorter line, was to join Wellington. With this precaution it was hoped the place might be taken. But though no operation in war is so certain as a modern siege, if the rules of art are strictly followed, no operation is less open to irregular daring: the engineer can neither be hurried nor delayed without danger. Now the time required by the French to gather in force depended on Marmont, whose march from Salamanca by the mountain passes could not be stopped by Spencer: it was also possible for him to pass the Tagus on the shortest line by fords near Alcantara. But Beresford's siege had damaged the carriages of the battering guns, eleven days were required to repair them, and the scanty means of transport for stores was diminished by carrying the wounded from Albuera: hence more than fifteen days of open trenches, including nine days of fire, could not be expected. With good guns, plentiful stores and regular sappers and miners, this time would have sufficed; but none of these things were in the camp, and it was a keen jest of Picton to say, " *Lord Wellington sued Badajos in forma pauperis.*" His guns were of soft brass, false in their bore, and the shot of different sizes, the largest being too small; the Portuguese gunners were inexperienced, there were few British artillery-men, few engineers, no sappers or miners, and no time to teach the troops of the line how to make fascines and gabions.

Regular and sure approaches against the body of the place,

first reducing the outworks, could not now be attempted; yet Beresford's lines against the castle and Fort Christoval might be renewed, avoiding his errors; that is to say, by pushing the attacks simultaneously and with more powerful means. This plan was adopted, and something was hoped from the inhabitants, something from the effect of Soult's retreat after Albuera. The battering train was of fifty pieces, a convoy of engineers' stores came up from Alcacer do Sal, and a company of British artillery was on the march from Lisbon to be mixed with the Portuguese, making a total of six hundred gunners. Volunteers from the line acted as assistant engineers, and a draft of three hundred intelligent infantry soldiers, including twenty-five artificers of the staff corps, were employed as sappers.

Hamilton's Portuguese first invested the place on the left bank, and, the 24th of May, General Houston, having five thousand men, invested San Christoval; a flying bridge was then laid down on the Guadiana below the town, and Picton, crossing that river by a ford above, joined Hamilton. Hill commanded the covering army, all the cavalry was pushed forward in observation of Soult, and when intelligence of Drouet's junction was obtained, two regiments of cavalry and two brigades of infantry, which had been quartered at Coria as posts of communication with Spencer, were called up to reinforce Hill. Phillipon had during the interval of siege levelled Beresford's trenches, repaired his own damages, mounted more guns and obtained a small supply of wine and vegetables from the people of Estremadura, who were still awed by the presence of Soult's army. Within the place all was quiet, the citizens did not now exceed five thousand souls, and many of them were seen, mixed with soldiers, working at the defences; hence, as retrenchments in the castle behind the intended points of attack would have prolonged the siege beyond the calculated period, Lord Wellington to obtain timely notice of such works had a large telescope placed in the tower of La Lyppe near Elvas, by which the interior of the castle could be searched.

In the night of the 29th the engineers broke ground for a false attack, and the following night sixteen hundred work men, with a covering party of twelve hundred, sunk a parallel against the castle without being discovered; at the same time twelve hundred workmen, covered by a guard of eight hundred, opened a parallel four hundred and fifty yards from San Christoval and seven hundred yards from the bridge-head. On this line, one breaching and two counter batteries were raised against the fort and bridgehead, to prevent a sally from the last point; a fourth battery was also commenced to search the defences of the castle, but the workmen were discovered and a heavy fire struck down many.

On the 31st the attack against the castle, where the soil was soft, advanced rapidly; but Christoval being on a rock, earth had to be brought from the rear and the attack proceeded slowly and with considerable loss. This day the British artillery company came up on mules from Estremos, the engineer hastened his work, and, to save time, prematurely traced a work for fourteen twenty-four pounders with six large howitzers to batter the castle. On the Christoval side the batteries were not finished until the night of the 1st of June, for the soil was so rocky the miner had to level ground for platforms, while mortars, of eighteen inches' diameter, sent shells from the castle unerringly amongst, the workmen; these huge missiles would have ruined the works on that side if they had not been on the edge of a ridge, down which most of the shells rolled before bursting: yet so difficult is it to judge rightly in war, that Phillipon stopped this fire, thinking it was thrown away!* The progress of the works was so delayed by bringing up earth, that woolpacks purchased at Elvas were adopted as a substitute, and on the 2nd, all the batteries being completed and armed with forty-three pieces of different sizes, twenty were pointed against the castle. The shot being too small for the guns the fire was very ineffectual at first, and five pieces became unserviceable; but towards evening the practice became steadier, the fire of Christoval was nearly silenced, and the covering of masonry fell from the castle-wall, discovering a perpendicular bank of clay.

In the night of the 3rd a fresh battery for seven guns

---

* All Phillipon's views and preparations are taken from his original journal of siege in manuscript.

was traced against the castle, about six hundred yards from the breach, but the 4th the garrison's fire was also increased by additional guns, six of the besiegers' pieces were disabled, principally by their own fire, and the batteries only slightly marked the bank of clay. At Christoval, the fort was much injured, and some damage done to the castle also from the batteries on that side, yet the guns were so soft that the rate of firing was much reduced. In the night the new battery was armed, the damaged works repaired, and next day, as the enemy had caused a gun from Christoval to plunge into the trenches on the castle side, the parallel was deepened and traverses constructed to protect the troops.

Fifteen uninjured pieces still played against the castle, and the bank of clay fell away in flakes, yet it remained perpendicular.

In the night the parallel against the castle was extended, a fresh battery was traced out five hundred and twenty yards from the breach, and on the Christoval side new batteries were opened and some old ones abandoned. The garrison now began to retrench the castle breach, and their workmen were soon covered, while from Christoval two pieces of artillery plunged directly into the trenches with great effect: on the other hand the clay bank took a slope nearly practicable, and stray shells set fire to the houses nearest the castle.

On the 6th, one of two breaches in Christoval being judged practicable, a company of grenadiers with twelve ladders was ordered to assault, a second turned the fort to divert the enemy's attention, three hundred men cut the communication between the fort and the bridge, and a detachment with a six-pounder moved into the valley of the Gebora to prevent any passage of the Guadiana by boats.

FIRST ASSAULT OF CHRISTOVAL.

Major McIntosh of the 85th Regiment led the stormers, preceded by a forlorn hope under Lieutenant Dyas of the 51st, and that gallant gentleman, guided by the engineer Forster, a young man of uncommon bravery, reached the glacis and descended the ditch without being discovered; but the French had cleared the rubbish away, seven feet of perpendicular wall remained, carts and pointed beams of wood chained together were placed above, and shells were ranged along the ramparts to roll down. The forlorn hope finding the opening impracticable was retiring, when the main body, which had been exposed to a flank fire from the town as well as a direct fire from the fort, came leaping into the ditch with ladders and strove to escalade; but the ladders were too short, the garrison, seventy-five men besides the cannoneers, made a stout resistance, the confusion and mischief occasioned by the bursting of the shells was great, and the stormers were beaten off with the loss of more than a hundred men.

Bad success produces disputes. The failure was attributed by some to the breach being impracticable from the first, by others to the confusion which arose after the main body had entered. French writers affirm that the breach, practicable on the night of the 5th was not so on the 6th, because the besiegers did not attack until midnight and thus gave the workmen time to remove the ruins and raise fresh obstacles: the bravery of the soldiers, who were provided with three muskets each, did the rest. The combinations for the assault were however not well calculated: the storming party was too weak, the ladders too few and short, the breach not sufficiently scoured by the fire of the batteries, and the leading troops were repulsed before the main body had descended the ditch. In such attacks the supports should almost form one body with the leaders, for the sense of power derived from numbers is a strong incentive to valour, and obstacles, insurmountable to a few, vanish before a multitude.

During the storm six iron guns were placed in battery against the castle, but two brass pieces became unserviceable, and the following day three others were disabled. However the bank of clay seemed to offer now a good slope, and in the night the engineer Patton examined it closely; he was mortally wounded in returning, yet lived to report it practicable. At Christoval the garrison continued to clear away the ruins at the foot of the breach, made interior retrenchments with bales of wool and other materials, ranged huge shells and barrels of powder with matches along the ramparts, and gave the defenders, chosen men, four muskets each. In this state of affairs news came that Drouet was close to Llerena, and Marmont on the move from Salamanca, wherefore Wellington ordered another assault on Christoval at both breaches. Four hundred men, carrying sixteen long ladders, were employed, the supports were better closed up, the appointed hour was nine instead of twelve, and more detachments were planted on the right and left to cut off communication with the town; but Phillipon, in opposition, made the garrison two hundred strong.

SECOND ASSAULT OF CHRISTOVAL.

Major McGeechy commanded the stormers, the forlorn hope, again led by the gallant Dyas, was accompanied by the engineer Hunt, and a little after nine o'clock the leading troops bounded forward, followed by the support, amidst a shattering fire of musketry which killed McGeechy, Hunt, and many men upon the glacis. Loudly shouted the British as they jumped into the ditch, but the French scoffingly called them on, and rolling down the barrels of powder and shells made fearful and rapid havoc. A column had been designed for each breach, yet both came together at the main breach, where some confusion about the ladders caused only a few to be reared, and the enemy, standing on the ramparts, bayoneted the foremost assailants, overturned the ladders, and again poured their destructive fire upon the crowd below until one hundred and forty fell and the rest retired.

The castle breach remained for assault, yet the troops could not form between the top and the retrenchments behind the opening unless Christoval was taken, and its guns used to clear the interior of the castle; but to take Christoval required several days; hence, as Soult was ready to advance, the stores were removed and the attack turned into a blockade, the allies having lost four hundred men and officers: the process of siege had been altogether false and irregular.

Marmont now joined Soult, Spencer joined Wellington,

and the 19th of June the French armies entered Badajos. The allies were only a few miles off holding both sides of the Caya, a small river flowing between Elvas and Campo Mayor into the Guadiana: yet their disposition was so skilfully concealed by undulating ground and woods, that on the 23rd the French marshals were forced to send out two exploring bodies of cavalry to obtain information. One column cut off a squadron of the 11th Light Dragoons, and the 2nd German Hussars escaped it with difficulty; the other column was checked by the heavy dragoons and Madden's Portuguese cavalry with a sharp skirmish, in which happened a single combat similar to that between Ariosto's Rogero and Mandricardo. An English horseman, standing high in his stirrups with raised sword, encountered a French officer who pierced him under the arm; slowly the weapon was driven through his body, yet no shrinking motion could be observed; he seemed only to give more force to his descending weapon, which bit into the Frenchman's brain and both fell dead together.

Soult and Marmont had above sixty thousand men in line, seven thousand being cavalry, with ninety guns. Wellington had only twenty-eight thousand sabres and bayonets, and the country, a cavalry one, furnished no position to compensate for inferior numbers: a battle gained would certainly have terminated the war. Yet the crisis passed without mischief, because Wellington so concealed his weakness, and outfaced his enemies with such audacity, such a blending of resolution and genius that the French marshals retired and separated without striking ! The political and military difficulties supported and overcome by the English general at this period were indeed most extraordinary, and must be sought for in my History of the War, from which this work, treating only of combats, is extracted.

BOOK VI.

Blockade of Ciudad Rodrigo—Combat of Elbodon—Combat of
Aldea de Ponte—Surprise of Aroyo de Molinos—Defence of Tarifa—
English Siege of Ciudad Rodrigo—Third English Siege of Badajos—
Assault of Picurina—Assault of Badajos.

BLOCKADE OF CIUDAD RODRIGO.

After the second siege of Badajos the contest in the Peninsula
presented a new phase. French reinforcements were poured into
Spain, forty thousand old soldiers entered by the northern line alone,
and General Dorsenne took command of the *Army of the North,*
which now contained seventeen thousand of Napoleon's young
guard. The king had a particular force about Madrid called the *Army
of the Centre;* Soult commanded the *Army of the South;* Marmont
the *Army of Portugal,* with which, by the emperor's orders, he took
post in the valley of the Tagus, leaving a division at Truxillo south of
that river, establishing a bridge of communication at Almaraz, which
he fortified on both sides strongly.

This disposition of the French armies was at once offensive and
defensive. Portugal was menaced from the north by Dorsenne, who
had Ciudad Rodrigo as an advanced place of arms; from the south by
Soult, who had Badajos for an advanced place of arms; in the centre
by Marmont, who could march on Abrantes, join Dorsenne, or unite
with Soult. In defence the French were still more powerful. If
Wellington assailed Dorsenne, the latter by retiring could concentrate
a great force, while Marmont acted on the English right flank; and
together they could present seventy thousand men in line. If he
assailed Soult, as he had indeed designed before the failure of
Badajos, Marmont could act on his left flank, and, united with Soult,
could present sixty-five thousand fighting men. If he marched
against Marmont by either bank of the Tagus, that marshal,
reinforced with detachments from Dorsenne, Soult, and the
king, could deliver battle with more than seventy thousand men.

The English general could not contend with such powerful armies beyond the mountains of Portugal, yet from political pressure he could not stand still, and there were defects in his adversaries' breast-plate through which he hoped to pierce. He saw that Badajos and Rodrigo were isolated and difficult to provision; that each depended for succour on the junction of armies under generals of equal authority, ill disposed to act together, and whose communications were long and uneasy, furnishing pretences for non-cooperation. Marmont had indeed a direct line of intercourse with Dorsenne across the Gredos mountains, by the fortified pass of Banos; but to reach Soult the Tagus was to be crossed at Almaraz, the defiles of Estremadura and the passes of the Morena to be threaded before a junction could be made in the plains of Badajos: wherefore, General Girard, having the remains of Mortier's army, called *the fifth corps,* was employed as a moving, column in Estremadura, to support Badajos and connect the army of Portugal with that of Soult.

In this state of affairs Wellington, who had received large reinforcements after the siege of Badajos, left General Hill, in August, with twelve thousand men of all arms to keep Girard in check, and in person marched to the north, under pretence of seeking healthy quarters for his sickly troops, really to blockade Ciudad Rodrigo, which an intercepted letter described as wanting provisions; it had however been previously supplied by Bessieres before he quitted his command, and this effort was frustrated. The army was then placed near the sources of the Agueda and Coa, close to the line of communication between Marmont and Dorsenne, and preparations were made for a siege, in the notion that the last general's force was weak: but that also was an error, and when discovered, a blockade was established. Almeida, whose renewed walls had been destroyed by Spencer when he marched to the south, was now repaired for a place of arms, the bridge over the Coa was restored, and with the utmost subtilty of combination and the most extensive arrangements the English general, while appearing only to blockade, secretly prepared for a siege. All his art was indeed required, for though the Anglo-Portuguese were at this time eighty thousand on paper, with ninety guns, twenty-two thousand men were in hospital; wherefore, Hill's corps being deducted, less than forty-five thousand were on the watch to snatch a fortress which was in the keeping of eighty thousand.

In September Rodrigo called for succour, whereupon Marmont and Dorsenne advanced to its relief with sixty thousand men, six thousand being cavalry, and they had a hundred pieces of artillery. Wellington could not fight this great army beyond the Agueda, but would not retreat until he had seen all their force, lest a detachment should relieve the place to his dishonour. In this view he took the following positions.

Picton's division, reinforced with three squadrons of German and British cavalry, was placed at the heights of Elbodon and Pastores, on the left of the Agueda, within three miles of Rodrigo. The light division with some squadrons of cavalry and six guns, were posted on the right of the Agueda, at the Vadillo, a river with a rugged channel falling into the Agueda three miles above Rodrigo: from this line an enemy coming from the eastern passes of the hills could be discerned. The sixth division and Anson's brigade of cavalry, forming the left of the army, was under General Graham at Espeja, on the Lower Azava, with advanced posts at Carpio and Marialva, from whence to Rodrigo was eight miles over a plain. Julian Sanchez's Partida watched the Lower Agueda, and the heads of columns were thus presented to the fortress on three points, namely, Vadillo, Pastores and Espeja. Two brigades of heavy cavalry on the Upper Azava, supported by Pack's Portuguese, connected Graham with Elbodon; but he was very distant from Guinaldo, the pivot of operations, and to obviate the danger of a flank march in retreat the first and seventh divisions were posted in succession towards Guinaldo. The army was thus spread out on different roads, like the sticks of a fan, having their point of union on the Coa

This disposition was faulty. Broad heights lining the left bank of the Agueda ended abruptly above the villages of Elbodon and Pastores, and were flanked in their whole length by woods and great plains, extending from Rodrigo to the Coa; they could not therefore be held against an enemy commanding those plains, and if the French pushed along them suddenly, beyond Guinaldo, the distant wings could be cut off. At Guinaldo however, three field redoubts had been constructed on high open ground, to impose upon the enemy and so gain time to assemble and feel his disposition for a battle, because a retreat beyond the Coa was to be avoided if possible.

On the 23rd the French encamped behind the hills northeast of Rodrigo, and a strong detachment, entering the plain, looked at the light division on the Vadillo and returned.

The 24th, six thousand cavalry and four divisions of infantry crossed the hills in two columns to introduce the convoy, while on the English side the fourth division occupied the position of Guinaldo, and the redoubts were completed. No other change was made, for it was thought the French would not advance further; but the 24th, soon after daybreak, fourteen squadrons of the imperial guards drove Graham's outpost from Carpio across the Azava; the Lancers of Berg then crossed that river in pursuit, but were flanked by some infantry in a wood and beaten back by two squadrons of the 14th and 16th Dragoons, who re-occupied the post of Carpio. During this skirmish, fourteen battalions of infantry and thirty squadrons of cavalry, with twelve guns, under Montbrun, passing the Agueda at Rodrigo marched towards Guinaldo; the road divided there, one branch turning the Elbodon heights on the French right the other leading through Pastores and Elbodon, and as the point of divarication was covered by a gentle ridge, it was doubtful which branch would be taken. Soon that doubt vanished. The cavalry pouring along the right-hand road leading to Guinaldo, drove in the advanced posts, and without waiting for their infantry fell on.

COMBAT OF ELBODON.

The action began disadvantageously for the allies. The left of the third division was turned, the 74th and 60th Regiments, being at Pastores, far on the right, were too distant to be called in, and Picton, having three other regiments at Elbodon, could take no immediate part in the fight Wellington sent to Guinaldo for a brigade of the fourth division, and meanwhile directed General Colville to draw up the 77th and 5th British Regiments, the 21st Portuguese and two brigades of artillery of the same nation, on a hill over which the road to Guinaldo passed, supporting their flanks with Alten s three squadrons. This position, convex towards the enemy, was covered, front and flanks, by deep ravines; but it was too extensive, and before Picton could come from Elbodon the crisis was over. Vainly the Portuguese guns sent their shot through Montbrun's horsemen, they crossed the ravine in half squadrons, and with amazing vigour rode up the rough height on three sides; neither the loose fire of the infantry nor the artillery stopped them, but they were checked by the fine fighting of the cavalry, who charged the heads of the ascending masses, not once but twenty times, and always with a good will maintaining the upper ground for an hour.

It was astonishing to see so few troopers resist that surging multitude even on such steep ground; but when Montbrun, obstinate to win, brought up his artillery, his horsemen, gaining ground in the centre, cut down some gunners and captured the Portuguese guns, and at the same time one German squadron, charging too far, got entangled in the ravines. The danger was then imminent, but suddenly the 5th Regiment, led by Major Ridge, a daring man, dashed bodily into the midst of the French cavalry and retook the artillery, which again opened, while the 77th, supported by the 21st Portuguese, vigorously repulsed the enemy on the left. These charges of infantry against a powerful cavalry, which had room to expand, could however only check the foe at particular points, and Montbrun pressed with fresh masses against the left of the allies, while other squadrons penetrated between their right and the village of Elbodon, from the inclosures and vineyards of which Picton was, with difficulty and some confusion, extricating his regiments. He could give no succour, the brigade of the fourth division was not in sight, the French infantry was rapidly approaching, and Wellington therefore directed both Picton and Colville to fall back and unite in the plain behind.

Colville, forming his battalions in two squares, descended at once from the hill, but Picton had a considerable distance to move, there was a great interval, and at that moment, the cavalry, fearing to be surrounded, galloped for refuge to the Portuguese regiment, which was farthest in retreat. Then the 5th and 7th, two weak battalions formed in one square, were quite exposed, and in an instant the whole of the French horsemen came thundering down upon them. But how vain, how fruitless to match the sword with the musket, send the charging horseman against the steadfast veteran ! The multitudinous squadrons, rending the skies with their shouts, closed upon the glowing squares like the falling edges of a burning crater, and were as instantly rejected, scorched and scattered abroad; then a rolling peal of musketry echoed through the hills, bayonets littered at the edge of the smoke, and with firm and even step the British regiments came forth like the holy men from the Assyrian's furnace.

Picton now effected his junction and the whole retired to Guinaldo, about six miles. The French would not renew the close attack, yet plied shot and shell until the entrenched camp was gained; there the fourth division presented a fresh front, Pack then came in from Campillo, the heavy cavalry from the Upper Azava, and as it was near dusk the action ceased. The 74th and 60th Regiments, posted at Pastores, were abandoned by this retreat, but they crossed the Agueda at a ford, and moving up the right bank reached Guinaldo in the night after a march of fifteen hours.

Graham had early received orders to fall back on the first division, yet to keep posts of observation on the Azava, while Sanchez's infantry went behind the Coa; the guerilla chief himself passed with his cavalry to the French rear, and the seventh division was withdrawn behind the left wing, which was now in line with the centre, though still distant. The light division should have come by Robledo to Fuente Guinaldo; Craufurd received the order at three o'clock, heard the cannonade, and might have reached it before midnight; but fearing a march in darkness he merely retired a league from the Vadillo, which was immediately passed by fifteen hundred French; Guinaldo was thus maintained by only fourteen thousand men, two thousand six hundred being cavalry. Graham was ten miles distant; the light division, debarred of a direct route by the enemy, was sixteen miles distant; the fifth division, posted at Payo in the mountains, was twelve miles distant; and during the night and the following day, Marmont united sixty thousand men in front of Guinaldo. The English general was thus in great danger, yet he would not abandon the light division, which, intercepted by the French cavalry at Robledo, did not arrive until after three o'clock in the evening. Marmont's fortune was fixed in that hour ! He knew not how matters really stood. He detached a strong column by the valley of the Azava to menace the allies' left, and made an ostentatious display of the Imperial Guards in the plain, instead of attacking an adversary who laughed to see him so employed, and soon changed the state of affairs.

In the night, by an able concentric movement, Wellington united his whole army on new ground between the Coa and the sources of the Agueda, twelve miles behind Guinaldo. Marmont, unconscious of his advantages, instead of troubling this difficult movement had also retired in the night, and was marching back when the scouts of his column in the valley of Azava reported that the allies were in retreat, and their divisions widely separated. Then discovering all the deceit of Guinaldo, and the escape of the light division, he prophetically exclaimed, alluding to Napoleon's fortune, *And Wellington, he also has a star.* In this mood he would have continued his retreat, but it is said Dorsenne forced him to wheel round and pursue: Wellington was then however in a strong position behind the stream of the Villa Maior, where he could not be turned, and where it covered all the practicable roads leading to the bridges and fords of the Coa.

COMBAT OF ALDEAPONTE.

The French moved by two roads against the right and centre. Checked on the first by the light division, on the second their horsemen drove the cavalry posts across the Villa Maior and took possession of Aldeaponte, where at twelve o'clock the head of their infantry attacked a brigade of the fourth division, posted on opposing heights, under General Pakenham. Wellington arriving at that moment directed a charge, and the French were driven back; they attempted to turn the brigade by a wood on their own left while their cavalry advanced to the foot of the hills, but the artillery sufficed to baffle the effort, and then the English general, taking the offensive, turned their left and seized the opposite hills: this finished the action and Aldeaponte was re-occupied. Wellington, who had been much exposed to fire, rode to another part, yet scarcely had he departed when the French from the other road joined those near Aldeaponte, and at five o'clock retook the village; Pakenham recovered it, but the enemy was very numerous, the country rugged, and so wooded he could not tell what was passing on the flanks: wherefore, knowing the chosen ground of battle was behind the Coa, he abandoned Aldeaponte for his original post.

In the night the allies retreated, and on the morning of the 28th occupied a new and strong position in a deep loop of the Coa, where it could only be attacked on a narrow front; but the French, who had brought only a few days' provisions and could gather none in that country, retired the same day. Dorsenne marched to Salamanca, a strong division was posted at Alba de Tormes to communicate with Marmont, and the latter resumed his old position in the valley of the Tagus. The light division, reinforced by some cavalry, now resumed the nominal blockade of Ciudad Rodrigo, in concert with Julian Sanchez; the rest of the army was cantoned on both sides of the Coa and head-quarters were fixed at Freneda.

Only three hundred men and officers fell in these combats on the British side. The French lost more, because of the unreturned fire at Elbodon, and here a fine chivalric action on their side merits notice. In one of the cavalry fights, an officer in the act of striking at Felton Harvey of the 14th Dragoons, perceived that he had but one arm and with a rapid change brought down his sword to a salute and passed on!

SURPRISE OF ARROYO DE MOLINOS.

While Rodrigo was being blockaded, General Hill co-operated with the Spaniards in Estremadura against General Drouet, who first joined Girard, but after various movements returned to the Morena, leaving his colleague at Caceres between the Tagus and the Guadiana. From that place Hill drove him the 26th of October, and hoping to cut him off from the bridge of Merida, moved by a cross road next day. On the march he heard Girard had halted in Arroyo de Molinos, leaving a rear-guard on the Caceres road —thus showing he knew not of the cross-road move-ment and looked for pursuit only from Caceres. With a rapid decision and a forced march the English general moved in the night upon Alcuesca, just one league from Arroyo, which was in a plain, and close behind it rose a rocky sierra, crescent-shaped, and about two miles wide on the chord. From Alcuesca one road led direct to Arroyo, another entered it on the left, and three led from it, the most distant of the last being the Truxillo road, which rounded the extrem-ity of the sierra; the nearest was the Merida road, and between them was that of Medellin. The weather was very stormy and wet, but no fires were permitted in the allies' camp, and at two o'clock in the morning of the 28th the troops moved to a low ridge half a mile from Arroyo, under cover of which they formed three bodies—the infantry on the wings, the cavalry in the centre. The left column marched straight upon the village, the right towards the extreme point of the sierra, where the Truxillo road turned the horn of the crescent, the cavalry kept the centre.

One brigade of Girard's division had marched at four o'clock by the road of Medellin, but Dombrouski's brigade and the cavalry of Briche were still in the place, and the horses of the rear-guard, unbridled, were tied to trees. The infantry were gathering on the Medellin road outside the village, and Girard was in a house waiting for his horse, when two British officers galloped into the street and in an instant all was confusion; hastily the cavalry bridled their horses and the infantry ran to their alarm-posts, but a tempest raged, a thick mist rolled down the craggy mountain, a terrific shout was heard amidst the clatter of the elements, and with the driving storm the 71st and 92nd Regiments came charging down. The French rear-guard of horsemen, fighting and struggling hard, were driven to the end of the village, where the infantry, forming their squares, endeavoured to cover the main body of the cavalry; but then the

71st, lining the garden walls, opened a galling fire on the nearest square, the 92nd, filing out of the streets, formed upon the French right, and the 50th Regiment, following closely, secured the prisoners.

The rest of the column, headed by the Spanish cavalry, skirted outside the houses to intercept the line of retreat, and soon the guns opened on the squares, and the 13th Dragoons captured the French artillery, while the 9th Dra goons and German Hussars dispersed their cavalry. Girard, an intrepid officer, although wounded, still kept his infantry together, retreating by the Truxillo road; but the right column of the allies was in possession of that line, the cavalry and artillery were close upon his flank, and the left column followed fast; his men fell by fifties and his situation was desperate, yet he would not surrender, and giving the word to disperse endeavoured to scale the almost inaccessible rocks of the sierra. His pursuers, not less obstinate, immediately divided. The Spaniards ascended the hills at an easier point beyond his left; the 39th Regiment and Ashworth's Portuguese turned the mountain by the Truxillo road; the 28th and 34th, led by General Howard, followed him step by step up the rocks, taking prisoners, but finally the pursuers, heavily loaded, were beaten in speed by men who had thrown away their arms and packs. Girard, Dombrouski, and Briche, escaped into the Guadalupe mountains, and then crossing the Guadiana at Orellana, on the 9th of November rejoined Drouet with six hundred men, the remains of three thousand: they were said to be the finest troops then in Spain, and their resolution in such an appalling situation was no mean proof of their excellence.

Thirteen hundred prisoners, including General Bron and the Prince of Aremberg, all the artillery, baggage, commissariat, and a contribution just raised, were taken. The allies had seventy killed and wounded, and one officer, Lieutenant Strenowitz, was taken. He was an Austrian, and distinguished for courage and successful enterprises, but he had abandoned the French to join Julian Sanchez, and was liable to death by the laws of war. Originally forced into the French service he was, in reality, no deserter, and General Hill applied frankly in his favour to

Drouet, who was so good-tempered that, while smarting under this disaster, he released his prisoner.

This exploit set all the French corps in motion to revenge it; yet on the 28th of November Hill, by a forced march, again surprised three hundred infantry and some hussars under Captain Neveux, who however lost only forty men, escaping the British cavalry, said his generous antagonist, by " *the intrepid and admirable manner in which he retreated.*"

DEFENCE OF TARIFA.

Soult had long resolved to reduce the maritime town of Tarifa, but General Campbell, governor of Gibraltar, equally resolute to prevent him, threw in an English garrison, under Colonel Skerrett. The defences were ancient, the place being encircled with towers connected by an archery wall, irregular, without a ditch, and too thin to resist even field artillery. It was commanded also by heights within cannon-shot, but the English engineer Smith* adapted the defence to the peculiarities of ground so skilfully as to fix the enemy's attention entirely to one point, which offered facilities for an internal resistance, to begin when the weak ramparts should be broken.

Tarifa was cloven by a periodical torrent, entering at the east and passing out at the west. It was barred at the entrance by a tower with a portcullis, in front of which palisades were planted across its bed. The houses within the walls were strongly built on inclined planes, rising from each side of the torrent; and at the exit of the water were two massive structures, called the tower and castle of the Gusmans, both looking up the hollow formed by the inclined planes. From these structures, a sandy neck, prolonged by a causeway for eight hundred yards, joined the town to an island, whose perpendicular sides forbade entrance save by the causeway which ended on an unfinished entrenchment and battery.

On the neck of land were sand hills, the highest, called the Catalina, being scarped and crowned with a field-work holding, a twelve-pounder. This hill masked the causeway towards the enemy, and with the tower of the Gusmans,

---

* Now Lieut.-General Sir C. Smith.

which was armed with a ship eighteen-pounder, flanked the western front of the tower. This tower gun also shot clear over Tarifa to the slope where the French batteries were expected, and there were a ship of the line, a frigate, and some gun-boats, anchored to flank the approaches.

Smith deterred the enemy from attacking the western front by the flanking fire of a fortified convent beyond the walls, by the Catalina hill, and by the appearance of the shipping; but he deceitfully tempted an attack on the eastern front and the line of the torrent, whose bed rendered the inner depth of wall greater than the outer. There he loopholed the houses behind, opened communications to the rear, and barricaded the streets; so that the enemy, after forcing the breach, would have been confined between the houses on the inclined planes, exposed on each side to musketry from loopholes and windows, and in front to a fire from the Gusmans, which looked up the bed of the torrent; finally the garrison could have taken refuge in that castle and tower, which, high and massive, were fitted to cover the evacuation, and were provided with ladders for the troops to descend and retreat to the island under protection of the Catalina.

There was no want of guns. Besides those of the Catalina, there were in the island twelve pieces, comprising four twenty-four pounders and two ten-inch mortars; in the town were six field-pieces, with four cohorns on the east front; an eighteen-pounder was on the Gusmans, a howitzer on the portcullis tower, and two field-pieces were in reserve for sallies: yet most of the island ordnance was mounted after the investment, and the walls and towers of the town were too weak and narrow to sustain heavy guns; hence only three field-pieces and the cohorns did in fact reply to the enemy's fire.

The garrison, including six hundred Spanish infantry and one hundred horse of that nation, amounted to two thousand five hundred men, of whom seven hundred were in the island, one hundred in the Catalina, two hundred in the convent, and fifteen hundred in the town. On the 19th of December, General Laval, having eight thousand men, drove in the advanced posts, but was with a sharp skirmish designedly led towards the eastern front.

The 20th the place was invested, and the 21st some French troops having incautiously approached the western front, Captain Wren of the 11th, suddenly descended from the Catalina and carried them off In the night the enemy approached close to the walls of that front, but in the morning Wren again fell on them; and at the same time a sally of discovery was made from the convent so vigorously that Lieutenant Welstead of the 82nd, entering one of the enemy's camps captured a field-piece; he was unable to bring it off in face of the French reserves, yet the latter were drawn by the skirmish under the fire of the ships, of the island, and of the town, whereby they suffered severely and with difficulty recovered the captured piece.

In the night of the 22nd the anticipations of the British engineer were realized. The enemy broke ground five hundred yards from the eastern front, and worked assiduously until the 26th, under a destructive fire, replying principally with wall-pieces, which would have done much mischief if the garrison had not been copiously supplied with sand-bags.

On the 23rd the ships were driven off in a gale; on the 29th the French guns opened against the town and their howitzers against the island; the piece at the Gusmans was dismounted, yet quickly re-established; but the ramparts came down by flakes, and in a few hours opened a wide breach a little to the English right of the portcullis tower. Skerrett then proposed to abandon the place, and though strenuously opposed by Major King and the engineer Smith, he would have done so, if General Campbell, hearing of this intention, had not called away the transports. Tarifa was indeed open to assault and escalade. But behind the breach the depth to the street was fourteen feet, and Smith had covered the ground below with iron gratings, having every second bar turned up; the houses were also prepared and garrisoned, and the troops well disposed on the ramparts, each regiment having its own quarter. The breach was held by the 87th under Colonel Gough.* On his left were some riflemen: on his right some Spaniards should have been, yet were not, and two companies of the 47th took their place.

* Now Lord Gough.

In the night of the 29th the enemy fired salvos of grape,but the besieged cleared the foot of the breach between the discharges.

The 30th the breaching fire was renewed, and the wall, broken for sixty feet, offered an easy ascent; yet the besieged again removed the rubbish, and in the night were augmenting the defences, when, flooded by rain, the torrent brought down from the French camp a mass of planks, fascines, gabions, and dead bodies, which broke the palisades, bent the portcullis back, and with the surge of waters injured the defences behind: a new passage was thus opened in the wall, yet the damage was repaired before morning, and the troops confidently awaited the assault.

In the night the torrent subsided as quickly as it had risen, and at daylight a living stream of French grenadiers gliding swiftly down its bed, as if assured of victory, arrived without shout or tumult within a few yards of the walls; but then, instead of quitting the hollow to reach the breach, they dashed like the torrent of the night against the portcullis. The 87th, previously silent and observant, as if at a spectacle, now arose and with a shout and a crashing volley smote the head of the French column; the leading officer, covered with wounds, fell against the portcullis grate and gave up his sword through the bars to Colonel Gough: the French drummer, a gallant boy, while beating the charge dropped lifeless by his officer's side, and the dead and wounded filled the hollow. The survivors breaking out right and left, and spreading along the slopes of ground under the ramparts, opened an irregular musketry, and at the same time men from the trenches leaped into pits digged in front and shot fast; but no diversion at other points was made and the storming column was dreadfully shattered. The ramparts streamed fire, and a field-piece sent a tempest of grape whistling through the French ranks in such a dreadful manner that, unable to endure the torment, they plunged once more into the hollow and regained their camp, while a shout of victory mingled with the sound of musical instruments passed round the wall of the town.

The allies had five officers wounded, and thirty-one men killed or hurt; the French dead covered the slopes in front of the rampart, and choked the bed of the river: ten wounded officers, of whom only one survived, were brought in by the breach, and Skerrett, compassionating the sufferings of the others, and admiring their bravery, permitted Laval to fetch them off. The siege was then suspended, for the rain had partially ruined the French batteries, interrupted their communications, and stopped their supplies; and the torrent, again swelling, broke the stockades of the allies and injured their retrenchments: some vessels also, coming from Gibraltar with ammunition, were wrecked on the coast. Nevertheless a fresh assault was expected until the night of the 4th, when frequent firing in the French camp without any bullets reaching the town, indicated that the enemy were destroying guns previous to retreating. Hence, at daylight the besieged, issuing from the convent, commenced a skirmish with the rear-guard, but were impeded by a heavy storm and returned, after making a few prisoners. Lavals misfortunes did not end there. His troops had contracted sickness, many deserted, and it was computed the expedition cost him a thousand men, while the allies lost only one hundred and fifty, and but one officer, Longley of the engineers, was killed.

Such is the simple tale of Tarifa, yet the true history of its defence cannot there be found. Colonel Skerrett obtained the credit, but he and Lord Proby, second in command, always wished to abandon both town and island. It was the engineer Smith's vigour and capacity which overmatched the enemy's strength without, and the weakness of those commanders within, repressing despondency where he failed to excite confidence. Next in merit was the artillery captain, Mitchel, a noble soldier who has since perished in the Syrian campaign against Ibrahim Pasha: his talent and energy at Tarifa were conspicuous.

ENGLISH SIEGE OF GIUDAD RODRIGO.

Lord Wellington, unable to maintain the blockade of Rodrigo, had withdrawn behind the Goa in November and widely spread his army for provisions; but the year 1812 opened favourably for his views. Napoleon, then preparing for his gigantic invasion of Russia, had recalled from Spain many old officers and sixty thousand of the best soldiers, including all the Imperial Guards. The Army *of the North,* thus reduced, was ordered to quarter about Burgos, while the Army *of Portugal,* leaving troops to guard Almaraz, moved across the Gredos mountains into the Salamanca country. It had been reinforced with eighteen thousand men, but was spread for subsistence from Salamanca to the Asturias on one side, and to the valley of the Tagus and Toledo on the other; Montbrun also had been detached from it to Valencia. The *Army of the Centre* was in a state of great disorder, and the king and Marmont were at open discord. In this state of affairs, seeing that Ciudad Rodrigo was weakly guarded, that Marmont, deceived by previous combination, had no suspicion of a siege, that Soult's attention was fixed on Tarifa; seeing in fine that opportunity was ripe, Lord Wellington leaped with both feet on Ciudad Rodrigo.

Thirty-five thousand men, cavalry included, were disposable for this siege, the materials for which were placed in villages on the left of the Azava river, and the ammunition in Almeida, where seventy pieces of ordnance had been secretly collected. Hired carts and mules were employed to bring up the stores, but for the guns the means of transport were so scanty that only thirty-eight could be brought to the trenches. A bridge was laid down on the Agueda, six miles below the fortress, on the 1st of January, and the investment was designed for the 6th, but the native carters took two days to travel ten miles of good road with empty carts, and it could not be made before the 8th: to find fault with them was dangerous, as they deserted on the slightest offence.

Rodrigo was on high ground overhanging the right bank of the Agueda; an old rampart thirty feet high, nearly circular and flanked with a few projections, formed the body of the fortress; a second bulwark, called a *Fausse-braye,* with a ditch and covered way, enclosed this rampart, yet was placed so low on the descent, as to give little cover to the main wall.

Beyond the walls, on the side farthest from the river, the suburb of Francisco was intrenched, and within it two large convents were fortified; the convent of Santa Cruz on the opposite side, near the river, was fortified as another outwork; and nearly between those points was an isolated ridge called the Little Teson, of less elevation than the place but only one hundred and fifty yards distant.

Behind the Little Teson and parallel to it, was another ridge called the Great Teson, which at six hundred yards overlooked the lesser one, and saw over it to the bottom of the ditch.

In the centre of the large Teson, on the edge towards the town, was an enclosed and palisadoed redoubt called Francisco, which was supported by the fire of two guns and a howitzer, placed on the flat roof of a convent in the fortified suburb. An old castle, forming part of the walls, gave access to the bridge at pistol-shot distance, but was of little value in defence.

On the side of the Tesons the ground was rocky, the front of the place better covered with outworks, and more fire could be directed on the trenches; yet that line of attack was adopted with reason, because elsewhere the batteries must have been constructed on the edge of the counterscarp to see low enough for breaching; whereas the lesser Teson would enable them to strike over the glacis, and a deep gully near the latter offered cover for the miner. It was therefore resolved to storm Fort Francisco, form a lodgement there, open the first parallel along the greater Teson, place thirty three pieces in counter-batteries, ruin the defences and drive the besieged from the convent of Francisco; then, working forward by the sap, breaching batteries were to be raised on the lesser Teson and the counterscarp blowed in, while seven guns demolished a weak turret on the left, and opened a second breach to turn retrenchments behind the principal one. Previous to breaking ground, Carlos Espana and Julian Sanchez were pushed to the Tormes, and then four British divisions and Pack's Portuguese commenced the siege; but as neither fuel nor cover were to be had on that side of the Agueda, the troops kept their quarters on the hither bank, cooking their provisions there and fording the river each day in severe frost and snow. Eight hundred carts drawn by horses had been constructed by the artificers, and were now the surest means for bringing up ammunition; but so many delays were anticipated from the irregularity of the native carters and muleteers, and the chances of weather, that Wellington calculated upon an operation of twenty-four days. He hoped to steal that time from his adversaries, yet knew, if he failed, the clash of arms would draw their scattered troops to this quarter as tinkling bells draw swarming bees: and to make them thus gather and consume their magazines was an essential part of his warfare.

On the 8th of January the light division and Pack's Portuguese forded the Agueda, three miles above the fortress, and took post beyond the great Teson, where they remained quiet, and as there was no regular investment the enemy did not think the siege was commenced. But in the evening the troops stood to their arms, and Colonel Colborne, now commanding the 52nd, taking two companies from each regiment of the light division stormed the redoubt of Francisco. This he did with so much fury that the assailants appeared to be at one and the same time in the ditch, mounting the parapets, fighting on the top of the rampart, and forcing the gorge of the redoubt, where the explosion of a French shell had burst the gate open. Of the defenders, a few were killed and forty made prisoners. The post being thus taken with a loss of only twenty-four men and officers, a lodgement was begun on the right, because the fort was instantly covered with shot and shells from the town. This tempest continued through the night, yet at daybreak the parallel, six hundred yards in length, was sunk three feet deep, four wide, and a communication over the Teson was completed: thus the siege gained several days by this well-managed assault.

On the 9th the first division took the trenches, and the place was encircled by posts to prevent any external communication. In the night twelve hundred workmen commenced three counter-batteries for eleven guns each, under a heavy fire of shells and grape; before daylight the labourers obtained cover, and a ditch was sunk in front to provide earth for the batteries, which were made eighteen feet thick at top to resist the powerful artillery of the place.

On the 10th the fourth division relieved the trenches, and a thousand men laboured, yet in great peril, for the beseiged had a superabundance of ammunition and did not spare it. In the night a communication from the parallel to the batteries was opened, and on the 11th the third division undertook the siege.

This day the magazines in the batteries were excavated and the approaches widened; but the enemy's fire was destructive, and shells fell so on the ditch in front of the batteries that the troops were withdrawn, and earth raised from the inside. Great damage was also sustained from salvos of shells with long fuzes, whose simultaneous explosion cut away the parapets in a strange manner, and in the night a howitzer from the garden of the Francisco convent killed many men.

On the 12th the light division resumed work and the riflemen during a thick fog digged pits for themselves in front of the trenches, from whence they picked off the enemy's gunners; yet the weather was so cold and the besieged shot so briskly little progress was made. The 13th, the same causes impeded the labourers of the first division. The scarcity of transport also baulked the operations, for one third only of the native carts arrived, the drivers were very indolent, most of the twenty-four pound ammunition was still at Villa de Ponte, and intelligence arrived that Marmont was preparing to succour the place. Wellington, thus pressed, decided to open a breach with his counter-batteries, which were only six hundred yards from the curtain, and then storm without blowing in the counterscarp: in other words, to overstep the rules of science and sacrifice life rather than time, for the capricious Agueda might in one night flood and enable a small French force to relieve the place.

The whole army was now brought up and posted in villages on the Coa, ready to cross the Agueda and give battle. Hill also sent a division across the Tagus, lest Marmont, despairing to save Rodrigo, should fall on the communications by Castello Branco and Villa Velha.

In the night of the 13th the batteries were armed with twenty-eight guns, the approaches were continued by the flying sap, and the Santa Cruz convent was surprised by the Germans of the first division, which secured the right flank of the trenches.

On the 14th the enemy, who had observed that the men in the trenches, when relieved, went off in a disorderly manner, made a sally and overturned the gabions of the sap; they even penetrated to the parallel, and were upon the point of entering the batteries, when a few workmen getting together checked them until a support arrived. The guns were thus saved, but this sally, the death of the engineer on duty, and the heavy fire from the town, delayed the opening of the breaching-batteries. However, at half past four in the evening twenty-five heavy guns battered the fausse-braye and ramparts, while two pieces smote the convent of Francisco. Then was beheld a spectacle fearful and sublime. For the French replied with more than fifty pieces, and the bellowing of eighty large guns shook the ground far and wide; the smoke rested in heavy volumes upon the battlements of the place, or curled in light wreaths about the numerous spires, and the shells hissing through the air seemed fiery serpents leaping from the darkness; the walls crashed to the stroke of the bullet, and the distant mountains, faintly returning the sound, appeared to moan over the falling city. When night put an end to this turmoil, the quick clatter of musketry was heard like the pattering of hail after a peal of thunder, for the 40th Regiment assaulted and carried the convent of Francisco, and established itself in the suburb on the left of the attack.

Next day the ramparts were again battered, and fell so fast it was judged expedient to commence the small breach, wherefore in the night five more guns were mounted. The 16th, at daylight, the batteries recommenced, but at eight o'clock a thick fog compelled them to desist; nevertheless the small breach was open and the place was summoned, yet without effect. At night the parallel on the Lower Teson was extended, a sharp musketry was directed against the great breach, and the riflemen of the light division, from their pits, picked off the enemy's gunners.

The 17th the fire on both sides was heavy and the wall was beaten down in large cantles; but several of the besiegers' guns were dismounted, their batteries injured, many men killed, the general of artillery wounded, and the sap entirely ruined. The riflemen in the pits were overpowered with grape yet towards evening recovered the upper hand; the French could then only fire from distant embrasures and in the night a new battery against the lesser breach was armed, and that on the Lower Teson was raised to afford more cover.

On the 18th, the besiegers' fire being resumed with great violence, a turret was shaken at the small breach, and the large breach became practicable in the middle; the enemy commenced retrenching it and the sap made no progress, the engineer was badly wounded, and a twenty-four pounder, bursting, killed several men. In the night the battery on the Lower Teson was improved, and a field-piece and howitzer from thence played on the great breach to destroy the retrenchments.

On the 19th both breaches became practicable, the assault was ordered, the battering-guns were turned against the artillery of the ramparts, and the order of attack terminated with these remarkable words, " *Ciudad Rodrigo must be stormed this evening.*"—" *We will do it,*" was the soldiers' comment.

For the storm the third and light divisions and Pack's Portuguese were organized.in four parts.

1°. Right attack. On the extreme right, troops posted in some houses beyond the bridge were to cross the river and escalade an outwork in front of the castle, where there was no ditch, but where two guns commanded the junction of the counterscarp. On their left, two regiments, assembled behind the convent of Santa Cruz with a third in reserve, were to enter the ditch at the extremity of the counterscarp, escalade the fausse-braye, and scour it on their left as far as the great breach.

2°. Great breach. One hundred and eighty men carrying hay-bags were to move out of the second parallel, followed by a storming party, and supported by Mackinnon's brigade of the third division.

3°. Left attack. The light division, assembled behind the convent of Francisco, was to send three rifle companies to scour the fausse-braye on the right. At the same time a storming party, preceded by men carrying hay-sacks and followed by the division, was to assault the small breach, detaching men, when the fausse-braye should be passed, to their right to assist the main assault, to the left to force a passage at the Salamanca gate.

4°. *False attack.* An escalade, to be attempted by Pack's Portuguese at the opposite side of the town.

The right attack was conducted by Colonel O'Toole. Five hundred volunteers under Major Manners, with a forlorn hope under Lieut. Mackie, composed the storming party of the third division. Three hundred volunteers led by Major George Napier,* with a forlorn hope under Lieutenant Gurwood, composed the storming party of the light division.

The deserters, of which there were many, had told the governor the light division was come out of its turn, and it must be to storm, yet he took no heed, and all the troops reached their posts without seeming to attract attention; but before the signal was given, and while Wellington, who in person had pointed out the lesser breach to Major Napier, was still on the ground, the attack at the right commenced, and was instantly taken up along the whole line. The space between the trenches and the ditch was then suddenly covered with soldiers and ravaged by a tempest of grape from the ramparts; for though the storming parties in the centre jumped out of the parallel when the first shout arose, so rapid were the troops on their right, that before they could reach the ditch, Ridge, Dunkin, and Campbell, with the 5th, 77th, and 94th Regiments, had already scoured the fausse-braye, and pushed up the great breach amidst bursting shells, the whistling of grape and musketry, and the shrill cries of the French, who were driven fighting behind the inner retrenchments. There they rallied, and, aided by musketry from the houses, made hard battle for their post; none would go back on either side; yet the British could not get forward, and the bodies of men and officers, falling in heaps, choked up the passage, which from minute to minute was raked with grape, from two guns flanking the breach, at the distance of a few yards; yet striving and trampling alike upon dead and wounded these brave men maintained the combat.

Meanwhile the stormers of the light division, who had

*General Sir G. Napier.

three hundred yards of ground to clear, would not wait for the hay-bags, and with extraordinary swiftness running to the crest of the glacis jumped down the scarp, a depth of eleven feet, and rushed up the fausse-braye under a smashing discharge of grape and musketry. The ditch was dark and intricate, and the forlorn hope inclined to the left while the stormers went straight to the breach, which was so narrow at top that a gun placed across nearly barred the opening; then the forlorn hope rejoined, and the whole rushed up, yet the head, forcibly contracted as the ascent narrowed, staggered under the fire. With the instinct of self-preservation the men snapped their muskets though they had not been allowed to load, and Napier, his arm shattered by a grape-shot, went down, but in falling called aloud to use the bayonet, while the unwounded officers instantly and simultaneously sprung to the front: the impulse of victory was thus given and with a furious shout the breach was carried. The supporting regiments, coming up abreast, then gained the rampart, the 52nd wheeled to the left, the 43rd to the right, and the place was won. During this contest, which lasted about ten minutes, the fighting at the great breach was unabated: but when the stormers and the 43rd poured along the rampart towards that quarter, the French wavered, three of their expense magazines exploded, and the third division with a mighty effort broke through the retrenchments: the garrison still fought awhile in the streets indeed, but finally fled to the castle, where the governor surrendered.

Now plunging into the town from all quarters, and throwing off all discipline, the troops committed frightful excesses; houses were soon in flames, the soldiers menaced their officers and shot each other, intoxication increased the tumult to absolute madness, and a fire being wilfully lighted in the middle of the great magazine, the town would have been blown to atoms but for the energetic coolness of some officers and a few soldiers who still preserved their senses. To excuse these excesses it was said, " the soldiers were not to be controlled." Colonel McLeod of the 43rd, a young man of a noble and energetic spirit, proved the contrary. He placed guards at the breach and constrained his men to keep their ranks for a long time, but as no organized efforts were made by higher authorities, and the example was not followed, the regiment dissolved by degrees in the general disorder.

Three hundred French fell, fifteen hundred were made prisoners, and immense stores of ammunition with a hundred and fifty pieces of artillery, including the battering-train of Marmont's army, were captured. The loss of the allies was twelve hundred soldiers and ninety officers, of which six hundred and fifty men and sixty officers had been slain or hurt at the breaches. General Craufurd and General Mackinnon, the former a person of great ability, were killed, and with them died many gallant men; amongst others a captain of the 45th, of whom it has been felicitously said, that three generals and seventy other officers had fallen, yet the soldiers fresh from the strife only talked of Hardyman." General Vandeleur, commanding the light division after Craufurd fell, was badly wounded; so was Colonel Colborne, with a crowd of inferior rank; and unhappily the slaughter did not end with the storm; for as the prisoners and their escort were marching out by the breach, an accidental explosion killed numbers of both.

This siege lasted only twelve days, half the time originally calculated, yet from the inexperience of engineers and soldiers, and the extraordinarily heavy fire of the place, the works were rather slowly executed. The cold also impeded the labourers, yet with less severe frost the trenches would have been overflowed, because in open weather the water rises everywhere to within six inches of the surface. The greatest impediment was the badness of the cutting tools furnished from the storekeeper-general's office in England; the profits of the contractor seemed to be the only thing respected: the engineers eagerly sought for French cutlery, because the English was useless !

Marmont heard of the siege the 15th and made great efforts to collect his forces at Salamanca. The 26th he heard of its fall and retired to Valladolid, thus harassing his men by winter marches. Had he remained between Salamanca and Rodrigo with strong advanced guards he would have recovered the place; for on the 28th the Agueda flooded two feet over the stone bridge, and carried away the allies' trestle-bridge. The army was then on the left bank, the breaches not closed, and no resistance could be offered. The greatest captains are the very slaves of fortune.

When Ciudad Rodrigo fell, Wellington's eyes were turned towards Badajos. He desired to invest it again early in March, because the flooding of the rivers in Beira, from the periodical rains, would then render a French incursion into Portugal difficult, enable him to carry nearly all his forces to the siege, and impede the junction of Soult and Marmont in Estremadura. Many obstacles arose, some military, some political, some from the perverseness of coadjutors and the errors of subordinates; yet on the 5th of March the troops were well on their way towards the Tagus, and then the English general, who had remained on the Coa to the last moment that he might not awaken the enemy's suspicions, gave up Rodrigo to Castanos and departed for Elvas.

Victor Alten's cavalry was left on the Yeltes in advance of the Agueda to mask the movements, but Marmont was unable to measure his adversary's talent or fathom his designs. He had again spread his army far and wide, appeared to expect no further winter operations, and having lost all his secret friends and emissaries at Ciudad Rodrigo, where they had been discovered and put to death by Carlos Espana, with an overstrained severity that gave general disgust, knew nothing of the allies' march to the Tagus. On the other hand the projected siege was, by the incredibly vexatious conduct of the Portuguese Regency, delayed ten days, and thrown into the violent equinoctial rains, which greatly augmented the difficulties. It was in vain Wellington threatened, remonstrated and wasted his mental powers to devise remedies for those evils, and to impart energy and good faith to that extraordinary government. Insolent anger, falsehood or stolid indifference in all functionaries, from the highest to the lowest, met him at every turn, and the responsibility even in small matters became too onerous for subordinate officers; he was compelled to arrange every detail of service himself with the native authorities. His iron strength of body and mind were thus strained until all men wondered how they resisted, and indeed he did fall sick, but recovered after a few days.

On the 15th of March pontoons were laid over the Guadiana four miles from Elvas, where the current was dull, and two large Spanish boats being arranged as flying-bridges, Beresford crossed that river on the 16th to invest Badajos with fifteen thousand men.

Soult was then before Cadiz, but Drouet and Daricau were with ten thousand men in Estremadura; wherefore General Graham marched with three divisions of infantry and two brigades of cavalry upon Llerena, while Hill moved by Merida upon Almendralejos. These covering corps were together thirty thousand strong, five thousand being cavalry, and the whole army presented fifty-one thousand sabres and bayonets, of which twenty thousand were Portuguese. Castanos had gone to Gallicia, and the fifth Spanish army, under Morillo and Penne Villemur, four thousand strong, passed down the Portuguese frontier to the Lower Guadiana, intending to fall on Seville when Soult should march to succour Badajos.

As the allies advanced, Drouet moved by his right towards Medellin, to maintain the communication with Marmont by Truxillo. Hill and Graham then halted, the latter at Zafra, having Slade's cavalry in front. Marmont meanwhile recalled his sixth division from Talavera to Castile, and four other divisions and his cavalry, quartered at Toledo, marched over the Guadarama towards Valladolid.

It was therefore manifest that he would not act this time in conjunction with Soult.

THIRD ENGLISH SIEGE OF BADAJOS.

Badajos stands between the Rivillas, a small stream, and the Guadiana, a noble river five hundred yards broad. From the angle formed by their confluence the town spread out like a fan, having eight regular bastions and curtains, with good counterscarps, covered way, and glacis.

At the meeting of the rivers, the Rivillas being there for a short distance deep and wide, was a rock one hundred feet high, crowned with an old castle, the ascent to which was not steep. This was the extreme point of defence on the enemy's left, and from thence to the Trinidad bastion, terminating this the eastern front of resistance, an inundation protected the ramparts, one short interval excepted, which was defended by an outwork, beyond the stream, called the cunette of San Roque.

On the enemy's right of San Roque, also beyond the Rivillas and four hundred yards from the walls, another outwork called the Picurina was constructed on an isolated hill, about the same distance from San Roque as the latter was from the castle. These two outworks had a covered communication with each other, and the San Roque had one with the town, but the inundation cut the Picurina off from the latter, and it was an inclosed and palisadoed work.

The southern front, the longest, was protected in the centre by a crown-work, constructed on the lofty Sierra de Viento, the end of which, at only two hundred yards, overlooked the walls. The remainder of that front and the western front had no outworks.

On the right bank of the Guadiana there were no houses, but the twice-besieged fort of San Christoval, three hundred feet square, stood there on a rocky height, and from its superior elevation looked into the castle, which was exactly opposite to it and consequently but five hundred yards distant. This fort also commanded the works heading the stone bridge, a quarter of a mile below stream.

Phillipon's garrison, nearly five thousand strong, was composed of French and Hessian, and some Spanish troops in Joseph's service. He had since the last siege made himself felt in every direction, scouring the country, defeating small guerilla bands, carrying off cattle almost from under the guns of Elvas and Campo Mayor, and pushing his spies to Ciudad Rodrigo, Lisbon, and even to Ayamonte, by which he gained a knowledge of the forces, material and personal, combined against his fortress, and prepared accordingly. He had formed an interior retrenchment at the castle, and mounted more guns there; he had strengthened San Christoval on the side before attacked, and made a covered communication to the bridge-head; he had constructed two ravelins on the south front, and commenced a third with counterguards for the bastions. At the eastern front he had dug a cunette at the bottom of the great ditch, which was in some parts filled with water. The gorge of the Pardaleras was enclosed and connected with the body of the place, from whence it was overlooked by powerful batteries the glacis of the western front was mined, and the arch of a bridge behind the San Roque was built up to cause the inundation. The inhabitants had been compelled to store food for three months, and provisions and ammunition had come in on the 10th and 16th of February, yet the supply of powder was inadequate, and there were not many shells.

Lord Wellington desired to assail the western front, but the engineer had not mortars, miners, or guns enough, or the means of bringing up stores for that attack: indeed the want of transport had again compelled the drawing of stores from Elvas, to the manifest hazard of that fortress. Hence, here, as at Ciudad Rodrigo, time was paid for with the loss of life, and the crimes of politicians were atoned by the blood of soldiers.

It was finally agreed to attack the bastion of Trinidad, because the counterguard there was unfinished, and the bastion could be battered from the Picurina. The first parallel was therefore to embrace that fort, the San Roque and the eastern front, so as to enable the counter-batteries to destroy the armaments of the southern fronts, which bore against the Picurina hill. The Picurina was to be stormed, and from thence the Trinidad and the next bastion, called the Santa Maria, were to be breached. The guns were then to be turned against the connecting curtain, known to be of weak masonry, and to open a third breach, whereby a storming party might turn any retrenchments behind the other breaches. In this way the inundation could be avoided. A French deserter declared, and truly, that the ditch was eighteen feet deep at the Trinidad, yet Wellington was so confident that he resolved to storm the place there without blowing in the counterscarp.

The battering train was of fifty-two pieces, including sixteen twenty-four-pound howitzers for throwing Shrapnel shells; but this species of missile, much talked of at the time, was little prized by Lord Wellington, who had detected its insufficiency, save with large guns and as a common shell; and partly to avoid expense, partly from a dislike to injure the inhabitants, neither in this, nor in any former siege did he use mortars. Here indeed he could not have brought them up, for the peasantry, and even the ordenança, employed to move the battering train, although well paid, deserted. Of nine hundred gunners present three hundred were British, the rest Portuguese; there were one hundred and fifty sappers, volunteers from the third division, unskilled, yet of signal bravery.

The engineer's park was established behind the heights of St. Michael which faced the Picurina, and in the night of the 17th, eighteen hundred men broke ground one hundred and sixty yards from that fort. A tempest stifled the sound of the pickaxes, and a communication four thousand feet long, with a parallel of six hundred yards, three feet deep and three feet six inches wide, was opened without hindrance; but when day broke the fort was reinforced, and a sharp musketry, interspersed with discharges from some field-pieces and aided by heavy guns from the body of the place, was directed on the trenches.

In the night of the 18th two batteries were traced, the parallel pro-longed, and the previous works improved; but the garrison raised the parapets of the Picurina, lined the top of the covered way with sand-bags, and planted musketeers to gall the men in the trenches.

The 19th, secret notice of a sally being received, the guards were reinforced; nevertheless, at one o'clock some cavalry came out by the Talavera gate, and thirteen hundred infantry under General Vielland, second in command, filed unobserved into the communication be-tween the Picurina and San Roque; one hundred men were also ready in the former, and all these troops, jumping out at once, drove the workmen off and began to demolish the parallel. Previous to this outbreak the French cavalry had commenced a sham fight on the right of the trenches, and the smaller party, pretending to fly toward the besiegers, answered Portuguese to the challenge of the picquets and were allowed to pass. Elated by their stratagem, they galloped to the engineer's park, a thousand yards in rear, where they killed some men before succour came; meanwhile the troops at the parallel rallied on the relief and beat the infantry back along the front of the ramparts even to the castle.

In this fight the besieged lost three hundred men and officers, the besiegers one hundred and fifty; but the chief engineer, Fletcher, was badly wounded, and several hundred intrenching tools were carried off; Phillipon had promised a high price for each, which turned out ill, because the soldiers, instead of pursuing briskly, dispersed to gather the tools. After the action a squadron of dragoons and six field-pieces were placed behind the St. Michael ridge, and a signal-post was established on the lofty Sierra de Viento, to give notice of the enemy's motions.

The weather continued wet and boisterous, making the labour very severe, yet in the night of the 19th the parallel was opened on its whole length; the 20th it was enlarged, and though the rain, flooding the trenches, greatly impeded progress, the work was extended to the left. Three counterbatteries were then commenced in its rear, because the ground was too soft in front to sustain the guns, and the San Roque was within three hundred yards; hence, the parallel, eighteen hundred yards long, being only guarded by fourteen hundred men, a few bold soldiers might by a sudden rush have spiked the guns in front of the trench.

A slight sally was this day repulsed, and a shoulder was given to the light of the parallel to cover that flank; in good time, for next day two field-pieces placed on the right bank of the Guadiana, tried to rake the trenches and were baffled by this shoulder. Indications of a similar design against the left flank, from the Pardaleras hill, were then observed, and three hundred men with two guns were posted on that side in some broken ground.

In the night, though the works went on, rain again impeded progress, and the besiegers, failing to drain the lower parts of the parallel by cuts, made an artificial bottom of sand-bags. On the other hand the besieged, thinking the curtain adjoining the castle was the object of attack, threw up earth in front and removed the houses behind; they also made a covered communication from the Trinidad gate to the San Roque, to take this supposed attack in reverse; and as the labour of digging was great, hung up brown cloth which appeared like earth, by which ingenious expedient they passed unseen between those points.

Vauban's maxim, that a perfect investment is the first requi-site in a siege, had been neglected to spare labour, yet the great master's art was soon vindicated by his countryman. Phillipon, finding the right bank of the Guadiana free, made a battery in the night for three field-pieces, which at daylight raked the trenches, the shots sweeping the parallel destructively; the loss was great and would have been greater but for the soft ground, which prevented the touch and bound of the bullets. Orders were therefore sent to the fifth division, then at Campo Mayor, to invest the place on the other bank, but those troops were distant and misfortunes accumulated. Heavy rain filled the trenches, the Guadiana run the fixed bridge under water, sunk twelve pontoons, and broke the tackle of the flying bridges; the provisions of the army could not be brought over, the battering-guns and ammunition were still on the right bank, and the siege was on the point of being raised. In a few days however the river subsided, some Portuguese craft were brought up to form another flying bridge, the pontoons saved were employed as row-boats, and the communication thus secured for the rest of the siege.

On the 23rd rain again filled the trenches, the works crumbled and the attack was entirely suspended. next day the fifth division invested the place on the right bank, the weather cleared, and the batteries, armed with twenty-one guns and seven five-and-a-half-inch howitzers, opened on the 25th, but were so vigorously answered, that one howitzer was dismounted, and several artillery and engineer officers killed. Nevertheless the San Roque was silenced, the garrison of the Picurina so galled by marksmen that none dared look over the parapet, and as the external appearance of that fort did not indicate much strength General Kempt was charged to assault it in the night.

This outward seeming of the Picurina was fallacious: it was very strong. The fronts were well covered by the glacis, the flanks deep, the rampart, fourteen feet perpendicular from the bottom of the ditch, was guarded with slanting pales above, and from thence to the top was an earthen slope of sixteen feet. A few palings had been knocked off at the covered way, and the parapet, slightly damaged, was repaired with sand-bags, but the ditch was deep, narrow at the bottom, and flanked by four splinterproof casemates. Seven guns were mounted. The entrance in the rear was protected with three rows of thick paling, the garrison was above two hundred strong, and every man had two muskets; the top of the rampart was garnished with loaded shells, a retrenched guard-house formed a second internal defence, and small mines, with a loopholed gallery under the counter-scarp to take the assailants in rear, were begun but not finished.

Five hundred men of the third division assembled for the attack. Two hundred under Major Rudd were to turn the fort on the left, an equal force under Major Shaw to turn it by the light, each being to detach half their force to seize the communication with San Roque and intercept succour coming from the town. The remainder were to attack Picurina by the gorge, leaving one hundred under Captain Powis as a reserve. The engineers, Holloway, Stanway, and Gipps, with twenty-four sappers bearing hatchets and ladders, guided these columns, and fifty men of the light division, likewise provided with axes, were to move out of the trenches at the moment of attack.

ASSAULT OF PICURINA.

The night was fine and the stormers quickly reached the fort, which, black and silent before, then seemed a mass of fire, under which the stormers run up to the palisades in rear and endeavoured to break through; the destructive musketry and thickness of the pales rendered their efforts nugatory, wherefore, turning against the sides of the work they strove to get in there, but the depth of the ditch and the slanting stakes at the top of the brickwork again baffled them. At this time, the French shooting fast and dangerously, the crisis appeared so imminent that Kempt sent the reserve headlong against the front. The fight was thus supported and the carnage terrible. A battalion which came from the town to succour the fort was beaten back by the men in the communication, the guns from the town and castle then opened, the guard of the trenches replied with musketry, rockets were thrown up by the besieged, and the shrill sound of alarm-bells mixing with the shouts of the combatants increased the tumult.

Still the Picurina sent out streams of fire, by the light of which dark figures were seen furiously struggling on the ramparts; for Powis had escaladed in front where the artillery had broken the pales; and the other assailants, throwing their ladders in the manner of bridges from the brink of the ditch to the slanting stakes thus passed, and all were fighting hand to hand with the enemy. Meanwhile the axemen of the light division, compassing the fort like prowling wolves, discovered the gate, and hewing it down broke in by the rear. Nevertheless the struggle continued. Powis, Holloway, Gipps, and Oates fell wounded on or beyond the rampart, Nixon of the 52nd was shot two yards within the gate, Shaw, Rudd, and nearly all the other officers of the 79th had fallen outside, and it was not until half the garrison were killed, that Gaspar Thiery, the commandant, surrendered with eighty-six men, while others, not many, rushing out of the gate endeavoured to cross the inundation and were drowned.

Phillipon had thought to delay the siege five or six days by the resistance of Picurina, and one day later this would have happened; for the mines and loop-holed gallery in the counterscarp would have been completed, and the work was too well covered by the glacis to be quickly ruined by fire. His calculations were baffled by this heroic assault, which, lasting only an hour, cost four officers and fifty men killed, fifteen officers and two hundred and fifty men wounded; and so vehement was the fight throughout, that the garrison forgot or had no time to roll over the shells and combustibles on the ramparts. Phillipon did not conceal the danger accruing to Badajos from the loss of the Picurina, but he stimulated his soldiers' courage, by calling to their recollection, how infinitely worse than death it was to be the inmate of an English prison-hulk—an appeal which must have been deeply felt, for the annals of civilized nations furnish nothing more inhuman towards captives of war than the prison-ships of England.

When Picurina was taken three battalions advanced to secure it, and though a great turmoil and firing from the town continued until midnight, a lodgement in the works and communication with the first parallel were established; the second parallel was also begun, but at daylight the redoubt was overwhelmed with fire, no troops could remain and the lodgement was destroyed. In the evening the sappers effected another lodgement on the flanks, the second parallel was then opened in its whole length, and next day the counter-batteries on the right of Picurina exchanged a vigorous fire with the town.

In the night of the 27th three breaching-batteries were traced out. The first, between the Picurina and the inundation, to breach the right face of the Trinidad. The second, on the Picurina, to breach the Santa Maria. The third, on a prolonged line of the front attacked, contained three Shrapnel howitzers to scour the ditch and prevent the garrison working in it; for Phillipon, having now discovered the true line of attack, was raising the counterguard of the Trinidad and the imperfect ravelin. At daybreak these works being well furnished with gabions and sandbags were lined with musketeers, who severely galled the workmen employed on the breaching-batteries, and the artillery practice was brisk on both sides. Two of the besiegers' guns were dismounted, the gabions placed in front of the batteries to protect the workmen were knocked over, and the musketry became so destructive the men were withdrawn to throw up earth from the inside.

In the night of the 27th the second parallel was extended on the right, to raise batteries against San Roque and the dam which held up the inundation, and to breach the curtain behind: but the ground was hard, the moon shone brightly, the labourers were quite exposed and the work was relinquished.

On the 28th the screen of gabions before the batteries was restored, the workmen resumed their labours outside and the parallel was improved. The besieged then withdrew their guns from San Roque, yet their marksmen still shot from thence with great exactness, and the plunging fire from the castle dismounted two howitzers in one of the counter-batteries. During the night the French observed the tracing-string, marking the direction of the sap in front of San Roque, and a daring fellow, creeping out before the workmen arrived, brought it on the line of the castle fire, whereby some loss was sustained.

In the night the howitzer battery was re-armed with twenty-four pounders to play on the San Roque, and a new breaching-battery was traced on the site of the Picurina; the second parallel was extended by sap, and a trench was digged for riflemen in front of the batteries.

The 29th a slight sally made on the right bank of the river was re-pulsed by the Portuguese; but the sap at San Roque was ruined by the enemy's fire, and the besieged continued to raise the counterguard and ravelin of the Trinidad, and to strengthen the front attacked. The besiegers armed two batteries with eighteen-pounders, which opened next day against Santa Maria, yet with little effect, and the explosion of an expense magazine killed many men.

While the siege was thus proceeding, Soult, having little fear for the town but designing a great battle, was carefully organizing a powerful force to unite with Drouet and Daricau. Those generals had endeavoured to hold the district of La Serena and keep open the communication with Harmont by Medellin and Truxillo, but Graham and Hill forced them into the Morena; and on the other side of the country Morillo and Penne-Villemur descended to the Lower Gua-diana, to fall on Seville when Soult should advance. Nor were there wanting other combinations to embarrass and delay that marshal. In February, a Spanish army had assembled in the Ronda to fall on Seville from that side also, which compelled Soult to send troops there, and fatally delayed his march to Estremadura. Marmont was however concentrating his army in the Salamanca country, and it was rumoured he meant to attack Ciudad Rodrigo. This disquieted Wel-lington: for though Marmont had no battering-train, the Spanish generals and engineers had neglected the repairs of the place, and had not even brought up from St. Jao da Pesqueira the provisions given to them from the British stores: the fortress therefore had only thirty days' supply, and Almeida was in as bad a state.

On the 30th, it being known that Soult was advancing from Cordova, the fifth division was brought over the Guadiana as a reserve to the covering army, leaving a Portuguese brigade with some cavalry of the same nation to maintain the investment on the right bank. The siege was then urged on, forty-eight pieces of artillery being in constant play, and the sap against San Roque advancing: the French fire was however destructive, and their progress in strength-ening the front attacked was visible.

On the 1st of April the sap was pushed close to San Roque, the Trinidad bastion crumbled under the stroke of the bullet, and the flank of the Santa Maria, which was casemated, also began to yield. next day the face of the Trinidad was broken, but the Santa Maria casemates being laid open the bullets were lost in their cavities, and Phillipon commenced a retrenchment to cut off the whole of the attacked front from the town.

In the night a new battery against San Roque being armed, two officers with some sappers glided behind that outwork, gagged the sentinel, placed powder-barrels and a match against the dam of the inundation and retired undiscovered. The explosion did not destroy the dam, the inundation remained and the sap made no progress, because of the French musketeers; for though the besiegers' marksmen slew many, reinforcements were sent across the inundation by means of a raft with parapets, and men also passed unseen behind the cloth communication, from the Trinidad. But the crisis of the siege was now approaching rapidly. The breaches were nearly practicable, Soult had effected his junction with Drouet and Daricau; and Wellington, who had not sufficient force to assault the place and give battle at the same time, resolved to leave two divisions in the trenches and fight at Albuera. In this view Graham fell back towards that place, and Hill, destroying the bridge at Merida, marched to Talavera Real.

Time was now, as in war it always is, a great object, and the anxiety on both sides redoubled. Soult was however still at Llerena when, the breaches being declared practicable, the assault was ordered for that evening, and Leith's division recalled to the siege; yet a careful personal examination caused Wellington to doubt, and he delayed the storm, until a third breach, as originally projected, should be formed in the curtain between Trinidad and Maria. This could not be commenced before morning, and during the night the French workmen laboured assiduously at their retrenchments, despite of the showers of grape with which the batteries scoured the ditch and the breach. On the 6th all the batteries were turned against the curtain, the bad masonry crumbled rapidly away, in two hours a yawning breach appeared and Wellington renewed his order for the assault. Eagerly then the soldiers got ready for a combat, so fiercely fought, so terribly won, so dreadful in all its circumstances, that posterity can scarcely be expected to credit the tale: but many are still alive who know that it is true.

Wellington spared Phillipon the affront of a summons, and seeing the breach strongly intrenched, the flank fire still powerful, he would not in that dread crisis trust his fortune to a single effort. Eighteen thousand daring soldiers burned for the signal of attack, he was unwilling to lose the service of any, and therefore to each division gave a task such as few generals would have the hardihood even to contemplate.

On the right, Picton's division was to file out of the trenches, cross the Rivillas, and scale the castle walls, from eighteen to twenty-four feet high, furnished with all means of destruction, and so narrow at top that the defenders could easily reach and as easily overturn the ladders.

On the left, Leith's division was to make a false attack on the Pardaleras, but a real assault on the distant bastion of San Vincente, where the glacis was mined, the ditch deep, the scarp thirty feet high, the parapet garnished with bold troops: Phillipon also, following his old plan, had three loaded muskets placed beside each man that the first fire might be quick and deadly.

In the centre, the fourth and light divisions, under Colville and Andrew Barnard, were to march against the breaches. Furnished like the third and fifth divisions with ladders and axes, they were preceded by storming parties of five hundred men, having each their separate forlorn hopes. The light division was to assault the Santa Maria, the fourth division the Trinidad and the curtain, both columns being divided into storming and firing parties, the former to enter the ditch, the latter to keep the crest of the glacis.

Between these attacks, Major Wilson of the 48th was to storm the San Roque with the guards of the trenches; and on the other side of the Guadiana General Power was to make a feint at the bridge-head.

At first only one brigade of the third division was to have attacked the castle, but just before the hour fixed, a sergeant of sappers deserted from the enemy and told Wellington there was but one communication from the castle to the town, whereupon he ordered the whole division to advance.

Many nice arrangements filled up this outline, and some

were followed, some disregarded, for it is seldom all things are attended to in a desperate fight. The enemy was not idle. While it was yet twilight some French cavalry rode from the Pardaleras, under an officer who endeavoured to look into the trenches with the view to ascertain if an assault was intended, but the picquet there drove him and his escort back into the works, darkness then fell and the troops awaited the signal.

ASSAULT OF BADAJOS.

Dry but clouded was the night, the air was thick with watery exhalations from the rivers the ramparts and trenches unusually still; yet a low murmur pervaded the latter, and in the former lights flitted here and there, while the deep voices of the sentinels proclaimed from time to time that all was well in Badajos. The French, confiding in Phillipon's direful skill, watched from their lofty station the approach of enemies they had twice before baffled, and now hoped to drive a third time blasted and ruined from the walls. The British, standing in deep columns, were as eager to meet that fiery destruction as the others were to pour it down, and either were alike terrible for their strength, their discipline, and the passions awakened in their resolute hearts.

Former failures there were to avenge on one side, and on both leaders who furnished no excuse for weakness in the hour of trial; the possession of Badajos was become a point of personal honour with the soldiers of each nation; but the desire for glory on the British part was dashed with a hatred of the citizens from an old grudge, and recent toil and hardship, with much spilling of blood, had made many incredibly savage: for these things, which render the noble-minded averse to cruelty, harden the vulgar spirit. Numbers also, like Caesar's centurion, who could not forget the plunder of Avaricum, were heated with the recollection of Rodrigo and thirsted for spoil. Thus every passion found a cause of excitement, while the wondrous power of discipline bound the whole together as with a band of iron, and in the pride of arms none doubted their might to bear down every obstacle that man could oppose to their fury.

At ten o'clock, the castle, the San Roque, the breaches,

the Pardaleras, the distant bastion of San Vincente, and the bridge-head on the other side of the Guadiana, were to be simultaneously assailed. It was hoped the strength of the enemy would quickly shrivel within that fiery girdle, but many are the disappointments of war. An unforeseen accident delayed the attack of the fifth division, and a lighted carcass, thrown from the castle, falling close to the third division, exposed its columns and forced it to anticipate the signal by half an hour. Thus everything was suddenly disturbed, yet the double columns of the fourth and light divsions moved silently and swiftly against the breaches, and the guard of the trenches, rushing forward with a shout, encompassed the San Roque with fire and broke in so violently that scarcely any resistance was made.

Soon however a sudden blaze of light and the rattling of musketry indicated the commencement of a more vehement combat at the castle. There Kempt, for Picton, hurt by a fall in the camp and expecting no change in the hour, was not present; there Kempt, I say, led the third division. Passing the Rivillas in single files by a narrow bridge under a terrible musketry, he re-formed his men, and run up the rugged hill with great fury, but only to fall at the foot of the castle severely wounded. Being carried back to the trenches, he met Picton at the bridge hastening to take the command, and meanwhile the troops, spreading along the front, had reared their heavy ladders, some against the lofty castle some against the adjoining front on the left, and with incredible courage ascended amidst showers of heavy stones, logs of wood, and bursting shells rolled off the parapet, while from the flanks musketry was plied with fearful rapidity, and in front the leading assailants were with pike and bayonet stabbed and the ladders pushed from the walls: and all this was attended with deafening shouts, the crash of breaking ladders, and the shrieks of crushed soldiers answering to the sullen stroke of the falling weights.

Still swarming round the remaining ladders those undaunted veterans strove who should first climb, until all were over-turned when the French shouted victory, and the British, baffled, yet untamed, fell back a few paces to take shelter under the rugged edge of the hill. There the broken ranks were re-formed, and the heroic Colonel Ridge, again springing forward, called with stentorian voice on his men to follow, and seizing a ladder raised it against the castle to the right of the former attack, where the wall was lower and where an embrasure offered some facility: a second ladder was placed alongside by the grenadier officer Canch, and the next instant he and Ridge were on the rampart, the shouting troops pressed after them, and the garrison, amazed and in a manner surprised, were driven fighting through the double gate into the town: the castle was won. Soon a reinforcement from the French reserve came to the gate, through which both sides fired and the enemy retired; but Ridge fell, and no man died that night with more glory—yet many died, and there was much glory.

All this time the tumult at the breaches was such as if the earth had been rent asunder and its central fires bursting upwards uncontrolled. The two divisions reached the glacis, just as the firing at the castle had commenced, and the flash of a single musket, discharged from the c-overed way as a signal, showed them the French were ready: yet no stir followed, and darkness covered the breaches. Some haypacks were then thrown, some ladders placed, and the forlorn hopes and storming parties of the light division, five hundred in all, descended into the ditch without opposition: but then a bright flame, shooting upwards, displayed all the terrors of the scene. The ramparts crowded with dark figures and glittering arms were on one side, on the other the red columns of the British, deep and broad, coming on like streams of burning lava: it was the touch of the magician's wand, a crash of thunder followed, and the storming parties were dashed to pieces by the explosion of hundreds of shells and powder-barrels.

For an instant the light division soldiers stood on the brink of the ditch, amazed at the terrific sight, but then, with a shout that matched even the sound of the explosion they flew down the ladders, or, disdaining their aid, leaped, reckless of the depth, into the gulf below; and nearly at the same moment, amidst a blaze of musketry that dazzled the eyes, the fourth division came running in to descend with a like fury. There were only five ladders for both columns, which were close together, and the deep cut made in the bottom of the ditch, as far as the counterguard of the Pardaleras, the Trinidad was filled with water from the inundation: into this miry snare the head of the fourth division fell, and it is said above a hundred of the fusileers, the men of Albuera, were there smothered. Those who followed, checked not, but, as if the disaster had been expected, turned to the left and thus came upon the face of the unfinished ravelin, which, rough and broken, was mistaken for the breach and instantly covered with men; a wide and deep chasm was however still between them and the ramparts, from whence came a deadly fire wasting their ranks. Thus baffled, they also commenced a rapid discharge of musketry, and disorder ensued; for the men of the light division, whose conducting engineer had been disabled early, having their flank confined by an unfinished ditch, intended to cut off the Santa Maria, rushed towards the breaches of the curtain and the Trinidad, which were indeed before them, but which the fourth division had been destined to storm.

Great was the confusion, the ravelin was crowded with men of both divisions, and while some continued to fire, others jumped down and run towards the breach; many also passed between the ravelin and the counterguard of the Trinidad; the two divisions got mixed, and the reserves, which should have remained at the quarries, also came pouring in until the ditch was quite filled, the rear still crowding forward and all cheering vehemently. The enemy's shouts also were loud and terrible, and the bursting of shells and of grenades, the roaring of guns from the flanks, answered by the iron howitzers from the parallel, the heavy roll and horrid explosion of the powder-barrels, the whizzing flight of the blazing splinters, the loud exhortations of the officers, and the continual clatter of the muskets made a maddening din.

Now a multitude bounded up the great breach as if driven by a whirlwind: but across the top glittered a range of sword-blades, sharp-pointed, keen-edged, immovably fixed in ponderous beams chained together and set deep in the ruins; and for ten feet in front the ascent was covered with loose planks studded with iron points, on which the feet of the foremost being set the planks slipped, and the unhappy soldiers falling forward on the spikes rolled down upon the ranks behind. Then the Frenchmen, shouting at the success of their stratagem and leaping forward, plied their shot with terrible rapidity, for every man had several muskets, and each musket in addition to its ordinary charge contained a small cylinder of wood stuck full of wooden slugs, which scattered like hail when they were discharged.

Once and again the assailants rushed up the breaches, but the sword-blades, immovable and impassable, always stopped the charge, and the hissing shells and thundering powder-barrels exploded unceasingly. Hundreds of men had fallen, hundreds more were dropping, yet the heroic officers still called aloud for new trials, and sometimes followed by many, sometimes by few, ascended the ruins; and so furious were the men themselves, that in one of these charges the rear strove to push the foremost on to the swordblades, willing even to make a bridge of their writhing bodies; the others frustrated the attempt by dropping down, yet men fell so fast from the shot it was hard to say who went down voluntarily, who were stricken, and many stooped unhurt that never rose again. Vain also would it have been to break through the sword-blades; for a finished trench and parapet were behind the breach, where the assailants, crowded into even a narrower space than the ditch was, would still have been separated from their enemies, and the slaughter have continued.

At the beginning of this dreadful conflict, Andrew Barnard had with prodigious efforts separated his division from the other, and preserved some degree of military array; but now the tumult was such, no command could be heard distinctly except by those close at hand, while the mutilated carcases heaped on each other, and the wounded, struggling to avoid being trampled upon, broke the formations; order was impossible! Nevertheless officers of all stations, followed more or less numerously by the men, were seen to start out as if struck by a sudden madness and rush into the breach, which yawning and glittering with steel seemed like the mouth of some huge dragon belching forth smoke and flame. In one of these attempts Colonel MacLeod of the 43rd, whose feeble body would have been quite unfit for war if it had not been sustained by an unconquerable spirit, was killed. Wherever his voice was heard there his soldiers gathered, and with such strong resolution did he lead them up the ruins, that when one, falling behind him, plunged a bayonet into his back, he complained not, but continuing his course was shot dead within a yard of the sword-blades. There was however no want of gallant leaders or desperate followers, until two hours passed in these vain efforts convinced the soldiers the Trinidad was impregnable; and as the opening in the curtain, although less strong, was retired, and the approach impeded by deep holes and cuts made in the ditch, the troops did not much notice it after the partial failure of one attack, which had been made early. Gathering in dark groups and leaning on their muskets they looked up with sullen desperation at the Trinidad, while the enemy stepping out on the ramparts and aiming their shots by the light of the fireballs which they threw over, asked, as their victims fell, *Why they did not come into Badajos ?*

In this dreadful situation, while the dead were lying in heaps, and others continually falling, the wounded crawling about to get some shelter from the merciless shower above, and withal a sickening stench from the burnt flesh of the slain, Captain Nicholas of the engineers, was observed by Lieut. Shaw of the 43rd, making incredible efforts to force his way with a few men into the Santa Maria. Collecting fifty soldiers of all regiments he joined him, and passing a deep cut along the foot of this breach, these two young officers, at the head of their band, rushed up the slope of the ruins, but ere they gained two-thirds of the ascent, a concentrated fire of musketry and grape dashed nearly the whole dead to the earth: Nicholas was mortally wounded, and the intrepid Shaw stood alone ! * After this no further effort was made at any point, and the troops remained passive, but unflinching, beneath the enemy's shot, which streamed without intermission: for many of the riflemen on the glacis, leaping early into the ditch, had joined in the assault, and the rest, raked by a cross-fire of grape from the distant bas-

---

* Now Major-General Shaw Kennedy. Captain Nicholas when dying, told the story of this effort, adding that he saw Shaw, while thus standing alone, deliberately pull out his watch and repeating the hour aloud declare that the breach could not be carried that night.

tions, baffled in their aim by the smoke and flames from the explosions, and too few in number, had entirely failed to quell the French musketry.

About midnight, when two thousand brave men had fallen, Wellington, who was on a height close to the quarries, sent orders for the remainder to retire and re-form for a second assault; he had just then heard that the castle was taken, and thinking the enemy would still hold out in the town was resolved to assail the breaches again. This retreat from the ditch was not effected without further carnage and confusion; for the French fire never slackened, and a cry arose that the enemy were making a sally from the flanks, which caused a rush towards the ladders. Then the groans and lamentations of the wounded, who could not move and expected to be slain, increased; and many officers who did not hear of the order endeavoured to stop the soldiers from going back, some would even have removed the ladders but were unable to break the crowd.

All this time the third division lay close in the castle, and either from fear of risking the loss of a point which insured the capture of the place, or that the egress was too difficult, made no attempt to drive away the enemy from the breaches. On the other side however, the fifth division had commenced the false attack on the Pardaleras, and on the right of the Guadiana the Portuguese were sharply engaged at the bridge: thus the town was girdled with fire. For Walker's brigade had, during the feint on the Pardaleras, escaladed the distant bastion of San Vincente. Moving up the bank of the river, he reached a French guard-house at the barrier-gate undiscovered, the ripple of the waters smothering the sound of the footsteps; but then the explosion at the breaches took place, the moon shone out, the French sentinels discovering the column fired, and the British soldiers, springing forward under a sharp musketry, began to hew down the wooden barrier at the covered way; the Portuguese, panic-stricken, threw down the scaling- ladders, but the others snatched them up, forced the barrier and jumped into the ditch; there the guiding engineer was killed, a *cunette* embarrassed the column, and when the foremost men succeeded in rearing the ladders they were found too short, for the walls Were generally above thirty feet high.

The fire of the French was deadly, a small mine was sprung beneath the soldiers' feet, beams of wood and live shells were rolled over on their heads, showers of grape from the flank swept the ditch, and man after man dropped dead from the ladders.

At this critical moment some of the defenders being called away to aid in recovering the castle, the ramparts were not entirely manned, and the assailants, having discovered a corner of the bastion where the scarp was only twenty feet high, placed three ladders under an embrasure which had no gun, and was only stopped with a gabion. Some men got up with difficulty, for the ladders were still too short, but the first man being pushed up by his comrades drew others after him, and thus many had gained the summit; and though the French shot heavily against them from both flanks and from a house in front they thickened and could not be driven back. Half the 4th Regiment then entered the town itself, while the others pushed along the rampart towards the breach, and by dint of hard fighting successively won three bastions. In the last, General Walker, leaping forwards sword in hand just as a French cannonier discharged a gun, fell with so many wounds that it was wonderful how he survived, and his soldiers seeing a lighted match on the ground cried out a mine ! At that word, such is the power of imagination, those troops whom neither the strong barrier nor the deep ditch, nor the high walls, nor the deadly fire of the enemy could stop, staggered back, appalled by a chimera of their own raising. While in that disorder a French reserve under General Veillande drove on them with a firm and rapid charge, pitching some over the walls, killing others outright, and cleansing the ramparts even to the San Vincente: but there Leith had placed a battalion of the 38th, and when the French came up, shouting and slaying all before them, it arose and with one close volley destroyed them. This stopped the panic, and in compact order the soldiers once more charged along the walls towards the breaches; yet the French, although turned on both flanks and abandoned by fortune, would not yield.

Meanwhile the detachment of the 4th Regiment which had entered the town when the San Vincente was first carried, was strangely situated; for the streets though empty were brilliantly were brilliantly illuminated, no person was seen, yet a low buzz and whisper were heard around, lattices were now and then gently opened, and from time to time shots were fired from underneath the doors of the houses by the Spaniards, while the regiment, with bugles sounding, advanced towards the great square of the town. In its progress several mules going with ammunition to the breaches were taken, but the square was as empty and silent as the streets, and the houses as bright with lamps. A terrible enchantment seemed to prevail, nothing to be seen but light, and only low whispers heard, while the tumult at the breaches was like the crashing thunder: there the fight raged, and quitting the square the regiment attempted to take the enemy in reverse, but they were received with a rolling musketry, driven back with loss, and resumed their movement through the streets.

At last the breaches were abandoned by the French, other parties entered the place, desultory combats took place in various parts, and finally Veillande and Phillipon, both wounded, seeing all ruined, passed the bridge with a few hundred soldiers and entered San Christoval. Early next morning they surrendered upon summons to Lord Fitzroy Somerset, who with great readiness had pushed through the town to the drawbridge ere the French had time to organize further resistance; yet even at the moment of ruin, this noble governor with an imperturbed judgment had sent horsemen out from the fort in the night to carry the news to Soult's army, which they reached in time to prevent a greater misfortune.

Now commenced that wild and desperate wickedness, which tarnished the lustre of the soldier's heroism. All indeed were not alike, hundreds risked, and many lost their lives in striving to stop violence; but madness generally prevailed, and the worst men being leaders all the dreadful passions of human nature were displayed. Shameless rapacity, brutal intemperance, savage lust, cruelty and murder, shrieks and piteous lamentations, groans, shouts, imprecations, the hissing of fires bursting from the houses, the crashing of doors and windows, and the reports of muskets used in violence resounded for two days and nights in the streets of Badajos ! On the third, when the city was sacked, when the soldiers were exhausted by their own excesses, the tumult

tumult rather subsided than was quelled: the wounded men were then looked to, the dead disposed of !

Five thousand men and officers fell during the siege, including seven hundred Portuguese; three thousand five hundred were stricken in the assault, sixty officers and more than seven hundred men slain on the spot. Five generals,Kempt, Harvey, Bowes, Colville, and Picton were wounded, the first three severely; six hundred men and officers fell in the escalade of San Vincente, as many at the castle, and more than two thousand at the breaches: each division there lost twelve hundred ! But how deadly the strife was at that point may be gathered from this; the 43rd and 52nd regiments of the light division, alone lost more men than the seven regiments of the third division engaged at the castle !

Let it be remembered that this frightful carnage took place in a space of less than a hundred yards square. That the slain died not all suddenly nor by one manner of death. That some perished by steel, some by shot, some by water; that some were crushed and mangled by heavy weights, some trampled upon, some dashed to atoms by the fiery explosions; that for hours this destruction was endured without shrinking and that the town was won at last: these things considered, it must be admitted that a British army bears with it an awful power. And false would it be to say the French were feeble men, the garrison stood and fought manfully and with good discipline, behaving worthily. Shame there was none on any side. Yet who shall do justice to the bravery of the British soldiers ? the noble emulation of the officers? Who shall measure out the glory of Ridge, of Macleod, of Nicholas, of O'Hare of the rifles, who perished on the breach at the head of the stormers, and with him nearly all the volunteers for that desperate service? Who shall describe the springing valour of that Portuguese grenadier who was killed, the foremost man, at the Santa Maria ? or the martial fury of that desperate rifleman, who, in his resolution to win, thrust himself beneath the chained sword-blades, and there suffered the enemy to dash his head to pieces with the ends of their muskets ? Who can sufficiently honour the intrepidity of Walker, of Shaw, of Canch, or the resolution of Ferguson of the 43rd, who having at Rodrigo received two deep wounds was here, with his hurts still open, leading the stormers of his regiment, the third time a volunteer and the third time wounded ! Nor are these selected as pre-eminent; many and signal were the other examples of unbounded devotion, some known some that will never be known; for in such a tumult much passed unobserved, and often the observers fell themselves ere they could bear testimony to what they saw: but no age, no nation ever sent forth braver troops to battle than those who stormed Badajos.

When the havoc of the night was told to Wellington, the pride of conquest sunk into a passionate burst of grief for the loss of his gallant soldiers.

BOOK VII.

Beira—Grant—Surprise of Almaraz—Siege of the Salamanca Forts—
Combats between the Duero and the Tormes—Combats of Castrejon
and the Guarena—Battle of Salamanca—Combat of La Serna.

BEIRA.

After the storming of Badajos the English general desired to fight
Soult in Andalusia, and his cavalry under Sir Stapleton Cotton very
soon overtook the French horse and defeated them near Usagre with
a loss to the victors of fifty or sixty men, to the vanquished of two or
three hundred, one half being prisoners. Had that action been rapidly
followed up by a powerful army a great victory would probably have
crowned this extraordinary winter campaign, but obstacles, untimely
and unexpected, arose. Carlos Espana's oppressions had created a
dangerous spirit in the garrison of Rodrigo, the people of the vicinity
were alarmed, both that fortress and Almeida were insecure, and
Marmont was on the Coa. These things were to be remedied before
Andalusia could be invaded. Yet the danger was not absolute, and
Wellington lingered about Badajos, hoping Soult, in anger for its fall,
would risk a blow north of the Morena. That marshal was indeed
deeply moved, but the Spanish armies were menacing Seville, and the
allies were double his numbers; hence he returned to Seville and
Wellington marched to Beira, which Marmont was now ravaging
with great violence.

Following the letter not the spirit of Napoleon's orders, for he was
discontented at being debarred a junction with Soult, Marmont had
reluctantly made this diversion, and seemed to have exhaled his ill-
will by a savage warfare contrary to his natural disposition. Carlos
Espana fled before him, the Portuguese militia were dispersed
in a skirmish near Guarda, Victor Alten retreated across the Tagus
at Villa Velha though the French were still fifty miles distant;
and though personally a very brave man was so disturbed in

judgment that he meditated burning the bridge there, which would have ruined Lord Wellington's combinations. The whole country was in commotion, the population flying before the ravaging enemy, and all things in disorder; the Portuguese general Lecor alone preserved a martial attitude:he checked the French cavalry, saved the magazines and hospitals, and hung upon the French rear when they retired.When the allies came on from Badajos Marmont was, at first, inclined to fight, but found it too dangerous from the flooding of the rivers behind him, and it was only by the interposition of fortune that he avoided a great disaster. Finally he retired to Salamanca, carrying with him as a prisoner Captain Colquhoun Grant, a scouting officer of great eminence, whose escape furnished an episode in this war more surprising even than that of Colonel Waters.

Grant, in whom the utmost daring was so mixed with subtlety of genius, and both so tempered by discretion that it is hard to say which quality predominated, had been sent from Badajos to watch the French movements. Attended by Leon, a Spanish peasant, faithful and quick of apprehension, who had been his companion on many former occasions, he reached the Salamanca district, passed the Tormes during the night in uniform, for he never assumed any disguise, and remained three days in the midst of the French camps. He thus obtained exact information of Marmont's object, of his provisions and scaling-ladders, making notes, which he sent to Wellington from day to day by Spanish agents. The third night, some peasants brought him an order thus worded— " The notorious Grant is within the circle of cantonments, the soldiers are to strive for his capture, and guards will be placed in a circle around the army." Grant consulted the peasants, and before daylight entered the village of Huerta close to a ford on the Tormes, where there was a French battalion, and on the other bank of the river cavalry videttes, patrolling back and forward for the space of three hundred yards, yet meeting always at the ford.

At daylight, when the soldiers were at their alarm-post, he was secretly brought with his horse behind the gable of a house, which hid him from the infantry and was near the ford. The peasants, standing on loose stones, spread their large cloaks to hide him from the videttes until the latter were seperated the full extent of their beat; then putting spurs to his horse he dashed through the ford between them, received their cross fire without damage, and reaching a wood baffled pursuit, and was soon rejoined by Leon.

Grant had before ascertained that ladders for storming Rodrigo were prepared, and the French officers openly talked of doing so; but desiring further to test this, and ascertain if Marmont's march might not finally be for the Tagus, wishing, also, to discover the French force, he placed himself on a wooded hill near Tamames where the road branched off to the passes and to Rodrigo. There lying perdue while the army passed in march, he noted every battalion and gun, and finding all went towards Rodrigo entered Tamames, and found the greatest part of their scaling-ladders had been left there, showing that the intention to storm Rodrigo was not real. This it was which had allayed Wellington's fears for that fortress when he sought to entice Soult to battle.

Marmont then passed the Coa, but Grant preceded him, with intent to discover if his further march would be by Guarda upon Coimbra, or by Sabugal upon Castello Branco; for to reach the latter it was necessary to descend from a very high ridge, or rather succession of ridges, by a pass at the lower mouth of which stands Penamacor. Upon one of the inferior ridges of this pass he placed himself, thinking the dwarf oaks which covered the hill would secure him from discovery; but from the higher ridge the French detected his movements with their glasses, and in a few moments Leon, whose lynx eyes were always on the watch, called out, *the French ! the French !* Some dragoons came galloping up, Grant and his follower darted into the wood for a little space and then suddenly wheeling rode off in a different direction; but at every turn new enemies appeared, and at last the hunted men dismounted and fled on foot through the low oaks; again they were met by infantry, detached in small parties down the sides of the pass, and directed in their chase by the waving of hats on the ridge above: Leon fell exhausted, and those who first came up killed him in despite of his companion's entreaties: a barbarous action ! Grant they carried to Marmont, who invited him to dinner, and the conversation turned on the prisoner's exploits.

The French marshal said he had been long on the watch, knew all his captive's haunts and disguises, had discovered that only the night before he slept in the French head-quarters, with other adventures which had not happened, for this Grant never used any disguise; but there was another Grant, also very remarkable in his way, who used to remain for months in the French quarters, using all manner of disguises; hence the similarity of names caused the actions of both to be attributed to one, and that is the only palliative for Marmont's subsequent conduct.

Treating his prisoner with apparent kindness, he exacted from him an especial parole, that he would not admit a rescue by the Partidas while on his journey through Spain to France: this secured his captive, though Wellington offered two thousand dollars to any guerilla chief who should recover him. The exaction of such a parole was a tacit compliment to the man; but Marmont sent a letter with the escort to the governor of Bayonne, in which, still in error as to there being but one Grant, he designated his captive as a dangerous spy who had done infinite mischief, and whom he had not executed on the spot out of respect to something resembling uniform which he wore: he therefore desired, that at Bayonne he should be placed in irons and sent to Paris: this was so little in accord with French honour, that before the Spanish frontier was passed Grant was made acquainted with the treachery.

At Bayonne, in ordinary cases, the custom was for prisoners to wait on the authorities and receive passports for Verdun; this was done; the letter was purposely delayed, and Grant with sagacious boldness refrained from escaping towards the Pyrenees. Judging, that if the governor did not recapture him at once he would entirely suppress the letter, and let the matter drop, he asked at the hotels if any French officer was going to Paris, and finding General Souham, then on his return from Spain, was so bent, he introduced himself, requesting permission to join his party. The other readily assented, and while thus travelling the general, unacquainted with Marmont's intentions, often rallied his companion about his adventures, little thinking he was then an instrument to forward the most dangerous and skilful of them all.

In passing through Orleans, Grant by a species of intuition discovered a secret English agent, and from him received a recommendation to another in Paris. He looked upon Marmont's double-dealing, and the expressed design to take away his life, as equivalent to a discharge of his parole, which was moreover only given with respect to Spain; hence on reaching Paris he took leave of Souham, opened an intercourse with the Parisian agent, and obtained money. He would not go before the police to have his passport examined, but took lodgings in a public street, frequented the coffee-houses and visited the theatres boldly, for the secret agent, intimately connected with the police, soon ascertained that his escape had been unnoticed.

After several weeks, the agent told him a passport was ready for one Jonathan Buck, an American who had died suddenly on the day it was to be claimed. Grant coolly demanded this passport as for Jonathan Buck and instantly departed for the mouth of the Loire, where, for reasons not necessary to mention, he expected more assistance. New difficulties awaited him, yet they were overcome by fresh exertions of his surprising talent, which fortune seemed to delight in aiding. Having taken a passage in an American ship its departure was unexpectedly delayed; then he frankly told his situation to the captain, who desired him to become a discontented seaman, gave him sailor's clothing with forty dollars, and sent him to lodge the money in the American consul's hands, as a pledge that he would prosecute for ill usage when he reached the United States: this being the custom, the consul gave him a certificate to pass from port to port as a discharged sailor seeking a ship.

A promise of ten Napoleons induced a French boatman to row him in the night to a small island, where, by usage, English vessels watered unmolested, and, in return, permitted the few inhabitants to fish and traffic without interruption. The masts of the British ships were dimly seen beyond the island, and the termination of all Grant's toils seemed at hand, when the boatman from fear or malice returned to port. Some men would have strived in desperation to force fortune and so have perished, others would have sunk in despair, for the money promised was Grant's all, and the boatman demanded full payment; but with admirable coolness he gave him one piece and a rebuke for his misconduct; the other threatened a reference to the police yet found himself overmatched in subtlety: his opponent replied that he would then denounce him as aiding the escape of a prisoner of war, and adduce the price of his boat as a proof of his guilt !

An old fisherman was afterwards engaged, and faithfully performed his bargain, but there were then no English vessels near the island; however the fisherman caught some fish, with which he sailed towards the southward, having heard of an English ship of war being there. A glimpse was obtained of her, and they were steering that way when a shot from a coast-battery brought them to, and a boat with soldiers put off to board. The fisherman was steadfast and true. He called Grant his son, and the soldiers were only sent to warn them not to pass the battery because an English vessel, the one they were in search of, was on the coast. The old man bribed the soldiers with his fish, assuring them he must go with his son or they would starve, and he was so well acquainted with the coast he could easily escape the enemy. Being desired to wait till night and then depart, he, under pretence of avoiding the English vessel, made the soldiers point out her bearings so exactly that when darkness fell he run her straight on board, and the intrepid Grant stood in safety on the quarter deck.

In England he got permission to choose a French officer for an exchange, that no doubt might remain as to the propriety of his escape; great was his astonishment to find in the first prison he visited the old fisherman and his real son, who had been captured notwithstanding a protection given to them for their services. Grant, whose generosity and benevolence were as remarkable as the qualities of his understanding, soon obtained their release, sent them with a sum of money to France, returned to the Peninsula, and within four months from the date of his first capture was again on the Tormes, watching Marmont's army as before ! Other adventures could be mentioned of this generous and spirited, yet gentle-minded man, who, having served his country nobly in every climate, died a victim to continual hardships aided by a mortified spirit, for he had not been rewarded as he deserved.

SURPRISE OF ALMARAZ.

So many obstacles, military and political, were to be overcome before Andalusia could be invaded, 1812, that Lord Wellington finally resigned that project and meditated instead, operations against Marmont's army. To obtain success it was essential to isolate him as much as possible, and in that view various combinations were matured; but the most important stroke was to destroy the bridge and forts at Almaraz on the Tagus. Strong in works, that place was also a great depot for stores and boats, and not only facilitated the passage of the Tagus for reinforcements coming from Soult, but was sufficient to serve as a base and place of arms for an army to operate on the rear and flank of the British, if they engaged with Marmont in Castile. General Hill, who remained with a force in the Alemtejo, was charged with this great and dangerous enterprise, for a clear understanding of which the nature of the country must be described.

The left bank of the Tagus, from Toledo to Almarag, is lined with rugged mountains, difficult for small bodies, impracticable for an army. From Almarag to the frontier of Portugal the banks are more open, yet still difficult, and the Tagus was only to be crossed at certain points, to which bad roads led. From Almaraz to Alcantara the bridges, both those included, were ruined, and those of Arzobispo and Talavera above Almaraz were of little value because of the rugged mountains. Soult's pontoon equipage had been captured in Badajos, and the French could only cross the Tagus between Toledo and the frontier of Portugal by Marmont's boat bridge at Almaraz, to secure which he had constructed three strong forts and a bridge-head.

The first, called Ragusa, contained stores and provisions, and was, though not finished, exceedingly strong; it had a loopholed stone tower twenty-five feet high within, and was flanked without by a field-work near the bridge. This was on the north bank. On the south bank the bridge had a fortified head of masonry, which was again flanked by a redoubt called Fort Napoleon, placed on a height a little in advance; imperfectly constructed, however, inasmuch as a wide berm in the middle of the scarp furnished a landing-place for troops escalading. It was yet strong, because it contained a second interior defence or retrenchment, with a loopholed stone tower, a ditch, drawbridge, and palisades.

These forts and the bridge-head were armed with eighteen guns and garrisoned with eleven hundred men, which insured command of the river; but the mountains on the left bank precluded the passage of an army towards Lower Estremadura, save by the royal road to Truxillo, which, five miles from the Tagus, went over the lofty rugged Mirabete ridge: to secure the summit of this, the French had drawn a line of works across the throat of the pass; that is to say, a large fortified house was connected by smaller posts with the ancient watch-tower of Mirabete, which contained eight guns and was surrounded by a rampart twelve feet high.

If all these works, and a road, which Marmont, following the traces of an ancient Roman way, was now opening across the Gredos mountains had been finished, the communication of the French, though circuitous, would have been very good and secure. Wellington feared that accomplishment and designed to surprise Almaraz previous to the siege of Badajos, when the redoubts were far from complete; but the Portuguese government then baffled him by neglecting to furnish the means of transporting the artillery from Lisbon. Hill now marched to attempt it with a force of six thousand men, including four hundred cavalry, two field brigades of artillery, a pontoon equipage, and a battering-train of six iron twenty-four-pound howitzers. The enterprise was become more difficult. For when the army was round Badajos, only the resistance of the forts was to be looked to; now Foy's division of Marmont's army was in the valley of the Tagus, and troops from the king's army occupied Talavera. Drouet was also with eight or nine thousand men near Medellin, and closer to Merida than Hill was to Almaraz; he might therefore intercept the latter's retreat—and the king's orders were imperative that he should hang on the English force in Estremadura. Hill had therefore to steer, going and coming, through all these forces with an unwieldy convoy, and as it were, blot out the strong place without a battle; but Wellington took many precautions to divert the French attention to other points, and to furnish support without indicating the true object.

Hill, though dangerously delayed by the difficulty of restoring the bridge of Merida, which he had himself destroyed during the siege of Badajos, crossed the Guadiana with six thousand men, twelve field-pieces, pontoons, battering-train and fifty country carts, conveying material and ammunition. On the 15th he reached Truxillo, and during his march the guerillas of the Guadalupe mountains made demonstrations at different points, between Almaraz and Arzobispo, as if seeking a place to cast a bridge that he might join Wellington. Foy was deceived by these feints, for his spies at Truxillo, while reporting the passage of the Guadiana, said Hill had fifteen thousand men, and that two brigades of cavalry were following: one report even stated that thirty thousand men had entered Truxillo, whereas there were less than six thousand of all arms.

Early on the 16th the armament reached Jaraicejo. formed three columns, and made a night march, intending to surprise at the same moment, the tower of Mirabete, the fortified house in the pass, and the forts at the bridge of Almaraz. The left column, directed against the tower, was commanded by General Chowne. The centre, with the dragoons and artillery, moved by the royal road under General Long. The right, composed of the 50th, 71st, and 92nd Regiments, under Hill in person, was to penetrate by the narrow and difficult way of Roman Gordo against the forts of the bridge; but day broke before any column reached its destination, and all hopes of a surprise were extinguished. This was an untoward beginning, unavoidable with the right and centre column because of the bad roads, but Chowne was negligent, for the Mirabete tower might have been assaulted before daylight.

Hill now saw that to reduce the Mirabete works in the pass he must incur more loss than was justifiable, and be in such plight that he could not finally carry the forts below; yet it was only through the pass the artillery could move against the bridge. In this dilemma, after losing the 17th and part of the 18th, in fruitless attempts to discover some opening through which to reach Almaraz with his guns, he resolved to leave them on the Sierra with the centre

column, make a false attack on the tower with Chowne's troops, and
in person, with the right column, secretly penetrate by the scarcely
practicable line of Roman Gordo to the bridge, intent, with infantry
alone, to storm works which were defended by eighteen pieces of
artillery and powerful garrisons !

This resolution was even more hardy than it appears, without a
reference to the general state of affairs. His march had been one of
secrecy, amidst various divisions of the enemy; he was four days'
journey from Merida, his first point of retreat; he expected Drouet to
be reinforced and advance, and hence, whether defeated or victorious
at Almaraz, his retreat would be very dangerous; exceedingly so if
defeated, because his fine British troops could not be repulsed with
a small loss, and he would have to fall back through a difficult
country, with his best soldiers dispirited by failure and burthened by
numbers of wounded men. Then, harassed on one side by Drouet,
pursued by Foy and D'Armagnac on the other, he would have been
exposed to the greatest misfortunes, every slanderous tongue would
have been let loose on the rashness of attacking impregnable forts,
and a military career, hitherto so glorious, might have terminated in
shame. Devoid of interested ambition, he was unshaken by such
fears, and remained concealed until the evening of the 18th, when he
commenced the descent, with design to escalade the Fort Napoleon
before daylight. The march was less than six miles, but the head of
the troops only reached the fort a little before daylight, the rear was
distant, and it was doubtful if the scaling ladders, cut in halves to
thread the short narrow turns in the precipitous descent, would serve
for an assault. Some small hills concealed the head of the column, and
at that moment Chowne commenced his false attack at Mirabete.
Pillars of white smoke rose on the lofty brow of the Sierra, the heavy
sound of artillery came rolling over the valley, and the garrison of Fort
Napoleon, crowding on the ramparts, were gazing at those portentous
signs of war, when, quick and loud, a British shout broke on their ears,
and the 50th Regiment with a Wing of the 71st, came bounding over
the low hills.

Surprised the French were to see an enemy so close while
the Mirabete was still defended, yet they were not unprepared

a patrol of English cavalry had been seen from the fort on the 17th, and in the evening of the 18th a woman had given exact information of Hill's numbers and designs. 'This intelligence had caused the, commandant, Aubert, to march in the night with reinforcements to Fort Napoleon, which was therefore defended by six companies ready to fight, and when the first shout was heard they smote with musketry and artillery on the British front, while the guns of Fort Ragusa took them in flank. A rise of ground, twenty yards from the ramparts, soon covered the assailants from the front fire, and General Howard, leading the foremost into the ditch, commenced the escalade. The breadth of the berm kept off the ends of the shortened ladders from the parapet, but the first men jumped on to the berm itself and drawing up the ladders planted them there; then with a second escalade they won the rampart and, closely fighting, all went together into the retrenchment round the stone tower. Aubert was wounded and taken, and the garrison fled towards the bridge-head, but the victorious troops would not be shaken off, they entered that work also in one confused mass with the fugitives, who continued their fight over the bridge itself. Still the British soldiers pushed their headlong charge, slaying the hindmost, and would have passed the river if some of the boats had not been destroyed by stray shots from the forts, which were now sharply cannonading each other, for the artillerymen had turned the guns of Napoleon on Fort Ragusa.

Many French, leaping into the water, were drowned, but the greatest part were made prisoners, and to the amazement of the conquerors the panic pervaded the other side of the river, where the garrison of Ragusa, though perfectly safe, fled with the others! Some grenadiers of the 92nd, then swimming over, brought back boats, with which the bridge was restored and the towers and works of Ragusa were destroyed, and the stores, ammunition, provisions and boats,burned. In the night the troops returned to the Mirabete ridge with the colours of the foreign regiment, and two hundred and fifty prisoners, including a commandant and sixteen other officers, their own loss being a hundred and eighty men. One officer of artillery was killed by his own mine, placed for the destruction of the tower, but the only officer slain in the assault was Captain Candler, of the 50th, a brave man, who fell leading the grenadiers of that regiment on to the rampart of Fort Napoleon.

Rapidity was an essential cause of this success. Foy had ordered D'Armagnac to reinforce the forts with a battalion, which might have entered Fort Ragusa early in the morning of the 19th; but instead of marching before day-break, it did not move until eleven o'clock, and meeting the fugitives on the road caught the panic.

Hill was about to reduce the works at Mirabete, when Sir W. Erskine, confused by the French movements, gave a false alarm, which caused a retreat on Merida; Wellington, in reference to this error of Erskine, told the ministers, that his generals, stout in action as the poorest soldiers, were overwhelmed with fear of responsibility when left to themselves: the slightest movement of an enemy deprived them of judgment. Erskine was a miserable officer; but all officers knew, that without powerful interest future prospects and past services would wither under the blight of a disaster; that a selfish government would instantly offer them as victims to a misjudging public and a ribald press, with which success is the only criterion of merit. English generals are, and must be, prodigal of their blood to gain reputation; but they are timid in command, because a single failure without a fault consigns them to shame and abuse.

Having resumed his former position, Hill engaged in a series of marches and countermarches against Drouet, yet no action occurred, save one between General Slade and General Lallemande, with two regiments of dragoons on each side. Slade, contrary to orders, drove back the French horsemen for eight miles, and through the defile of Maquilla followed in disorder; but in the plain beyond stood Lallemande's reserves, with which he broke the disorderly mass, killed or wounded fifty, pursued for six miles and took a hundred prisoners. Two days after, the Austrian Strenowitz, having but fifty men of Slade's dragoons, recovered all the wounded prisoners, defeated eighty French, killed many and took twenty-six such is the difference between mere dash and military skill.

In the summer of 1812 Lord Wellington resolved to fight Marmont. There were many reasons for this, but the principal one was, that Napoleon was in the heart of Russia, that his own army was stronger, especially in cavalry, than it had yet been or was likely to be, and if he did not then strike no better opportunity could be expected. He had ninety thousand men, British and Portuguese, but six thousand were in Cadiz, and the Walcheren expedition was still to be atoned for; the regiments which had served there were so sickly that only thirty-two thousand British were in line; yet to these he could join twenty-five thousand Portugese, making fifty-seven thousand sabres and bayonets, which he judged sufficient. Of this force Hill had seventeen thousand, two thousand being cavalry with twenty-four guns. General D'Urban was with twelve hundred Portuguese horsemen in the Tras Os Montes, and was to cooperate with Wellington, who had therefore nearly forty thousand of all arms, three thousand five hundred being cavalry, with fifty-four guns.

Almaraz bridge had been destroyed to lengthen the French lateral line of communication, Alcantara was now repaired to shorten the British line; and though the break in that stupendous structure was ninety feet wide and one hundred and fifty above the water, the genius of Colonel Sturgeon overcame the difficulty. Hill's army was thus brought a fortnight nearer to Wellington than Drouet was to Marmont, if both marched with artillery; and as the army of the centre was, by the king's misrule, in a state of great disorder, Marmont was for a time isolated from all the other armies save that of the north, now under General Caffarelli, who was however occupied by maritime expeditions from Coruna.

Marmont was a man to be feared. He was quick of apprehension, morally and physically brave, scientific, used to war, strong of body, in the prime of life, eager for glory; and though neither a great nor a fortunate commander, such a one as could bear the test of fire. He had strongly fortified three convents at Salamanca, and having about twenty five thousand men in hand, demanded aid from the King, from Soult, and from the army of the north. His design was to dispute the Tormes and Duero in succession, the first by his forts, the second with an army, which he could augment to forty six thousand without extraneous aid by calling Bonet's division from the Asturiae.

On the 13th of June Wellington advanced to the Tormes.

The bridge of Salamanca was barred by the French forts, all the others had been destroyed save that of Alba de Tolmes, the castle of which was garrisoned; the allies however passed the river above and below Salamanca by the fords of Santa Marta and Los Cantos, and General Clinton invested the forts with the sixth division. Marmont, who had two divisions and some cavalry, retired by the road of Toro. Salamanca then became a scene of rejoicing. The houses were illuminated, the people, shouting, singing and weeping for joy, gave Wellington their welcome while his army took a position on the hill of San Christoval five miles in advance.

SIEGE OF THE SALAMANCA FORTS.

Clinton had only four heavy guns and three twenty-fourpound howitzers, but the train used by Hill at Almaraz had passed the Tagus at Alcantara on its way up. The strength of the forts had however been under-estimated, they contained eight hundred men. San Vincente, placed on a perpendicular cliff overhanging the Tormes, had a fortified convent within, and was well flanked and separated by a deep ravine from the other forts; and these last, called San Cajetano and La Merced, though smaller and of a square form, were bomb-proof and with deep ditches.

The engineer Burgoyne, directing the siege, commenced a battery two hundred and fifty yards from Vincente, and as the ruins of convents all around which had been destroyed to make the forts, rendered it impossible to excavate, earth was brought from a distance; but the moon was up, the night short, the French musketry heavy, the sixth division inexperienced, and at daybreak the battery was still imperfect. An attempt had been made to attach the miner secretly to the counterscarp, but the vigilance of a trained dog baffled this design: it was then openly made, yet defeated by a plunging fire from the top of the convent.

On the 18th eight hundred Germans, placed in the ruins, mastered all the enemy's fire save that from loop-holes, and two field-pieces were placed on a neighbouring convent to silence the French artillery, but failed.

In the night the first battery was armed; at daybreak on

the 19th seven guns opened, and by nine o'clock the wall of the convent was cut away to the level of the rampart; a second breaching battery of iron howitzers, which saw lower down the scarp, then commenced its fire, but that ordnance was unmeet for battering, and the enemy's musketry brought down a captain and more than twenty gunners.

The 20th Colonel Dickson arrived with more iron howitzers from Elvas, and the second battery, reinforced with additional pieces, revived its fire, striking only the convent, a huge cantle of which came to the ground, crushing many of the garrison and laying bare the inside of the building; carcasses were immediately thrown into the opening, but the enemy extinguished the flames. A lieutenant and fifteen gunners were lost this day, ammunition failed, and the attack was suspended.

During this siege the aspect of affairs had changed on both sides. Wellington, deceived as to the strength of the forts, now found by intercepted returns that both Soult and Marmont were far stronger than he had expected; he had calculated also that Bonet's division would not quit the Asturias, but that general was in full march for Leon; Caffarelli was likewise preparing to reinforce Marmont, and thus the brilliant prospect of the campaign was suddenly clouded. Meanwhile Marmont, having united four divisions of infantry and a brigade of cavalry, twenty-five thousand men, came to the succour of the forts. His approach, over an open country, being descried at a considerable distance, a brigade was called from the siege, the battering train was sent across the Tormes, and the army formed in order of battle on the top- of San Christoval. This position was four miles long, rather concave, and the steep descent in front tangled with hollow roads, stone inclosures and villages; the summit was broad, even, and covered with ripe corn, the right was flanked by the Upper Tormes, the left dipped into the country bordering the Lower Tormes; for in passing Salamanca that river took a sweep round the back of the position. The infantry, heavy cavalry and guns, crowned the summit of the mountain, but the light cavalry was in a low country on the left, where there was a small stream and a marshy flat. In front of the left, centre, and right, the

Castillanos, and Moresco, were nearly in a line at the foot of the position, which overlooked the country for many miles, yet had neither shade nor fuel to cook with, nor water nearer than the Tormes, and the heat was very oppressive.

At five o'clock in the evening the enemy's horsemen approached, pointing towards the left of the position, as if to turn it by the Lower Tormes; to check this the light cavalry made a short forward movement and a partial charge took place, but the French opened six guns and the others retired to their own ground. The light division immediately closed towards the left, and the French cavalry halted. Meanwhile the main body of the enemy bore with a rapid pace in one dark volume against the right, and halting at the foot of the position sent a flight of shells on to the lofty summit; nor aid this fire cease until after dark, when Marmont, taking possession of Moresco, established himself behind that village and Castillanos, within gunshot of the allies.

That night the English general slept amongst the troops, and the first streak of light saw both sides under arms. Some signals were interchanged between Marmont and the forts, yet all remained quiet until evening, when Wellington detached the 68th Regiment to drive the French from Moresco. This attack, made with vigour, succeeded, but the troops being recalled just as daylight failed, a body of French, passing unperceived through standing corn, broke into the village unexpectedly and did considerable execution. In the skirmish an officer, named Mackay, being surrounded, refused to surrender, and, fighting against a multitude, received more wounds than the human frame was thought capable of sustaining; yet he lived to show his honourable scars.

Next day three divisions and a brigade of cavalry joined Marmont, who, having now forty thousand men, extended his left and seized a part of the height in advance of the allies' right wing. From thence he could discern the whole of their order of battle, and attack their right on even terms; but Graham, using the seventh division, dislodged his detachment with a sharp skirmish before it could be formidably reinforced, and in the night the French withdrew to some heights six miles in rear.

It was thought Marmont's tempestuous advance to Moresco on the evening of the 20th should have been his ruin; but Wellington argued, that if he came to fight it was better to defend a strong position than descend to combat in the plain; for the French inferiority was not such as to insure a result decisive of the campaign, and in case of failure, a retreat across the Tormes would have been very difficult. To this may be added, that during the first evening there was some confusion amongst the allies; the troops, of different nations, had formed their order of battle slowly; the descent of the mountain towards the enemy was by no means easy; walls, hollow ways and villages, covered the French front, and Marmont, having plenty of guns and troops ready of movement, could have evaded the action until night. This reasoning however failed on the 21st. The allies, whose infantry was a third more, their cavalry three times as numerous and much better mounted, might have poured down by all the roads at daybreak, and then Marmont, turned on both flanks and followed vehemently, could never have made his retreat to the Duero through the open country: on the 22nd, when his other troops came up, the chances were no longer the same.

Marmont now withdrew his right, abandoning the road of Toro, but keeping that of Tordesillas, and placing his left on the Tormes at Huerta, where the river took a sudden bend, descending perpendicularly towards the allies. Thus commanding the ford of Huerta he could pass the river and communicate by the left bank with his forts. Wellington made corresponding dispositions. Closing towards the river, he placed the light division at the ford of Aldea Lengua, sent Graham down with two divisions to the nearer ford of Santa Marta, and General Bock's heavy German cavalry over the Tormes to watch the ford of Huerta

On the 23rd all was tranquil, but at break of day on the 24th some dropping pistol-shots, and now and then a shout, came faintly from a mist covering the lower ground beyond the river; the heavy sound of artillery succeeded, and the hissing of bullets cutting through the thickened atmosphere told that the French were over the Tormes. Soon the fog vanished, and the German horsemen were seen retiring in close and beautiful order before twelve thousand French infantry, advancing in battle array. At intervals, twenty guns would start forwards and send their bullets whistling and tearing up the ground beneath the Germans, while scattered parties of light cavalry scouting out capped all the hills in succession, peeling abroad and giving signals to the main body. Wellington then sent Graham over the river with two divisions and a brigade of English cavalry, concentrating the rest of his troops near Moresco to await the event.

Bock continued his retreat in fine order, regardless alike of the cannonade and of the light horsemen on his flanks, until the enemy's scouts gained a height, from whence, at the distance of three miles, they for the first time perceived Graham's twelve thousand men, ranged with eighteen guns on an order of battle perpendicular to the Tormes. From the same point Wellington's heavy columns were seen clustering on the height above the fords of Santa Marta, and the light division at Aldea Lengua, ready either to advance against the French troops left on the right bank, or to pass the river in aid of Graham. At this sight Marmont hastily faced about, repassed the Tormes, and resumed his former ground.

Wellington, unwilling to stir before the forts fell, here again refused an accidental advantage; for it is not easy to see how the French could have avoided a defeat if he had moved with all the troops on the right bank against the French divisions on that side.

The forts were now closely pressed. On the 23rd, the heavy guns being brought back, a battery to breach San Cajetano was armed with four pieces; yet the line of fire being oblique only beat down the parapet and knocked away the palisades. An escalade of that fort and La Merced was tried at ten o'clock, yet failed in half an hour with a loss of one hundred and twenty men and officers; the wounded were brought off next day under truce, and the enemy had all the credit of the fight. General Bowes, whose rank might have excused his leading so small a force, being wounded early in this assault, was having his hurt dressed when he heard the troops were yielding, whereupon he returned to the fight and fell.

Want of powder now suspended the siege until the 26th, when a convoy arrived. Then the second and third batteries were re-armed, and the field-pieces replaced on the neighbouring convent. The iron howitzers, throwing hot shot, soon set the convent within San Vincente on fire; but the garrison extinguished the flames and this balanced combat continued during the night. In the morning the besiegers' fire was redoubled, the convent was in a blaze, the breach of Cajetano improved, and a fresh storming party was assembled, when the white flag waved from Cajetano. Negotiation ensued, but Wellington, judging it an artifice to gain time, ordered a double assault, to oppose which Cajetano scarcely fired a shot, and the flames raged so at Vincente no opposition could be made. Seven hundred prisoners, thirty pieces of artillery, provisions, arms, clothing, and a secure passage over the- Tormes, were the immediate fruits of this capture: not the less prized that the breaches were found more formidable than those at Rodrigo, and a storm would have been very doubtful if the garrison could have gained time to extinguish the flames in San Vincente. The allies had ninety killed, and their whole loss was five hundred men and officers, of which one hundred and sixty men with fifty horses fell outside Salamanca, the rest in the siege.

COMBATS BETWEEN THE DUERO AND THE TORMES.

When the forts were taken Marmont retreated. Wellington pursued by easy marches, and on the 2nd of July inflicted a slight loss on the rearguard at the bridge of Tordesillas; it would have been a great one if he had not been deceived by a false report that the French had broken the bridge the night before.

Marmont then took the line of the Duero, having fortified posts at Zamora and Toro, and broken the bridges there and at Puente Duero. and Tudela also, preserving only that of Tordesillas. His left was at Simancas on the Pisuerga, which was unfordable, and the bridges at that place and Valladolid were commanded by fortified posts. His centre was at Tordesillas and very numerous; his right on heights opposite the ford of Pollos, which Wellington seized instantly as it gave him a passage, though a difficult one and unfit for a large force. Head-quarters were then fixed at Rueda, and the army disposed with a head against the ford of Pollos and bridge of Tordesillas, the rear on the Zapardiel and Trabancos rivers to meet any outbreak from the Valladolid side. Marmont's line of defence, measured from Valladolid to Zamora, was sixty miles; from Simancas to Toro above thirty; but the actual occupation was not above twelve; the bend of the river gave him the chord, the allies the arc, and the fords were few and difficult.

It was Wellington's design to force Marmont by the cooperation of the Gallician and other Spanish forces to live on his fixed magazines; Castanos however, like all Spanish generals, failed in the hour of need. Marmont had then the means of rendering the campaign futile if not disastrous to the British general, but with a false judgment threw away his actual advantages by striving to better them. Bonet's recall from the Asturias was a great error. Napoleon and Wellington had alike foreseen the importance of holding that province; the one ordered, the other calculated on its retention, and their judgment was now vindicated. The Gallicians and Asturians immediately moved by the coast towards Biscay, where the maritime expedition from Coruna, a large one under Sir Home Popham, had descended on several points; Caffarelli therefore retained the reinforcement destined for Marmont, and that marshal, by gaining six thousand men under Bonet, lost twelve or thirteen thousand of the army of the north, and opened all the northern provinces to the Spaniards.

In this state of affairs neither Wellington nor Marmont had reason to fight on the Duero. The latter because his position was so strong he could safely wait for Bonet's and Caffarelli's troops, while the king operated against the allies' communications. The former because he could not attack the French, except at great disadvantage; for the fords of the Duero were little known, and that of Pollos very deep. To pass the river there and form within gunshot of the enemy's left, without other combinations, promised nothing but defeat, for the strength of ground was with the French. While they had the bridge at Tordesillas, an attempt to force a passage would have enabled Marmont to fall on the front and rear, if the operation was within his reach; if beyond his reach, that is to say, near Zamora, he could cut the communication with Rodrigo and yet preserve his own with Caffarelli and the king. Wellington therefore resolved to wait until the fords should become lower, or the Gallicians and Partidas should be persuaded to act, and thus force the French to detach men or dislodge for want of provisions.

D'Urban's Portuguese cavalry, which was on the French side of the river, now incommoded Marmont's light, and Foy marched to drive them off; General Pakenham, commanding the third division, immediately crossed the ford of Pollos, which brought Foy back, and Marmont then augmented the efficiency of his cavalry by taking a thousand horses from the infantry officers and sutlers.

On the 8th Bonet arrived, and the French marshal, extending his right to Toro, commenced repairing the bridge there. Wellington, in like manner, stretched his left to the Guarena, keeping his centre still on the Trabancos and his right at Rueda, with posts near Tordesillas and the ford of Pollos. In this situation the armies remained for some days, during which Graham and Picton went to England in bad health, and the principal powder magazine at Salamanca exploded with hurt to many. No other events worth recording occurred. The weather was fine, the country rich, the troops received their rations regularly, and wine was so plentiful it was hard to keep the soldiers sober; the caves of Rueda, natural or cut in the rock below the surface of the earth, were so immense, and held so much wine, that the drunkards of two armies failed to make any very sensible diminution in the quantity, and many men perished in that labyrinth. The soldiers of each army also, passing the Duero in groups, held amicable intercourse, conversing of battles that were yet to be fought, and the camps on the banks of the Duero seemed at times to belong to one general, so difficult is it to make brave men hate each other.

To the officers of the allies all looked prosperous, they w ere impatient for the signal of battle, and many complained that the French had been permitted to retreat from Christoval; had Wellington been finally forced back to Portugal, his reputation would have been grievously assailed by his own people. The majority, peering forward with misty political vision, overlooked the difficulties close at hand, but their general was fretted with general was fretted with care and mortification, for all cross and evil circumstances seemed to combine against him. The Spanish cooperation had failed in all quarters, the enemy in front was growing stronger, Soult was seriously menacing Cadiz, and the king was said to have been joined by Drouet; the Portuguese troops were deserting in great numbers from misery; the English government had absurdly and perniciously interfered with the supply of the military chest; there was no money and the personal resources of Wellington alone kept the army in its forward position. " I have never," said he, "been in such distress as at present, and some serious misfortune must happen if the government do not attend seriously to the subject and supply us regularly with money. The arrears and distresses of the Portuguese government are a joke to ours, and if our credit was not better than theirs we should certainly starve. As it is, if we don't find means to pay our bills for butcher's meat there will be an end to the war at once."

Thus stript as it were to the skin, he was going once more to hide his nakedness in the mountains of Portugal, when Marmont, proud of his own unripened skill, and perhaps, from the experience of San Christoval, undervaluing his adversary's tactics; desirous also, it was said, to gain a victory, without the presence of a king; Marmont, pushed on by fate, madly broke the chain which restrained his enemy's strength.

To understand the remarkable movements which were now about to commence, it must be borne in mind that the French army, while the harvest was on the ground, had no regard to lines of communication; it had supports on all sides, and the troops were taught to reap the standing corn, and grind it themselves if the cavalry could not seize flour in the villages. This organization, approaching the ancient Roman military perfection, baffled the irregular, and threw the regular force of the allies entirely upon the defensive; their flanks once turned a retreat must follow to save the communications; but the French offered no point for retaliation.

Wherefore, with a force composed of four different nations, Wellington was to make difficult evolutions in an open country, his only chances of success being the casual errors of his adversary, an able general, who knew the country perfectly disciplined, and of one nation. The game would have been quite unequal if the English had not been so strong in cavalry.

In the course of the 15th and 16th Marmont, who had previously made deceptive movements, concentrated his beautiful and gallant army on its right towards Toro, which place, intercepted letters, reports of deserters and the talk of the peasants, had for several days assigned as his point of passage. On the morning of the 16th English exploring officers, passing the Duero near Tordesillas, found only the garrison there, and in the evening the reports stated, that two French divisions had already crossed by the bridge of Toro; wherefore Wellington united his centre and left at Canizal, on the Guarena, during the night, intending to attack; but as he had still some doubts of the real object, he left Sir Stapleton Cotton on the Trabancos with the right wing, composed of the fourth and light divisions and Anson's cavalry. Suddenly Marmont recalled his troops, returned to Tordesillas and Pollos, passed the Duero and concentrated at Nava del Rey in the evening of the 17th, some of his men having marched forty, some fifty miles without a halt. Wellington was then near Toro, and Cotton remained behind the Trabancos during the night without orders, in a bad position; Wellington however hastened to his aid, bringing up Bock's, Le Marchant's, and Alten's cavalry, while the fifth division took post six miles in rear of the Trabancos.

COMBATS OF CASTREJON AND THE GUARENA.

At daybreak Cotton's outposts were driven in, yet the bulk of his cavalry and a troop of horse artillery showed a front, having the two infantry divisions in support; the fourth behind his left, the light division behind his right, but widely separated by a valley. The country was open, like the downs of England, with here and there watergullies, dry hollows and naked heads of land, behind one of which, on the other side of the Trabancos, lay the French army. Cotton, seeing only horsemen, pushed his cavalry towards the river, advancing cautiously by his right along some high tableland, where his troops were lost at first in the morning the morning fog, then thick on the stream. Very soon the deep tones of artillery shook the ground, the sharp ring of musketry was heard in the mist, and the 43rd Regiment was hastily brought through the village of Castrejon to support the advancing cavalry; for besides the deep valley separating the fourth from the light division, there w as a ravine with a marshy bottom between the cavalry and infantry, and the village furnished the only good passage.

The cannonade became heavy, and the spectacle surprisingly beautiful. The lighter smoke and mist, mingling and curling in fantastic pillars, formed a huge and glittering dome tinged with many colours by the rising sun, and through the gross vapour below the restless horsemen were seen or lost, as the fume thickened from the rapid play of the artillery; the bluff head of land beyond the Trabancos, now covered with French troops, appeared by an optical deception close at hand, dilated to the size of a mountain, and crowned with gigantic soldiers, who were continually breaking off and sliding down into the fight. Suddenly a dismounted English cavalry officer stalked from the midst of the smoke towards the line of infantry; his gait was peculiarly rigid, and he appeared to hold a bloody handkerchief to his heart; but that which seemed a cloth was a broad and dreadful wound: a bullet had entirely effaced the flesh from his left shoulder and breast and carried away part of his ribs, his heart was bared and its movement plainly discerned. It was a piteous and yet a noble sight, for his countenance though ghastly was firm, his step scarcely indicated weakness, and his voice never faltered. This unyielding man's name was Williams. He died a short distance from the field of battle, it was said in the arms of his son, a youth of fourteen, who had followed his father to the Peninsula in hopes of obtaining a commission, for they were not in affluent circumstances.

Cotton maintained this exposed position until seven o'clock, when Wellington and Beresford came up, and both were like to have been slain together. For a squadron of French cavalry, breaking away from the head of land beyond the Trabancos, had just before come with such speed across the valley that it was for a moment thought they were deserting; but with headlong course they mounted the tableland on which Cotton's left wing was posted, and drove a whole line of British cavalry skirmishers back in confusion. The reserves then came up from Alaejos, and these furious swordmen, scattered in all directions, were in turn driven away or cut down; yet thirty or forty, led by their gallant officer, suddenly appeared above the ravine separating the British wings, just as Wellington and Beresford arrived on the slope beneath them. Some infantry picquets were in the bottom, higher up were two guns covered by a squadron of light cavalry disposed in perfect order, and when the French officer saw this squadron he reined in his horse with difficulty, his men gathering in a confused body round him; they seemed lost, but their daring leader waving his sword soused down with a shout on the English troopers, who turning, galloped through the guns, and the whole mass, friends and enemies, went like a whirlwind to the bottom, carrying away in the tumult Wellington and Beresford. The French horsemen were now quite exhausted and a reserve of heavy dragoons cut most of them to pieces; yet their invincible leader, assaulted by three enemies at once, struck one dead from his horse, and with surprising exertions saved himself from the others, though they rode hewing at him on each side for a quarter of a mile.

Scarcely was this over when Marmont, having ascertained that a part only of Wellington's army was before him, crossed the Trabancos in two columns, and penetrating between the light and fourth divisions marched straight upon the Guarena. The British retired in three columns, the light division being between the fifth division and the French, close to the latter, the cavalry on the flanks and rear. The air was extremely sultry, the dust rose in clouds, and the close order of the troops was rendered very oppressive by a siroc wind; but where the light division marched the military spectacle was strange and grand. Hostile columns of infantry, only half musket-shot from each other, were marching impetuously towards a common goal, the officers on each side pointing forwards with their swords, or touching their caps and waving their hands in courtesy, while the German cavalry, huge men, on huge horses, rode between in a close compact body as if to prevent a collision: at times the loud tones of command to hasten the march were heard passing

from the front to the rear on both sides, and now and then the rush of
French bullets came sweeping over the columns, whose violent pace
was continually accelerated.

Thus moving for ten miles, yet keeping the most perfect order,
both parties approached the Guarena, and the enemy seeing the light
division, although more in their power than the others, was yet
outstripping them in the march, increased the fire of their guns and
menaced an attack with infantry: the German cavalry instantly drew
close round, the column plunged suddenly into a hollow dip of ground
on the left, and ten minutes after the head of the division was in the
stream of the Guarena between Osmo and Castrillo. The fifth division
entered it at the same time higher up on the left, and the fourth division
passed on the right. The soldiers of the light division, tormented with
thirst yet long used to their enemy's mode of warfare, drunk as they
marched; those of the fifth division, less experienced, stopped a few
moments, and on the instant forty French guns gathering on the
heights above sent a tempest of bullets amongst them. So nicely timed
was the operation.

The Guarena, flowing from four distinct sources which united
below Castrillo, offered a very strong line of defence; yet Marmont,
hoping to carry it in the first confusion, brought up all his artillery and
pushed the head of his right column over an upper branch. Wellington, expecting this, had previously ordered up the other divisions of
his army, and they were in line before Marmont's infantry, oppressed
with heat and long marches, could gather strength to attempt the
passage of the other branch. Carier's brigade of cavalry first crossed,
and was followed by a column of infantry, just as the fourth division
had gained the table-land above. Carier's horsemen entered the
valley on the left, the infantry in one column menaced the front, but
the sedgy banks of the stream would have been difficult to force,
if Victor Alten, slow to perceive an advantage, had not suffered
the French cavalry to cross first in considerable numbers without
opposition. Then he assailed them by successive squadrons instead
of regiments, and when the 14th and German Hussars were
hard-pressed, brought up the 3rd Dragoons, who were however
driven back by the fire of the infantry, and many fell.

Finally Carier being wounded and taken, the French retired, and meanwhile the 27th and 40th Regiments, coming down the hill, broke the enemy's infantry with an impetuous bayonet charge: Alten's horsemen then sabred some of the fugitives.

Marmont lost a general and five hundred soldiers by this combat, but, though baffled at one point, and beaten at another, he concentrated his army and held both banks of the branch he had gained. Wellington also concentrated, and as the previous operations had only cost him six hundred men and the French but eight hundred, the day being still young, the positions open and within cannon-shot, a battle was expected. Marmont's troops had however been marching for two days and nights, and Wellington's plan did not admit of fighting unless in defence, or with such advantage as that he could crush his opponent and keep the field afterwards against the king.

The French marshal had passed a great river, surprised the allies' right, and pushed it back above ten miles: he had nevertheless failed as a general. His aim had been, by menacing the communication between Salamanca and Rodrigo, to draw the allies back; yet on the evening of the 16th, having passed the Duero at Toro, he was nearer to Salamanca than they were, and, persisting, Wellington must have fought him at disadvantage, or passed the Tormes at Euerta to regain the road of Rodrigo. Marmont however relinquished this stroke to march eighty miles in forty-eight hours, and after many nice evolutions, in which he lost a thousand men by the sword and fatigue, found his adversary on the 18th facing him in the very position he had turned on the evening of the 16th!

On the 19th the armies were quiet until evening, when the French were suddenly concentrated in one mass on their left. Wellington made a corresponding movement on the tableland above, which caused the light division to overlook the enemy's main body, then at rest round the bivouac fires; it would have remained so if Sir Stapleton Cotton coming up had not turned a battery upon a group of French officers. At the first shot they seemed surprised—for it was a discourteous and ill-considered act—at the second their gunners run to their pieces, and a reply from twelve heavier guns wounded an artillery-officer, killed several British soldiers, swept away a whole section of Portuguese, and compelled the division to withdraw in a mortifying manner to avoid unnecessary blood-spilling.

Wellington now expected a battle, because the heights he occupied trended backwards to the Tormes on the shortest line, and as he had thrown a Spanish garrison into the castle of Alba de Tormes he thought the French could not turn his right; if they attempted it, he could shoulder them off the Tormes at the ford of Huelta. At daybreak however, instead of crossing the Guarena in front to dispute the high land, Marmont marched rapidly up the river-and crossed the stream, though the banks were difficult, before any disposition could be made to oppose him. He thus turned the right and gained a new range of hills trending also towards the Tormes, and parallel to those which Wellington possessed. Then commenced a scene similar to that of the 18th but on a greater scale. The allies moving in two lines of battle within musket shot of the French endeavoured to cross their march, the guns on both sides exchanged rough salutations as the accidents of ground favoured their play, and the officers, like gallant gentlemen who bore no malice and knew no fear, made their military recognitions, while the horsemen on each side watched with eager eyes for an opening to charge: but the French, moving as one man along the crest of the heights, preserved the lead and made no mistake.

Soon it became evident that the allies would be outflanked, wherefore Wellington, falling off a little, made towards the heights occupied by Marmont during the siege of the forts, intending to halt there while an advanced guard, forcing a march, secured the position and fords of Christoval. But he made no effort to seize the ford of Huerta, for his own march had been long, the French had passed over nearly twice as much ground, and he thought they could not reach the Tormes that day. When night approached he discovered this error. His second line had indeed got the heights of Vellosa, but his first line was heaped up in low ground near the French army, whose fires, crowning all the opposite hills, showed they commanded the ford of Huerta. Wellington then ordered the bivouac fires to be made with much smoke, under cover of which he filed the troops off with great celerity towards Vellosa; but the Portuguese cavalry, coming in from the front, were mistaken for French and lost some men by cannon-shot ere they were recognised.

Very much disquieted by this day's operations was the English leader. Marmont, perfectly acquainted with the country, had out-flanked and outmarched him, and gained the command of the Tormes, thus securing his junction with the king's army, and enabled to fight or wait for reinforcements, while the scope of the allies' operations would hourly become more restricted. Meanwhile Caffarelli having finally detached eighteen hundred cavalry with guns to aid Marmont, they were coming on, and the king also was taking the field; hence though a victory should be won, unless it was decisive, Wellington's object would not be advanced. That object was to deliver the Penin-sula by a course of solid operations, incompatible with sudden and rash strokes unauthorized by anything but hope; wherefore, yielding to circumstances, he resolved to retreat on Portugal and abide his time; yet with a bitter spirit, nothing soothed by the recollection that he had refused to fight at advantage exactly one month before upon the very hills he now occupied. Nevertheless that steadfast temper which then prevented him from seizing an adventitious chance would not now let him yield to fortune more than she could ravish from him: he still hoped to give the lion's stroke, and resolved to cover Salamanca and the communication with Ciudad Rodrigo to the last moment. The uncertainty of war was now known. This inability to hold his ground was made known to Castanos by a letter, which Marmont intercepted, and immediately decided to push on without waiting for the king, who afterwards announced this accident as a subtle stroke by Wellington to draw on a premature battle !

On the 21st, the allies being on San Christoval, the French threw a garrison into Alba de Tormes, from whence the Spaniards had been withdrawn by Carlos Espana, without the knowledge of the English general. Marmont then passed the Tormes by the fords, between Alba and Huerta, and moving up the valley of the Machechuco encamped at the outer edge of a forest. Wellington also passed the Tormes in the evening by the bridge of Salamanca and the fords of Santa Marta and Aldea Lengua; but the third

division and D'Urban's cavalry remaining on the right bank, intrenched themselves, lest the French, who had left a division on the
heights of Babila Fuente, should recross the Tormes in the night and
overwhelm them.

When the light division descended the rough side of the Aldea
Lengua mountain to cross the river night had come down suddenly,
and with more than common darkness, for a storm, that usual
precursor of a battle in the Peninsula, was at hand. Torrents of rain
deepened the ford, the water foamed and dashed with increasing
violence, the thunder was frequent and deafening, and the lightning
passed in sheets of fire close over the column, playing upon the points
of the bayonets. One flash falling amongst the cavalry near Santa
Marta killed many men and horses, while hundreds of frightened
animals, breaking loose and galloping wildly about, were supposed
to be the enemy charging in the darkness, and some of their patrols
were indeed at hand, hovering like birds of prey: but nothing could
disturb the beautiful order in which the serene veterans of the light
division were seen by the fiery gleams to pass the foaming river,
pursuing their march amidst this astounding turmoil, alike regardless
of the storm and the enemy.

The position now taken was nearly the same as that occupied by
General Graham a month before, when the forts of Salamanca were
invested. The left wing rested in low ground on the Tormes, having
a cavalry post in front. The right wing was extended on a range of
heights, which ended also in low ground, near the village of Arapiles:
this line, perpendicular to the Tormes from Euerta to Salamanca, was
parallel to it from Alba to Euerta, and covered Salamanca. Meanwhile
the enemy, extending his left along the edge of the forest, menaced the
line of communication with Rodrigo and in the night advice came that
General Chauvel, bringing up Caffarelli's horsemen and twenty
guns, had reached Pollos the 20th, and would join Marmont the 22nd
or 23rd. Hence Wellington, feeling he must now retreat to Rodrigo,
and fearing the French cavalry thus reinforced would hamper his
movements, determined, unless they attacked him or committed
some flagrant fault, to retire before Chauvel's horsemen could arrive.

At daybreak on the 22nd, Marmont called the troops at

Babila Fuente over the Tormes, brought Bonet's and Maucune's divisions out of the forest, and took possession of the ridge of Calvariza Ariba; he also occupied in advance of it on his right, a wooded height on which was an old chapel called Nuestra Senora de la Pena. But at a little distance from his left and from the English right, stood a pair of solitary hills, called indifferently the *Arapiles* or the *Hermanitos*. Steep and savagely rugged, about half cannon-shot from each other, their possession would have enabled Marmont to cross Wellington's right, and force a battle with every advantage. Nevertheless they were neglected by the English at first until Colonel Waters, having observed an enemy's detachment stealing towards them, informed Beresford, who thought it of no consequence, but Waters then rode to Wellington who immediately sent troops to seize them. A combat similar to that which happened between Caesar and Afranius at Lerida now ensued; for the French, seeing this detachment, broke their own ranks and running to the encounter gained the first Arapiles and kept it, yet were repulsed in an endeavour to seize the second. This skirmish was followed by one at Nuestra Senora de la Pena, half of which was gained, the enemy keeping the other half: Victor Alten, aiding the attack with a squadron of German hussars, was there wounded by a musket-shot.

The loss of the distant Arapiles rendered a retreat difficult to the allies during daylight; for though the one gained was a fortress in the way of the French army, Marmont, by extending his left and gathering a force behind his own rock, could frame a dangerous battle during the movement. Wellington therefore extended his troops on the right of his own Hermanito, placing the light companies of the Guards at the village of Arapiles in low ground, and the fourth division, with exception of the 27th Regiment, on a gentle ridge behind them. The fifth and sixth divisions he gathered in one mass upon the internal slope of the English Hermanito, where the ground being hollow, hid them from the enemy.During these movements a sharp cannonade was exchanged from the tops of those frowning hills, on whose crowning rocks the two generals sat like ravenous vultures watching for their quarry.

Marmont's project was not yet developed. His troops

from Babila Fuente were still in the forest some miles off, and he had only two divisions close up. The occupation of Calvariza Ariba and Nuestra Senora de la Pena might be therefore only a daring defensive measure to cover the formation of his army; but the occupation of the Hermanito was a start forward for an advantage to be afterwards turned to profit, and seemed to fix the operations on the left of the Tormes. In this doubt Wellington brought up the first and light divisions to confront the French on Calvariza Ariba, and calling the third division and D'Urban's cavalry over the river, posted them in a wood near Aldea Tejada, entirely refused to the enemy and unseen by him, yet securing the main road to Rodrigo. Thus the position was suddenly reversed. The left now rested on the English Hermanito, the right on Aldea Tejada; that which was the rear became the front, the interval between the third and fourth divisions being occupied by Bradford's Portuguese infantry, a Spanish division, and the British cavalry.

Breaks and hollows so screened the men that few could be seen by the French, and those seemed pointing to the Rodrigo road in retreat; moreover, the commissariat and baggage had been ordered to the rear and the dust of their march was seen many miles off: nothing indicated an approaching battle. Such a state of affairs could not last long. At twelve o'clock Marmont, thinking the important bearing of his Hermanito on Wellington's retreat would induce the latter to drive him thence, brought up Foy's and Ferey's divisions in support, placing the first, with some guns, on a wooded height between the Hermanito and Nuestra Senora de la Pena; the second, with Boyer's dragoons, on a ridge behind Foy. Nor was this ill-timed, for Wellington, thinking he could not insure a safe retreat in daylight, was going to attack, but on the approach of these troops gave counter-orders lest he should bring on a general battle disadvantageously.

The French from Babila Fuente had not then reached the edge of the forest, yet Marmont resolved to fight, and fearing the allies would retreat before his own dispositions were completed, ordered Thomieres' division, covered by fifty guns and supported by the light cavalry, to make a flank movement by its left and-menace the Rodrigo road.

Then hastening the march of his other divisions, he watched when Wellington should move in opposition to Thomieres, designing to fall upon him by the village with six divisions of infantry and Boyer's dragoons, which he now ordered to take fresh ground on the left of the Hermanito rock, leaving only one regiment of cavalry with Foy.

In these new circumstances the two armies embraced an oval basin, formed by different ranges of hills that rose like an a amphitheatre, the Arapiles rocks appearing like the doorposts. Around this basin, which was more than a mile from north to south and more than two miles from east to west, the hostile forces were grouped. The northern and western half formed the allies' position; the eastern heights were held by the French right; their left, consisting of Thomieres' division, the artillery and light cavalry, moved along the southern side of the basin, but with a wide loose march; for there was a long space between Thomieres' division and those in the forest destined to form the centre; a longer space between him and the divisions about the French Hermanito. The artillery, fifty guns, massed on Thomieres' right flank, opened its fire grandly, taking ground to the left by guns in succession as the infantry moved on; and these last marched eagerly, continually contracting their distance from the allies and bringing up their left shoulders as if to envelope Wellington's position and embrace it with fire. At this time also, Bonet's troops, one regiment of which held the French Arapiles, carried the village of that name, and although soon driven from the greatest part of it again maintained a fierce struggle.

Marmont's first arrangements had occupied several hours, but as they gave no positive indication of his designs, Wellington, ceasing to watch them, had retired from his Hermanito; but when he was told the French left was in motion pointing towards the Ciudad Rodrigo road, he returned to the rock and observed their movements for some time with a stern contentment. Their left wing was entirely separated from the centre, the fault was flagrant, and he fixed it with the stroke of a thunderbolt. A few orders issued from his lips like the incantations of a wizard, and suddenly the dark mass of troops which covered the English Hermanito, as if possessed by some mighty spirit, rushed violently down the interior slope of the mountain and entered the great basin, amidst a storm of bullets which seemed to shear away the whole surface of the earth over which they moved. The fifth division instantly formed on the right of the fourth, connecting the latter with Bradford's Portuguese, who hastened forward at the same time from the right of the army, and then the heavy cavalry, galloping up on the right of Bradford, closed this front of battle. The sixth and seventh divisions, flanked on the right by Anson's light cavalry, were ranged at half cannon shot on a second line, which was prolonged by the Spaniards in the direction of the third division; and this last, reinforced by two squadrons of the 14th Dragoons, and D'Urban's Portuguese horsemen, formed the extreme right of the army. Behind all, on the highest ground, the first and light divisions and Pack's Portuguese were disposed in heavy masses as a reserve.

When this grand disposition was completed, the third division and its attendant horsemen, formed in four columns and flanked on the left by twelve guns, received orders to cross Thomieres' line of march. The remainder of the first line, including the main body of the cavalry, was to advance when the attack of the third division should be developed; and as the fourth division must in this forward movement necessarily lend its flank to the enemy's troops stationed on the French Hermanito, Pack was to assail that rock the moment the left of the British line passed it. Thus, after long coiling and winding, the armies came together, and drawing up their huge trains like angry serpents mingled in deadly strife.

BATTLE OF SALAMANCA

Marmont from his Hermanito saw the country beneath him suddenly covered with enemies at a moment when he was in the act of making a complicated evolution, and when, by the rash advance of his left, his troops were separated into three parts too dispersed to assist each other, those nearest the enemy being neither strong enough to hold their ground nor aware of what they had to encounter. The third division was however still hidden by the western heights, and he hoped the tempest of bullets in the basin beneath would check the British line until he could bring up his other divisions and by the village of Arapiles fall on what was now the left of the allies' position. But even this his only resource for saving the battle was weak, for there were in reserve the first and light divisions and Pack's Portuguese, in all twelve thousand troops, with thirty pieces of artillery; the village was also well disputed, and the English rock stood out as a strong bastion of defence. However, nothing daunted, Marmont despatched officer after officer, some to hasten the troops from the forest, others to stop the progress of his left wing; and with a sanguine expectation he still. looked for victory, until Pakenham shot with the third division like a meteor across Thomieres' path; then pride and hope alike died within him, and desperately he was hurrying in person to that fatal point, when an exploding shell stretched him on the earth with a broken arm and two deep wounds in his side. Confusion ensued, and the troops, distracted by ill-judged orders and counter-orders, knew not where to move, whom to fight, or whom to avoid.

It was five o'clock when Pakenham fell upon Thomieres; and it was at a moment when that general, whose column had gained an open isolated hill, expected to see the allies in. full retreat towards the Rodrigo road, closely followed by Marmont from the Arapiles. The counter-stroke was terrible ! Two batteries of artillery, placed on the summit of the western heights, suddenly took his troops in flank, Pakenham's massive columns, supported by cavalry, were in his front, and two-thirds of his own division, lengthened out and unconnected, were still in a wood, where they could hear but could not see the storm now bursting; from the chief to the lowest soldier all felt they were lost, and in an instant Pakenham, the most frank and gallant of men, commenced the battle.

As the British masses came on, forming lines while in march, the French gunners, standing up manfully, sent out showers of grape, and a crowd of light troops poured in a fire of musketry, under cover of which the main body endeavoured to display a front. But bearing onwards through the skirmishers with the might of a giant Pakenham broke the half-formed lines into fragments, and sent the whole in confusion upon the advancing supports; one only officer remained by the artillery; standing alone he fired the last gun at the distance of a few yards, but whether he lived or there died could not be seen for the smoke. Some squadrons of light cavalry fell on the right of the third division; the 5th Regiment repulsed them, and then D'Urban's Portuguese horsemen, reinforced by two squadrons of the 14th Dragoons under Felton Harvey, gained the enemy's flank, while the Oporto regiment, led by the English Major Watson, charged his infantry, but Watson fell deeply wounded and his men retired.

Pakenham continued his tempestuous course against the remainder of Thomieres' troops, which were now arrayed on the wooded heights behind the first hill, yet imperfectly and offering two fronts; the one opposed to the third division and its attendant horsemen, the other to the fifth division, Bradford's brigade, and the main body of cavalry and artillery, all of which were now moving in one great line across the basin. Mean while Bonet, repulsed from the village of Arapiles, was sharply engaged outside with the fourth division, Maucune kept a menacing position behind the French Hermanito, Clausel's division came up from the forest, and the connection of the centre and left was in some measure restored: two divisions were however yet in the rear, and Boyer's dragoons were still in march. Thomieres had been killed, Bonet succeeding Marmont was disabled, hence more confusion; but the command then devolved on Clausel, and he was of a capacity to sustain this terrible crisis, which may be thus described. The fourth and fifth divisions and Bradford's brigade, hotly engaged, were steadily gaining ground on the English left; the heavy cavalry, Anson's light dragoons, and Bull's troop of artillery were next in line, advancing at a trot on Pakenham's left, and on that general's right D'Urban's horsemen overlapped the enemy. Thus in less than half an hour, and before an order of battle had even been formed by the French, their commander-in-chief and two other generals had fallen, and the left of their army was turned, thrown into confusion and enveloped.

Clausel's division had now joined Thomieres', and a new front had been spread on the southern heights, yet loosely and unfit to resist; for the troops were. some in double lines, some in columns, some in squares, a powerful sun struck on their eyes, and the light soil, stirred up and driven forward by a breeze, which arose in the west at the moment of the attack, came mingled with smoke full upon them in such stifling volumes, that scarcely able to breathe and quite unable to see their fire was given at random. In this situation, while Pakenham, bearing onward with conquering violence was closing on their flank, and the fifth division advancing with a storm of fire on their front, the interval between the two attacks was suddenly filled with a whirling cloud of dust, moving swiftly forward and carrying within its womb the trampling sound of a charging multitude. As it passed the left of the third division, Le Marchant's heavy horsemen, flanked by Anson's light cavalry, broke out at full speed, and the next instant twelve hundred French infantry, formed in several lines, were trampled down with a terrible clangour and tumult. Bewildered and blinded they cast away their arms and run through the openings of the British squadrons, stooping and demanding quarter, while the dragoons, big men on big horses, rode onward, smiting with their long glittering swords in uncontrollable power, and the third division, following at speed, shouted as the French masses fell in succession before this dreadful charge.

Nor were these valiant swordsmen yet exhausted. Le Marchant and many officers had fallen, but Cotton and all his staff were still at their head, and with ranks confused and blended in one mass, still galloping forward, they sustained from a fresh column an irregular stream of fire which emptied a hundred saddles; yet with fine courage and downright force, the survivors broke through this the third and strongest body of men that had encountered them, and Lord Edward Somerset, continuing his course at the head of one squadron with a happy perseverance, captured five guns. The French left was thus entirely broken, more than two thousand prisoners were taken, their light horsemen abandoned that part of the field, and Thomieres' division no longer existed as a military body. Anson's cavalry, which had passed quite over the hill and had suffered little in the charge, was now joined by D'Urban's troopers and took the place of Le Marchant's exhausted men; the heavy German dragoons followed in reserve, forming with the third and fifth divisions and the guns one formidable line, two miles in advance of where Pakenham had first attacked: and that impetuous officer with unmitigated strength still pressed forward spreading terror and disorder on the enemy's left.

But while these signal events, which occupied about forty minutes, were passing on the allies' right, a terrible battle raged in the centre. For when the first shock of the third division had been observed, the fourth division, moving in a line with the fifth, had passed the village of Arapiles under a prodigious cannonade, and vigorously driving Bonet's troops step by step to the southern and eastern heights, had compelled them to mingle with the broken remains of Clausel's and Thomieres' divisions. This combat having opened the French Hermanito about the time of the cavalry charge, enabled Pack's Portuguese to assail that rock, and the front of battle was thus completely defined, for Foy's division was then exchanging a distant cannonade with the first and light divisions. However Bonet's troops, notwithstanding Marmont's fall and the loss of their own general, fought strongly, and Clausel made a surprisingly vigorous effort and beyond all men's expectations to restore the battle. Soon a great change was visible. Ferey's division, drawn off from the height of Calvaraza, arrived in the centre behind Bonet's men; the light cavalry, Boyer's dragoons, and two divisions of infantry from the forest, were also united there; and on this mass of fresh men Clausel rallied the remnants of his own and Thomieres' division. Thus Sarrut's, Brennier's and Ferey's unbroken divisions, supported by all the cavalry, were suddenly massed to cover the line of retreat on Alba do Tormes, while Maucune still held the French Hermanito, having Foy on his right.

But Clausel, not content with having thus got the army together in a condition to effect a retreat, attempted to turn the tide of victory, founding hope on a misfortune which had befallen Pack. For that officer, ascending the French Hermanito in one heavy column, was within thirty yards of the summit, believing himself victorious, when the enemy leaped suddenly forward from the rocks upon his front and upon his left flank; the hostile masses closed, there was a thick cloud of smoke, a shout, a stream of fire, and the side of the hill was covered with the dead, the wounded and flying Portuguese. They were unjustly scoffed at for this failure, no troops could have withstood that crash upon such steep ground, and the propriety of attacking the hill at all seems questionable. The result went nigh to shake the whole battle. For the fourth division had just then reached the southern ridge of the basin, and one regiment had actually gained the summit when twelve hundred French, arrayed on the reverse slope, charged up hill when the British were quite breathless and disordered by the previous fighting; the French came up resolutely and without a shot won the crest, and even pursued down the other side until two supporting regiments below checked them.

This counter-blow took place at the moment of Pack's defeat, and then Maucune, no longer in pain for the Hermanito, menaced the left flank and rear of the fourth division with skirmishers, until a wing of the 40th Regiment, wheeling about with a rough charge, cleared the rear. Maucune would not engage more deeply at that time, yet Ferey's troops pressed vigorously against the front of the fourth division, and Brennier did the same by the first line of the fifth division; Boyer's dragoons also came on rapidly, and the allies outflanked and over-matched lost ground. Fiercely and fast the French followed, and the fight once more raged in the basin below. General Cole had before this fallen deeply wounded, Leith had the same fortune, but Beresford promptly drew Spry's Portuguese brigade from the second line of the fifth division, and thus flanked the advancing columns of the enemy: yet he also fell desperately wounded, and Boyer's dragoons came freely into action, because Anson's cavalry had been checked, after Le Marchant's charge, by a heavy fire of artillery.

Now the crisis of battle arrived, victory was for the general who had the strongest reserves in hand, and Wellington, seen that day at every point where and when his presence was most required, brought up the sixth division, and turned the scale by a charge, rough, strong, and successful. Nevertheless the struggle was no slight one. Hulse's brigade, which was on the left, went down by hundreds, and the 61st and 11th Regiments won their way desperately and through such a fire as British soldiers only can sustain. Some of Boyer's dragoons also, breaking in between the fifth and sixth divisions, slew many men and caused some disorder in the 53rd; yet that brave regiment lost no ground, nor did Clausel's impetuous counter-attack avail at any point, after the first burst, against the steady courage of the allies. The southern ridge was thus regained, the French generals Menne and Ferey were wounded, the first severely, the second mortally; Clausel himself was hurt, Boyer's reserve of dragoons, coming on at a canter, were met and broken by the fire of Hulse's noble brigade, and the current of the fight once more set for the British. The third division continued to outflank the enemy's left, Maucune abandoned the Hermanito, Foy retired from Calvariza, and the allied host, righting itself as a gallant ship after a sudden gust, again bore onwards in blood and gloom: for though the air, purified by the storm of the night before, was peculiarly clear, one vast cloud of smoke and dust rolled along the basin, and within it was the battle with all its sights and sounds of terror.

When Wellington had thus restored the fight in the centre, he directed the first division to push between Foy and the rest of the French army, which would have rendered it impossible for the latter to rally or escape; but this order was not executed, and Foy's and Maucune's divisions were skilfully used by Clausel to protect his retreat. Foy, posted on undulating ground and flanked by dragoons, covered the roads to the fords of Huerta and Encina; Maucune, reinforced with fifteen guns, was on a steep ridge in front of the forest, covering the road to Alba de Tormes; and behind this ridge, the rest of the army, then falling back in disorder before the third, fifth and sixth divisions, took refuge. Wellington immediately sent the light division in two lines, flanked by dragoons, against Foy, and supported them with the first division in columns, flanked on the right by two brigades of the fourth division, which he drew from the centre when the sixth division had restored the fight. The seventh division and the Spaniards followed in reserve, the country was covered with troops, and a new army seemed to have arisen out of the earth.

Foy, throwing out a cloud of skirmishers, retired by wings, firing heavily from every rise of ground upon the light division, which returned no shot, save by its skirmishers; for three miles this march was under his musketry, occasionally thickened by a cannonade, but the French aim was baffled by the twilight and rapid gliding of the lines. Meanwhile the French general Desgraviers was killed, the flanking brigades from the fourth division penetrated between Maucune and Foy, and it seemed difficult for the latter to extricate his troops. Yet he did so thus. Augmenting his skirmishers on the last defensible ridge, along the foot of which run a marshy stream, he redoubled his musketry and made a menacing demonstration with his horsemen just as the darkness fell; the British guns immediately opened, a squadron of dragoons galloped forwards from the left, the infantry impetuously hastened to the summit of the hill, and a rough shock seemed at hand, but there was no longer an enemy: the main body had gone into the forest on their left during the firing, and the skirmishers fled swiftly after covered by the smoke and coming night.

Maucune was now maintaining a noble battle. He was outflanked and outnumbered, yet the safety of the French army depended on his courage, he knew it, and Pakenham, marking his bold demeanour, advised Clinton, who was immediately in his front, not to assail him until the third division should have turned his left. Nevertheless Clinton plunged his troops into action under great disadvantage; for after remaining some time unnecessarily under Maucune's batteries, which ploughed heavily through their ranks, they were suddenly directed to attack the hill, and aided by a brigade of the fourth division they rushed up; but in the darkness of the night the fire showed from afar how the battle went. On the English side a sheet of flame was seen, sometimes advancing with an even front, sometimes pricking forth in spear-heads, now falling back in waving lines, anon darting upwards in one vast pyramid, the apex of which often approached yet never gained the actual summit of the mountain; but the French musketry, rapid as lightning, sparkled along the brow of the height with unvarying fulness and with what destructive effects the dark gaps and changing shapes of the adverse fire showed too plainly: meanwhile Pakenham turned the left, Foy glided into the forest, and Maucune's task being then completed, the effulgent crest of the ridge became black and silent and the whole French army vanished as it were in the darkness.

During this fight Wellington in person made the light division advance towards the ford of Huerta, having the forest on his right; for he thought the Spanish garrison was still in the castle of Alba, and that the enemy must be found at the fords. For this final stroke he had strengthened his left wing; nor was he diverted from it by Foy's retreat into the forest, because it pointed towards the fords of Encina and Gonzalo, where the right wing of the allies would find him; moreover a squadron of French dragoons, busting from the forest soon after dark and firing their pistols, had passed at full gallop across the front of the 43rd Regiment towards the ford of Huerta, indicating great confusion in the defeated army, and confirming Wellington's notion as to the direction: yet the troops were then marching through standing corn, where no enemy could have preceded them!

Had the castle of Alba been held the French could not have carried off a third of their army; nor would they have been in much better plight if Carlos Espana, who soon discovered his error in withdrawing the garrison, had informed Wellington of the fact; but he suppressed it and suffered the colonel who had only obeyed his orders to be censured. The left wing therefore reached the fords without meeting any enemy, and, the night being far spent, was there halted. The right wing, exhausted by long fighting, halted after the action with Maucune, and thus the French gained Alba unmolested; yet the action did not terminate without two remarkable accidents. While riding close behind the 43rd Regiment, Wellington was struck in the thigh by a spent ball which passed through his holster; and in the night Sir Stapleton Cotton, who had gone to the ford of Huerta, was, in returning, shot through the arm by a Portuguese sentinel whose challenge he disregarded. These were the last events of this famous battle in which the English general, to use a French officer's expression, *defeated forty thousand men in forty minutes!* Yet he fought it as if his genius disdained such trial of its strength. Late in the evening of that great day I saw him behind my regiment, then marching towards the ford. He was alone, the flush of victory was on his brow, his eyes were eager and watchful, but his voice was calm and even gentle. More than the rival of Marlborough, for he had defeated greater generals than Marlborough ever encountered, he seemed with prescient pride only to accept the victory as an earnest of greater glory.

COMBAT OF LA SERNA.

During the few hours of darkness succeeding the battle of Salamanca, Clausel with a wonderful diligence passed the Tormes at Alba; but Wellington also crossed that river with his left wing at daylight, and moving up stream overtook the French on the Almar rivulet, near the village of La Serna, and launched his cavalry against them. Their squadrons fled from Anson's troopers, abandoning three battalions of infantry, who in separate columns were making up a hollow slope, hoping to gain the crest of some heights before the pursuing cavalry could fall on, and the two foremost did reach the higher ground and there formed squares; the last, when half-way up, seeing Bock's heavy German dragoons galloping hard on, faced about and commenced a disorderly fire, and the squares above also plied their muskets on the Germans, who, after crossing the Almar, had to pass a turn of narrow road and clear rough ground before opening a charging front. They dropped fast under the fire. By twos, by threes, by tens, by twenties they fell, yet the mass, surmounting the difficulties of the ground, hurtled on the column and went clean through it: then the squares above retreated and several hundred prisoners were made by those able and daring horsemen.

  This charge was successful even to wonder, and the victors standing in the midst of captives and admiring friends seemed invincible; yet those who witnessed the scene, nay the actors themselves remained with the conviction of the military truth,—that cavalry are not able to cope with veteran infantry, save by surprise. The hill of La Serna offered a frightful spectacle of the power of the musket. The track of the Germans was marked by their huge bodies. A few minutes only had the combat lasted, and above a hundred had fallen—fifty-one were killed outright. In several places man and horse had died simultaneously, and so suddenly, that falling together on their sides they appeared still alive, the horse's legs stretched out as in movement, the rider's feet in the stirrups, the bridle in hand, the sword raised to strike, and the large hat fastened under the chin, giving to the grim yet undistorted countenance a supernatural and terrible expression.

When the French found their rear-guard attacked they turned to its succour, but seeing the light division coming up recommenced the retreat, and were soon joined by Caffarelli's horsemen and guns, under General Chauvel: too late they joined for the battle, yet covered the retreat with a resolution that deterred the allied cavalry from meddling with them. Clausel then carried his army off with such celerity that his head-quarters were that nitght forty miles from the field of battle.

King Joseph was at this time at Blasco Sancho, one short march from the beaten army: he came to aid Marmont with fourteen thousand men, and so early as the 24th could easily have effected a junction, but he then knew only of Marmont's advance from the Duero, not of his defeat. Next day he received, from that marshal and Clausel, letters describing the battle and saying the army must go over the Duero to establish new communications with the Army of the North. A junction with them was still possible, but the king retreated in haste, leaving behind two officers and twenty seven horsemen, who were next day attacked and captured by seven troopers of the 14th Dragoons led by Corporal Hanley,* a noble soldier, thus described by an officer under whom he had many times charged. " A finer fellow never rode into the field. His feats, besides the one at Blasco Sancho, were extraordinary. He was a very handsome man, rode magnificently, and had altogether such a noble bearing before the enemy as is not often seen."

Clausel marched upon Valladolid, abandoning the garrisons of Toro, Tordesillas and Zamora, and, being still pressed by the British, went up the Arlazan river. Then the king passed over the Guadarama mountains to Madrid and Wellington entered Valladolid, where he found large stores, seventeen pieces of artillery, and eight hundred sick and wounded men. This terminated the Salamanca operations, which present the following remarkable results. On the

*Now Serjeant-major at the Tower.

18th of July Marmont's army, forty-two thousand sabres and bayonets with seventy-four guns, passed the Duero to attack the allies. On the 30th it repassed that river in retreat, having in those twelve days marched two hundred miles, fought three combats, and a general battle, in which one marshal of France, seven generals, and twelve thousand five hundred men and inferior officers were killed, wounded or taken, together with two eagles, several standards and twelve guns, exclusive of those found at Valladolid. In the same period the allies, who had forty-six thousand sabres and bayonets, with sixty guns, the excess of men being Spanish, marched one hundred and sixty miles, and had one marshal, Beresford, four generals and six thousand men and officers killed or wounded.

BOOK VIII.

Madrid—Siege of Burgos—Retreat from Burgos—Combat of Venta de
Pozo—Combat on the Carion—Retreat from Madrid—Alba de Tormes—
Combat of the Huebra.

MADRID.

Wellington, having entirely separated the king's army from Marmont's, had to choose between pursuing the latter and besieging
Burgos, or marching on Madrid. He adopted the last, and crossing the
Guadarama mountains descended on the Spanish capital, leaving
General Clinton with twelve thousand men to watch Clausel and co-
operate with Spaniards from Gallicia. Joseph had good troops, and
being unwilling to fly before a detachment occupied the Escurial,
placing detachments on all the roads. In this state D'Urban's Portuguese cavalry drove back Trielhard's outposts and entered Majadahonda. Some German infantry, Bock's heavy cavalry, and a troop of
horse-artillery then entered Las Rozas, a mile in D'Urban's rear; but
in the evening, Trielhard, reinforced by Schiazzetti's Italian dragoons and the lancers of Berg, returned; D'Urban called up the horse
artillery and would have charged, but his Portuguese fled, and three
of the guns being overturned on rough ground were taken. The victorious cavalry passed through Majadahonda in pursuit, and though
the German dragoons, albeit surprised in quarters, stopped the
leading French squadrons, yet, when Schiazzetti's horse came up, the
fight would have ended badly if Ponsonby's cavalry and the seventh
division had not arrived. Trielhard then retired, carrying away captive, the Portuguese general, Visconde de Barbacena, the colonel of
the German cavalry, and others of less rank. The whole loss war
above two hundred, and the German dead lay very thickly in the
streets; many were stretched in their shirts and trousers across the sills
of the doors, thus manifesting the suddenness of the action and their
own bravery.

After this combat the king crossed the Tagus with his court, but in the most horrible confusion, for his army, composed of Spaniards, French and Italians, began to plunder the convoy. Marshal Jourdan threw himself into the midst of the disorderly troops, and being aided by other generals, with great personal risk arrested the mischief, and succeeded in making the multitude file over the bridge of Aranjuez; yet the procession was lugubrious and shocking; crowds of weeping women and children and despairing men, courtiers of the highest rank, desperately struggling with savage soldiers for the animals on which they were endeavouring to save their families. Lord Wellington did not molest them. Ignorant of their situation, or more probably, compassionating their misery and knowing the troops could escape over the Tagus, he would not strike. Perhaps also he thought it wise to leave Joseph with the burthen of a court.

The king, expecting to find a strong reinforcement from Soult at Toledo, was inclined to march towards the Morena; instead of troops he found a positive refusal, and a plan for uniting his own and Suchet's army to Soult's in Andalusia. From thence all were to menace Lisbon, but this was too vast for the king's genius, and his personal anger at being denied the troops, overcoming prudence, he directed his march on Valencia, peremptorily commanding Soult to aban. don Andalusia and join him there. Meanwhile Wellington entered Madrid and was met by the whole population—not with feigned enthusiasm to a conqueror, for there was no tumultuous exultation, famine was amongst them and misery had subdued their spirit: but with tears and every sign of deep emotion they crowded around his horse, hung by his stirrups, touched his clothes, and throwing themselves on their knees blessed him aloud !

Madrid was still vexed by the presence of an enemy in the Retiro, which was garrisoned with two thousand good soldiers besides convalescents, and contained enormous stores, twenty thousand stand of arms, one hundred and eighty pieces of artillery, and the eagles of two French regiments. The works however were bad, and the French yielding on terms were sent to Portugal, but on the way were basely robbed and many murdered by the escort: an infamous action perpetrated by Spaniards, far from Madrid.

It was strange to see French generals, used to war, thus. giving up armies as it were to their enemies; for including the garrisons of Toro, Tordesillas, Astorga and Zamora, all of which might have been saved but were not, and this of the Retiro, which should not have been left, six thousand good soldiers were absolutely given as a present to swell the loss of Salamanca.

Some time Wellington remained in Madrid, apparently occupied with balls and bull-fights, yet really watching events to decide whether he should operate in the north or south. The hour of action came at last. Soult abandoned Andalusia, and the 29th of August his rear-guard lost two hundred men in Seville, where it was attacked by Colonel Skerrett and some Spaniards from Cadiz; the former then joined Hill, who after a series of operations against Drouet, in one of which he defeated the French cavalry, now came to La Mancha. The south of Spain was for the enemy then a scene of confusion which gave Wellington time for action in the north, where his presence war. absolutely required; for Clausel had re-occupied Valladolid with a renovated force of twenty-two thousand men and fifty guns, Clinton had made some serious errors, and the Spanish generals had as usual failed on all points.

Leaving Hill a powerful force to co-operate with all the southern Spanish armies beyond the Tagus, Lord Wellington quitted Madrid the 1st of September, and at Arevalo concentrated twenty-one thousand men, three thousand being cavalry; yet the Portuguese soldiers were ill equipped, and could scarcely be fed, because of the continued misconduct of their government.

On the 6th he passed the Duero to fight Clausel, and called on Castanos to join him with the Gallicians; but seldom did a Spanish general deviate into activity; Castanos delayed and Clausel retreated slowly up the beautiful valleys of the Pisuerga and Arlanzan, which, in denial of the stories about French devastation, were carefully cultivated and filled to repletion with corn, wine and oil. Nor were they deficient in military strength. Off the high road ditches and rivulets impeded the troops, while cross-ridges continually furnished strong positions, flanked with lofty hills on either side, by means of which Clausel baffled his adversary in a surprising manner. Each day he offered battle, yet on ground Wellington was unwilling to assail, partly because he momentarily expected the Gallicians; chiefly because of the declining state of his own army from sickness, and that the hope of ulterior operations in the south made him unwilling to lose men. By flank movements he dislodged the enemy, yet each day darkness fell ere they were completed and the morning's sun always saw Clausel again in position. Thus he barred the way at eight places, and finally covered Burgos the 16th, by taking the strong position of Cellada del Camino.

But eleven thousand Spanish infantry, three hundred cavalry, and eight guns, had now joined Wellington, who would have fallen on frankly the 17th, if Clausel, alike wary and skilful, had not observed the increased numbers and retired in the night to Frandovinez; he was however next day pushed sharply back to the heights of Burgos, and the following night passed through that town leaving behind large stores of grain. Caffarelli, who had come down to place the castle in a state of defence, now joined him and both retreated upon Briviesca.

The allies entered Burgos amidst great confusion. The garrison of the castle had set fire to some houses impeding the defence, the conflagration spread, and the Partidas, gathering like wolves round a carcass, entered the town for mischief Mr. Sydenham, an eye-witness not unused to scenes of war, thus described their proceedings: " What with the flames and plundering of the guerillas, who are as bad as Tartars and Cossacks of the Kischack or Zagatay hordes, I was afraid Burgos would be entirely destroyed, but order was at length restored by the manful exertions of Don Miguel Alava."

SIEGE OF BURGOS.

Caffarelli had placed eighteen hundred infantry, besides artillery-men, in the castle; and Dubreton, the governor, in courage and skill surpassed even the hopes of his sanguine countrymen. The works inclosed a rugged hill, between which and the river the city of Burgos was situated. An old wall with a new parapet and flanks offered the first line of defence; the second line, within the other, was of earth, a kind of field-retrenchment, but well palisaded; the third line, similarly constructed, contained two elevated points, on one of which was an intrenched building called the White Church, on the other the ancient keep of the castle. This last, the highest point, was intrenched and surmounted with a casemated work called the Napoleon battery, which commanded everything around save on the north. There the hill of San Michael, only three hundred yards distant and scarcely less elevated than the fortress, was defended by a horn-work with a sloping scarp twenty-five, and a counterscarp ten feet high. This work was merely closed by strong palisades, but was under the fire of the Napoleon battery, well flanked by the castle, and covered in front by intrenchments for out picquets. Nine heavy guns, eleven fieldpieces and six mortars or howitzers, were mounted in the fortress; and as the reserve artillery and stores of the Army of Portugal were deposited there the armament could be augmented.

FIRST ASSAULT.

So completely commanded were all the bridges and fords over the Arlanzan by the castle guns, that two days elapsed ere the allies could cross; but on the 19th, the passage being effected above the town, Major Somers Cocks with the 79th, supported by Pack's Portuguese, drove in the French outposts on the hill of San Michael, and in the night, reinforced with the 42nd Regiment, assailed the horn-work. The conflict was murderous. The main storming column was beaten off, and the attack would have failed if Cocks had not forced an entrance by the gorge. The garrison was thus cut off, but the assailants not being closely supported the French broke through them. The troops complained of each other, and the loss was above four hundred, while that of the enemy was less than one hundred and fifty.

The defences of the castle were feeble and incomplete, yet Wellington's means were so scant that he relied more upon the enemy's weakness than his own power. However, it was said water was scarce, and that the provision-magazines might be burned; wherefore twelve thousand men were set to the siege while twenty thousand formed the covering army.

For the attack, the trenches were to be opened on the right of San Michael towards the town, and a battery for five guns established on the right of the captured horn-work. A sap was then to be pushed from the trenches towards the first wall, and from thence the engineer was to proceed by gallery and mine.

When the first mine should be completed, the battery from San Michael was to open against the second line of defence, and the assault given on the first line. Approaches were then to be continued against the second line, and the battery turned against the third line, in front of the White Church, where the defences were exceedingly weak. Meanwhile a trench for musketry was to be dug along the brow of San Michael, and a concealed battery prepared within the horn-work for a final attack on the Napoleon battery; but the artillery consisted of only three eighteen-pounders with five iron twenty-four-pound howitzers: slender means which, rather than the defects of the fortress, governed the line of attack.

When the horn-work fell, a lodgement was commenced in the interior, and continued vigorously under a destructive fire from the Napoleon battery, but good cover was obtained in the night.

On the 21st the garrison mounted several field-guns, and at night fired heavily with grape and shells on the workmen digging the musketry trench. The 22nd this fire was redoubled, yet the besiegers worked with little loss, and their musketeers galled the enemy. In the night the battery was armed with two eighteen-pounders and three howitzers, and the secret battery within the horn-work was commenced; but Wellington, now deviating from his first plan, directed an escalade against the first line. In this view, at midnight four hundred men with ladders were secretly posted in a hollow road, fifty yards from the wall, which was from twenty-three to twenty-five feet high without flanks; and to aid this main column, a Portuguese battalion was assembled in the town of Burgos for a flank attack.

SECOND ASSAULT.

In this assault, although the Portuguese were repelled by the fire of the common guard, the principal party, composed of detachments under Major Lawrie, entered the ditch, yet altogether and confusedly; Lawrie was killed, the soldiers who mounted the ladders were bayoneted, combustible missiles were thrown down in abundance. and the men gave way, leaving half their number behind. The wounded were brought off next day under a truce, and it is said, that on the body of an officer the French found a complete plan of the siege. It was a very disastrous attempt, which delayed the regular progress for two days, increased the enemy's courage and produced a bad effect upon the troops, some of whom were already dispirited by the storm of the horn-work.

The original plan being now resumed, the hollow way from whence the escaladers had advanced, running along the front of defence, was converted into a parallel, and the trench made deep and narrow to secure them from the plunging shot of the castle. Musketeers were also planted to keep down the enemy's fire. But heavy rains incommoded the troops, and the French raised a palisaded work on their own right, which flanked this parallel, and from thence they killed so many of the besiegers' marksmen that the latter were withdrawn.

In the night a flying sap from the right of the parallel was pushed within twenty yards of the first line; but the directing engineer was killed, and with him many men, for the French plied their musketry sharply, and rolled large shells down the steep side of the hill. The head of the sap was indeed so commanded as it approached the wall, that a six feet trench, added to the height of the gabions above, scarcely protected the workmen; wherefore the gallery for a mine was worked as rapidly as the inexperience of the miners would permit.

When the secret battery in the horn-work of San Michael was completed two eighteen-pounders were removed from the first battery to arm it, being replaced by two iron howitzers. The latter were used to drive the French marksmen from their offensive palisaded wall, but after firing one hundred and forty rounds without success the attempt was relinquished; and ammunition was so scarce that the soldiers were paid to collect the enemy's bullets.

A zigzag was now commenced in front of the first battery, down the face of San Michael, to obtain footing for a musketry trench to overlook the enemy's defences below: the workmen were exposed to the whole fire of the castle at the distance of two hundred yards, and were knocked down fast, yet the work went steadily on.

On the 26th the gallery was advanced eighteen feet and the soil found favourable; but the men, in passing the sap, were hit by the French marksmen, and an assistant engineer was killed. In the night the parallel was prolonged on the light to within twenty yards of the ramparts, in the view of driving a second gallery and mine; musketeers were then planted there and at the same time the zigzag was continued, and the musket trench completed with little loss, though the whole fire of the castle was concentrated on the spot.

The 27th the French strengthened their second line, cut a step along the edge of the counterscarp for a covered way, and palisaded the communication. The besiegers finished the musketry trench on the right of their parallel, and opened a gallery for the second mine; but the first mine went on slowly, the men in the sap being galled by stones, grenades, and small shells, which the French threw into the trenches by hand; the artillery fire also knocked over the gabions of the musketry trench on San Michael so fast that the troops were withdrawn during the day.

In the night a trench of communication, forming a second parallel behind the first, was begun and nearly completed from the hill of San Michael, but at day light the French fire was heavy, and the shells which passed over came rolling down the hill again into the trench. The completion of the work was therefore deferred until night, and though the back roll of the shells continued to gall the troops, this, and the other trenches in front of the horn-work, above and on the right of the parallel below, were filled with men whose fire was incessant: the first mine also was completed, and being loaded with a thousand pounds of powder, and the gallery strongly tamped for fifteen feet with bags of clay, another storm was ordered.

THIRD ASSAULT.

At midnight, the hollow road being lined with men to fire on the defences, the storming party, three hundred strong, was assembled there, attended by others who carried tools and materials to secure a lodgement when the breach should be carried. The mine was then exploded, the wall fell, and an officer with twenty men rushed forward to the assault. The effect of the explosion was disappointing, yet it cast the wall down, the enemy was stupefied, and the forlorn hope, a sergeant and four daring soldiers, gained the summit of the breach; soon however the French recovered, and threw them over pierced with bayonet wounds. Meanwhile the officer, with his twenty men, missed the breach in the dark, and finding the wall unbroken returned, saying there was no breach; then the main body regained the trenches, and before the sergeant and his comrades came in with streaming wounds to tell their tale the enemy was reinforced: the scarcity of ammunition would not permit a fire to be directed upon the work during the night, and the French, raising a parapet behind it, placed obstacles on the ascent which deterred the besiegers from renewing the assault at daylight.

Twelve days had now elapsed since the siege commenced, one assault had succeeded, two had failed, twelve hundred men had been killed or wounded, little progress was made, and the troops were dispirited, notably the Portuguese, who seemed to be losing their ancient spirit. Discipline was relaxed, ammunition was wasted, work in the trenches avoided and neglected by officers and men, insubordination was gaining ground, and reproachful orders were issued, the Guards only being noticed as presenting an honourable exception.

The French marksmen in the flanking palisaded work were so expert that everything which could be seen from thence was hit, until the howitzer battery on San Michael was reinforced with a captured French eighteen-pounder, and this mischievous post was at last demolished. At the same time the gallery of the second mine was pushed forward, and a new breaching battery for three guns constructed behind it, so close to the enemy's defences that they screened it from the artillery fire of their upper fortress. To arm this work the three eighteen-pounders were dragged in the night from San Michael, and next day were, under a musketry fire which thinned the workmen, placed in battery; but the watchful Dubreton brought a howitzer down, with which he threw shells into the battery, and making a hole through a flank wall, thrust out a light gun also, which sent its bullets whizzing through the thin parapet of the work at every round. The allies were thus driven from their post, more French cannon were brought from the upper works, and the battery was demolished; two of the gun-carriages were disabled, a trunnion was knocked off one of the guns, and the muzzle of another split: and vainly the marksmen endeavoured to quell this fire, the French eventually remained masters.

In the night a more solid battery was made on the left of the ruined one, but at daylight the French fire, plunging from above, made the parapet fly off so rapidly, that the besiegers relinquished it also, returning to their mines and breaching battery on San Michael. The two guns still serviceable were now remanded to the upper battery, to beat down a retrenchment formed by the French behind the old breach; but the weather was so wet and stormy that the workmen, those of the Guards excepted, abandoned the trenches, and at daylight the guns were still short of their destination. However, on the 2nd of October they were placed, and at four o'clock in the evening, their fire having cleansed the old breach, and the second mine being tamped for explosion, a double assault was ordered. For this operation a battalion of the 24th British Regiment, under Captain Hedderwick, was formed in the hollow way, having one advanced party under Lieut. Holmes near the new mine, and a second under Lieut. Frazer towards the old breach.

FOURTH ASSAULT.

At five o'clock the mine exploded with terrific effect, sending many of the French into the air and breaking down one hundred feet of the wall; the next instant Holmes and his brave men went rushing through the smoke and crumbling ruins; and Frazer, as quick and brave, was already fighting with the defenders on the summit of the old breach. The supports followed closely, and in a few minutes both points were carried with a loss of thirty-seven killed and two hundred wounded, seven being officers,—amongst them the conducting engineer.

During the night lodgements were formed on the ruins of the new breach, imperfectly and under a destructive fire from the upper defences; but the previous happy attack had revived the spirits of the army, vessels with powder were coming coastwise from Coruna, a convoy was expected by land from Rodrigo, and a supply of ammunition, sent by Sir Home Popham, reached the camp from Santander. This promising state of affairs was of short duration. On the evening of the 5th three hundred French came swiftly down the hill, and, sweeping away labourers and guards from the trenches, killed or wounded a hundred and fifty men, got possession of the old breach, destroyed the works and carried off all the tools.

In the night the allies repaired the damage and pushed saps from each flank, to meet in the centre near the second French line and serve as a parallel to check future sallies. Meanwhile the howitzers on San Michael continued their fire, and the breaching battery in the horn-work opened; but the guns, being unable to see the wall sufficiently low soon ceased to speak, and the embrasures were masked. On the other hand the besieged could not, from the steepness of the castle-hill, depress their guns to bear on the lodgement at the breaches in the first line; yet their musketry was murderous, and they rolled down large shells to retard the approaches towards the second line.

On the 7th the besiegers were so close to the wall that the howitzers above could not play without danger to the workmen, and two French field-pieces taken in the horn-work were substituted. The breaching battery on San Michael being amended renewed its fire and at five o'clock had beaten down fifty feet from the parapet of the second line, yet the enemy's return was heavy and another eighteen-pounder lost a trunnion. In the night block-carriages with supports for the broken trunnions were provided, and the disabled guns again fired with low charges; but rain now filled the trenches, the communications were injured, the workmen negligent, the approaches to the second line went on slowly, and again Dubreton came thundering down from the upper ground, driving the guards and workmen from the new parallel at the lodgements, levelling all the works, carrying off all the tools, and killing or wounding two hundred men. Colonel Cocks, promoted for his gallant conduct at the storming of San Michael, restored the fight and repulsed the French, but fell dead on the ground recovered: he was a young man of a modest demeanour, brave, thoughtful and enterprising: he lived and died a good soldier.

After this severe check the approaches to the second line were abandoned, the trenches were extended to embrace the whole of the front attacked, and as the battery on San Michael had now formed a practicable breach twenty-five feet wide the parallel was prolonged towards it, and a trench was opened for marksmen at thirty yards' distance. Nevertheless another assault could not be risked, because the powder was nearly exhausted and the troops, if unsuccessful, would have been without ammunition in front of the French army, then gathering head near Briviesca. Heated shot were however thrown at the White Church to burn the magazines, and the miners were directed to drive a gallery on the other side of the castle against the church of San Roman, a building occupied by the French beyond their line.

On the 10th a supply of ammunition arrived from Santander, but Dubreton had meanwhile strengthened his works, and isolated the new breach on one flank by a stockade, extending at right angles from the second to the third line of defence. The fire from the Napoleon battery then compelled the besiegers again to withdraw their guns within the horn-work, and the attempt to burn the White Church was relinquished, yet the gallery against San Roman was continued.

On the 15th the battery in the horn-work was rearmed against the Napoleon battery, but was silenced in threequarters of an hour. The embrasures were then altered, that the guns might bear on the breach in the second line, and the besiegers worked to repair the mischief done by rain, and to push the gallery under San Roman, where the mine was loaded with nine hundred pounds of powder.

The 17th the battery of the horn-work cleared away the temporary defences at the breach, the howitzers damaged the rampart on each side, and, a small mine being sprung, a cavalier or mound from which the enemy had killed many men in the trenches was taken, yet the French soon recovered that work.

On the 18th the new breach being practicable, the storm was ordered, the explosion of the mine under San Roman to be the signal; that church was also to be assaulted, and between these attacks the works covering the ancient breach were to be escaladed.

FIFTH ASSAULT.

At half-past four o'clock the mine at San Roman exploded, with little injury to the church itself; but the latter was resolutely attacked by some Spanish and Portuguese troops, and though the enemy sprung a countermine which brought the building entirely down the assailants lodged themselves in the ruins. Meanwhile two hundred of the Foot-Guards, with strong supports, pouring through the old breach in the first line escaladed the second, and between that and the third line were strongly met by the French. A like number of Germans under Major Wurmb, similarly supported, simultaneously stormed the new breach, and some men mounting the hill above actually gained the third line. Unhappily at neither point did the supports follow closely, and the Germans, cramped on their left by the enemy's stockade, extended their right towards the Guards; but at that moment Dubreton came dashing like a torrent from the upper ground and in an instant cleared the breaches. Wurmb and many other brave men fell, and the French gathering round the Guards forced them also beyond the outer line. More than two hundred men and officers were killed or wounded in this combat, and next night the enemy recovered San Roman by a sally.

The siege was now virtually terminated, for though the French were beaten out of San Roman again, and a gallery was opened from that church against the second line, these were mere demonstrations. The fate of Burgos was fixed outside. For while the siege was going on, Caffarelli and Clausel had

Clausel had received a reinforcement of twelve thousand men from France, and thus forty-four thousand good troops were prepared to relieve the Castle before October, although they could not act until Souham, appointed to command in chief, had arrived. It was also essential to combine their operations with the king, who had formed a great army to recover Madrid; but all the lines of correspondence were so circuitous and beset by the Partidas that the most speedy and certain communication was through the minister of war at Paris, who found the information he wanted in the English newspapers ! These, while deceiving the British public by accounts of battles never fought, victories never gained, enthusiasm and vigour nowhere existing. with great assiduity enlightened the enemy upon the numbers, situation, movements and reinforcements of the allies.

Souham arrived the 3rd of October with more reinforcements from France, but he imagined that sixty thousand troops were around Burgos, exclusive of the Partidas, and that three divisions were coming up from Madrid; whereas none were coming, and little more than thirty thousand were around Burgos, eleven thousand being Gallicians, scarcely so good as the Partidas. Wellington's real strength was in his Anglo-Portuguese, now only twenty thousand; for besides those killed or wounded at the siege, the sick had gone to the rear faster than the recovered men came up. Some unattached regiments and escorts were near Segovia and other points north of the Guadarama, and a reinforcement of five thousand men had been sent from England in September; but the former belonged to Hill's army, and of the latter the Life-Guards and Blues had gone to Lisbon: hence a regiment of Foot-Guards, and some detachments of the line, in all three thousand, were the only available forces in the rear.

During the first part of the siege, the English general, seeing the French scattered and only reinforced by conscripts, did not fear interruption; the less so, that Sir Home Popham was again menacing the coast line; and now, when they were concentrating, he was willing to fight; for he thought Popham and the guerillas would keep Caffarelli employed, and he was himself a match for Clausel. Souham however, over-rating the allies' force, feared a defeat, as being the only barrier between Wellington and France; and far from meditating an advance dreaded an attack; hence, as want of provisions forbad a concentration of his army permanently near Burgos, he prepared to fight on the Ebro. Soon however, the English newspapers told him Soult was in march from Andalusia— that the king intended to move upon Madrid,— that no English troops had left that capital to join Wellington, that the army of the latter was not numerous, and the castle of Burgos was sorely pressed: then he resolved to raise the siege.

On the 13th a skirmish took place on a stream beyond Monasterio, where Captain Perse of the 16th Dragoons, twice forced from the bridge twice recovered it and maintained his post until F. Ponsonby, who commanded the Cavalry reserves, arrived. Ponsonby and Perse were both wounded, and this demonstration was followed by various others until the evening of the 18th, when the whole French army was united and the advanced guard captured a picquet of Brunswickers. This sudden movement prevented Wellington taking, as he designed, the advanced position of Monasterio, Falling back, therefore, he took ground covering the siege, where, on the 20th, Maucune, advancing with two divisions of infantry and one of cavalry, gained some advantage, yet, having no supports, was finally outflanked and beaten back to Monasterio by two divisions under Sir Edward Paget.

There were now in position, twenty-one thousand Anglo-Portuguese infantry and cavalry, eleven thousand Gallicians, and the guerilla horsemen of Marquinez and Julian Sanchez. Four thousand were troopers, but only two thousand six hundred were British and German, and the Spanish horsemen, regular or irregular, could scarcely be reckoned as combatants. The artillery counted forty-two pieces, including twelve Spanish guns extremely ill equipped and scant of ammunition. The French had nearly five thousand cavalry, and more than sixty guns. Wellington stood therefore at great disadvantage in numbers, composition, and real strength. In his rear was the castle and the river Arlanzan, the fords and bridges of which were commanded by the guns of the fortress: his generals of division, Paget excepted, were not of marked ability, and his troops were somewhat desponding, and deteriorated in discipline. His situation was altogether dangerous. Victory could scarcely be expected, defeat would be destruction, and he had provoked a battle not knowing Caffarelli's troops were united to Souham's.

Souham should have forced an action, because his ground was strong, his retreat open, his army powerful and compact, his soldiers full of confidence, his lieutenants, Clausel, Maucune, and Foy, men of distinguished talents, able to second, and able to succeed him in the chief command: the chances of victory were great, the chances of defeat comparatively small. It was thus he judged the matter himself, for Maucune's advance was designed as the prelude to a great battle, and the English general was then willing to stand the trial. But generals are not absolute masters of events. Extraneous events here governed both sides. The king by the junction of Soult's army was at the head of a great force, and had designed not only to drive Hill from Madrid, but to cut Wellington off from Portugal: hence he had ordered Souham not to fight. Hill at the same time gave notice of the king's advance; and Wellington, fearing to be isolated when Hill was forced from Madrid, raised the siege and resolved to retreat.

Some fighting had meanwhile taken place at Burgos. Dubreton had again got possession of the ruins of San Roman but was driven away next morning; but then, the order to raise the siege being received the guns and stores were removed from the batteries. The greatest part of the draught animals had however gone to fetch powder and artillery from Santander, and the eighteen-pounders could not be carried off. Thus the siege was raised after five assaults, several sallies and thirty-three days of investment, during which the besiegers lost more than two thousand, and the besieged six hundred men killed or wounded; the latter also suffered severely from continual labour, want of water, and bad weather; for the fortress was too small to afford shelter for the garrison, and the greater part had bivouacked between the lines of defence.

RETREAT FROM BURGOS.

It was commenced in the night of the 21st by the following daring enterprise. The army quitted its position after dark, the artillery, the wheels being muffled with straw, passed the bridge of Burgos under the castle guns with such silence and celerity, that Dubreton, watchful and suspicious as he was, knew nothing of the march until the Partidas, failing in nerve, commenced galloping, when he poured a destructive fire down but soon lost the range. By this delicate operation Souham was compelled to follow, instead of using the castle to intercept the line of retreat; for if Wellington had avoided the fortress, the French by passing through it could have forestalled him at Cellada del Camino.

The 23rd the infantry crossed the Pisuerga, but while the main body made this long march, Souham having passed through Burgos in the night of the 22nd, vigorously attacked the rear-guard under Sir Stapleton Cotton, which was composed of cavalry and horse-artillery, two battalions of Germans and the Partidas of Marquinez and Sanchez.

At seven o'clock the picquets were first driven from the bridge of Baniel, and then from the Hormaza stream, after which the whole rear-guard drew up in a large plain behind Cellada del Camino. It had on the left a range of hills occupied by Marquinez, on the right the Arlanzan, and across the middle of the plain a marshy rivulet cut the main road, being only passable by a little bridge near a house called the Venta de Pozo. In front, about half-way between this stream and Cellada, there was a broad ditch with a second bridge and a hamlet. Cotton retired over the marshy stream, but left Anson's horsemen and Halket's infantry as a rear-guard beyond the ditch, and then Anson, placing the 11th Dragoons and the guns in advance at Cellada del Camino on a gentle eminence, likewise prepared to pass the stream.

COMBAT OF VENTA DE POZO.

When the French approached Cellada, two squadrons of the 11th beat back their leading horsemen, and the artillery plied them briskly with shot; yet the main body, advancing at a trot along the road, compelled the whole to retire beyond the bridge of Venta de Pozo. Meanwhile the French general Curto, leading a brigade of hussars and followed by Boyer's dragoons, ascended the hills and drove Marquinez from them towards a ravine at the foot, which could only be passed at particular points; towards one of those the Partida galloped, just as the French on the plain, after a sharp struggle had forced the 11th Dragoons across the ditch between Cellada and Venta de Pozo. The German riflemen were in the hamlet, and the ditch might have been disputed if it had not been thus turned by Curto; but that event compelled Anson to retire on the Venta de Pozo stream. His movement was covered by the 16th Dragoons, and while passing the bridge there, the Partidas, pouring down from the hills, were so closely pursued by the French hussars that the mixed mass hurtled on the flank of the 16th at the moment it was charged in rear by the enemy pursuing in the plain: Colonel Pelley and many men were taken, and the regiment was driven back on the reserves, which however stood fast, and while the French were reforming the whole got over the bridge of Venta de Pozo.

Cotton now formed a new line. Anson was on the left of the road, the German infantry and guns were in support, the heavy German cavalry on the right—the whole presenting an imposing order of battle. But then Caffarelli's cavalry, composed of the lancers of Berg, a regiment of chasseurs, and several squadrons of gens d'armes, all fresh men, entered the line on the French left. At first they tried the stream on a wide front, and finding it impassable wheeled with a quick daring decision to their right, trotting under the heavy pounding of the English artillery over the bridge and forming beyond in opposition to the German cavalry. The latter charged with a rough shock and broke their right, but they had let too many come over, the French left gained an advantage, and their light, full of mettle, rallied; a furious sword combat had place, in which the gens d'armes fought so fiercely that the Germans, maugre their size and courage and the superiority of their horses, were beaten back in disorder. The French followed on the spur with shrill and eager cries, and Anson being outflanked and menaced on both sides retreated also; not happily, for

Boyer's dragoons had now crossed the ravine at the foot of the hills and came thundering in on his left, breaking the ranks and sending all to the rear in a confused mass.

The Germans first extricated themselves and formed a fresh line on which the others rallied, the gens d'armes and lancers who had suffered severely from the artillery as well as in the sword fight having halted; but Boyer's dragoons, ten squadrons, then attacked the new line which was still confused and wavering, and though the German officers rode gallantly to meet the charge their men followed but a short way and finally turned, when the swiftness of the English horses alone prevented a terrible catastrophe.

Some favourable ground enabled the line to reform once more, yet only to be again broken. Meanwhile Wellington in person placed Halket's infantry and the guns in a position to cover the cavalry, and they remained tranquil until the enemy, in full pursuit after the last charge, came galloping down, lending their left flank, when the power of the musket was again manifested. A tempest of bullets emptied the French saddles by scores, and their hitherto victorious horsemen, after three fruitless charges, drew off to the hills, while the British cavalry, covered by the infantry, made good its retreat to the Pisuerga. The loss in this combat was considerable on both sides. The French suffered most, but took a colonel and seventy other prisoners; and before the fight they had captured a commissariat store near Burgos.

While the rear-guard was thus engaged, drunkenness and insubordination, the usual concomitants of an English retreat, were exhibited at Torquemada, where the well-stored winevaults became the prey of the soldiery: twelve thousand men were at one time in a state of helpless inebriety. This was bad, and Wellington having now retreated fifty miles, resolved to check the pursuit. His previous arrangements had been well combined, but the means of transport were scanty, the weather severe, and his convoys of sick and wounded were still on the wrong side of the Duero: wherefore, crossing the Carion river at its confluence with the lower Pisuerga, he turned and halted.

Here he was joined by a regiment of Guards and detachments coming from Coruna, and his ground, extending from Villa

Muriel to Duenas below the meeting of the waters, was strong; for though the upper Pisuerga was parallel to the Carion, the lower part turned suddenly, to flow at a right angle from the confluence. Hence his position, a range of hills, lofty yet descending with an easy sweep, was covered in front by the Carion, and on the right by the lower Pisuerga. A detachment was left to destroy the bridge of Banos on this last river, and a battalion was sent to aid the Spaniards in destroying the bridges high up on the Carion at Palencia. On the immediate front some houses and convents, lying beyond both rivers, furnished posts to cover the destruction of the bridges of Muriel and San Isidro on the Carion, and that of Duenas on the lower Pisuerga.

Souham cannonaded the rear-guard at Torquemada on the 24th, and then passing the upper Pisuerga sent Foy's division against Palencia, but ordered Maucune to pursue the allies to the bridges of Banos, Isidro, and Muriel, halting himself, however, if fame does not lie, because the number of French drunkards were even more numerous than those of the British army.

COMBAT OF THE CARION.

Before the enemy appeared the summits of the hills were crowned, the bridges mined, and that of San Isidro strongly protected by a convent filled with troops. The left of the position was equally strong, but the advantage of a dry canal with high banks, running parallel with the Carion, was overlooked, and the village of Muriel was not occupied in sufficient strength. Foy meanwhile reached Palencia, where, according to some French writers, a treacherous attempt was made, under cover of a parley, to kill him; he however drove the allies with loss from the town, and in such haste that all the bridges were abandoned in a perfect condition, and the French cavalry, spreading abroad, gathered baggage and prisoners.

This untoward event compelled Wellington to throw back his left at Muriel, thus offering two fronts, the one facing Palencia, the other the Carion; in that state Maucune, having dispersed some caçadores defending a ford, fell with a strong body of infantry and guns on the troops at Muriel, just as a mine was exploded and the party covering the bridge were passing the broken arch by means of ladders. The play of the mine checked the advance of the French, but suddenly a horseman, darting at full speed from their column, rode down to the bridge under a flight of bullets from his own people, calling out he was a deserter. When he reached the chasm made by the explosion, he violently checked his foaming horse, held up his hands, exclaimed that he was a lost man, and with hurried accents asked if there was no ford near. The good-natured soldiers pointed to one a little way off, whereupon the gallant fellow looked earnestly for a few moments to fix the exact point, then wheeling sharply round, kissed his hand in derision, and bending low over his saddlebow dashed back to his own comrades, amidst showers of shot and shouts of laughter from both sides. Maucune's column, covered by a concentrated fire of guns, then passed the river at the ford thus discovered, made some prisoners in the village and lined the dry bed of the canal.

At this moment Wellington came up, and turning some guns upon the enemy desired that the village and canal might be retaken; General Oswald said they could not be held afterwards; but Wellington, whose retreat was endangered by the presence of the enemy on that side of the river, peremptorily ordered one brigade to attack the main body and another brigade to clear the canal, strengthening the last with Spanish troops and Brunswickers. A sharp fire of artillery and musketry ensued, and the allies suffered some loss, especially by cannon-shot, which from the other side of the river plumped into the reserves and threw the Spaniards into confusion: they were falling back, when their fiery countryman, Miguel Alava, with exhortation and example, for though wounded he would not retire, urged them forward until the enemy was driven over the river.

During these events other French troops attempted unsuccessfully to seize the bridge of San Isidro; but at that of Banos on the Pisuerga the mine failed, and their cavalry galloping over made both working and covering party prisoners. Wellington's position was thus sapped. For Souham could concentrate on the allies' left by Palencia and force them to fight with their back upon the lower Pisuerga; or he could pass that river on his own left and forestall them on the

Duero at Tudela. If the allies pushed over the Pisuerga by the bridge of Duenas, Souham, having the initial movement, might be first on the ground while Foy fell on their rear. If Wellington sought by a rapid movement down the right of the Pisuerga to cross at Cabezon, the nest bridge, and so gain the Duero, Souham, moving by the left bank, might fall on him while in march and hampered between the Duero, Pisuerga, and Esquevilla: he must then have retired through Valladolid and Simancas, giving up his communications with Hill. In this critical state of affairs, keeping good watch on the left of the Pisuerga, and knowing the ground there was rugged and the roads narrow and bad, while on the right bank they were good and wide, the English general sent his baggage in the night to Valladolid, withdrew all the troops before day-break on the 26th, made a sixteen-mile march to Cabezon, passed to the left of the Pisuerga and mined the bridge: it was a fine stroke of generalship.

Being then master of his own movements he sent a detachment to hold the bridge of Tudela on the Duero, immediately behind him, and employed the seventh division to secure the more distant bridges of Valladolid, Simancas, and Tordesillas. The line of that great river, now in full water, being thus assured, he again halted, partly because the ground was favourable, partly to give the commissary-general Kennedy time to remove the sick men and other incumbrances from Salamanca. This operation was attended with great disasters from the negligence of medical and escorting officers conducting the convoys, and the consequent bad conduct of the soldiers. Outrages were perpetrated on the inhabitants along the whole line of march, terror was predominant, and the ill-used drivers and muleteers deserted by hundreds, some with, some without their cattle. Great sufferings were endured by the sick, the commissariat lost nearly the whole of the animals and carriages employed, the villages were abandoned, and the under-commissaries were bewildered, or paralyzed by the terrible disorder thus spread along the line of communication .

Souham pursued on the 26th by the right of the Pisuerga, being deterred from taking the left bank by the rugged nature of the ground, and by the King's orders not to risk a serious action. In the morning of the 27th his whole army was collected in front of Cabezon, but he contented himself with a cannonade and an unmeaning display: the former killed Colonel Robe of the artillery; the latter enabled Wellington for the first time to discover the numbers he had to contend with, and taught him that he could hold neither the Pisuerga nor the Duero permanently. Nevertheless he kept his actual position, and when the French, leaving a division in his front, extended their right by Valladolid to Simancas, he caused the bridges at those places to be destroyed. Congratulating himself that he had not fought in front of Burgos with so powerful an army, he now resolved to retire behind the Duero and, if pressed, even behind the Tormes. Meanwhile as General Hill would then be liable to a flank attack, and the more certainly if any disaster happened on the Duero, he ordered him to retreat at once from Madrid, giving the discretion as to the line, yet desiring him, if possible, to come by the Guadamara passes: for he still designed, if all went well, to unite with Hill in a central position, keep Souham in check with a part of his force, and with the remainder fall upon Soult who was now directing the king's army.

On the 28th Souham, still extending his right, endeavoured to force the bridges at Valladolid and Simancas on the Pisuerga, and that of Tordesillas on the Duero. The first was defended by the seventh division, but the French being strong and eager at the second it was destroyed, and the regiment of Brunswick Oels was detached to ruin that of Tordesillas. This was effected, and a tower behind the ruins being occupied, the remainder of the Brunswickers took post in a pine wood at some distance. The French arrived and seemed baffled, yet very soon sixty officers and non-commisioned officers, headed by Captain Guinret, a daring man, formed a small raft to hold their arms and clothes, and then plunged into the water with their swords between their teeth, swimming and pushing the raft before them. Under protection of a cannonade they thus crossed this a great river, though it was in full and strong water and the weather very cold, and having reached the other side, naked as they were, stormed the tower, whereupon the Brunswickers,

Brunswickers, amazed at the action, abandoned their ground, leaving the gallant Frenchmen masters of the passage.

When Wellington heard of the attack at Simancas and saw the whole French army in march to its right down the Pisuerga he destroyed the bridges at Valladolid and Cabeçon, and crossed the Duero at Tudela and Puente de Duero on the 29th; but scarcely had he effected this when intelligence of Guingret's splendid action at Tordesillas reached him. Critical then was his position, but with the decision of a great captain he marched instantly by his left, reached the heights between Rueda and Tordesillas on the 30th, and there fronting his powerful enemy forbad further progress. The bridge had been repaired by the French, yet their main body had not arrived, and Wellington's menacing position was too significant to be misunderstood. The bridges of Toro and Zamora were now destroyed by detachments, and though the French, spreading along the river, commenced repairing the former, the junction with Hill's army was insured; the English general, therefore, thinking the bridge of Toro could not be restored for several days, again hoped to maintain the line of the Duero permanently, because Hill, of whose operations it is now time to speak, was fast approaching.

RETREAT FROM MADRID.

The king, having fifty thousand veteran infantry, eight thousand cavalry and eighty-four pieces of artillery, came to drive the allies from Madrid. Soult and Jourdan acted under him, and the former first attacked General Cole at the Puente Largo, near Aranjuez on the Tagus; but though the English mines failed to destroy the bridge the French were vigorously repulsed. General Hill being thus menaced resolved to retreat by the Guadarama and join Wellington, whom he knew to be pressed by superior forces: he also thought the valley of the Tagus, although opened, could not furnish provisions for the French; but the commissary who had the care of that line had not removed the great magazines formed for the allies' advance to Madrid: they were full, and Soult might have used them to interpose between Wellington and Portugal while Souham pressed him in retreat; yet neither he, nor Hill, nor Wellington, knew of their existence ! Such is war.

Hill burned his pontoons and then causing the fort of the Retiro in Madrid to be blown up with all its stores, retreated by easy marches across the Guadarama, followed gently by the French; for Soult did not know his actual force, and, suspecting Wellington's design to unite and fight a battle, moved cautiously. When near Arevalo, fresh orders, founded on new combinations, changed the direction of Hill's march. Souham had repaired the bridge of Toro several days sooner than Wellington expected, and thus his design to join Hill on the Adaja and attack Soult was baffled; for Souham, possessing Toro and Tordesillas, could fall upon his rear; and he could not bring Hill up to attack Souham, because, having destroyed the bridges, he had no means to repass the Duero, and Soult moving by Fontiveros would reach the Tormes on his rear. His central position was therefore no longer available for offence or defence, and he directed Hill to gain Alba de Tormes at once by the road of Fontiveros. On the 6th of November he fell back himself to San Christoval, covering Salamanca.

Joseph, thinking to prevent Hill's junction, had gained Arevalo by the Segovia road, and on the 8th, Souham's scouts being met with at Medina del Campo, the king, for the first time since he had quitted Valencia, obtained news of the army of Portugal. One hundred thousand combatants, of which above twelve thousand were cavalry, with a hundred and thirty pieces of artillery, were then assembled on plains, over which, three months before, Marmont had marched with such confidence to his own destruction; and Soult, then expelled from Andalusia by Marmont's defeat, was now, after having made half the circuit of the Peninsula, come to drive into Portugal that very army whose victory had driven him from the south. Wellington had foreseen, and foretold, that the acquisition of Andalusia, though politically important and useful, would prove injurious to himself at the moment. The prophecy was fulfilled. The French had concentrated a mighty power, from which it required both skill and fortune to escape. Meanwhile the Spanish armies let loose by this union of all the French troops kept aloof, or, coming to aid, were found a burden rather than a help.

On the 7th Hill passed the Tormes at Alba, and the bridge there was mined; for Wellington, holding Christoval and being still uncertain of the real numbers of the enemy, was desirous to maintain the line of the Tormes permanently and give his troops repose. His own retreat had been of two hundred miles; Hill had marched a greater distance; Skerrett had come from Cadiz; the soldiers who besieged Burgos had been in the field with scarcely an interval of repose since January; all were barefooted, their equipments were spoiled, the cavalry were weak, the horses out of condition, and discipline was generally failing.

The excesses committed on the retreat from Burgos have been touched upon; and during the first day's march from the Tagus to Madrid, five hundred of the rear-guard, chiefly of one regiment, finding the inhabitants of Valdemoro had fled, plundered the houses; drunkenness followed and two hundred and fifty fell into the hands of the enemy. The conduct of an army can never be fairly judged by following in the wake of a retreat. Here there was no want of provisions, no hardships to exasperate, yet the author of this history counted on the first day's march from Madrid seventeen bodies of murdered peasants; by whom killed, or for what, whether by English or Germans, by Spaniards or Portuguese, whether in dispute, in robbery, or in wanton villany, was unknown; but their bodies were in the ditches, and a shallow observer might thence have drawn most foul and false conclusions against the English general and nation.

Wellington desired a battle. Christoval was strong, the Arapiles glorious as well as strong; and by the bridge of Salamanca and the fords he could concentrate on either position on a shorter line than the French. Yet he prepared for retreat, sending sick men and stores to the rear, ordering up small convoys of provisions on the road to Rodrigo, and destroying spare ammunition. He gave clothing, arms and accoutrements to the Spanish troops, but an hour after had the mortification to see them selling their equipments under his own windows! At this time, indeed, the Spaniards, civil and military, began to evince hatred of the British. Daily did they attempt or perpetrate murder, and one act of peculiar atrocity merits notice. A horse, led by an English soldier, being frightened, backed against a Spanish officer commanding at a gate; he caused the soldier to be dragged into his guard-house and there bayoneted him in cold blood, and no redress could be had for this or other crimes, save by counterviolence, which was not long withheld. A Spanish Colonel while wantonly stabbing at a rifleman was shot dead by the latter; and a British volunteer slew another officer at the head of his own regiment in a sword fight, the troops of both nations looking on, but here there was nothing dishonourable on either side.

The civil authorities, not less savage, treated every person with intolerable arrogance. The Prince of Orange, remonstrating about his quarters with the sitting junta, they ordered one of their guards to kill him; and he would have been killed, had not Lieut. Steele of the 43rd, a bold athletic person, felled the man before he could stab, but then both had to fly. The exasperation caused by these things was leading to serious mischief, when the enemy's movements gave another direction to the rising passions.

On the 10th Soult opened a concentrated fire of eighteen guns against the castle of Alba de Tormes, which, crowning a bare rocky knoll and hastily intrenched, furnished scarcely any shelter from this tempest; for two hours the garrison could only reply with musketry, but eventually it was aided by the fire of four pieces from the left bank of the river; the post was thus defended until dark with such vigour that the enemy would not assault. During the night the garrison was reinforced, the damaged walls were repaired, barricades were made, and in the morning the enemy withdrew. This combat cost the allies a hundred men.

On the 11th the king reorganised his army. Uniting his own troops with the army of the south, he placed the whole under Soult and removed Souham to make way for Drouet. Caffarelli had before returned to Burgos with his divisions and guns, and what with garrisons, stragglers, and losses, scarcely ninety thousand combatants were on the Tormes; but twelve thousand were cavalry, nearly all were veteran troops, and they had one hundred and twenty pieces of artillery. Such a mighty power could not remain idle, the country was exhausted of provisions, the soldiers wanted bread

and the king, eager enough for battle, for he was of a brave spirit and
had something of his brother's greatness of soul, sought counsel how
to deliver it with most advantage.

Jourdan was for the boldest and shortest mode. He said Wellington's position was composed of three parts, namely, a right wing at
Alba; a centre at Calvariza Ariba; a left wing at San Christoval,
separated from the centre by the Tormes. This line was fifteen miles
long, the Tormes was still fordable in many places above Salamanca,
and therefore the French army might assemble in the night, pass the
river at day-break by the fords between Villa Gonzalo and Huerta,
and make a concentrated attack upon Calvariza Ariba, which would
force on a decisive battle.

Soult opposed this. He objected to attacking a position Wellington knew so well, which he might have fortified, and where the army
must fight its way even from the fords to gain room for an order of
battle. He proposed instead, to move by the left to certain fords, three
in number, between Exeme and Galisancho, seven or eight miles
above Alba de Tormes. Easy in themselves their banks were suited to
force a passage, and by a slight circuit the troops in march would not
be seen by the enemy. The army would thus gain two marches, would
be placed on the flank and rear of the allies, and would fight on ground
chosen by its own generals, instead of ground chosen by the enemy;
or it could force an action in a new position whence the enemy could
with difficulty retire in the event of disaster: Wellington must then
fight to disadvantage, or retire hastily, sacrificing part of his army to
save the rest, and the effect, militarily and politically, would be the
same as if he was beaten by a front attack.

Jourdan observed, that this was prudent, and might be successful
if Wellington accepted battle; but that general could not thereby be
forced to fight, which was the great object; he would have time to
retreat before the French could touch his communication with Rodrigo,
and it was supposed by some generals that he would retreat on
Almeida at once by San Felices and Barba de Puerco.*

Neither Soult nor Jourdan knew the position of the Arapiles,

---

* For this council of war, and the opinions, I have the personal authority of
Marshal Jourdan.

and the former, while urging his plan, offered to yield if the king was so inclined; but though Jourdan's proposition was supported by all the generals of the army of Portugal, except Clausel, who leaned to Soult's opinion, the last marshal commanded two-thirds of the army, and the question was finally decided agreeably to his counsel. Nor is it easy to determine which was right, for though Jourdan's reasons were strong and the result conformable, the failure was only in the execution. Nevertheless it would seem, so great an army and so confident, for the French soldiers eagerly demanded a battle, should have grappled in the shortest way.

Wellington, well acquainted with his ground, desired a battle on either side of the Tormes. His hope was indeed to prevent the passage of that river until the rains, rendering it unfordable, should force the French to retire from want of provisions, or engage him on the position of Christoval: yet he also courted a fight on the Arapiles, those rocky monuments of his former victory. He had sixty-eight thousand combatants under arms, fifty-two thousand of which, including four thousand British cavalry, were Anglo-Portuguese, and he had nearly seventy guns. With this force concentrated upon the strong ridges of Calvariza Ariba and the two Arapiles, the superiority of twenty thousand men would scarcely have availed the French.*

Soult's project was adopted, trestle bridges were made for the artillery, and at daybreak on the 14th were thrown, while the cavalry and infantry passed by the upper fords; the army then took a position at Mozarbes, having the road from Alba to Tamames under the left flank. Wellington remained in Salamanca, and when the first report came that the enemy was over the Tormes, he made the caustic observation, that he would not recommend it to some of them. Soon however the concurrent testimony of many reports convinced him of his mistake, he galloped to the Arapiles, ascertained the direction of Soult's march, and drew off the second division, the cavalry, and some guns to attack the head of the French column. The fourth division and Hamilton's Portugese remained at Alba

---

* For the Duke's secret views here I have his own authority.

to protect this movement; the third division secured the Arapiles until the troops from Christoval should arrive; and he was still so confident that the bulk of the troops did not quit Christoval that day. But at Mozarbes he found the French already too strong to be seriously meddled with, and when under cover of a cannonade which kept off their cavalry, he examined their position, discovered that the evil was without remedy. Wherefore he destroyed the bridge of Alba, leaving only three hundred Spaniards in the castle, with orders, if the army retired, to save themselves as they could.

He still hoped the French would give battle at the Arapiles, but placed the first division at Aldea Tejada on the Junguen stream, to secure a passage in case Soult should finally compel him to choose between Salamanca and Rodrigo. Meantime Clausel's army, now under Drouet, finding the bridge of Alba broken and the castle occupied, also crossed the Tormes at Galisancho, and then Soult, who had commenced fortifying Mozarbes, extended his left towards the Rodrigo road: yet slowly, because the ground was heavy and crossed by the many sources of the Junguen and Valmusa streams, which were flooded with the rain. This movement was like that of Marmont at the battle of Salamanca, but on a wider circle, and an outward range of heights, beyond a sudden attack and catastrophe. The result in each case was remarkable. Marmont closing with a short quick turn, a falcon striking at an eagle, received a buffet that broke his pinions and spoiled his flight. Soult, a wary kite, sailing slowly and with a wide wheel to seize his prey, lost it altogether.

When Wellington saw the French cavalry pointing to the Rodrigo road, he judged the design was first to establish a fortified head of cantonments at Mozarbes, from whence to operate against the communication with Rodrigo; wherefore suddenly casting his army into three columns he crossed the Junguen, and covering his left flank with cavalry and guns, defiled in order of battle with a wonderful boldness and facility at little more than cannon-shot from his enemy. He had good fortune however to aid: for there was a thick fog and a heavy rain which rendered the bye-ways and fields nearly impassable to the French while he used the high roads.

Then he took his army in one mass quite round the French left, and having gained the Valmusa river halted for the night, in rear of those who had been threatening him in front only a few hours before !

This was truly a surprising exploit, yet it was not credit able to the generalship on either side. The English commander, having suffered Soult to pass the Tormes and turn his position, waited too long on the Arapiles, or this dangerous movement would have been unnecessary; and a combination of bad roads, bad weather, and want of vigour on the other side, rendered it possible and no more. It has been said by a great master, that the defect of Soult's military genius was a want of promptness to strike at the decisive moment, and here he was certainly slack.

On the 16th the allies retired by three roads, all of which led, by Tamames, San Munos, and Martin del Rio, to Rodrigo, through a forest penetrable in all directions: in the evening they halted behind the Matilla river. This march was only of twelve miles, yet stragglers were numerous, and the soldiers finding vast herds of swine quitted their colours by hundreds to shoot them; indeed such a rolling musketry echoed through the forest, that Wellington thought the enemy was upon him. Every effort was made to stop this excess, and two offenders were hanged; still the hungry men broke from the columns, the property of whole districts was swept away in a few hours, and the army was in some degree placed at the mercy of the enemy; who were however content to glean the stragglers, of whom they captured two thousand: they did not press the rear until evening, when their lancers fell on, but were checked by the 28th Regiment and the Light Dragoons.

During the night, the light division having the rear-guard, the cavalry in the front, for some unknown reason, filed off by the flanks without giving any intimation of the movement, and at daybreak as the soldiers of the division were rolling their blankets some strange horsemen were seen behind the bivouac; they were taken for Spaniards, until their cautious movements and vivacity of gesture showed them to be French. The troops run to arms, in good time, for five hundred yards in front the wood opened on a large plain, where eight thousand French horsemen were discovered advancing in one solid mass, yet carelessly, and without suspecting the vicinity of the British. The division immediately formed columns, two squadrons of dragoons came hastily up from the rear, and Julian Sanchez' cavalry also appeared in small parties on the right flank. This checked the enemy's march while the infantry retired, but the French, though fearing to close, sent many squadrons to the right and left, some of which rode on the flanks near enough to bandy wit in the Spanish tongue with the British soldiers, and very soon mischief was visible: the road was strewed with baggage, the batmen came running in for protection, some wounded, some without arms, and all breathless as just escaped from a surprise.

The thickness of the forest had enabled the French horsemen to pass unperceived on the flanks, and, as opportunity offered, they galloped from side to side, sweeping away the baggage and sabring the conductors and guards; they even menaced one of the columns but were checked by the fire of the artillery. In one of these charges General Paget was carried off, and it might have been Wellington's fortune, for he also was continually riding between the columns and without an escort. The main body of the army soon passed the Huebra river at three places and took post behind it; but when the light division arrived at the edge of a tableland which overhung the fords, the French cavalry suddenly thickened, and the sharp whistle of musket-bullets with the splintering of branches gave notice that their infantry were also up; for Soult, hoping to forestal the allies at Tamames, had pushed a column towards that place from his left, but finding Hill's troops there in position, turned short to his right in hopes to cut off the rear-guard.

COMBAT OF THE HUEBRA.

The English and German cavalry, warned by the musketry, crossed the fords in time, and the light division should have followed without delay; for the forest ended at the edge of the table-land, and the descent to the river, eight hundred yards, was quite open and smooth, the fords of the Huebra deep. Instead of this General C. Alten ordered the division to form squares ! All persons were amazed, but then Wellington happily came up and caused the astonished troops to glide off to the fords. Four companies of the 43rd and one of riflemen, left by him to cover the passage, were instantly assailed on three sides with a fire showing that a large force was at hand; a driving rain and mist prevented them from seeing their adversaries, they were forced through the wood, and thrown out on the open slope, where they maintained their ground for a quarter of an hour, and then swiftly running to the fords passed them under a sharp musketry. Only twenty-seven fell, for the tempest, beating in the Frenchmen's faces, baffled their aim, and the division guns, playing from the low ground with grape, checked the pursuit: yet the deep bellow from thirty pieces of heavy French artillery in reply, showed how critically timed was the passage.

The banks of the Huebra were steep and broken, but the French infantry spread to the right and left and there were several fords to be guarded; the 52nd and the Portugese defended those below; the guns, supported by the riflemen and 43rd, defended those above, and behind the right of the light division, on higher ground, was the seventh division. The bulk of the army was massed on the right of this position, covering all the roads leading to Rodrigo.

One brisk attempt to force the fords guarded by the 52nd was vigorously repulsed by that regiment, but the skirmishing, and the cannonade, which never slackened, continued until dark; and heavily the French guns played on the light and 7th divisions. The former was of necessity held near the fords and in column, lest a sudden rush of cavalry should carry off the division pieces from the flat ground, and it was plunged into at every round, yet suffered little loss, because the clayey soil, saturated with rain, swallowed the shot and smothered the shells. But the 7th division was, with astonishing want of judgment, kept by Lord Dalhousie on open and harder ground, in one huge mass, tempting havoc for hours, when a hundred yards in his rear the rise of the hill and the thick forest would have entirely protected it, without in any manner weakening the position ! Nearly three hundred men were thus lost.

On the 18th the army was to have drawn off before daylight

and Wellington was uneasy, because the Huebra, good for defence, was yet difficult to remove from at that season, inasmuch as the roads, hollow and narrow, led up a steep bank to table-land, open, flat, marshy, and scored with water-gullies. Moreover from the overflowing of one stream the principal road was impassable at a mile from the position; hence to get off in time, without jostling and without being attacked, required nice management. All the baggage and stores had marched in the night, with orders not to halt until they reached the high lands near Rodrigo; but if the preceding days had produced some strange occurrences, the 18th was not less fertile in them.

Wellington, knowing the direct road was impassable from the flood, had directed several divisions by another, longer and apparently more difficult; this seemed so extraordinary to some generals, that, after consulting together, they deemed him unfit to conduct the army, and led their troops by what appeared to them the fittest line of retreat ! The condemned commander had before daylight placed himself on his own road, and waited impatiently for the arrival of the leading division until dawn; then, suspecting something of what had happened, he galloped to the other road and found the would-be leaders, stopped by that flood. which his arrangements had been made to avoid. The insubordination and the danger to the whole army were alike glaring; yet the practical rebuke was so severe and well timed, the humiliation so complete and so deeply felt, that, with one proud sarcastic observation, indicating contempt more than anger, he led back the troops and drew off all his forces safely.*

Some confusion and great danger still attended the operation, for even on the true road one water-gully was so deep that the light division, covering the rear, could only pass it man by man over a felled tree; but Soult, unable to feed his troops a day longer, stopped on the Huebra with his main body and only sent some cavalry to Tamames. Thus the allies retired unmolested, yet whether from necessity, or from negligence in the subordinates, the means of transport were too scanty for the removal of the wounded men, most

* The details of this curious event were told to me by the Duke of Wellington

of whom were hurt by cannon-shot; many were thus left behind; and as the enemy never passed the Huebra, those miserable creatures perished by a horrible lingering death.

The marshy plains over which the army was now marching exhausted the strength of the wearied soldiers, thousands straggled, the depredations on the herds of swine were repeated, and the temper of the troops generally prognosticated the greatest misfortunes if the retreat should be continued. This was however the last day of trial. Towards evening the weather cleared up, the hills near Rodrigo furnished dry bivouacs and fuel, good rations restored the strength and spirits of the men, and next day Rodrigo and the neighbouring villages were occupied in tranquillity. The cavalry was then sent out to the forest, and being aided by Sanchez' Partida, brought in from a thousand to fifteen hundred stragglers who must otherwise have perished.

Such was the retreat from Burgos. The French gathered good spoil of baggage, but what the exact loss of the allies in men was cannot be exactly determined, because no Spanish returns were ever seen. An approximation may however be easily made, and the whole loss of the double retreat cannot be set down at less than nine thousand. including the siege of Burgos.

BOOK IX.

March to Vittoria—Battle of Vittoria.

MARCH TO VITTORIA.

In England, the retreat from Burgos produced anger and fear; for the public had been taught to believe the French weak and dispirited, and the reverses were unexpected. Lord Wellesley justly attributed them to the imbecile, selfish policy of Mr. Perceval and his colleagues, which he characterized as having *"nothing regular but confusion."* Lord Wellington alone supported the contest, for the Portuguese and Spanish Governments had become absolutely hostile to him, and were striving to make the people of those countries hostile also. However, in 1813, the aspect of the war, not in the Peninsula only, but all over the civilized world, was changed by the failure of Napoleon's gigantic expedition to Russia, and the English General, morally strengthened by this great event, and seeing time ripe for a decisive blow, successfully exerted all his mental vigour to overbear the folly and vices of the govermnents he had to deal with. He renovated discipline, repressed the intrigues of the Portuguese Regency, and, going to Cadiz, obtained of the Spanish Cortes paramount military authority, with its assent to a general combination all over the Peninsula. The three nations gave him two hundred thousand men; the Anglo-Portuguese army furnishing seventy thousand, with ninety pieces of artillery, and sixteen thousand Anglo-Sicilians were at Alicant. His flanks rested on the Biscay and Mediterranean seas, on each of which floated British fleets; now effective auxilliaries, because the French lines of retreat being close to and parallel with the coast on both sides of Spain, every port abandoned by them, furnished a storehouse to the allies, and the navy became a moveable base of operations.

To oppose him were great armies on the French side, yet

all in confusion. Napoleon had drawn off thousands of the old soldiers
and experienced officers, to give stability to the new levies with
which he was striving to restore his failing fortunes; to compensate
for the weakness thus occasioned, he directed the king to concentrate
on the northern line of invasion and act, not as the monarch of a
subdued country but as the general of an army in the field, having to
contend with an equal power. This view demanded promptness and
vigour to clear the communication of insurgents, judgment to adopt
suitable positions, and one imperious command over all the generals.
Thus governed the French soldiers were numerous enough to hope for
victory against greater numbers than Wellington could employ
against them; for though reduced by drafts, and the secondary war of
the Spaniards after the retreat of Burgos, to two hundred and thirty
thousand men, of which seventy-eight thousand were on the southern
line of invasion and thirty thousand in hospital, a hundred and twenty
thousand men with a hundred guns, including a reserve at Bayonne,
were on the northern line of invasion. This was a great power, of one
nation, one spirit, one discipline, and the emperor with comprehensive genius had explained how it was to be made available. Joseph
could not comprehend the spirit of the great master's instructions, and
was unwilling to obey. Quarrelling with his subordinates, he would
be still a king, lost time, made false movements, and at the opening
of the campaign, instead of being concentrated on the right point and
under one head, his troops were scattered over all the north of Spain,
under generals who agreed in nothing but opposition to his military
command.

Such was the state of affairs when Wellington, forming two
masses, gave one of forty thousand fighting men to General Graham,
with orders to penetrate through the Portuguese province of Tras
os Montes to the Esla river, in Spain, thus turning that line of the
Duero which Marmont had the year before made an iron barrier. With
the other mass, thirty thousand, he designed to force the Tormes,
pass the Duero, unite with Graham, augment his army to ninety
thousand, by calling down the Gallicians under Castanos, and
then ranging the whole on a new front march all abreast upon
the scattered French and drive them refluent to the Pyrenees.

A grand design and grandly executed. For strong of heart and strong of hand his veterans marched to the encounter, the glories of twelve victories playing about their bayonets, and he their leader, so proudly confident, that in crossing the stream which marks the frontier of Spain, he rose in his stirrups, and waving his hand cried out *Adieu Portugal !*

How were the French employed and disposed at this critical moment, when the serpent they had pursued only a few months before, slowly trailing his exhausted length into Portugal, had thus cast his slough, and with glistening crest and rattling scales was again rolling forward in voluminous strength ?

The king was at Valladolid with his guards, holding a mock court instead of a general's orderly room.

Drouet with the army of the centre was in march from Segovia towards the Duero above Valladolid.

General Leval who commanded ten thousand men at Madrid, was preparing to move with a large convoy of pictures and other property towards Segovia.

General Gazan with the army of the south, was moving his troops in a state of uncertainty between the Upper Tormes and the Duero, having an advanced division of infantry and cavalry at Salamanca under General Villatte.

General Reille with the army of Portugal was on the Duero and the Esla.

The position of the French was therefore defined by the three rivers. The Esla covered their right wing, the Duero their centre, the Tormes their left, and the point of concentration was Valladolid. But Leval's troops at Madrid were isolated, and that was not all the extent of the dissemination. Clausel, now commanding the army of the north, was engaged in Navarre warring down the insurgents, Foy as his lieutenant was in Biscay with a large detachment, and half of Reille's army was on the march to join Clausel. Add many false reports, false conjectures, and continued disputes as to the real plan of the English general, and the confusion of the king's command will be comprehended.

On the 22nd of May, Graham being well advanced, Lord Wellington put his right wing in motion towards the Tormes, and the 26th at 10 o'clock in the morning the heads of his columns appeared with excellent concert close to that river on all the roads.

Villatte, a good officer, barricaded the bridge, sent his baggage to the rear, and called in a detachment from Alba, yet wishing to discover the real force of his enemy waited on the heights above the ford of Santa Marta too long; for the ground enabled Wellington to conceal his movements, and Fane's horsemen with six guns passed the ford of Santa Marta in Villatte's rear unseen, while Victor Alten's cavalry removed the barricades on the bridge and pushed through the town to attack in front. The French general indeed gained the heights of Cabrerizos, marching towards Babila Fuente, before Fane got over the river, but at the defile of Aldea Lengua was overtaken by both columns of cavalry, and being first battered by the guns was charged. But horsemen are no match for such infantry, whose courage and discipline nothing could quell. They fell before the round shot in sections, and one hundred died in the ranks without a wound from intolerable heat; yet they beat off the cavalry, and in the face of thirty thousand enemies made their way to Babila Fuente, where, being joined by the detachment from Alba, the whole disappeared from the sight of their admiring and applauding opponents. Two hundred had fallen dead in the ranks, a like number, unable to keep up, were captured, and a leading gun being overturned in the defile retarded six others, all of which were taken.

On the 28th, having approached the point on the Duero where he proposed to throw the bridge for communication with Graham's corps, Wellington left Hill in command, and went off suddenly to the Esla, being uneasy for his combination there. Passing the Duero at Miranda, by means of a basket moving on a rope stretched from rock to rock, the river foaming hundreds of feet below, he on the 30th reached Carvajales.

Graham had met with many difficulties in the rugged Tras os Montes, and though the Gallicians did not fail here, the combination was retarded by the difficulty of crossing the Esla. It was to have been effected the 29th, at which time the right wing, continuing its march from the Tormes, could have been near Zamora and the passage of the Duero insured; the French would then have been surprised, separated, and overtaken in detail; now, though still ignorant that a whole army was on the Esla, they were alarmed, and had planted the opposite bank with picquets of cavalry and infantry; moreover, the stream was full and rapid, the banks steep, the fords hard to find, difficult and deep, and the appearance of the allies on the Tormes was known through all the cantonments. Nevertheless Wellington, early on the 31st, caused some squadrons of hussars with infantry holding by their stirrups, to pass a ford, and Graham approached the right bank with all his forces; a French picquet was thus surprised by the hussars, the pontoons were immediately laid, and the columns commenced crossing, but several men, even of the cavalry, were drowned.

On the 1st of June the rear was still on the Esla, yet the van entered Zamora, the French retiring on Toro. Next day their rear-guard of cavalry being overtaken by the hussars gave battle, was broken, and driven back on the infantry with a loss of two hundred men.

Wellington halted the 3rd to bring the Gallicians down on his left, and to close up his own rear, for he thought the French, who were concentrating, might give battle; but he had entirely mastered the line of the Duero, and those who understand war may say, whether it was an effort worthy of the man and his army. Some of his columns had marched a hundred and fifty, some above two hundred and fifty miles in the wild Tras os Montes, through regions thought to be impracticable even for small corps; forty thousand men, infantry, cavalry, artillery, and even pontoons, all had passed, and been suddenly placed as if by a supernatural power upon the Esla before the enemy knew that they were in movement.

The field was now clear for the shock of arms, but the forces were unequally matched. Wellington had ninety thousand men, and more than one hundred pieces of artillery in hand. Twelve thousand were cavalry, the British and Portuguese were seventy thousand; and this mass of regulars was aided by all the Partidas. Sanchez' horsemen, a thousand strong, were on the right beyond the Duero; Porlier, Barcena, Salazar and Manzo on the left between the Upper Esla and the Carion; Saornil menaced Avila, the Empecinado hovered about Leval; and the Spanish reserve of Andalusia, having crossed the Tagus on the 30th, drew all the numerous small bands swarming around as it advanced. On the other hand, though the French could collect nine or ten thousand horsemen and one hundred guns, their infantry was less than half the number of the allies, being only thirty-five thousand strong, exclusive of Leval. The way to victory was therefore open, and on the 4th Wellington marched forward with a conquering vehemence, pouring a torrent of war, whose depth and violence the king was even now ignorant of.

It was thought Joseph would fight on the Carion. But though he had then fifty-five thousand fighting men, exclusive of a Spanish division escorting the convoys and baggage, he did not judge that river a good position and retired behind the upper Pisuerga. Meanwhile he sent Jourdan to examine Burgos castle, and expedited fresh letters, having before written from Valladolid, to Foy, Sarrut and Clausel, calling them towards the plains of Burgos, and others to Suchet, directing him to march upon Zaragoza: but Suchet w as then engaged in Catalonia, Clausel was in Aragon, Foy on the coast of Guipuscoa, and Sarrut pursuing Longa in the Montana.

Joseph was still unacquainted with his enemy. Higher than seventy or eighty thousand he did not estimate his force, and proposed to fight on the elevated plains of Burgos. But more than a hundred thousand men were before and around him; for all the Partidas of the Asturias and Montana were drawing together on his right, Julian Sanchez and the Partidas of Castile were closing on his left, and Abispal having passed the Gredos mountains with the Andalusian reserve and Frere's cavalry was in full march for Valladolid. Joseph was however hopeful to win if he could rally Clausel's and Foy's divisions in time, and his despatches to the former were frequent and urgent. Come with the infantry of the army of Portugal ! Come with the army of the north, and we shall drive the allies over the Duero ! Such was his cry, but he was not a general to contend with Wellington, and recover the initiatory movement at such a crisis.

While still on the Pisuerga he received Jourdan's report. The castle of Burgos was untenable, there were no magazines of provisions, the new works were unfinished and commanded the old, which were unable to hold out a day. Of Clausel's and Foy's divisions nothing had been heard. This intelligence was decisive, and he resolved to retire behind the Ebro. All the French outposts in the Bureba and Montana were immediately withdrawn, and the great depot of Burgos was evacuated upon Vittoria, which was thus encumbered with the artillery depots of Madrid, Valladolid and Burgos, and with the baggage and stores of many armies and many fugitive families; and at that moment also arrived, from France, a convoy of treasure which had long waited for escort at Bayonne.

Meanwhile the tide of war flowed onwards with terrible power. The allies having crossed the Carion the 7th, Joseph retired to Burgos with his left wing, composed of the armies of the south and centre, while Reille's army, forming the right wing, moved by Castro Xerez. Wellington followed hard: conducting his operations continually on the same principle, he pushed his left wing and the Gallicians along bye-roads, and passed the upper Pisuerga on the 8th, 9th, and 10th. Having thus turned the line of the Pisuerga entirely, and outflanked Reille, he made a short journey the 11th, and on the 12th halted his left wing to arrange the supplies; yet he still pushed forward the right wing, resolved to make the French yield the castle of Burgos or fight for possession.

Reille, who had regained the great road to Burgos the 9th, was now strongly posted behind the Hormaza stream, barring the way to Burgos; the other armies were in reserve behind Estepar. In this situation they had been for three days, cheered by intelligence of Napoleon's victory at Bautzen, and the consequent armistice; but on the 12th, Wellington's columns came up, and the light division, preceded by the hussars and dragoons, turned Reille's right, while the rest of the troops attacked the whole range of heights to Estepar. Reille, finding horsemen acting behind his right flank while his front was strongly menaced, made for the bridge of Baniel under the fire of Gardiner's horse-artillery, losing Some prisoners and a gun; an effort was made to cut him off from the bridge, but he bore the artillery fire without shrinking, and, evading a serious attack, passed the Arlanzan with a loss of only thirty men killed.

The three French armies being then covered by the Urbel and
Arlanzan rivers could not be easily attacked, all the stores of Burgos
were removed, and in the night the king, having mined the castle,
retreated along the high road to Pancorbo, into which he threw a
garrison. Everything was done confusedly. The mines under the
castle exploded outwardly at the moment a column of infantry was
defiling beneath, several streets were laid in ruins, thousands of shells
and other combustibles were driven upwards with a horrible crash,
the hills rocked above the devoted column, and a shower of iron,
timber, and stony fragments falling on it, in an instant destroyed more
than three hundred men ! Fewer deaths might have sufficed to
determine the crisis of a great battle ! Such and so fearful is the
consequence of error, so terrible the responsibility of a general !

Wisely did Napoleon speak when he told Joseph, if he would
command he must give himself up entirely to the business, labouring
day and night, thinking of nothing else. Here was a noble army driven
like sheep before prowling wolves, yet in every action the inferior
generals had been prompt and skilful, the soldiers brave, ready and
daring, and in a country very favourable for defence; but the mind of
a great commander was wanting, and the Esla, the Tormes, the Duero,
the Carion, the Pisuerga, the Arlanzan, seemed to be dried up, the
rocks, the mountains, the deep ravines to be levelled. Clausel's strong
positions, Dubreton's thundering castle, all disappeared like a dream,
and sixty thousand veteran soldiers, willing to fight, were hurried
with all the confusion of defeat across the Ebro: nor was that barrier
found of more avail to mitigate the rushing violence of their formidable adversary.

Joseph, having placed the defile and fort of Pancorbo between
him and his enemy, thought he could safely await his reinforcements,
and extended his wings for the sake of subsistence. Hence on the 16th
Drouet marched to Aro on the left, while Gazan held the centre,
having a strong advanced guard beyond Pancorbo; for as the king's
hope was to retake the offensive, he retained the power of issuing
beyond the defiles, and his scouting parties were pushed forward on
all sides. The rest of the army was cantoned by divisions in rear, and
Reille, from behind the Ebro, was to watch the road to Bilbao, being

there joined by Sarrut.

While these movements were in progress, all the incumbrances of the armies were assembled in the basin of Vittoria, and many small garrisons of the army of the north came in; for Clausel, having received the king's first letter on the 15th of June, had gathered his scattered columns to rejoin by the way of Logrono, yet his garrisons were many, and he could only concentrate fourteen thousand men. The king was nevertheless confident in the strength of his front, and had no doubt of retaking the offensive when all his forces came in.

His dream was short-lived. On the 13th, while the explosion at Burgos was still ringing in the hills, Wellington was marching by his left towards the country about the sources of the Ebro. This great movement, masked by the cavalry and the Spanish irregulars who infested the rear of the French, suddenly placed the army between the sources of the Ebro and the great mountains of Reynosa; this cut the French entirely off from the sea-coast, and all the ports, except Santona and Bilbao, were immediately evacuated. Santona was then invested by the Spaniards, and the English ships entered Sant Andero, where a depot and hospital station was established; the connection of the army with Portugal was thus severed: she was cast off as a heavy tender is cast from its towing-rope, and all the British military establishments were transferred by sea to the coast of Biscay.

The English general had now to choose between a march down the left bank of the Ebro to seek a battle; or to place the army on the great communication with France, while the fleet, keeping pace, furnished fresh depots at Bilbao and other ports. The first was an uncertain operation, because of the many narrow and dangerous defiles which were to be passed; the second was secure even if the first should fail; but both were compatible to a certain point; for to gain the great road leading from Burgos to Bilbao, was a good step for either, and, failing of that, there was a road leading by Valmaceda to Bilbao in reserve. Wherefore with an eagle's sweep Wellington brought his left wing round, and poured his numerous columns through all the deep narrow valleys and rugged defiles towards the great road of Bilbao. At Medina de Pomar, a central point, he left the sixth division to guard his stores and supplies, but the march of the other divisions was unmitigated; neither the winter gullies, nor the ravines, nor the precipitous passes amongst the rocks, retarded the march even of the artillery; where horses could not draw men hauled, when the wheels would not roll the guns were let down or lifted up with ropes; and strongly did the rough veteran infantry work their way through those wild and beautiful regions: six days they toiled unceasingly; on the seventh, swelled by Longa's Spaniards, and all the smaller bands which came trickling from the mountains, they burst like raging streams from every defile and went foaming into the basin of Vittoria.

During this movement many reports reached the French, some absurdly exaggerated, as that Wellington had one hundred and ninety thousand men, yet all indicating the true direction of his march; and as early as the 15th, Jourdan, warning Joseph that the allies would turn his light, pressed him to place Reille at Valmaceda and close the other armies towards the same quarter. Joseph yielded so far, that Reille was ordered to concentrate at Osma and gain Valmaceda by Orduna if it was still possible; if not he was to descend rapidly upon Bilbao, and rally Foy's division and the garrisons of Biscay upon his army: but no general decided dispositions were made.

Reille called in Maucune from Frias, and having fears for his safety gave him a choice between a direct road across the hills, or the circuitous route of Puente Lara. Maucune started late in the night of the 17th by the direct road; and meanwhile Reille having reached Osma on the morning of the 18th, found a strong English column issuing from the defiles in his front, and in possession of the high road to Orduna. This was Graham. He had three divisions and a considerable body of cavalry, and the French general, who had eight thousand infantry and fourteen guns, engaged him with a sharp skirmish and cannonade, wherein fifty men fell on the side of the allies, above a hundred on that of the enemy; but at half-past two o'clock, Maucune had not arrived, and beyond the mountains, on the left of the French, the sound of a battle arose and seemed to advance along the valley of Boveda in rear of Osma. Reille, suspecting the truth, instantly retired fighting towards Espejo, where the mouths of the two valleys opened on each other, and then suddenly, from that of Boveda Maucune's troops rushed forth, begrimed with dust and powder, breathless and broken.

That general had, as before said, marched over the Araçena ridge instead of going by the Puente Lara, and his leading brigade, after clearing the defiles, halted near the village of San Millan in the valley of Boveda, without planting picquets; he was there awaiting his other brigade and the baggage, when suddenly the light division, moving on a line parallel with Graham's march, appeared on some rising ground in front. The surprise was equal on both sides, but the British riflemen instantly dashed down the hill with loud cries and a bickering fire, the 52nd followed in support, and the French retreated fighting as they best could. The rest of the English regiments remained in reserve, thinking all their enemies before them, but then the second French brigade, followed by the baggage, came hastily out from a narrow cleft in some perpendicular rocks on their right hand, and a confused action ensued. For the reserve scrambled over rough intervening ground to attack this new foe, who made for a hill a little way in front, and then the 52nd, whose rear was thus menaced, quitting their first enemies, wheeled round and running full speed up the hill met them on the summit; so pressed, the French cast off their packs, and half flying, half fighting, escaped along the side of the mountains, while their first brigade, still retreating on the road towards Espejo, were pursued by the riflemen. Meanwhile the sumpter animals, sadly affrighted, run about the rocks with a wonderful clamour; and though the escort, huddled together, fought desperately, all the baggage became the spoil of the victors, and four hundred of the French fell or were taken: the rest with unyielding resolution and activity escaped, though pursued through the mountains by some Spanish irregulars: Reille then retreated behind Salinas de Anara.

Neither Reille nor the few prisoners he had made could account for more than six Anglo-Portugese divisions at these defiles; hence, as no enemy had been felt on the great road from Burgos, the king judged that Hill was marching with the others byValmaceda into Guipuscoa, to menace the great communication with France. It was however clear that six divisions were on the right and rear of the French position, and no time was to be lost; wherefore Gazan and D'Erlon marched in the night to unite behind the Zadora river, up the left bank of which they had to file into the basin of Vittoria. But their way was through the pass of Puebla de Arganzan, two miles long, and so narrow as scarcely to furnish room for the great road: wherefore to cover the movement, Reille fell back during the night to Subijana Morillas on the Bayas river. His orders were to dispute the ground vigorously, for by that route Wellington could enter the basin before the others could thread the pass of Puebla; or he might send a corps from Frias, to attack the king on the Miranda side in rear while his front was engaged in the defile. One of these things the English general should have endeavoured to accomplish, but the troops had made long marches on the 18th, and it was dark before the fourth division reached Espejo: D'Erlon and Gazan, therefore, without difficulty passed the defile, and the head of their column appeared on the other side just as the allies drove Reille back from the Bayas.

Wellington had reached that river before mid-day the l9th, and, if he could have forced it at once, the other two armies, then in the defile, would have been cut off; Reille was however well posted, his front covered by the stream, his right by the village of Subijana de Morillas, which was occupied as a bridge-head; his left was secured by rugged heights, and it was only by a combat in which eighty French fell that he was forced beyond the Zadora; but the other armies had then passed the defile, the crisis was over, and the allies pitched their tents on the Bayas. The king now heard of Clausel at Logrono, and called him to Vittoria; he also directed Foy, then in march for Bilbao, to rally the garrisons of Biscay and Guipuscoa and join him on the Zadora. These orders were received too late.

The basin into which the king had thus poured all his troops, his parcs, convoys and incumbrances, was eight miles broad by ten long, Vittoria being at the further end.

The Zadora, narrow and with rugged banks, after passing that town, flows through the Puebla defile towards the Ebro, dividing the basin unequally,—the largest portion being on the left bank. A traveller, coming from the Ebro by the royal Madrid road, would enter the basin by the Puebla defile, breaking through a rough mountain ridge. On emerging from the pass, at the distance of six miles on the left he would see the village of Subijana de Morillas, facing the opening into the basin which Reille had defended on the Bayas. The spires of Vittoria would appear eight miles in front, and radiating from that town, the road to Logrono would be on his right hand; that to Bilbao by *Murgia* on the left hand, crossing the Zadora at a bridge near the village of Ariaga. Further on, the road to Estella and Pampeluna would be seen on the right, the road to Durango on the left, and between them the royal causeway leading over the great Arlaban ridge by the defiles of Salinas. Of all these roads, though some were practicable for guns, especially that to Pampeluna, the royal causeway alone could suffice for such an incumbered army; and as the allies were behind the ridge, bounding the basin on the right bank of the Zadora, and parallel to the causeway, they could by prolonging their left cut off that route.

Joseph, feeling this danger, thought to march by Salinas to Durango, there to meet Foy's troops and the garrisons of Guipuscoa and Biscay; but in the rough country, neither his artillery nor his cavalry, on which he greatly depended, though the cavalry and artillery of the allies were scarcely less powerful, could act or subsist, and he must have sent them into France: moreover, if pressed by Wellington in that mountainous region, so favourable for irregulars, he could not long remain in Spain. It was then proposed to retire to Pampeluna and bring Suchet's army up to Zaragoza; but Joseph desired to keep open the great communication with France; for though the Pampeluna road was practicable to wheels, it required something more for the enormous mass of guns and carriages of all kinds now heaped around Vittoria.

One large convoy had marched the 19th, and the fighting men in front were thus diminished, while the plain was still covered with artillery parcs and equipages, and the king, infirm of purpose continued to waste time in vain conjectures about his adversary's movements. And on the 21st, at three o'clock in the morning, Maucune's division, more than three thousand good soldiers, also marched with a second convoy. The king then adopted a new line of battle.

Reille, reinforced by a Franco-Spanish brigade of infantry and Digeon's dragoons, took the extreme right to defend the passage of the Zadora, where the Bilbao and Durango roads crossed it by the bridges of Gamara Mayor and Ariaga. The centre, under Gazan and Drouet, was distant six or eight miles from Gamara, lining the Zadora also; but on another front, for the stream, turning suddenly to the left round the heights of Margarita, descended thence to the Puebla defile nearly at right angles with its previous course. There covered by the river, on an easy open range of heights, Gazan's right was extended from an isolated hill in front of the village of Margarita to the royal road; his centre was astride of the royal road in front of the village of Arinez; his left occupied rugged ground behind Subijana de Alava, facing the Puebla defile, and a brigade under Maransin was on the Puebla ridge beyond the defile. Drouet was in second line; the mass of cavalry, many guns, and the king's guards formed a reserve behind the centre about the village of Gomecha, and fifty pieces of artillery were pushed in front, pointing to the bridges of Mendoza, Tres Puentes, Villodas, and Nanclares.

While the king was making conjectures, Wellington had made a new disposition of his forces; for thinking Joseph would not fight on the Zadora, he sent Giron with the Gallicians on the 19th to seize Orduna; Graham was to have followed him, but finally penetrated through difficult mountain ways to Murguia, thus cutting the enemy off from Bilbao and menacing his communications with France. The army had been so scattered by the previous marches that Wellington halted on the 20th to rally the columns, and took that opportunity to examine the French position, where, contrary to his expectation, they seemed resolved to fight, wherefore he gave Graham fresh orders and hastily recalled Giron from Orduna. The long-expected battle was then at hand, and on neither side were the numbers and courage of the troops of mean account. The sixth division, six thousand five hundred strong, had been left at Medina de Pomar, and hence only sixty thousand Anglo-Portuguese sabres and bayonets, with ninety pieces of cannon, were actually in the field; but the Spanish auxiliaries raised the numbers to eighty thousand combatants. The regular muster-roll of the French was lost with the battle, yet a careful approximate reckoning gives about sixty thousand sabres and bayo-nets, and in number and size of guns they had the advantage: but their position was visibly defective.

Their best line of retreat was on the prolongation of Reille's right, at Gamara Mayor; yet he was too distant to be supported by the main body, and therefore the safety of the latter depended on his good fighting. Many thousand carriages and other impediments were heaped about Vittoria, blocking all the roads and disordering the artillery parcs; and on the extreme left, Maransin's brigade, occupy-ing the Puebla ridge, was isolated and too weak to hold its ground. The centre was indeed on an easy range of hills, its front open, with a slope to the river, and powerful batteries bore on all the bridges; nev-ertheless, many of the guns being advanced in the loop of the Zadora, were exposed to musketshot from a wood on the right bank.

Seven bridges were within the scheme of operations, yet none were broken or retrenched. The bridge of La Puebla, facing the French left, was beyond the defile; that of Nanclares, facing Subijana de Alava, was at the French end of the defile; three bridges around the deep loop of the river opened upon the right of the French centre, that of Mendoza being highest up the stream, Vellodas lowest down, Tres Puentes in the centre: the bridges of Gamara Mayor and Ariaga were. as already said, guarded by Reille.

Wellington projected three distinct battles. Graham, moving by the Bilbao road, was to force a passage with twenty thousand men against Reille, and Giron's Gallicians were called up to his support; the design being to shut up the French centre and left between the Zadora and the Puebla mountain. Hill, having Morillo's Spaniards, Sylviera's Portuguese and the second British division, with cavalry and guns, in all twenty thousand men, was to force the passage of the Zadora river beyond the Puebla defile, assailing Maransin there with his right, while his left, threading the pass to enter the basin on that side, turned and menaced the French left and secured the bridge of Nanclares.

In the centre battle, the third, fourth, seventh and light divisions of infantry, the great mass of artillery, the heavy cavalry and Portuguese horsemen, in all thirty thousand combatants, were led by Wellington in person. Being encamped along the Bayas, these bodies had only to march over the ridge which bounded the basin of Vittoria on that side, and come down to their respective points on the Zadora, namely, the bridges of Mendoza, Tres Puentes, Villodas and Nanclares; but the country was so rugged exact concert could not be maintained, and each general of division was left in some degree master of his own movements.

BATTLE OF VITTORIA.

At daybreak on the 21st, the weather being rainy with a thick vapour, the troops moved from the Bayas, crossed the ridge and slowly approached the Zadora, while Hill on the other side of the ridge commenced the passage of that river beyond the defile of Puebla. On his side Morillo's Spaniards led, and their first brigade assailed the mountain to the right of the great road; but the ascent proved so steep the soldiers appeared to climb rather than walk up, and the second brigade, which was to connect the first with the British troops below, ascended only half-way. Little opposition was made until the first brigade was near the summit, when skirmishing commenced and Morillo was wounded; his second brigade then joined him, and the French, feeling the importance of the height, reinforced Maransin. Hill soon succoured Morillo with the 71st regiment and a battalion of light infantry, both under Colonel Cadogan, yet the fight was doubtful; for though the British won the summit and gained ground along the side of the mountain, Cadogan fell, and Gazan having sent Villatte's division to aid Maransin, the French fought so strongly that the allies could scarcely hold their ground. Hill sent more troops, and with the remainder of his corps passed the Zadora, threaded the Puebla defile, and fiercely issuing forth on the other side won the village of Subijana de Alava in front of Gazan's line, and then connecting his right with the troops on the mountain, maintained that forward position, despite of the enemy's efforts, until the centre battle was begun on his left.

Meanwhile Wellington, keeping all his cavalry in mass as a reserve, placed the fourth division opposite the bridge of Nanclares, the light division at the bridge of Villodas, both being covered by rugged ground and woods, and the light division so close to the water, that the skirmishers could have killed the French gunners in the loop of the river. The weather had now cleared up, and then Hill's battle was prolonged by the riflemen of the light division, with a biting fire on the enemy's skirmishers; but no serious effort was made, because the third and seventh divisions, meeting with rough ground, had not reached their point of attack, and it would have been imprudent to push the fourth division and cavalry over the bridge of Nanclares, with the Puebla defile in their rear, before the other divisions were ready.

While thus waiting, a Spanish peasant told Wellington the bridge of Tres Puentes on the left of the light division was unguarded, and offered to lead the troops over it. General Kempt's brigade was on the instant directed towards that quarter, and being concealed by some rocks, passed the narrow bridge at a running pace, mounted a steep rise of ground and halted close under the crest, being then actually behind the king's advanced posts, and within a few hundred yards of his line of battle. Some French cavalry approached, and two round shots were fired by the enemy, one of which killed the poor peasant to whose courage and intelligence the allies were so much indebted, but no movement of attack was made, and Kempt called the 15th Hussars over the river: they came at a gallop, crossing the narrow bridge one by one, horseman after horseman, and still the French remained torpid, showing an army but no general.

It was now one o'clock, Hill's assault on the village of Subijana was entirely developed, and a curling smoke, faintly seen far up the Zadora on the extreme left, and followed by the sound of distant guns, told that Graham's attack had also commenced. Then the king, finding both flanks in danger, caused his reserve to file off towards Vittoria, and gave Gazan orders to retire by successive masses; but at that moment the third and seventh divisions were seen moving rapidly down to the bridge of Mendoza, whereupon Gazan's artillery opened, a body of his cavalry drew near the bridge, and the French light troops, very strong there, commenced a vigorous musketry. Some British guns replied to the French cannon from the opposite bank, and the value of Kempt's forward position was instantly made manifest; for Andrew Barnard, springing forward, led the riflemen of the light division in the most daring manner between the French cavalry and the river, taking their light troops and gunners in flank, and engaging them so closely that the English artillerymen, thinking his dark-clothed troops enemies, played on both alike.

This singular attack enabled a brigade of the third division to pass the bridge of Mendoza without opposition, while the other brigade forded the river higher up, followed by the seventh division and Vandeleur's brigade of the light division. The French now abandoned the ground in front of Villodas; and the battle, which had slackened, was revived with extreme violence; for Hill pressed the enemy in his front, the fourth division passed the bridge of Nanclares, the smoke and sound of Graham's guns became more distinct, and the banks of the Zadora presented a continuous line of fire. Thus the French, weakened in the centre by the draft made of Villatte's division, and shaken in resolution by the king's order to retreat, became perplexed and could make no regular retrograde movement, because the allies were too close.

The seventh division and Colville's brigade of the third division, having forded the river, formed the left of the British, and were immediately engaged with the French right; but then Wellington, seeing the hill in front of Arinez nearly denuded of troops by the withdrawal of Villatte's division, led Picton and the rest of the third division in close column at a running pace, diagonally, across the front of both armies, towards that central point. This attack was headed by Barnard's riflemen, and followed by the remainder of Kempt's brigade and the hussars ;* and at the same time, when the fourth division had passed the bridge of Nanclares, the heavy

---

* The conception and execution of this movement has been repeatedly given to Picton. Erroneously so. My authority is the Duke of Wellington.

cavalry, a splendid body, galloped over also, squadron after squadron into the plain ground between Cole and Hill.

Thus caught in the midst of their dispositions for retreat, the French threw out a prodigious number of skirmishers, and fifty pieces of artillery played with astonishing activity. To answer this fire Wellington brought over most of his guns, and both sides were shrouded by a dense cloud of smoke and dust, under cover of which the French retired by degrees to the second range of heights in front of Gomecha, on which their reserve had been posted, yet still holding the village of Arinez on the main road. Picton's troops, always headed by the riflemen of the light division, then plunged into that village amidst a heavy fire of muskets and artillery, and three guns were captured; but the post was important, fresh French troops came down, and for some time the smoke and dust and clamour, the flashing of the fire-arms, and the shouts and cries of the combatants, mixed with the thundering of the guns, were terrible: finally the British troops issued forth victorious on the other side. During this conflict the seventh division, reinforced by Vandeleur's brigade of the light division, was heavily raked by a battery at the village of Margarita, until the 52nd regiment with an impetuous charge carried that village, and the 87th won the village of Hermandad, and, so fighting, the whole line advanced.

When the village of Arinez was won, the French opposed to Hill, at Subijana de Alava, were turned, and being hard pressed in front, and on their left by the troops of the Puebla mountain, fell back two miles in disorder, striving to regain the line of retreat to Vittoria. It was thought some cavalry launched at the moment would have disorganized the whole French battle, but none moved, and the confused multitude shooting ahead recovered order.

The ground was exceedingly diversified with woods and plains, here covered with corn, there broken by ditches, vineyards and hamlets; hence the action, for six miles, resolved itself into a running fight and cannonade, the dust and smoke and tumult of which, filling all the basin, passed onwards towards Vittoria. Many guns were taken, and at six o'clock the French reached the last defensible height, one mile in front of Vittoria. Behind them was the plain in which the city stood, and beyond the houses thousands of carriages, animals and non-combatants, men, women, and children, huddling together in all the madness of terror; and as the English shot went booming over head, the vast crowd started and swerved with a convulsive move-ment, while a dull and horrid sound of distress arose: but there was no hope, no stay for army or multitude. It was the wreck of a nation.

French courage was not yet quelled. Reille, on whom every thing now depended, maintained his post at the Upper Zadora, and the armies of the south and centre, drawing up on their last heights between the villages of Ali and Armentia, made their muskets flash like lightning, while more than eighty pieces of artillery, massed to-gether, pealed with such a horrid uproar, that the hills laboured and shook and streamed with fire and smoke, amidst which the dark figures of the French gunners were seen bounding with a frantic energy. This terrible cannonade and musketry checked the allies. The third division, having the brunt of the storm, could scarcely maintain its ground, and the French generals began to draw off their infantry from the right wing, when suddenly the fourth division rushing forward carried the hill on the French left; then the heights were all abandoned, for at that moment Joseph, finding the royal road so blocked by carriages the artillery could not pass, indicated the road of Salvatierra for retreat, and the troops at once went off in a confused mass. The British followed hard, and the light cavalry galloped through the town to intercept the new line, which passed a marsh, and was likewise choked with carriages and fugitive people, for on each side there were deep drains. Disorder and mischief then prevailed en-tirely. The guns were left on the edge of the marsh, the artillerymen fled with the horses, and the infantry, breaking through the miserable multitude, went clean off: the cavalry however still acted with order, and many generous horsemen were seen to carry children and women from the dreadful scene.

This retreat placed Reille in great danger. His advanced troops under Sarrut had been originally posted at the village of Aranguis, beyond the Zadora, hold in some heights which covered the bridges of Ariaga and Gamara Mayor. They were driven from thence by Graham's vanguard under General Oswald, who seized Gamara Menor on the Durango road, and forced the Franco-Spaniards from Durano on the royal causeway: thus the first blow on this side deprived the king of his best line of retreat and confined him to the road of Pampeluna. Sarrut however recrossed the river in good order, taking post with one brigade at the bridge of Ariaga and the village of Abechuco covering it; the other was in reserve to support him and General La Martiniere, who defended the bridge of Gamara Mayor and the village of that name, also on the right of the river. Digeon's dragoons were behind the village of Ariaga; Reille's own dragoons were behind the bridge of Gamara; one brigade of light cavalry was on the extreme right to sustain the Franco-Spanish troops, higher up the river; another, under General Curto, was on the French left, extending down the Zadora.

Longa's Spaniards were to have attacked Gamara at an early hour, when it was feebly occupied, but they did not stir, and the village being reinforced, Robinson's brigade of the fifth division assaulted it instead. He made the attack at a running pace at first, but the French fire became so heavy, that his men stopped to reply, and the columns got intermixed; however, encouraged by their officers, and especially by the example of General Robinson, an inexperienced man but of a daring spirit, they renewed the charge, broke through the village and even crossed the bridge. One gun was captured and the passage seemed to be won, when Reille suddenly turned twelve pieces upon the village, and then La Martiniere, rallying his men under cover of this cannonade retook the bridge: it was with difficulty the allied troops could even hold the village until they were reinforced.

Now a second British brigade came down, and the bridge was again carried, but the new troops were soon driven back as the others had been, and the bridge remained forbidden ground. Graham had meanwhile attacked the village of Abechuco, covering the bridge of Ariaga; it was carried at once by the German riflemen, who were supported by Bradford's Portuguese and the fire of twelve guns; yet here, as at Gamara, the French maintained the bridge, so that at both places the troops on each side remained stationary under a reciprocal fire of artillery and small arms. Reille, with inferior numbers, thus continued to interdict the passage until the tumult of Wellington's battle, coming up the Zadora, reached Vittoria itself, and a part of the British horsemen rode out of that city upon Sarrut's rear. Digeon's dragoons kept this cavalry in check for the moment, and Reille had previously formed a reserve of infantry, which now proved his safety; for Sarrut was killed at the bridge of Ariaga, and Menne, next in command, could scarcely draw off his troops while Digeon's dragoons held the British cavalry at point; but with the aid of his reserve Reille finally rallied all his troops at Betonio. He had now to make head on several sides, because the allies were coming down from Ariaga, from Durano, and from Vittoria; yet he fought his way to Metauco on the Salvatierra road and there covered the general retreat with some degree of order. Vehemently and closely did the British pursue, and neither the bold demeanour of the French cavalry, which made several vigorous charges, nor darkness, which now fell, could stop their victorious career until the flying masses had passed Metauco.

This was the battle of Vittoria. The French had, comparatively, few men slain, but to use Gazan's words, " *lost all their equippages, all their guns, all their treasure, all their stores, all their papers; no man could even prove how much pay.was due to him: generals and subordinate officers alike were reduced to the clothes on their backs, and most of them were barefooted.*" Never was an army more hardly used by its commander. The soldiers were not half beaten; yet never was a victory more complete. The French carried off but two pieces of artillery from the battle. Jourdan's baton, a stand of colours, one hundred and forty-three brass pieces, one hundred of which had been used in the fight, all the parcs and depots from Madrid, Valladolid, and Burgos, carriages, ammunition, treasure, every thing, fell into the hands of the victors. The loss in men did not exceed six thousand; the loss of the allies was five thousand one hundred and seventy six, killed, wounded, and missing. Of these one thousand and forty-nine were Portuguese; five hundred and fifty-three

Spanish. Hence the English lost more than double what Portuguese and Spaniards did together; yet both fought well, and especially the Portuguese: but British troops are the soldiers of battle. The spoil was immense, yet so plundered, principally by the followers and non-combatants, for with some exceptions the fighting troops may be said to have marched upon gold and silver without stooping to pick it up, that of five millions and a half of dollars, indicated by the French accounts to be in the money-chests, not one dollar came to the public. Wellington sent fifteen officers with power to examine all loaded animals passing the Ebro and the Duero yet very little was recovered; and this robbery was not confined to ignorant and vulgar people: officers were seen mixed with the mob contending for the disgraceful gain.

On the 22nd, Giron and Longa pursued the convoy which had moved under Maucune on the morning of the battle; the heavy cavalry and Portuguese horsemen remained at Vittoria; Pakenham came with the sixth division from Medina Pomar, and Wellington pursued Joseph, who had been flying up the Borundia and Araquil valleys all night. Reille, who covered the retreat, reached Huerta in the valley of Araquil, thirty miles from the field of battle, on the evening of the 22nd. Joseph attained Yrursun, from which roads branched off to Pampeluna on one side, and to Tolosa and St. Esteban on the other, from thence on the 23rd, expediting orders to different points on the French frontier to prepare provisions and succours for his suffering army; meanwhile he sent Reille by St. Esteban to the Lower Bidassoa with his infantry, six hundred select cavalry, the artillery-men and horses: Gazan's and D'Erlon's troops marched upon Pampeluna, intending to cross the frontier at St. Jean Pied de Port.

At Pampeluna the army bivouacked on the glacis of the fortress, but in such destitution and insubordination that the governor would not suffer them to enter the town.

Wellington, who had sent Graham's corps into Guipuscoa by the pass of St. Adrian, overtook the French rear and captured one of the two guns saved from Vittoria, and on the 28th the king fled into France by the Roncesvalles. Foy and Clausel were thus isolated on each flank and in great danger.

The first had a strong country, but his troops were disseminated, and the fugitives from the battle spread such alarm that the forts of Arlaban, Montdragon, and Salinas, blocking the passes into Guipuscoa, were abandoned to Longa and Giron. Foy, who had only one battalion in hand, rallied the fugitive garrisons, advanced, and from some prisoners acquired exact intelligence of the battle. Then he ordered the two convoys from Vittoria to march day and night towards France, and reinforcing himself with Maucune's escort gave battle to the Spanish general, who, having three times his force, worsted him with a loss of six guns and two hundred men. He retreated to Villafranca, where, late in the evening of the 24th, Graham came upon him from the side pass of San Adrian: he had now rallied a considerable force and gave battle on the Orio with Maucune's troops and St. Pol's Italian division: the first were beaten, yet the Italians gained some advantages, and the position was so strong that Graham had recourse to flank operations; Foy then retired to Tolosa, and again offered battle; whereupon Graham turned his flank with the Spaniards, broke his front with the Anglo-Portuguese, drove his wings beyond Tolosa on each side, and bursting the gate of the town forced a passage through his centre by the main road. Nevertheless Foy retreated with a loss of only four hundred men, and he had killed and wounded more than four hundred Anglo-Portuguese in the two days' operations. The Spanish loss was not known, but must have been considerable, and Graham, who was himself hurt, halted two days to hear of Wellington's progress. During that time the convoys reached France in safety, and Foy, his force increased by the junction of detachments to more than sixteen thousand men, threw a garrison into San Sebastian and joined Reille on the Bidassoa: twenty-five thousand men were then on that river, and Graham halted to invest Sebastian.

While these events passed in Guipuscoa, Clausel was more hardly pressed on the other flank of the allies. He had approached Vittoria with fourteen thousand men on the 22nd, but finding Pakenham there with the 6th division, retired to Logrono and halted until the evening of the 23rd, thus enabling Wellington, who thought he was at Tudela, to discover his real situation and march against him.

He fled to Tudela, reached it the 27th, after a march of sixty miles in forty hours, and thinking he had outstripped his pursuers proposed to enter France by Taffalla and Olite, but an alcalde told him Wellington had forestalled him at those places and he marched upon Zaragoza. He could have been intercepted again, yet Wellington, fearing to drive him on Suchet, only launched Mina in pursuit, and Clausel after destroying guns and baggage finally escaped by Jacca into France. The king had meanwhile caused Gazan to re-enter Spain by the Bastan, from whence Hill quickly drove him. Joseph's reign was over. After years of toils and combats, admired rather than understood, Lord Wellington, emerging from the chaos of the Peninsula struggle, crowned the Pyrenees—a recognized conqueror. From that pinnacle the clangour of his trumpets was heard, and the splendour of his genius blazed out, a flaming beacon for warring nations.

BOOK X.

Battle of Castalla—English Siege of Taragona—Siege of San Sebastian
—Storming of San Bartolomeo—First Storm of San Sebastian.

While the main armies strove in the north of Spain, the Mediterranean coast was the scene of a secondary contest maintained by an English expedition sent from Sicily in 1812. Destined at first for Catalonia, it finally landed at Alicant, where it remained inactive until April, 1813, but then Sir John Murray, whose want of vigour on the Douro was overbalanced by aristocratic influence at home, assumed command. Acting in conjunction with the Spanish general Elio, he commenced a series of petty enterprises, and broached several projects which he had not nerve to execute, and only roused Suchet to serious action. That marshal, previously inert, concentrated in the night of the 11th all his disposable force, and next morning falling upon Mijares, Elio's lieutenant, defeated him with a loss of fifteen hundred prisoners. Then he marched against Murray, who retreated through the pass of Biar to a position of battle, leaving Colonel F. Adam with two thousand five hundred men and six guns in the defile. The ground was very strong, but the French light troops crowned the rocks on each side and after two hours' fighting the allies abandoned the pass, with a loss of two guns and some prisoners besides killed and wounded, yet made their retreat, three miles, to the main position, in good order, and were not pursued.

This double success in one day indicated the approach of a decisive battle, in anticipation of which Murray had studied and chosen his ground with judgment. His left, composed of Whittingham's Spanish division, was intrenched on a rugged sierra, and the troops coming from Biar prolonged the line on a front of two miles, until the ridge ended abruptly over the town of Castalla. That place with its old castle, crowning an isolated sugar-loaf hill, was prepared for defence, having all the approaches commanded by batteries, and being strongly occupied with Mackenzie's British division. The cavalry was disposed on a plain, partly in front, partly behind the town. Clinton's English and Roche's Spanish divisions were in reserve in rear of the right, on a lower height nearly perpendicular to the main front; and their line as well as the town was covered by the dry bed of a torrent called a *baranco*, having precipitous sides and in many places a hundred feet in depth: that front was therefore refused and scarcely attackable.

On the 12th Suchet's cavalry, issuing cautiously from the defile of Biar, extended to its left on the plain; the infantry, following, took possession of a low ridge facing the Sierra, and then the cavalry, passing the baranco, turned the town as if to menace the divisions in reserve. This movement alarmed Murray, and notwithstanding the impregnable strength of his ground he shrunk from the encounter; even while Suchet was advancing he thrice gave orders to the quartermaster general Donkin to put the army in retreat; the last time so peremptorily, that obedience must have followed if at that moment the French light troops in advance had not commenced firing.

BATTLE OF CASTALLA.

Suchet's dispositions were slowly made, as if he feared to commence. A mountain spur, jutting from the Sierra between Whittingham and the troops from Biar, hid two-thirds of the allies from his view, and he first sent an exploring column of infantry towards Castalla, to turn the intercepting spur and discover all the conditions of the position; when that was effected his cavalry closed towards the baranco. Then he formed two powerful columns of attack and sent them against Whittingham and Adam on each side of the spur, retaining a reserve on his own ridge, and keeping his exploring column towards Castalla to meet any sally from that point.

The ascent against Whittingham was so ruggedly steep, and the upper part so intrenched, that the battle resolved itself there at once into a stationary skirmish of light troops; but on the other side of the spur the French mounted the height, slowly indeed and with many skirmishers, yet so resolutely, that it was evident good fighting only would send them down again. Their light troops, spreading over the face of the Sierra and in some places attaining the summit, were met and held in play by the Anglo-Sicilian troops with changing fortune; but where the main column came on the 27th Regiment there was a terrible crash of battle, and preceded by a singular encounter. For an abrupt declination of ground enabled the French to halt and re-form for the decisive assault, out of fire, yet close to that regiment which was by order lying down in expectation of the charge. Suddenly a grenadier officer, rising alone to the upper ground, challenged Waldron the captain of the 27th Grenadiers to single combat; he, an agile Irishman of boiling courage, instantly leaped forward to the duel, and the hostile lines though ready to charge awaited the result. Rapidly the champions' swords clashed and glittered in the sun, but Waldron cleft his adversary's head in twain, and the 27th springing up with a deafening shout charged and sent the French, maugre their numbers and courage, down the mountain side, covering it with their dead and wounded. It was a glorious exploit, erroneously attributed in the despatch to Colonel Adam, though entirely conducted by the colonel of the regiment, Reeves.

Suchet seeing his principal column thus broken, and having the worst of the fight in other parts, made two secondary attacks with his reserve to cover a rally, yet failed in both and his army was thus separated in three parts without connection; for the column beaten by Reeves was in great confusion at the foot of the Sierra, the exploring column was on the left, and the cavalry beyond the baranco, the only passage across it being commanded by the allies. A vigorous sally from Castalla, and a general advance, would then have compelled the French infantry to fall back upon Biar in confusion before the cavalry could come to their assistance, and the victory would have been completed; but Murray, who had remained during the whole action behind Castalla, first gave Suchet time to rally and retire in order towards the pass of Biar, and then gradually passing out Clinton's and Roche's divisions by the right of the town, with a tedious pedantic movement, changed his own front, keeping his left at the foot of the heights, and extending his right, covered by the cavalry, towards another sierra called Onil: General Mackenzie however, moving out by the left of Castalla with four battalions and eight guns, followed the enemy without orders.

Suchet had by this time plunged into the pass with his infantry, cavalry and tumbrils, in one mass, leaving the rearguard of three battalions and eight guns to cover the passage; these being pressed by Mackenzie and sharply cannonaded, turned and offered battle, answering gun for gun; but they were heavily crushed by the English shot, the clatter of musketry commenced, and one well-directed vigorous charge would have overturned and driven them in mass upon the other troops, then wedged in the narrow defile. Mackenzie was willing, but his advance had been directed by the quartermaster-general Donkin, not by Murray, and he was now compelled by the latter, despite of all remonstrances and the indignant cries of the troops, to retreat! Suchet, thus relieved from ruin by his adversary, immediately occupied a position across the defile, having his flanks on the ridges above; and though Murray finally sent some light companies to attack his left he retained his position until night.

This battle, in which the allies had about seventeen thousand men of all arms, the French about fifteen thousand, was, Suchet says, brought on against his wish by the impetuosity of his light troops, and that he lost only eight hundred men. His statement is confirmed by Vacani the Italian historian. Murray affirmed that it was a pitched battle, and that the French lost above three thousand men. In favour of Suchet's version it may be remarked, that neither the place, nor the time, nor the mode of attack was answerable to his talents and experience in war, if he had really intended a pitched battle; and though the fight was strong at the principal point, it was scarcely possible to have so many as three thousand killed and wounded. Eight hundred seems too few, because the loss of the victorious troops, with all advantages of ground, was more than six hundred. This however is certain; if Suchet lost three thousand men, which would have been at least a fourth of his infantry, he must have been so disabled, that what with the narrow defile of Biar in the rear, and the distance of his cavalry in the plain, to have escaped at all was extremely discreditable to Murray's generalship.

ENGLISH SIEGE OF TARRAGONA.

It has been shown that Lord Wellington put every armed body of the Peninsula in movement against the French when he commenced the march to Vittoria; and under his combinations the Duke del Parque should have joined Elio from Andalusia, before the battle of Castalla, which would have raised the allied forces there to fifty thousand men, including the irregulars. Del Parque with the usual Spanish procrastination delayed his arrival until the end of May; and then Murray had to execute his part of the following plan, sketched by Wellington to hamper Suchet and prevent him from moving to the king's assistance. The Spaniards, numerous but unwieldy, were to oppose that marshal in front on the Xucar, while Murray with the Anglo-Sicilians was to embark and sail for the siege of Tarragona in his rear: if he detached men to raise the siege the Spaniards were to advance, and Murray was to return and aid them to keep the country thus gained: if Suchet came back to recover his ground this operation was to be repeated.

On the 31st of May Murray, in pursuance of this arrangement, sailed with fifteen thousand men under arms, his British and Germans being about eight thousand, his cavalry seven hundred. His battering-train was complete and powerful, the materials for gabions and fascines were previously collected at Iviça, and the naval part, under Admiral Hallowel, was strong in ships of the line, frigates, bomb-vessels, gun-boats and transports. There was however no cordiality between General Clinton, the second in command, and Murray; nor between the latter and his quartermaster general Donkin; nor between Donkin and the admiral: subordinate officers also, adopting false notions, some from vanity, some from hearsay, added to the uneasy state of the leaders, and there was much tale-bearing. Neither admiral nor general was very sanguine as to success, and in no quarter was there a clear comprehension of Lord Wellington's ably devised plan.

When the fleet passed Valencia with a fair wind Suchet

knew the expedition aimed at Catalonia, and prepared to aid that principality, but he could not march before the 7th of June. Murray's armament however, having very favourable weather, anchored on the evening of the 2nd in the Bay of Tarragona, whence five ships of war were sent with two battalions of infantry and some guns, under Colonel Prevost to attack San Felippe de Balaguer, a fort garrisoned by a hundred men and only sixty feet square. But it was on a steep isolated rock in the gorge of a pass, blocking the only carriage-way from Tortoza to Tarragona, and though the mountains on either hand commanded it, they were nearly inaccessible themselves, and great labour was required to form the batteries.

Prevost, landing the 3rd, was joined by a Spanish brigade, and in concert with the navy placed two six-pounders on the heights south of the pass, from whence at seven hundred yards' distance they threw shrapnel-shells. Next day two twelve-pounders and a howitzer, brought to the same point by the sailors, opened also, and at night the seamen with extraordinary exertions dragged up five twenty-four pounders and their stores. The troops then constructed their batteries with great labour, for the earth was carried up from below, and everything else, even water, brought from the ships, the landing-place being more than a mile and a half off; wherefore, time being valuable, favourable terms were offered to the garrison. They were refused and the fire continued, yet with slight success, one battery was relinquished, and a violent storm retarded the construction of the others

Colonel Prevost had early warned Murray that his means were insufficient, and a second Spanish brigade was now sent to him; but, so severe was the labour, that the breaching batteries were still incomplete on the 6th, and out of three guns mounted one was disabled. Suchet, who was making forced marches to Tortoza, ordered the governor of that place to succour San Felippe, and he would certainly have raised the siege, if Captain Peyton of the Thames frigate had not brought up two eight-inch mortars, with which, on the 7th, he exploded a small magazine, whereupon the garrison surrendered. The besiegers then occupied the place, and meanwhile Murray had commenced the siege of Tarragona.

Bertoletti, an Italian, commanded the fortress and was

supposed to be disaffected, yet he proved himself a loyal and energetic officer. His garrison, sixteen hundred strong, five hundred being privateer seamen and Franco-Spaniards, served him well, and when Murray occupied the Olivo and Loretto heights the first day, and the town was bombarded in the night by the navy, the fire was returned so sharply that the flotilla suffered most. Two batteries were then opened the 6th, but were found too distant, and a third was commenced six hundred yards from Fort Royal. The 8th a practicable breach was made in that outwork, yet the assault was deferred, and some pieces removed to play from the Olivo; whereupon the besieged, finding the fire slacken, repaired the breach at Fort Royal and increased the defences. The subsequent proceedings cannot be understood without reference to the relative positions of the French and allied armies.

Tarragona was situated on one of a cluster of rocks terminating a range descending to the sea, but, with the exception of that range, surrounded by an open country called the *Campo de Taragona*, itself environed by very rugged mountains, through which several roads descend into the plain.

Westward there were only two carriage-ways from Tortoza. One direct, by the Col de Balaguer to Tarragona; the other circuitous, leading by Mora, Falcet, Momblanch and Reus. The capture of San Felippe blocked the first, the second was in bad order, and at best only available for small mountain-guns.

Northward there was a carriage-way leading from Lerida, which united with that from Falcet at Momblanch.

Eastward was the royal causeway from Barcelona, running through Villa Franca and Torredembarra, and after passing Villa Franca sending two branches to the right, one through the Col de Cristina, the other through Col de Leibra.

Between these various roads the mountains were too rugged to permit cross communications; troops coming from different sides could only unite in the Campo de Tarragona; where Murray, who had fifteen thousand fighting men, and Copons, who had six thousand regulars and the irregular division of Manso, could present twenty-five thousand combatants.

Copons indeed told Murray, that his troops could only fight in position, and he would not join in any operation to endanger his retreat into the mountains; but his force, the best in Spain, was now at Reus and the Col de Balaguer, ready to harass and oppose any French corps which should attempt to descend into the Campo. Murray could also calculate upon seven or eight hundred seamen and marines to aid him in the siege, or in a battle near the shore, and he expected three thousand fresh troops from Sicily. Sir Edward Pellew, commanding the great Mediterranean fleet, promised to' distract the French by a descent eastward of Barcelona, and a general rising of the Somatenes might have been effected: those mountaineers were indeed all at his disposal, to procure intelligence, to give timely notice of the French marches and impede them by breaking up the roads.

The French power was greater yet more scattered. On the west Suchet, coming with nine thousand men from Valencia, was to be reinforced by Pannetier's brigade and some troops from Tortoza, up to eleven or twelve thousand men with artillery; but the fall of San Felippe de Balaguer barred his only carriage-way, and the road by Mora and Momblanch, which remained open, was long and bad. On the eastern side Maurice Mathieu could bring seven thousand men with artillery from Barcelona; Decaen could move from the Ampurdam with an equal number, and thus twenty-five thousand men in all might finally bear upon the allied army.

Suchet had more than a hundred and sixty miles to march, and Maurice Mathieu was to collect his forces from various places, and march seventy miles after Murray had disembarked; nor could he stir at all until Tarragona was actually besieged, lest the allies should reembark and attack Barcelona Decaen had in like manner to look to the security of the Ampurdam, and was one hundred and thirty miles distant. Wherefore the English general could calculate upon ten days' clear operations after investment, before even the heads of the enemy's columns could issue from the hills bordering the Campo; and it was possible that Suchet might endeavour to cripple the Spaniards in his front at Valencia before he marched to the succour of Tarragona.

Eastwards and westward also, the royal causeway was in places exposed to the fire of the naval squadron; and though the first siege of Tarragona had shown that an army could not be there stopped by this fire, it was an impediment not to be left out of the calculation. Thus, a central position, possession of the enemy's point of junction, the initial movement, the good-will of the people, and the aid of powerful flank diversions belonged to Murray: superior numbers and better soldiers to the French, since the allies, brave and formidable to fight in a position, were not well constituted for general operations.

Tarragona, if the resources for an internal defence be disregarded, was a weak place. A simple revetment three feet and a half thick, without ditch or counterscarp, covered it on the west; the two outworks of Fort Royal and San Carlos, slight obstacles at best, were not armed or even repaired until after the investment; and the garrison, too weak for the extent of rampart, was oppressed with labour. Here then, time being precious to both sides, ordinary rule should have been set aside for daring operations, and Murray's troops were brave. They had been acting together for nearly a year, and after the fight at Castalla became so eager, that an Italian regiment, which at Alicant was ready to go over bodily to the enemy, now volunteered to lead the assault on Fort Royal. This confidence was not shared by their general: up to the 8th his proceedings were ill judged, and his after operations disgraceful to the British army.

False reports had made Suchet reach Tortoza on the 5th, and put two thousand Frenchmen in motion from Lerida, whereupon Murray avowed alarm and regret at having left Alicant; yet he constructed heavy counter-batteries near the Olivo, sent a detachment to Valls on the Lerida road, and placed Manso on that of Barcelona.

On the 9th the emissaries said the French were coming from the east and from the west, and would, when united, exceed twenty thousand. Murray sought an interview with the admiral, and declared his intention to raise the siege, and though his views changed during the conference, he was discontented, and the two commanders were evidently at variance, for Hallowel would not join in a summons to the governor, and again bombarded the place.

On the 10th spies in Barcelona gave notice that ten thousand French with fourteen guns would march from that city next day, whereupon Copons joined Manso; but Murray landed several mortars, armed the batteries at the Olivo, and on the 11th opened their fire in concert with the ships of war. Professing also a desire to fight the column coming from Barcelona, he sent the cavalry under Lord Frederick Bentinck to Altafalla, and pretending to seek a position of battle to the eastward left orders to storm the out works that night; he returned however before the hour appointed, extremely disturbed by intelligence that Maurice Mathieu was at Villa Franca with eight thousand combatants, and Suchet closing on the Col de Balaguer. His infirmity of mind was now apparent. At eight o'clock he repeated the order to assault, and the storming party was awaiting the signal, when a countermand arrived; the siege was then to be raised and the guns removed immediately from the Olivo; the commandant of artillery remonstrated, and the general promised to hold the batteries until next night, but meanwhile called in the detachment at Valls and the cavalry, without any notice to Copons, though he depended on their support.

All the artillery stores and the heavy guns of the batteries on the low ground, were removed to the beach for embarkation on the morning of the 12th, and at twelve o'clock Lord Frederick Bentinck arrived with the cavalry: it is said he was ordered to shoot his horses, but refused to obey and moved towards the Col de Balaguer. The detachment from Valls arrived next, the infantry marched to Cape Salou to embark, the horsemen followed Lord Frederick, and were themselves followed by fourteen pieces of artillery; yet each body moved independently, and all was confused, incoherent, afflicting, and dishonourable.

When the seamen were embarking the guns, orders were sent to abandon that business and collect boats for the reception of troops, the enemy being supposed close at hand; and notwithstanding Murray's previous promise to hold the Olivo he now directed the artillery officer to spike the guns and burn the carriages. Then loud murmurs arose, army and navy were alike indignant, and so excited, that it is said personal insult was offered to the general.

Three staff-officers repaired in a body to his quarters to offer plans and opinions, and the admiral, who did not object to raising the siege but to the manner of doing it,.would not suffer the seamen to discontinue the embarkation of artillery; he however urged an attack upon the column coming from Barcelona, and opposed the order to spike the guns at the Olivo, offering to be responsible for carrying all clear off during the night.

Murray again wavered. Denying he had ordered the battering-pieces to be spiked, he sent counter-orders, and directed a part of Clinton's troops to advance towards the Gaya river; yet a few hours afterwards he peremptorily renewed the order to destroy the guns. Even this unhappy action was not performed without confusion. General Clinton, forgetful of his own arrangements, with an obsolete courtesy took off his hat to salute an enemy's battery which had fired upon him, forgetting that this action from that particular spot was the conventional signal for the artillery to spike the guns: they were thus spiked prematurely. All the troops were embarked in the night of the 12th, and many stores and horses on the 13th, without interruption from the enemy; but nineteen battering-pieces, whose carriages had been burnt, were, in view of the fleet and army, carried in triumph, with all the platforms, fascines, gabions, and small ammunition, into the fortress ! Murray, seemingly unaffected by this misfortune, shipped himself on the evening of the 12th and took his usual repose in bed !

During these proceedings, the French, unable to surmount the obstacles opposed to their junction, unable even to communicate by their emissaries, were despairing of the safety of Tarragona. Suchet did not reach Tortoza before the 10th, but a detachment from the garrison had on the 8th attempted to succour San Felippe, and nearly captured the naval Captain Adam, Colonel Prevost, and other officers, who were examining the country. On the other side Maurice Mathieu reached Villa Franca the 10th, announcing that Decaen was close behind with a powerful force; he drove Copons from Arbos the 11th, and sent his scouting parties into Vendrills, as if he was resolved singly to attack Murray. Sir Edward Pellew had however landed his marines at Rosas, which arrested Decaen's march; and Maurice

Mathieu, alarmed at the cessation of fire about Tarragona, knowing nothing of Suchet's movements and too weak to fight the allies alone, fell back in the night of the 12th to the Llobregat.

Suchet's operations to the westward were even less decisive. His advanced guard under Panettier reached Perillo the 10th. Next day, hearing nothing from his spies, he caused Panettier to pass by his left over the mountains to some heights terminating abruptly on the Campo; on the 12th therefore that officer was but twenty-five miles from Tarragona, and a patrol, descending into the plains, met Lord Frederick Bentinck's troopers, and reported that Murray's whole army was at hand: Panettier would not then enter the Campo, but at night kindled large fires to encourage the garrison. These signals were unobserved, the country people had disappeared, no intelligence could be procured, and Suchet could not follow him with a large force in those wild hills, where there was no water. Thus on both sides of Tarragona the succouring armies were quite baffled at the moment chosen by Murray for flight.

Suchet now received alarming intelligence from Valencia, yet still anxious for Tarragona, pushed towards Felippe de Balaguer on the 14th, thinking to find Prevot's division alone; but the head of his column was suddenly cannonaded by the Thames frigate, and he found the British fleet anchored off San Felippe and disembarking troops. Murray's operations were indeed as irregular as those of a partizan, yet without partizan vigour. He had heard in the night of the 12th of Panettier's march, and to protect the cavalry and guns under Lord Frederick, sent Mackenzie's division by sea to Balaguer on the 13th, following with the whole army on the 14th. Mackenzie drove back the French posts at both sides of the pass, the embarkation of the cavalry and artillery then commenced, and Suchet, still uncertain if Tarragona had fallen, marched to bring off Panettier.

At this moment Murray heard that Maurice Mathieu's column, which he always erroneously supposed to be under Decaen, had retired to the Llobregat, that Copons was again at Reus, and Tarragona had not been reinforced. Elated by this information, he revolved various projects in his mind, at one time thinking to fall upon Suchet, at another to cut off Panettier; now resolving to march upon Cambrills, and even to menace Tarragona again by land; then he was for sending a detachment by sea to surprise the latter, yet finally disembarked the army on the 15th, and being ignorant of Suchet's last movement decided to strike at Panettier. With that object, he detached Mackenzie by a rugged valley against Valdillos, which he reached on the 16th; but Suchet had then carried off Panettier's brigade, and next day the detachment was recalled by Murray, who now only thought of re-embarking.

This determination was caused by a fresh alarm from the eastward. Maurice Mathieu, hearing the siege was raised, and the allies had re-landed at the Col de Balaguer, retraced his steps and boldly entered Cambrills the 17th, on which day, Mackenzie having returned, Murray's whole army was concentrated in the pass. Suchet was then behind Perillo, and as Copons was at Reus, by Murray's desire, to attack Maurice Mathieu, the latter was in danger, if the English general had been capable of a vigorous stroke. On the other hand Suchet, too anxious for Valencia, had disregarded Mackenzie's movement on Valdillos, and taught by the disembarkation of the army at San Felippe that the fate of Tarragona, for good or evil, was decided, had on the 16th retired to Perillo and Amposta, attentive only to the movement of the fleet.

Meanwhile Maurice Mathieu endeavoured to surprise Copons, who was led into this danger by Murray; for having desired him to harass the French general's rear with a view to a general attack, he changed his plan without giving the Spaniard notice. However he escaped, and Murray was free to embark or remain at Col de Balaguer. He called a council of war, and it was concluded to reembark; but at that moment the great Mediterranean fleet appeared in the offing, and Admiral Hallowel, observing the signal announcing Lord William Bentinck's arrival, answered with more promptitude than decorum, *"we are all delighted."* Thus ended an operation perhaps the most disgraceful that ever befel the British arms.

Murray's misconduct deeply affected Lord Wellington's operations. The English battering train being taken, Suchet had nothing to fear for Catalonia, which was full of fortresses, and he could therefore move by Zaragoza to disturb the siege of Pampeluna, which was consequently relinquished for a blockade, and the siege of San Sebastian undertaken This involved the adoption of an immense line of covering positions along the Pyrenees from Roncesvalles to the Bidassoa, and along the left bank of that river to the sea; and the siege, itself a difficult one, was rendered more so by the culpable negligence of the English naval administration.

Passages, the only port near the scene of operations suited for the supply of the army, being between the covering and besieging forces, the stores and guns once landed were in danger from every movement of the enemy; and no permanent magazines could therefore be established nearer than Bilbao, at which port and at St. Ander and Coruna the great depots of the army were fixed; the stores being transported to them from the establishments in Portugal. But the French held Santona, whence their privateers interrupted the communication along the coast of Spain; American privateers did the same between Lisbon and Coruna; and the intercourse between Sebastian and the ports of France was scarcely molested by the English vessels of war: because Wellington's urgent remonstrances could not procure a sufficient naval force on the coast of Biscay !

SIEGE OF SAN SEBASTIAN.

Built on a low sandy isthmus, having the harbour on one side, the river Urumea on the other, Sebastian was strong; and behind it rose the Monte Orgullo, a rugged cone four hundred feet high, washed by the ocean and crowned with the small castle of La Mota. This hill was cut off from the town by a line of defensive works, and covered with batteries; but was itself commanded at a distance of thirteen hundred yards by the Monte Olia, on the other side of the Urumea.

The land front of the town, three hundred and fifty yards wide, stretching quite across the isthmus, consisted of a high curtain or rampart, very solid, with half bastions at either end and a lofty casemated flat bastion or cavalier in the centre.

A regular horn-work was pushed out from this front, and six hundred yards beyond the horn-work the isthmus was closed by the ridge of San Bartolomeo, at the foot of which stood the suburb of San Martin.

On the opposite side of the Urumea were certain sandy hills called the *Chofres,* through which the road from Passages passed to a wooden bridge over the river, and thence, by a suburb called Santa Catalina, along the top of a sea-wall which formed *a fausse-braye* for the horn-work.

The flanks of the town were protected by simple ramparts, washed on one side by the water of the harbour, on the other by the Urumea, which at high tide covered four of the twenty-seven feet comprised in its elevation. This was the weak side of the fortress, though protected by the river; for it had only a single wall, which was ill flanked by two old towers and a half-bastion called San Elmo, close under the Monte Orgullo. There was no ditch, no counterscarp, no glacis; the wall could be seen to its base from the Chofre hills, at distances varying from five hundred to a thousand yards; and when the tide was out the Urumea left a dry strand under the rampart as far as St. Elmo. However the guns from the batteries at Monte Orgullo, especially that called the Mirador, could rake this strand. The other flank of the town was secured by the harbour, in the mouth of which was a rocky island, called Santa Clara, where the French had established a post of twenty-five men.

Previous to the battle of Vittoria Sebastian was nearly dismantled; there were no bomb proofs, no palisades, no outworks; the wells were foul, the place only supplied with water by an aqueduct. Joseph's defeat restored its importance as a fortress. General Emanuel Rey entered it the 22nd of June, bringing with him the convoy which had quitted Vittoria the day before the battle. The town was thus filled with emigrant Spanish families, and the ministers and other persons attached to the court; the population, ordinarily eight thousand, was increased to sixteen thousand, and disorder and confusion were predominant. Rey, pushed by necessity, forced all persons not residents to march at once to France; the people of quality went by sea, the others by land, and fortunately without being attacked, for the Partidas would have given them no quarter.

On the 27th Foy threw a reinforcement into the place, and next day Mendizabal's Spaniards appeared; whereupon Rey burned the wooden bridge with both the suburbs, and commenced fortifying the heights of San Bartolomeo.

The 29th the Spaniards having slightly attacked San Bartolomeo were repulsed.

The 1st of July the governor of Gueteria abandoned that place, and his troops, three hundred, entered San Sebastian; at the same time a vessel from St. Jean de Luz arrived with fifty-six cannoniers and some workmen. The garrison was thus increased to three thousand men, and all persons not able to provide subsistence for themselves were ordered away: meanwhile Mendizabal cut off the aqueduct.

On the 3rd an English frigate and sloop with some small craft arrived to blockade the harbour, but French vessels from St. Jean de Luz continued to enter by night.

On the 4th Rey sallied to obtain news, and after some hours' skirmishing returned with prisoners.

The 6th, French vessels with a detachment of troops and a considerable convoy of provisions from St. Jean de Luz entered the harbour.

The 7th Mendizabal tried, unsuccessfully, to set fire to the convent of San Bartolomeo.

The 9th Graham arrived with British and Portuguese troops, and on the 13th the Spaniards marched away.

At this time Reille was at Vera and Echallar, in a menacing position, but Wellington drove him thence on the 15th and established the seventh and light divisions there; thus covering the passes over the Pena de Haya mountain, by which the siege might have been interrupted.

Before Graham arrived the French had constructed a redoubt on San Bartolomeo, connecting it with the convent of that name, which they also fortified. These outworks were supported by posts in the ruined houses of the San Martin suburb, and by a circular redoubt, formed of casks, on the main road, half-way between the convent and horn-work. Hence, working along the isthmus, it was necessary to carry in succession three lines covering the town, and a fourth behind it, at the foot of Monte Orgullo before the castle of La Mota could be assailed: seventy-six pieces were mounted on the walls.

The beseiging army consisted of the fifth division under General Oswald, and the Portugese brigades of J. Wilson and Bradford, reinforced by detachments from the first division. Including the artillery-men, some seamen commanded by Lieutenant O'Reilly of the Surveillante, and one hundred regular sappers and miners, now for the first time used in the sieges of the Peninsula, nearly ten thousand men were employed, with forty pieces of artillery. The seige depot was at Passages, from whence to the Chofre sand-hills was only one mile and a half of good road, and a pontoon bridge was laid over the Urumea river above the Chofres; but from thence to the height of Bartolomeo was more than five miles of very bad road.

Early in July, Major Smith, the engineer of Tarifa, proposed a plan of siege, founded upon the facility furnished by the Chofre hills to destroy the flanks, rake the principal front, and form a breach with the same batteries; the works would, he observed, be secured, except at low water, by the Urumea, and counter-batteries could be constructed on the left of that river, to rake the line in which the breach was to be formed. Against the castle and its out-works he relied principally upon the vertical fire, instancing the reduction of Fort Bourbon inthe West Indies as proof of its efficacy. This plan would probably have reduced Sebastian in a reasonable time without any remarkable loss of men, and Lord Wellington approved of it, though he erroneously doubted the efficacy of the vertical fire. He renewed his spproval after examining the works in person, and all his orders were in that spirit; but neither the plan nor his orders were followed, and the seige which should have been an ordinary event of war obtained a mournful celebrity. Wellington has been unjustly charged with a contempt for the maxims of the great masters of the art in his desire to save time: he did not urge the engineer here beyond the rules. *Take the place in the quickest manner, but do not from over speed fail to take it,* was the sense of his instructions. The haste was with Graham, one of England's best soldiers, but of a genius intuitive rather than reflective, which, joined to great natural modesty and a certain easiness of temper, caused him at times to abandon his own correct conceptions for less judicious counsels of men who advised deviations from the original plan.

In the night of the 10th two batteries were raised against the convent and redoubt of San Bartolomeo; and in that of the 13th, four batteries, to contain twenty of the heaviest guns and four eight-inch howitzers, were marked out on the Chofre sand-hills, at distances varying from six hundred to thirteen hundred yards from the eastern rampart of the town. No parallel of support was made, because the river was supposed unfordable, but good trenches of communications and subsequently regular approaches were formed. Two attacks were thus established—one on the right bank of the Urumea by the Portuguese brigades; one on the left bank by the fifth division: yet most of the troops were encamped on the right bank to facilitate a junction with the covering army in the event of a general battle.

On the 14th a French sloop entered the harbour with supplies, and the batteries of the left attack opened against San Bartolomeo, throwing hot shot into the convent. The besieged responded with musketry from the redoubt, with heavy guns from the town, and with a field-piece which they had mounted on the belfry of the convent itself.

The 15th Colonel Fletcher took command of the engineers, but Major Smith retained the direction of the attack from the Chofre hills, and Wellington's orders continued to pass through his hands. This day, the convent being set on fire, the musketry of the besieged silenced, and the defences damaged, the Portuguese troops of the fifth division felt the enemy, but were repulsed with loss: the French then sallied, and the firing only ceased at nightfall.

A battery for seven additional guns was now commenced against Bartolomeo on the right of the Urumea, and the original batteries again set fire to the convent, yet the flames were extinguished by the garrison.

In the night of the 16th Rey sounded the Urumea, designing to cross and storm the batteries on the Chofres; but the fords discovered were shifting, and the difficulty of execution deterred him.

The 17th, the convent being nearly in ruins, an assault was ordered. Detachments from Wilson's Portuguese, supported by the light company of the 9th British Regiment and three companies of the Royals, composed one column, which under General Hay was to storm the redoubt; another column under General Bradford, composed of Portuguese, but supported by three companies of the 9th British Regiment under Colonel Cameron, assailed the convent.

STORMING OF SAN BARTOLOMEO.

At ten o'clock in the morning two six-pounders opened against the redoubt, and the French, reinforced and occupying the suburb of San Martin in support, announced with a sharp return of fire their resolution to fight. The Portuguese advanced slowly at both attacks, and the companies of the 9th, passing through them, first fell upon the enemy. Cameron's grenadiers going down the face of the hill were exposed to a heavy cannonade from the horn-work, yet soon gained the cover of a wall, fifty yards from the convent, and there awaited the second signal. This rapid advance, which threatened to cut off the garrison from the suburb, joined to the fire of the two six-pounders, and some other field-pieces on the farther side of the Urumea, caused the French to abandon the redoubt, whereupon Cameron jumped over the wall and assaulted both the convent and the houses of the suburb. At the latter a fierce struggle ensued, and Captain Woodman was killed in the upper room of a house, after fighting his way from below; yet the grenadiers carried the convent with such rapidity that the French could not explode some small mines, and hastily joined the troops in the suburb: there the combat continued, Cameron's force was much reduced and the affair was becoming doubtful, when the remainder of his regiment arrived and the suburb was with much fighting entirely won.

At the right attack the company of the 9th although retarded by a ravine, by a thick hedge, by the slowness of the Portuguese, and by a heavy fire, entered the abandoned redoubt with little loss; but the troops were then rashly led against the cask redoubt, contrary to orders, and were beaten back by the enemy. The loss was thus balanced. That of the French was two hundred and forty, and the companies of the 9th under Cameron, alone, had seven officers and sixty men killed or wounded. The operation, although successful, was an error; for the seven-gun battery on the right of the Urumea was not opened, wherefore the assault was precipitate or the battery was not necessary, but the loss justified the conception of the battery. When the action ceased the engineers made a lodgement in the redoubt, and commenced two batteries to rake the horn-work and the eastern rampart of the place. Two other batteries were also commenced on the right bank of the Urumea.

The 18th the besieged threw up traverses on the land front to meet the raking fire of the besiegers; and the latter dragged four pieces up the Monte Olia to plunge into the Mirador and other works on the Monte Orgullo. In the night a lodgement was made on the hills of San Martin, the two batteries at the right attack were armed, and two additional mortars dragged up the Monte Olia.

On the 19th all these batteries were armed, and in the night the French were driven from the cask redoubt.

All the batteries opened fire the 20th, and were principally directed to form the breach.

Smith's plan was similar to that followed by Marshal Berwick a century before. He proposed a lodgement on the horn-work before the breach should be assailed; but he had not then read the description of that siege, and unknowingly fixed the breaching-point precisely where the wall had been most strongly rebuilt after Berwick's attack. This was a fault, yet a slight one, because the wall did not resist the batteries very long; but it was a serious matter that Graham, at the suggestion of the commander of the artillery, began his operations by breaching. Smith objected to it, Fletcher acquiesced very reluctantly, on the understanding that the ruin of the defences was only postponed, a condition afterwards unhappily forgotten.

This first attack was not satisfactory, the weather proved bad, some guns mounted on ship-carriages failed, one twenty -four-pounder was rendered unserviceable by the enemy, another by accident, a captain of engineers was killed, and the shot had little effect on the solid wall. In the night however, the ship-guns were mounted on better carriages, and a parallel across the isthmus was projected; but the greatest part of the workmen, to avoid a tempest, sought shelter in the suburb of San Martin, and when day broke only one-third of the work was performed.

On the 21st the besiegers sent a summons, the governor refused to receive the letter, the firing was renewed, and though the main wall resisted the parapets crumbled; the batteries on Monte Olia also plunged into the horn-work at sixteen hundred yards' distance, with such effect that the besieged, having no bomb-proofs, were forced to dig trenches to protect themselves. The French fire, directed solely against the breaching batteries, was feeble, but at midnight a shell thrown from the castle into the bay gave the signal for a sally, during which French vessels with supplies entered the harbour. The besieged now isolated the breach by cuts in the rampart and other defences, yet the besiegers' parallel across the isthmus was completed, and in its progress laid bare the mouth of a drain four feet high and three feet wide, containing the pipe of the aqueduct cut off by the Spaniards. Through that dangerous opening Lieutenant Reid,* a young and zealous engineer, crept even to the counterscarp of the horn-work, where he found the passage closed and returned. Thirty barrels of powder were placed in this drain, and eight feet was stopped with sand-bags, forming a globe of compression to blow, as through a tube, so much rubbish over the counterscarp as might fill the narrow ditch of the horn-work.

On the 22nd the fire from the batteries, unexampled from its rapidity and accuracy, opened what appeared a practicable breach in the eastern flank wall, between two towers called Los Hornos and Las Mesquitas; but the descent into the town behind this breach was more than twelve feet perpendicular, and the garrison were seen from Monte Olia diligently working at the interior defences to receive the assault: they added also another gun to the battery of St. Elmo, just under the Mirador battery, to flank the front attack. On the other hand the besiegers had placed four sixty-eight pound carronades in battery to play on the defences of the breach, yet the fire was slack because the guns were now greatly enlarged at the vents.

On the 23rd, the sea blockade being null, the French vessels

---

* Now Sir W. Reid, Governor of Malta.

carried off the badly-wounded men. This day also the besiegers, judging the breach between the towers practicable, turned the guns, at the suggestion of General Oswald, to break the wall on the right of the main breach. Smith opposed this, urging, that no advantage would be gained by making a second opening, to get at which the troops must first pass the great breach; time would be thus lost, and there was a manifest objection on account of the tide and depth of water at the new point attacked. His counsel was overruled, and in the course of the day, the wall being thin, the stroke heavy and quick, a second breach thirty feet wide was rendered practicable.

The ten-inch mortars and sixty-eight-pound carronades were now turned upon the great breach, and a stockade, the latter separating the high curtain from the flank against which the attack was conducted. Under this fire the houses near the breach were soon in flames, which destroyed several defences and menaced the whole town with destruction, wherefore the assault was ordered for next morning: when the troops assembled the flames were still so fierce the attack was deferred, and the batteries again opened.

During the night the vigilant governor mounted two field-pieces on the cavalier, fifteen feet above the other defences and commanding the high curtain; and he still had on the horn-work a light piece, and two casemated guns on the flank of the cavalier. Two other field-pieces were mounted on an intrenchment, crossing the ditch of the land front and bearing on the approaches; a twenty-four pounder looked from the tower of Las Mesquitas, flanking the main breach; two four-pounders were in the tower of Hornos; two heavy guns on the flank of St. Elmo, and two others, on the right of the Mirador, looked on the breaches from within the fortified line of Monte Orgullo. Thus fourteen pieces were still available for defence, and the retaining sea-wall, or *fausse-braye,* between which and the river the storming parties must necessarily advance, was covered with live shells to roll over on the columns below. Behind the burning houses other edifices were loopholed and filled with musketeers; but as the flames forced the French to withdraw their guns until the moment of attack, and the British artillery officers were confident that in daylight they could silence the enemy's fire and keep the parapet clear of men, Graham renewed his order for the assault.

FIRST STORM OF SAN SEBASTI AN

In the night of the 24th two thousand men of the fifth division filed into the trenches on the isthmus. Of this force, a battalion of the Royals, under Major Frazer, was destined for the great breach; the 38th Regiment under Colonel Greville, was to assail the lesser and most distant breach; the 9th Regiment under Colonel Cameron, was to support the Royals. A detachment selected from the light companies of all those battalions was placed in the centre of the Royals, under Lieutenant Campbell* of the 9th Regiment, who was accompanied by the engineer Machel with a ladder party, being designed to sweep the high curtain after the breach should be won.

From the trenches to the points of attack was three hundred yards, the way being between the horn-work and the river, strewed with rocks slippery from sea-weed; the tide also had left large deep pools of water; the parapet of the horn-work was entire, the parapets of the other works and the two towers, closely flanking the breach, were far from being ruined, and every place was thickly garnished with musketeers. The difficulties were obvious, and a detachment of Portuguese was placed in a trench on the isthmus, only sixty yards from the ramparts, to quell, if possible, the fire of the horn-work.

It was still dark when the stormers moved out of the trenches, and when the globe of compression in the drain was exploded against the horn-work the astonished garrison abandoned the flanking parapet; the troops then rushed onwards, the stormers for the main breach leading, and suffering more from the fire of their own batteries on the right of the Urumea than from the enemy Frazer and the engineer Harry Jones first reached the breach, the enemy had fallen back behind the ruins of the burning houses, and those brave officers rushed up expecting their troops would follow; but not many followed, for it was extremely dark, the narrow

---

* Major-General Sir Colin Campbell in the Crimea.

way and the rocks had contracted the front and disordered the column, and the soldiers came straggling and out of wind to the foot of the breach. The foremost gathered near their gallant leaders, yet the deep descent into the town and volumes of flames and smoke still issuing from the houses awed the stoutest; more than two-thirds, irritated by the destructive flank fire, had broken off at the demi-bastion to commence a musketry battle with the enemy lining the rampart on their left, and the shells from Monte Orgullo fell rapidly. Then the French at the breach, recovering confidence, with a smashing musketry from the ruins and loopholed houses smote the head of the column, while those in the towers smote it on the flanks; and from every quarter came showers of grape and hand-grenades tearing the ranks in a dreadful manner.

Frazer was killed on the flaming ruins, the intrepid Jones stood there awhile longer amidst a few heroic soldiers, hoping for aid, but none came and he and those with him were struck down; the engineer Machel had been killed early, his ladderbearers fell or were dispersed, and the rear of the column had got disordered before the head was beaten. It was in vain Greville, Cameron, Captain Archimbeau, and other regimental officers, strove to rally their men and refill the breach; in vain Campbell, breaking through the tumultuous crowd with the survivors of his chosen detachment, mounted the ruins; twice he ascended, twice he was wounded, and all around him died. Then the Royals endeavoured to retire, but got intermixed with the 38th and some companies of the 9th, which were seeking to pass them and get to the lesser breach; and thus swayed by different impulses, pent up between the horn-work and the river, the mass, reeling to and fro, could neither advance nor go back until the shells and musketry, constantly plied in front and flank, thinned the concourse and the trenches were regained in confusion At daylight a truce was agreed to for an hour, during which the French, who had removed Jones and other wounded men from the breach, carried off the more distant sufferers, lest they should be drowned by the rising of the tide.

Five officers of engineers, including Sir Richard Fletcher, and forty-four officers of the line with five hundred and twenty men, were killed, wounded, or made prisoners in this assault, the failure of which was signal, yet the causes were obvious.

1°. Lord Wellington, on the 22nd, had given final directions for the attack, finishing thus: " *Fair daylight must be taken for the assault.*" These instructions and their emphatic termination were unheeded.

2°. Major Smith had ascertained that the ebb tide would serve exactly at daybreak on the 24th, but the assault was made the 25th, and before daylight, when the higher water contracted the ground, increased the obstacles, and forced the column, with a narrow front and uneasy progress, to trickle onwards instead of dashing with a broad surge against the breach.

3°. The troops filed tediously out of long narrow trenches in the night, and were immediately exposed to a fire of grape from their own batteries on the Chofres; this fire should have ceased when the globe of compression was sprung in the drain, but from the darkness and noise that explosion was neither seen nor heard.

4°. There was a neglect of moral influence, followed by its natural consequence, want of vigour in execution. No general went out of the trenches. Oswald had opposed the plan of attack, and his opinion, in which other officers of rank joined, was freely expressed out of council, it was said even in the hearing of the troops, abating that daring confidence which victory loves.

Wellington repaired immediately to St. Sebastian and would have renewed the attack, but there was no ammunition, and next day extraneous events compelled him to turn the siege into a blockade. The battering train was then sent to Passages, and at daybreak the garrison sallied and swept off two hundred Portuguese with thirty British soldiers. This terminated the first siege of San Sebastian, in which the allies lost thirteen hundred men.

BOOK XI.

Pyrenees—Combat of Roncesvalles—Combat of Linzoain—Combat of
Maya—Combat of Zabaldica—First Battle of Sauroren—
Combat of Buenza—Second Battle of Sauroren—Combat of Dona
Maria—Combats of Echallar and Ivantelly.

THE battle of Vittoria was fought the 21st of June, and on the 1st of
July Marshal Soult, under a decree issued at Dresden, succeeded
Joseph as lieutenant to the emperor.

The 12th, travelling with surprising expedition, that marshal
assumed command of the French troops, now reorganized in one
body, called *the army of Spain,* and he had secret orders to put Joseph
forcibly aside if necessary, but that monarch voluntarily retired.*
Reinforced from the interior, Soult's army was composed of nine
divisions of infantry, a reserve and two regular divisions of cavalry,
besides light horsemen attached to the infantry. Including garrisons,
and thirteen German, Italian, and Spanish battalions not belonging to
the organization, he had one hundred and fourteen thousand men: and
as the armies of Catalonia and Aragon numbered at the same period
above sixty-six thousand, the whole force still employed against
Spain exceeded one hundred and eighty thousand men, with twenty
thousand horses.

Soult was one of the few men whose energy rendered them worthy
lieutenants of the emperor, and with singular zeal and ability he
now served. Nominally he had ninety seven thousand men under
arms, with eighty-six pieces of artillery; but the foreign battalions,
most of which were to return to their own countries for the disciplin-
ing of new levies, only counted as part of the garrisons of Pampeluna,
San Sebastian, Santona and Bayonne: they amounted to seventeen
thousand, and the permanent *army of Spain,* furnished therefore, only
seventy-seven thousand five hundred men under arms, seven thousand being cavalry. Its condition was not satisfactory.

* For this fact Marshal Soult is my authority.

The military administration was disorganized, the soldiers were discouraged by disaster, discipline had been deteriorated, and the people were flying from the frontier.

To secure his base and restore order ere he retook the offensive was Soult's desire; but Napoleon's orders were imperative against delay, and he was compelled to immediate action, though Wellington's advance from Portugal had been so rapid that the great resources of the French frontier were not immediately available, and everything was reeling and rocking in terror from the blow given to the army at Vittoria.

Bayonne, a fortress of no great strength, had been entirely neglected. But the arming and provisioning that and other places; the restoration of an intrenched camp, originally traced by Vauban to cover Bayonne; the enforcement of discipline; the removal of the immense train of Joseph's wasteful court; the establishment of a general system for supplies, and judicious efforts to stimulate the civil authorities and excite the national spirit, soon indicated the presence of a great commander. The soldiers' confidence then revived, and some leading merchants of Bayonne zealously seconded the general: the people were however more inclined to avoid burdens than to answer calls on their patriotism.

Soult examined the line of military positions on the 14th, and ordered Reille, who then occupied the passes of Vera and Echallar, to prepare pontoons for throwing two bridges over the Bidassoa at Biriatou; Wellington, as before said, drove him from those passes next day, yet he prepared his bridges, and by the 16th, Soult was ready for a gigantic offensive movement.

His army was divided into three corps of battle and a reserve. Clausel with the left was at St. Jean Pied de Port, and in communication, by the French frontier, with a division under General Paris at Jaca, belonging to Suchet but under Soult's orders.

Drouet, Count D'Erlon, with the centre, occupied the heights near Espelette and Ainhoa.

Reille with the right wing was on the mountains overlooking Vera from the side of France.

The reserve, under Villatte, guarded the right bank of the Bidassoa from the mouth to Irun, at which place the stone bridge was destroyed. The heavy cavalry under Trielhard, and the light horsemen under Pierre Soult, the marshal's brother, were on the banks of the Nive and the Adour.

To oppose this force Wellington had in Navarre and Guipuscoa above a hundred thousand men. Of these the Anglo-Portuguese furnished fifty thousand infantry and seven thousand cavalry; the Spanish regulars under Giron, Abispal, and Carlos Espana, about twenty-five thousand infantry; the rest were irregular; and hence the troops in line were, of the allies, eighty-two thousand, of the French seventy-eight thousand.

The theatre of operations was quadrilateral, with sides from forty to sixty miles in length, having a fortress at each angle, namely, Bayonne, San Jean Pied de Port, San Sebastian and Pampeluna, all in possession of the French. The interior, broken and tormented by peaked mountains, narrow craggy passes, deep watercourses, dreadful precipices and forests, appeared a wilderness which no military combinations could embrace. The great spinal ridge of the Pyrenees furnished a clue to the labyrinth. Running diagonally across the quadrilateral, it entirely separated Bayonne, St. Jean Pied de Port and San Sebastian from Pampeluna, and the troops blockading the latter were thus cut off from those besieging San Sebastian, the only direct communication between them being a great road running behind the mountains from Tolosa, by Irurzun, to Pampeluna.

A secondary range of mountains on the French side of the Great Spine, inclosing the valley of Bastan and lining that of the Bidassoa, furnished positions for the centre and left of the covering armies, with interior but difficult lateral communications.

The troops covering Pampeluna were on the Great Spine of the Pyrenees. Behind them were valleys into which the passes across the spine led, descending at the other side in parallel lines, and giving to each division means for a concentric retreat on Pampeluna.

Wellington having his battering-train and stores about

San Sebastian, which was nearer and more accessible to the enemy than Pampeluna, made his army lean towards that side. His left wing, including, the army of siege, was twenty-one thousand, with singularly strong positions of defence; his centre, twenty-four thousand strong, could in two marches unite with the left to cover the siege or fall upon the flanks of an enemy advancing by the high road of Irun; but three days or more were required by those troops to concentrate for the security of the blockade of Pampeluna on the right.

Soult thought no decisive result would attend a direct movement upon San Sebastian, and by his seaboard intercourse he knew that place was not in extremity; but he had no communication with Pampeluna, and feared its fall. Wherefore he resolved rapidly to concentrate on his left by means of the great French roads leading to St. Jean Pied de Port, covering his movement by the Nivelle and Nive rivers, and by the positions of his centre: thus he hoped to gather on Wellington's right quicker than that general could gather to oppose him, and, compensating by numbers the disadvantage of assailing mountain positions, force a way to Pampeluna.

That fortress succoured, he designed to seize the road of Irurzun, and either fall upon the separated divisions of the centre in detail as they descended from the Great Spine, or operate on the rear of the troops besieging San Sebastian, while a corps of observation, left on the Lower Bidassoa, menaced it in front. The siege of San Sebastian and the blockade of Pampeluna would be thus raised, the French army united in an abundant country, and its communication with Suchet secured.

To mislead Wellington by vexing his right, simultaneously with the construction of the bridges against his left, Soult directed General Paris to march from Jaca, when time suited, by the higher valleys towards Sanguessa, to drive the partizans from that side, and join the left of the army when it should have reached Pampeluna. Clausel was directed to repair the roads in his own front, push the heads of columns towards the Roncesvalles pass, and with a strong detachment menace Hill's flank by the lateral passes of the Bastan.

On the 20th Reille's troops on the heights of Sarre and Vera, being cautiously relieved by Villatte, marched towards St. Jean Pied de Port, which they were to reach early on the 22nd; and on that day the two divisions of cavalry and parc of artillery were to concentrate at the same place. D'Erlon, with the centre, was to hold his positions in front of Hill while these great movements were taking place.

Villatte, having fifteen thousand sabres and bayonets, remained in observation on the Bidassoa. If threatened by superior forces he was to retire, upon the intrenched camp at Bayonne, halting successively on certain positions. If only a small corps crossed the river, he was to drive it vigorously back; and if the allies retired in consequence of Soult's operations he was to relieve San Sebastian and follow them briskly by Tolosa.

Rapidity was of vital importance to the French marshal, but heavy rains swelled the streams and ruined the roads in the deep country between Bayonne and the mountains; the headquarters which should have arrived at St. Jean Pied de Port on the 20th, were a few miles short of that place the 21st, and Reille's troops were forced to go round by Bayonne to gain the causeway. The cavalry was also retarded, and the army, men and horses, worn down by severe marches. Two days were thus lost, yet the 24th more than sixty thousand fighting men, including cavalry, national guards, and gendarmes, with sixty-six pieces of artillery, were assembled to force the passes of Roncesvalles and Maya; the former being in the Great Spine, the latter giving entrance to the Bastan. The main road leading to Roncesvalles was repaired, and three hundred sets of bullocks were provided to drag the guns; the national guards of the frontier on the left, ordered to assemble in the night on the heights of Yropil, were reinforced with regular troops to vex and turn the right of the allies at the foundry of Orbaiceta.

At St. Jean Pied de Port Soult was almost in contact with the allies at the passes of the Roncesvalles, which were also the points of the defence nearest to Pampeluna. He had thirty thousand bayonets, the frontier national guards to aid, and his artillery and cavalry were massed behind his infantry for here the great road from St. Jean Pied de Port to Pampeluna, the only one fit for cannon, entered the mountains: but to understand his movements a short description of the country is necessary, taking the point of departure from his camp.

Before him was the Val Carlos, formed by two descending shoots from the Great Spine of the Pyrenees. That on his left hand separated this valley from the valley of Orbaiceta; that on his right hand separated it from several conjoint valleys, known as the Alduides and Baygorry, the latter name being given to the lower, the former to the upper parts.

The great road to Pampeluna led up the left hand tongue by the remarkable rocks of Chateau Pignon, near which narrow branches went off to the village of San Carlos on the right, and to the foundry of Orbaiceta on the left. The main line, after ascending to the summit of the Great Spine, turned to the right and run along the crest until it reached the pass of Ibaneta, where, turning to the left, it led down by the famous Roncesvalles into the valley of Urros.

A lateral continuation however run along the magistral crest, beyond the Ibaneta, to another pass called the Mendichuri, which also led down into the Val de Urros; and from Mendichuri there was a way into the Alduides valley through a side pass called the Atalosti.

On Soult's right hand the Val Carlos was bounded by the ridge and rock of Ayrola, from the summit of which there was a way directly to the Mendichuri and the lateral pass of Atalosti; and the ground between those defiles, called the Lindouz, was an accessible mountain knot, tying all the valleys together and consequently commanding them.

Continuing along the Great Spine, after passing the Atalosti, there would be on the right hand, descending towards the French frontier, the Val de Ayra, the Alduides and the Bastan. On the left hand, descending to Pampeluna, would be the Val de Zubiri and the valley of Lanz, separated from each other by a lofty wooded range. All these valleys on each side were, in their order, connected by roads leading, over comparatively low portions of the Great Spine, called by the French *cols*, or necks, by the Spaniards *puertos*, or doors.

General Byng and Morillo, the first having sixteen hundred

British troops, the second four thousand Spaniards, were in position before Soult. Byng, reinforced with two Spanish battalions, held the rocks of Altobiscar, just above Chateau Pignon. On his right a Spanish battalion was posted at the foundry of Orbaiceta; on his left Morillo's remaining Spaniards were near the village of Val Carlos on a minor height called the Iroulepe.

Behind the Great Spine, in the valley of Urros, General Cole held the fourth division in support of Byng; but he was twelve miles off, separated by the Ibaneta pass, and could not come up under four hours. General Campbell, having a Portuguese division two thousand strong, watched the Alduides; but he was eight miles off, and separated by the lateral pass of Atalosti. General Picton, with the third division, was at Olague in the valley of Lanz, on the Spanish side of the Spine; and both he and Campbell could at pleasure gain the valley of Zubiri—Picton by a cross communication, Campbell by the pass of Urtiaga, which was directly in his rear; he could also join Cole in the valley of Urros by the pass of Sahorgain.

In this state of affairs Soult placed twelve thousand infantry within two miles of the Chateau Pignon, against Byng, and directed the national guards at Yropil, reinforced with regulars, to move into the valley of Orbaiceta and turn the Spaniards at the foundry. A second column, four thousand strong, was placed in the Val Carlos to assail Morillo at Iroulepe. A third column of sixteen thousand, under Reille, assembled, in the night, at the foot of the Ayrola rock, with orders to ascend at daylight and move along the crest of the ridge to seize the culminant Lindouz. From that point detachments were to be pushed through the passes of Ibaneta, Mendichuri, and Sahorgain, into the Roncesvalles, while others extended to the right as far as the pass of Urtiaga, thus cutting off Byng and Morillo from Cole and Hamilton.

COMBAT OF RONCESVALLES.

On the 23rd Soult issued an order of the day remarkable for its force and frankness. Conscious of ability he avowed a feeling of his own worth; but he was too proud to depreciate brave adversaries on the eve of battle.

"Let us not," he said to his soldiers, *" defraud the enemy of the praise which is due to him. The dispositions of the general have been prompt, skilful, and consecutive, the valour and steadiness of his troops have been praiseworthy."*

On the 25th at daylight he led up against the rocks of Altobiscar.

Byng, warned the evening before that danger was near, and jealous for the village of Val Carlos, had sent the 57th Regiment down there, yet kept his main body in hand and gave notice to Cole.

Soult, throwing out a multitude of skirmishers, pushed forward his supporting columns and guns as fast as the steepness of the road and difficult nature of the ground would permit; but the British fought strongly, the French fell fast among the rocks, and their musketry pealed in vain for hours along that cloudy field of battle, five thousand feet above the level of the plains. Their numbers however continually increased in front, and the national guards from Yropil, skirmishing with the Spaniards at the foundry of Orbaiceta, threatened to turn the right. Val Carlos was at the same time menaced by the central column, and Reille ascending the rock of Ayrola turned Morillo's left.

At mid-day Cole arrived in person at Altobiscar, but his troops were distant, and the French, renewing their attack, neglected the Val Carlos to gather more thickly against Byng. He resisted their efforts, yet Reille made progress along the summit of the Ayrola ridge, Morillo fell back towards Ibaneta, and the French were nearer that pass than Byng, when Ross's brigade, of Cole's division, coming up the Mendichuri pass, appeared on the Lindouz at the instant when the head of Reille's column was closing on the Atalosti to cut the communication with Campbell. This last-named officer had been early molested, according to Soult's plan, by the frontier guards of the Val de Baygorry, yet he soon detected the feint and moved by his right towards Atalosti when he heard the firing on that side. The Val d'Ayra separated him from the ridge of Ayrola, along which Reille was advancing, yet, noting that general's strength and seeing Ross's brigade labouring up the steep ridge of Mendichuri, he judged its commander to be ignorant of what was going on above, and, sending Cole notice of the enemy's proximity and strength, offered to pass the Atalosti and join battle, if he could be furnished afterwards with provisions and transport for his sick.

Before this message reached Cole, a wing of the 20th Regiment and a company of Brunswickers, forming the head of Ross's column, had gained the Lindouz, where suddenly they encountered Reille's advanced guard. The moment was critical, and Ross, an eager hardy soldier, called aloud to charge, whereupon Captain Tovey of the 20th run forward with a company, and full against the 6th French Light Infantry dashed with the bayonet. Brave men fell by that weapon on both sides, yet numbers prevailed and Tovey's soldiers were eventually pushed back. Ross however gained his object, the remainder of his brigade had time to come up and the pass of Atalosti was secured, with a loss of one hundred and forty men of the 20th Regiment and forty-one of the Brunswickers.

Previous to this vigorous action, Cole, seeing the French in the Val Carlos and the Orbaiceta valley, on both flanks of Byng, whose front was not the less pressed, had reinforced the Spaniards at the foundry, but now recalled his men to defend the Lindouz; and learning from Campbell how strong Reille was, caused Byng, with a view to a final retreat, to relinquish Altobiscar and approach Ibaneta. This movement uncovered the road leading down to the foundry of Orbaiceta, yet it concentrated all the troops; and Campbell, although he could not enter the line, Cole being unable to meet his demands, made such skilful dispositions as to impress Reille with a notion that his numbers were considerable.

During these operations the skirmishing never ceased, though a thick fog, coming up the valley, stopped a general attack which Soult was preparing; thus, when night fell Cole still held the Great Spine, having lost three hundred and eighty men killed and wounded. His right was however turned by Orbaiceta, he had only eleven thousand bayonets to oppose thirty thousand, and his line of retreat, five miles down hill and flanked by the Lindouz, was unfavourable; wherefore in the dark, silently threading the passes, he gained the valley of Urros, and his rear-guard followed in the morning. Campbell went off by Urtiaga into the Zubiri valley, and the Spanish battalion retreated from the foundry by a goat path.

The great chain was thus abandoned, yet the result of the day's operation was unsatisfactory to Soult. He had lost four hundred men, he had not gained ten miles, and was still twenty-two miles from Pampeluna, with strong positions in the way, where increasing numbers of intrepid enemies were to be expected.

His combinations had been thwarted by fortune, and by errors of execution which the most experienced generals know to be inevitable. Fortune sent the fog at the moment he was thrusting forward his heaviest masses; Reille failed in execution; for he was to have gained the Lindouz with all speed, but previous to ascending the rock of Ayrola lost time by reorganizing two newly arrived conscript battalions and serving out provisions; the two hours thus employed would have sufficed to seize the Lindouz before Ross got through the pass of Mendichuri. The fog would still have stopped the spread of his column to the extent designed by Soult, yet fifteen or sixteen thousand men would have been placed on the flank and rear of Byng and Morillo.

On the 26th Soult putting his left wing on Cole's track, ordered Reille to follow the crest of the mountains and seize the passes from the Bastan in Hill's rear, while D'Erlon pressed him in front. Hill would thus, Soult hoped, be crushed or thrown off from Pampeluna, and D'Erlon could thus reach the valley of Zubiri with his left, while his right, descending the valley of Lanz, would hinder Picton from joining Cole. A retreat by those generals, on separate lines, would then be inevitable, and the French army could issue in a compact order of battle from the mouths of the two valleys against Pampeluna.

COMBAT OF LINZOAIN.

All the columns were in movement at daybreak, but every hour brought its obstacle. The fog still hung heavy on the mountain-tops. Reille's guides were bewildered, refused to lead the troops along the crests, and at ten o'clock, having no other resource, he marched down the Mendichuri pass and fell into the rear of Soult's column, the head of which, though retarded also by the fog and rough ground, had overtaken Cole's rear-guard. The leading infantry struck hotly upon some British light companies under Colonel Wilson, while a squadron, passing their flank, fell on the rear; but Wilson, facing about, drove them off, and thus fighting Cole reached the heights of Linzoain. There Picton met him, with intelligence that Campbell had reached Eugui in the Val de Zubiri, and that the third division, having crossed the woody ridge, was also in that valley. The junction of all was thus secured, the loss of the day was less than two hundred, and neither wounded men nor baggage had been left behind; but at four o'clock the French seized some heights which endangered Cole's position, and he again fell back a mile, offering battle at a puerto, in the ridge separating the valley of Zubiri from that of Urros, which last, though descending on a parallel line, did not open on Pampeluna. During this skirmish, Campbell, coming from Eugui, showed his Portuguese on the ridge above the French right flank; he was however distant, Picton's troops were still further off, and there was light for an action if Soult had pressed one; but, disturbed with intelligence received from D'Erlon, and doubtful what Campbell's troops might be, he put off the attack until next morning, and after dark the junction of all the allies was effected.

This delay was an error. Cole was alone for five hours, and every action, by augmenting the wounded men and creating confusion, would have augmented the difficulties of a retreat for troops fatigued with incessant fighting and marching during two days and a night. Moreover Reille's failure from the fog, had reduced the primary combinations to D'Erlon's co-operation, and reports now brought the mortifying conviction that he also had gone wrong: by rough fighting only could Soult therefore attain his object, and, it is said, his manner discovered a secret anticipation of failure; yet his temper was too steadfast to yield, for he gave orders to advance next day, renewing his instructions to D'Erlon, whose operations must now be noticed.

That general, who had eighteen thousand fighting men, placed two divisions on the morning of the 25th near the passes of Maya, having previously caused the national guards of Val Baygorry to make demonstrations towards the lateral passes of Arriette, Yspeguy and Lorietta, on Hill's right. General William Stewart, commanding a division, and still the same daring but imprudent man he had shown

himself at Albuera, was deceived by these feints, and looked to that
quarter which was guarded by Sylviera's Portuguese more than to his
own front. His division, consisting of two British brigades, was
consequently neither posted as it should be, nor otherwise prepared
for an attack. His ground was strong, but however rugged a position
may be, if it is too extensive and the troops are not disposed with
judgment, the inequalties constituting its strength become advantageous to an assailant.

There were three passes over the Col de Maya to defend, Aretesque on the right, Lessessa in the centre, Maya on the left; and from
these entrances two roads led into the Bastan in parallel directions;
one down the valley through the town of Maya, the other along the
Atchiola mountain. General Pringle's brigade guarded the Aretesque, Colonel Cameron's brigade the Maya and Lessessa passes.
The Col itself was broad on the summit, three miles long, and on each
flank lofty rocks and ridges rose one above another; those on the right
blended with the Goramendi mountains, those on the left with the
Atchiola mountain, near the summit of which the 82nd Regiment,
belonging to the seventh division, was posted.

Cameron, encamped on the left, had a clear view of troops
coming from Urdax, one of D'Erlon's camps; but at Aretesque a
great round hill, one mile in front, masked the movements of an
enemy coming from Espelette, the other French camp. This hill
was not occupied at night, nor in the daytime, save by some Portuguese cavalry videttes, and the nearest guard was an infantry picquet
of eighty men posted on the French slope of the Col. Behind
this picquet there was no immediate support, but four light
companies were encamped one mile down the reverse slope, which
was more rugged and difficult of access than that towards the enemy.
The rest of Pringle's brigade was disposed at distances of two
and three miles in the rear, and the signal for occupying the position
was to be the fire of four Portuguese guns from the rocks above
the Maya pass. Thus of six British regiments, furnishing more than
three thousand fighting men, half only were in line, and chiefly
massed on the left of a position, wide, open, and of an easy ascent
from the Aretesque side. Stewart also, quite deceived as to the real

state of affairs, was at Elisondo, several miles off, when at midday D'Erlon commenced the battle.

COMBAT OF MAYA.

From the Aretesque pass at dawn a glimpse bad been obtained of cavalry and infantry in movement along the hills in front, and soon afterwards some peasants announced the approach of the French. At nine o'clock a staff officer, patrolling round the great hill in front, discovered sufficient to make him order up the light companies from the reverse slope, to support the picquet; and they formed on the ridge with their left at the rock of Aretesque, just as D'Armagnac's division, coming from Espelette, mounted the great hill in front; Abbe's division followed, while Maransin, with a third division, advanced from Ainhoa and Urdax against the Maya pass, seeking also to turn it by a narrow way leading up the Atchiola mountain.

D'Armagnac forced the picquet back with great loss upon the light companies, who sustained his assault with infinite difficulty; the alarm guns were then heard from the Maya pass, and Pringle hastened to the front; but his battalions, moving hurriedly from different camps, came up irregularly. The 34th arrived first at a running pace, yet by companies not in mass, and breathless from the length and ruggedness of the ascent; the 39th and 28th followed, but not immediately nor together, and meanwhile D'Armagnac, closely supported by Abbe, with domineering numbers and valour combined, maugre the desperate fighting of the light companies and the 34th, established his columns on the broad ridge of the position. Colonel Cameron sent the 50th from the left to the assistance of the overmatched troops, and that fierce and formidable old regiment, charging the head of an advancing, column drove it clear out of the pass of Lessessa in the centre. But the French were many, and checked at one point assembled with increased force at another; nor could Pringle restore the battle with the 39th and 28th Regiments, which, cut off from the others, were, though fighting strongly, forced back to a second and lower ridge crossing the main road into the Bastan. They were followed by D'Armagnac, while Abbe pushed the 50th and 34th towards the Atchiola road to the left, upon Cameron's brigade. That officer, still holding the pass of Maya with the left wings of the 71st and 92nd Regiments, now brought their right wings and the Portuguese guns into action: yet so dreadful was the slaughter, especially of the 92nd, that the enemy was, it is said, actually stopped for a time by the heaped mass of dead and dying; and then the left wing of that noble regiment, coming down from the higher ground, was forced to smite wounded friends and exulting foes alike, as mingled together they stood or crawled before its fire.*

Such was the state of affairs when Stewart reached the field by the mountain road of Atchiola. The passes of Lessessa and Aretesque were lost; that of Maya was still held by the left wing of the 71st, but Stewart, seeing Maransin's men gathered thickly on one side, and Abbe's men on the other, abandoned it for a new position on the first rocky ridge covering the road over the Atchiola. He called down the 82nd from the highest part of that mountain, sent messengers to demand further aid from the seventh division, and meanwhile, though wounded, made a strenuous resistance, for he was a very gallant man. During this retrograde movement, Maransin suddenly thrust the head of his division across the front of the British line and connected his left with Abbe, throwing as he passed a destructive fire into the wasted remnant of the 92nd, which even then gave way but sullenly, and still fought, though two-thirds had fallen: however, one after the other, all the regiments were forced back, the Portuguese guns were taken and the position lost.

Abbe now followed D'Armagnac on the road to the town of Maya, leaving Maransin to deal with Stewart's new position; and notwithstanding its extreme strength the French gained ground until six o'clock; for the British, shrunk in numbers, wanted ammunition, and a part of the 82nd defended the rocks on which they were posted with stones. In this desperate condition Stewart was upon the point of

---

* In my original work, misled by false information, I said the soldiers of the 92nd were all Irish: but their Colonel, McDonald, afterwards gave me irrefragable proof, by a list of names. that they were Scotchmen.

abandoning the mountain entirely, when Barnes' brigade of the seventh division, arriving from Echallar, charged and drove the French back to the Maya ridge. Stewart was then master of the Atchiola, and D'Erlon thinking greater reinforcements had come up, recalled his other divisions from the Maya road and re-united his whole corps on the *Col*. He had lost fifteen hundred men and a general, but he took four guns, and fourteen hundred British soldiers and one general were killed or wounded.

Such was the commencement of Soult's operations to restore the fortunes of France. Three considerable actions fought on the same day had each ended in his favour. At San Sebastian the allies' assault was repulsed; at Roncesvalles they abandoned the passes; at Maya they were defeated—but the decisive blow was still to be struck.

Lord Wellington heard of the fight at Maya on his way back from San Sebastian, after the assault, but with the false addition that D'Erlon was beaten. As early as the 22nd he had known that Soult was preparing a great offensive movement; yet the impassive attitude of the French centre, the disposition of their reserve, twice as strong as he at first supposed, together with the bridges prepared by Reille, were calculated to mislead, and did mislead him. Soult's combinations to bring his centre finally into line on the crest of the great chain being impenetrable, the English general could not believe he would throw himself with only thirty thousand men into the valley of the Ebro, unless sure of aid from Suchet. But that general's movements indicated a determination to remain in Catalonia, and Wellington, in contrast to Soult, knew that Pampeluna was not in extremity, and thought, the assault not having been made, that San Sebastian was. Hence the operations against his right, their full extent not known, appeared a feint, and he judged the real effort would be to raise the siege of San Sebastian. But in the night of the 25th, correct intelligence of the Maya and Roncesvalles affairs arrived. Graham was then ordered to turn the siege into a blockade, to embark the guns and stores, and hold his spare troops ready to join Giron, on a position of battle marked out near the Bidassoa. Cotton was directed to move the cavalry up to Pampeluna, and Abispal was instructed to hold some of his Spanish troops ready to act in advance of that fortress. Meanwhile Wellington, having arranged his lines of correspondence, proceeded to San Esteban, which he reached early in the morning.

While the embarkation of the guns and stores was going on it was essential to hold the posts at Vera and Echallar, because D'Erlon's object was not pronounced; and an enemy in possession of those places could approach San Sebastian by the roads leading over the Pena de Haya, or by the defiles of Zubietta leading round that mountain. But when Wellington reached Irueta, saw the reduced state of Stewart's division, and knew Picton had marched from Olague, he directed all the troops within his power upon Pampeluna, and to prevent mistakes indicated the valley of Lanz as the general line of movement. Of Picton's exact position, or of his intentions, nothing positive was known; but supposing him to have joined Cole at Linzoain, as indeed he had, Wellington judged their combined forces sufficient to check the enemy until assistance could reach them from the centre, or from Pampeluna, and he so advised Picton on the evening of the 26th.*

Following these orders the seventh division marched in the night of the 26th, the sixth division the next morning, and Hill in the following night. Meanwhile the light division, quitting Vera, reached the summit of the Santa Cruz mountain, and there halted to cover the defiles of Zubietta until Longa's Spaniards should block the roads leading over the Pena de Haya; that effected, it was to thread the passes and descend upon the great road of Irurzun, thus securing Graham's communication with the army round Pampeluna.

These movements spread fear and confusion far and wide. All the narrow valleys and roads were crowded with baggage, commissariat stores, artillery and fugitive families; reports of the most alarming nature were as usual rife; each division, ignorant of what had really happened to the other, dreaded that some of the numerous misfortunes related might be true; none knew what to expect, or where they were to meet the enemy, and one universal hubbub filled

---

* All these conjectures and proceedings are given on
the Duke's personal authority.

the wild regions through which the French army was working its fiery path towards Pampeluna.

D'Erlon's inactivity gave great uneasiness to Soult: he repeated his original orders to push forward by his left whatever might be the force opposed, and thus stimulated D'Erlon advanced to Elisondo the 27th; yet again halted there, and it was not until the morning of the 28th, when Hill's retreat had opened the way, that he followed through the pass of Vellate. His further progress belongs to other combinations, arising from Soult's direct operations which shall now be continued.

Picton having assumed command of all the troops, seventeen thousand, in the valley of Zubiri on the evening of the 26th, retreated before dawn the 27th, without hope or intention of covering Pampeluna; Soult followed in two columns down both banks of the Guy river, his cavalry and artillery closing the rear: both moved in compact order, the narrow valley was overgorged with troops, and a bicker of musketry alone marked the separation of the hostile forces. Meanwhile the garrison of Pampeluna attacked the Count of Abispal, who in great alarm spiked some of his guns, destroyed his magazines, and would have suffered a disaster, if Carlos Espana had not fortunately arrived from the Ebro with his division and checked the sally. Imminent was the crisis however, for Cole, first emerging from the Zubiri valley, had passed Villalba, three miles from Pampeluna, in retreat; Picton, following close, was at Huarte, and Abispal's Spaniards were in confusion: in fine Soult was all but successful, when Picton, feeling the importance of the crisis, suddenly turned on some steep ridges which stretched across the mouths of the Zubiri and Lanz valleys and screened Pampeluna.

Posting the third division on the right, he prolonged his left with Morillo's Spaniards, called upon Abispal to support him, and directed Cole to occupy some heights a little in advance. That general had however noted a salient hill one mile farther on, commanding the great road, where two Spanish regiments of the blockading troops were still posted, and towards them he directed his course. Soult had also marked this hill, and a French detachment was in full career to seize it, when the Spaniards, seeing the British so close, vindicated their ground by a sudden charge. This was for Soult the stroke of fate. His double columns, just then emerging exultant from the narrow valley, stopped at the sight of ten thousand men crowning the summit of the mountain in opposition, while two miles further back stood Picton with a greater number, for Abispal had now taken post on Morillo's left. To advance by the great road was then impossible, and to stand still was dangerous; for the French army, contracted to a span in front, was cleft in its whole length by the river Guy, and compressed on each side by mountains which there narrowed the valley to a quarter of a mile. In this difficulty Soult, with the promptness of a great commander, instantly shot the head of Clausel's columns to his right, across the ridge which separated the Zubiri from the Lanz valley, and threw one of Reille's divisions of infantry and a body of cavalry across the mountains on his left, beyond the Guy river, thus giving himself a strong position of battle and menacing Picton's right flank. Reille's remaining divisions he established at the village of Zabaldica in the Val de Zubiri, close under Cole's right, while Clausel seized the village of Sauroren as close under that general's left.

While Soult was thus establishing a line of battle, Wellington, who had quitted Hill's quarters in the Bastan early on the 27th, crossed the great mountain spine into the valley of Lanz, without being able to learn anything of Picton's movements or position until he reached Ostiz, a few miles from Sauroren. There he found Long's brigade of light cavalry, placed to furnish posts of correspondence in the mountains, and from him heard that Picton had abandoned the heights of Linzoain: whereupon, leaving instructions to stop all the troops coming down the valley of Lanz until the state of affairs near Pampeluna could be ascertained, he made at racing speed for Sauroren. As he entered that village he saw Clausel's divisions moving along the crest of the mountain, and thus knew the allied troops in the valley of Lanz were intercepted; then pulling up his horse, he wrote on the parapet of the bridge at Sauroren fresh instructions to turn everything from that valley to the light by a cross-road, which led out of it to Marcalain and thence round the hills, to enter the valley again at Oricain, in rear of the position occupied by Cole. Lord Fitzroy Somerset, who had kept up with him, galloped with these orders out of Sauroren by one road, the French light cavalry simultaneously dashed in by another, and Wellington rode alone up the mountain.

A Portuguese battalion on the left, first recognising him, raised a joyful cry, and soon the shrill clamour was taken up by the next regiments, swelling as it run along the line into that stern and appalling shout which the British soldier is wont to give upon the edge of battle, and which no enemy ever heard unmoved. In a conspicuous place he stopped, desirous that both armies should know he was there. A spy who was present pointed out Soult, then so near that his features could be plainly distinguished. Fixing his eyes attentively upon that formidable man, Wellington thus spoke, " *Yonder is a great commander, but he is a cautious one and will delay his attack to ascertain the cause of these shouts; that will give time for the sixth division to arrive and I shall beat him.*" The event justified the prediction.

Cole's position was the summit of a mountain mass, which filled all the space between the Guy and Lanz valleys, as far back as Huarte and Villalba. It was highest in the centre and well defined towards the enemy, yet the trace was irregular, the right being thrown back towards the village of Arletta so as to flank the great road, which was also swept by guns placed on a lower range behind.

Overlooking Zabaldica and the Guy river, was the bulging hill vindicated by the Spaniards, a distinct but lower point on the right of the position. The left, also abating in height, was yet extremely rugged and steep, overlooking the Lanz river, and Ross's brigade was posted on that side, having in front a Portuguese battalion, whose flank rested on a small chapel. Campbell was on the right of Ross. Anson was on the highest ground, partly behind, partly on the right of Campbell. Byng's brigade was on a second mass of hills in reserve, and the Spanish hill was further reinforced by a battalion of Portuguese.

This front of battle was less than two miles, and well filled, its flanks being washed by the Lanz and the Guy; and those torrents, pursuing their course, broke by narrow passages through the steep ridges screening Pampeluna which had been first occupied by Picton, and where the second line was now posted; that is to say, at the distance of two miles from, and nearly parallel to the first position, but on a more extended front. Carlos Espana maintained the blockade behind these ridges, and the British cavalry under Cotton stood on some open ground in the rear of Picton's right wing.

Soult's position was also a mountain filling the space between the two rivers. It was even more rugged than that of the allies, and was only separated from it by a deep narrow ravine. Clausel's three divisions leaned to the right on the village of Sauroren, which was down in the valley of Lanz, close under the chapel height; Reille's two divisions occupied the village of Zabaldica, quite down in the valley of Zubiri under the right of the allies. The remaining division of this wing and the light cavalry were, as before said, thrown forward on the mountains at the other side of the Guy river, menacing Picton and seeking to communicate with Pampeluna.

COMBAT OF ZABALDICA.

The French guns at Zabaldica first opened fire, but the elevation required to send the shot upward rendered it so ineffectual, that the greatest part of the artillery remained in the narrow valley of Zubiri. Soult had however made another effort to gain the Spaniards' hill and establish himself near the centre of the allies' line of battle, but had been valiantly repulsed just before the arrival of Wellington, who now reinforced the post with the 40th British Regiment. There was then a general skirmish along the front, under cover of which Soult examined the whole position, and the filing continued on the mountain side until a terrible storm, the usual precursor of English battles in the Peninsula, brought on premature darkness and terminated the dispute. This was the state of affairs at daybreak on the 28th, but a signal alteration had place before the great battle of that day commenced, and the movements of the wandering divisions by which this change was effected must now be traced.

Although the Lanz covered the left of the allies and the right of the French, the heights occupied by both were prolonged beyond that river; the continuation of the allies' range sweeping forward so as to look into the rear of Sauroren, while the continuation of the French range fell back in a direction nearly parallel to this forward inclination of the allies' ridge. On each side they were steep and high yet lower and less rugged than the heights on which the armies stood opposed; for on the latter, rocks piled on rocks stood out like castles, so difficult to approach and so dangerous to assail that the hardened veterans of the Peninsula only would have dared the trial: both sides •were therefore strong in defence. But Soult was forced to attack or retreat, and therefore Wellington looked anxiously for his sixth division, then coming from Marcalain by a road which run behind his ridge beyond the Lanz and fell into that valley at Oricain, one mile in rear of Cole's left. It had been turned into that road from the higher part of the Lanz valley by Lord Fitzroy Somerset, and was followed by General Hill when he arrived at the point of divarication the way was thus open for D'Erlon to join Soult, and the rapidity with which that marshal had seized Sauroren would thus have proved a masterstroke, if his lieutenant had pursued Hill vigorously: for the change of direction gave the sixth division a march of eighteen instead of four hours to join the army; and Hill, forced to take a position at Marcalain, covering the great road of Irurzun on Wellington's left, w as there joined by the seventh division and the whole were thrown out of the line of battle. During these important movements, which were not completed until the evening, of the 28th, and which finally placed all the allies in military communication, D'Erlon remained inactive in the Bastan !

The proximity of the sixth division on the morning of the 28th, with the certainty of Hill's co-operation, made Wellington think Soult would not venture an attack; and the latter, disquieted about D'Erlon, of whom he only knew that he had not followed his instructions, certainly viewed the British position with uneasy anticipations, and again with anxious eyes took cognizance of its rugged strength, seeming dubious and distrustful of fortune. He could not operate with advantage by his left beyond the Guy river, because the mountains ther e were rough, and his enemy, having shorter lines of movement, could meet him with all arms combined; moreover his artillery, unable to emerge from the Val de Zubiri, except by the great road, would thus have been exposed to a counter attack. In this dubious state he crossed the Lanz and ascended the prolongation of the allies' ridge, which, as he had possession of the bridge; of Sauroren, was for the moment his own ground; from thence he could see into the left and rear of Cole's position, but the country towards Marcalain was so broken that he could not discern the march of the sixth division. The deserters however told him that four divisions, namely, the second, sixth, and seventh British, and Sylviera's Portugese, which was under Hill, were expected from that side; he was thus influenced to attack, because the valley, widening as it descended, offered the means of assailing the allies in front and flank, and intercepting the divisions from Marcalain by the same combination.

One of Clausel's divisions already occupied Sauroren, and the other two were now posted on each side of that village; that on the right hand was ordered to send flankers to the ridge from whence Soult had made his observations, and upon signal to move down the valley, wheel to the left, and assail the rear of the allies while the other two divisions assailed their front: five thousand men would thus be enveloped by sixteen thousand, and Soult hoped to crush them not withstanding the strength of ground. Meanwhile Reille's two divisions on the side of Zabaldica., were each to send a brigade against the Spanish hill, and connect the right of their attack with Clausel's left. The remaining brigades were to follow in support, the division beyond the Guy was to keep Picton in check, and all were to throw themselves frankly into action.

FIRST BATTLE OF SAUROREN.

At midday on the 28th of July, the anniversary of the Talavera fight, the French gathered in masses at the foot of the position, and their skirmishers quickly spread over the face of the mountain, working upward like a conflagration; but the columns of attack were not all ready when Clausel's right-hand division, without awaiting the general signal of battle, threw out flankers on the ridge beyond the Lanz and pushed down the valley in one mass. With a rapid pace it turned Cole's left and was preparing to wheel up on his rear, when suddenly Madden's Portuguese brigade of the sixth division appeared on the crest of the ridge beyond the river, driving the flankers back and descending, as from the clouds, with a rattling fire upon the right and rear of the column; and not less suddenly the main body of that division, emerging from behind the same ridge near the village of Oricain, presented a line of battle across the front. It was the counter-stroke of Salamanca ! The French were, while striving to encompass Cole's left, themselves encompassed; for two brigades of Cole's division instantly turned and smote them on the left, the Portuguese smote them on the right, and thus scathed on both flanks with fire, they were violently shocked and pushed back with a mighty force by the sixth division, yet not in flight, but fighting fiercely and strewing the ground with their enemies' bodies as well as with their own.

Clausel's second division, on the other side of Sauroren, seeing this dire conflict, with a hurried movement assailed the chapel height to draw off Cole's fire from the troops in the valley, and gallantly did the French soldiers throng up the craggy steep; yet the general unity of the attack was ruined; neither the third division nor Reille's brigades had yet received the signal, and their attacks were made irregularly, in succession, running from right to left as the necessity of aiding others became apparent. It was however a terrible battle and well fought. One column darting out of the village of Sauroren, silently, sternly, without firing a shot, worked up to the chapel under a tempest of bullets, which swept away whole ranks without abating the speed and power of the mass; the Portuguese there shrunk abashed, and that part of the position was won; soon however they rallied on Ross's British brigade, and the whole, running forward, charged the French with a loud shout and dashed them down the hill. Heavily stricken the latter were, yet undismayed, they re-formed, and again ascended, to be again broken and overturned. But the other columns of attack now bore upwards through the smoke and flame with which the skirmishers covered the face of the mountain, and another Portuguese regiment, fighting on the right of Ross, yielded to their fury; thus a heavy body crowned the heights, and wheeling against Ross's exposed flank forced him back also, and his ground was instantly occupied by the enemies with whom he had been engaged in front. Now the fight raged close and desperate on the crest of the position, charge succeeding charge, each side yielding and advancing by turns. This astounding effort of French valour was however of no avail. Wellington brought Byng's brigade forward at a running pace, and calling the 27th and 48th British Regiments, from the higher ground in the centre, against the crowded masses, rolled them backward in disorder, and threw them, one after the other, violently down the mountain-side; yet with no child's play; the two British regiments had to fall upon the enemy three separate times with the bayonet, and lost more than half their own numbers.

During this battle on the mountain-top, the sixth division gained ground in the Lanz valley, and when it arrived on a front with the left of the victorious troops near the chapel, Wellington, seeing the momentary disorder of the enemy, ordered Madden's Portuguese brigade beyond the Lanz, which had never ceased its fire against the right flank of the French column, to assail the village of Sauroren in rear; but the state of the action in other parts and the exhaustion of the troops soon induced him to countermand this movement.

On the French left, Reille's brigades, connecting their right with Clausel's third division, had environed the Spanish hill and ascended it unchecked, at the moment then the fourth division was so hardly pressed from Sauroren; a Spanish regiment then gave way on the left of the 40th, but a Portuguese battalion, rushing forward, again covered the flank of that invincible regiment, which waited in stern silence until the French set their feet upon the broad summit. Scarcely did their glittering arms appear over the brow of the mountain when the charging British cry was heard, the fierce shock given, the French mass was broken to pieces and a tempest of bullets followed it down the mountain. Four times this assault was renewed, and the French officers were seen even to pull up their tired men by the belts, so fierce and resolute they were to win, but it was the labour of Sisyphus; the vehement shout and shock of the British soldier always prevailed, and at last, with thinned ranks, tired limbs, and fainting hearts, hopeless from repeated failures, the French were so abashed that three British companies sufficed to bear down a whole brigade.*

While the battle was thus being fought on the mountain, Soult's cavalry beyond the Guy river passed a rivulet, and with a fire of carbines forced the 10th Hussars to yield some rocky ground on Picton's right, but the 18th Hussars renewed the combat, killed two officers, and drove them over the rivulet again.

Such were the leading events of this sanguinary struggle, which Lord Wellington, fresh from the fight, with homely emphasis called " *bludgeon work.*" Two generals and eighteen hundred men had been killed or wounded on the French side, following their official reports; a number far below the estimate made at the time by the allies, whose loss amounted to two thousand six hundred. These discrepancies between hostile calculations ever occur, and there is little wisdom in disputing where proof is unattainable; yet the numbers actually engaged were twenty-five thousand French and twelve thousand allies; hence, if the strength of the latter's position did not save them from the greater loss, their steadfast courage is more to be admired.

The 29th the armies rested in position without firing a shot, and the wandering divisions on both sides were now entering the line.

Hill had sent all his baggage, artillery, and wounded men to Berioplano behind Picton's ridge, but still occupied his position, covering the Marcalain and Irurzun roads; thus posted, he likewise menaced the valley of Lanz in rear of Soult's right, his communication with Oricain being maintained by the seventh division; the light division was also approaching Hill's left, and therefore on Wellington's side the crisis was over. He had vindicated his position with only sixteen thousand combatants, and now, including the Spanish troops blockading Pampeluna, he had fifty thousand in close military combination. Thirty thousand flushed

* For this fact I had the authority of a French colonel of artillery.

with recent successes were in hand, and Hill's troops were well placed for re-taking the offensive.

Soult's situation was proportionably difficult Seeing he could not force the position, he had sent his artillery, part of his cavalry, and his wounded men, back to France immediately after the battle, ordering the two former to join Villatte on the Lower Bidassoa and await further instructions Having shaken off this burthen he awaited D'Erlon's arrival by the valley of Lanz, and that general did reach Ostiz, a few miles above ,Sauroren, at mid-day on the 29th, bringing intelligence, obtained indirectly during his march, that Graham had retired from the Bidassoa and Villatte had crossed that river. This gave Soult a hope that his first movements had disengaged San Sebastian, and he instantly conceived a new plan of operations, dangerous indeed, yet conformable to the critical state of his affairs.

No success was to be expected from another attack, yet he could not, being reinforced with eighteen thousand men, retire by the road he came without some dishonour; nor could he remain where he was, because his supplies of provisions and ammunition, derived from distant magazines by slow and small convoys, were unequal to the consumption. Two-thirds of the British troops, great part of the Portuguese and all the Spaniards, were, as he supposed, assembled in his front under Wellington, or on his right flank under Hill; and it was probable other reinforcements were on the march; wherefore he resolved to prolong his right with D'Erlon's corps, and cautiously drawing off the rest of his army place the whole between the allies and the Bastan, in military connection with his reserve and closer to his frontier magazines. Thus posted he could combine all his forces in one operation to relieve San Sebastian, and profit from new combinations.

In the evening of the 29th the second division of cavalry, which was in the valley of Zubiri, passed over to that of Lanz and joined D'Erlon, who was ordered to march early on the 30th by the cross road, leading on Marcalain, which Hill had followed to get out of that valley. During the night the first division of cavalry and La Martiniere's division of infantry, both on the extreme left of the French army, retired over the mountains to Eugui, in the upper part of the

Zubiri valley, having orders to cross the separating ridge there and join D'Erlon in the valley of Lanz The remainder of Reille's wing moved by the crest of the position to Sauroren, being gradually to relieve Clausel's troops, which were then to move up the Lanz valley, follow D'Erlon, and be followed in like manner by Reille, meanwhile Clausel detached two regiments to the ridges beyond the Lanz river, to cover his own march and open a military connection with D'Erlon, whose new line of operations was just beyond those heights.

In the night Soult again heard, from deserters, that three divisions were to make an offensive movement next day by the Marcalain road on his right, and at daylight he was convinced the men spoke truly; because from the ridges held by Clausel beyond Sauroren he descried columns descending from Picton's position and from above Oricain, while others were in movement apparently to turn Clausel's right flank. These columns were Morillo's Spaniards, Campbell's Portuguese, and the seventh division, marching to adopt a new disposition, which shall be presently explained.

Early in the morning Soult's combination was apparent Foy's division, the last of Reille's wing, was seen in march along the crest of the mountain to Sauroren, where Maucune's division had previously relieved Conroux's, and the latter, belonging to Clausel, was moving up the valley of Lanz Wellington was not a general to suffer a flank march across his front within cannon-shot. He immediately opened his batteries from the chapel height, and sent skirmishers against Sauroren; and soon this fire, spreading to the right, became brisk between Cole and Eoy; but it subsided at Sauroren, and Soult, relying on the strength of the ground, directing Reille to maintain that village until nightfall, went off himself to join D'Erlon. His design was to fall upon the troops he had seen moving to turn his right and crush them with superior numbers: a daring project, well and finely conceived, but he had to deal with a man more rapid of perception and of a rougher stroke than himself. Overtaking D'Erlon, who had three divisions of infantry and two of heavy cavalry, he found him facing, not the troops seen in march the evening before, but Hill who was in position with ten thousand men.

COMBAT OF BUENZA

Hill, occupying a very extensive mountain ridge, had his right strongly posted on rugged ground, but his left was insecure D'Erlon, who had not less than twenty thousand sabres and bayonets in line, was followed by La Martiniere's division of infantry. Soult's combination was therefore still extremely powerful, the light troops were already engaged when he arrived, and thus the same soldiers on both sides who had so strenuously combated at Maya were again opposed to each other.

D'Almagnac made a false attack on Hill's right, Abbe endeavoured to turn his left and gain the summit of the ridge in the direction of Buenza; Maransin followed Abbe, and the French cavalry, entering the line, connected the two attacks D'Armagnac pushed his feint too far, became seriously engaged and was beaten; but after some hard fighting Abbe turned the left flank, gained the summit of the mountain, and rendered the position untenable.

Hill, who had lost four hundred men, retired to the heights of Eguaros, drawing towards Marcalain with his right and throwing back his left; being there joined by Campbell and Morillo he again offered battle Soult, whose principal loss was in D'Almagnac's division, had however gained his main object; he had turned Hill's left, secured a fresh line of retreat, a shorter communication with Villatte by the pass of Dona Maria, and withal, the command of the great Irurzun road to Toloza, which was distant only one league. His first thought was to seize it and march upon Toloza or Ernani to raise the siege of San Sebastian; there was nothing to oppose this, except the light division, whose movements shall be noticed hereafter, but neither Hill nor Soult knew of its presence. If the French marshal's other combinations had been happily executed he would have broken into Guipuscoa on the 31st with fifty thousand men, thrust aside the light division in his march, and taken Graham in reverse while Villatte's reserve attacked him in front Wellington would have followed, yet scarcely in time, for he did not suspect his views, and was ignorant of his strength thinking D'Erlon's force to be only three divisions, whereas it was four divisions of infantry and two of cavalry. This error however did not prevent him from seizing the decisive point of operation and like a great captain giving a counter-stroke which Soult, trusting to the strength of Reille's position, little expected. For when La Martiniere's division and the cavalry had abandoned the mountains above Elcano, and that Zabaldica was evacuated, Picton, reinforced with two squadrons of cavalry and a battery of artillery, was directed to enter the Zubiri valley and turn the French left. Meanwhile the seventh division swept over the hills beyond the Lanz river upon Clausel's right, with safety, because Campbell and Morillo insured communication with Hill, who was ordered to push the head of his column towards Olague and menace Soult's rear in the valley of Lanz. He was in march to do this when D'Erlon, as shown, met and forced him back. During these movements Cole never ceased to skirmish with Foy on the mountain between Zabaldica and Sauroren, while the sixth division reinforced with Byng's brigade assaulted the latter village.

SECOND BATTLE OF SAUROREN.

Picton quickly gained the Val de Zubiri, and threw his skirmishers against Foy's left flank on the mountain, while on the other flank General Inglis, one of those veterans who purchase every step of promotion with their blood, advancing with only five hundred men of the seventh division, broke at one shock the two French regiments on the ridges covering Clausel's right, and drove them down into the valley of Lanz. He lost indeed one-third of his own men, but instantly spread the remainder in skirmishing order along the descent and opened a biting fire upon the flank of Conroux's division, which being, in march up the valley from Sauroren, was now thrown into disorder by having two regiments thus suddenly tumbled upon it from the top of the mountain.

Foy's division was marching along the crest of the position between Zabaldica and Sauroren at the moment of this attack; but he was too far off to give aid, and his own light troops were engaged with Cole's skirmishers; moreover Inglis had been so sudden that before the evil was well perceived it was past remedy; for

Wellington instantly pushed the sixth division under Pakenham to the left of Sauroren, and sent Byng headlong down from the chapel height against Maucune, who was in that village This vigorous assault was simultaneously enforced from the other side of the Lanz by Madden's Portuguese, and the battery near the chapel sent its bullets crashing through the houses, or booming up the valley towards Conroux's column, which Inglis never ceased to vex

The village and bridge of Sauroren and the straits beyond were soon covered with a pall of smoke, the musketry pealed frequent and loud, and the tumult and affray echoing from mountain to mountain filled all the valley. Byng with hard fighting carried Sauroren, four-teen hundred prisoners were made, and the two French divisions, being entirely broken, fled, partly up the valley towards Clausel's other divisions, partly up the original position, to seek refuge with Foy, who remained on the summit a helpless spectator of this rout He rallied the fugitives in great numbers, but had soon to look to himself, for his own skirmishers were now driven up the mountain by Cole's men, and his left was infested by Picton's detachments. Thus pressed, he fell back along the hills separating the valley of Zubiri from that of Lanz, and the woods enabled him to effect his retreat without much loss; yet he dared not descend into either valley, and thinking himself entirely cut off, sent advice to Soult and went over the Great Spine into the Alduides by the pass of Urtiaga. Clausel meanwhile had been driven up the valley of Lanz to Olague, where, being joined by La Martiniere, he took a position; and Wellington, whose pursuit had been damped by hearing of Hill's action, also halted.

The allies lost nineteen hundred men killed, wounded, or taken in this and Hill's battle, and nearly twelve hundred were Portuguese, for the soldiers of that nation bore the brunt of both fights. On the French side the loss was enormous Conroux's and Maucune's divi-sions were completely disorganized. Eight thousand men under Foy were entirely separated from the main body, two thousand at the lowest computation were killed or wounded, many were dispersed in the woods and ravines, and three thousand prisoners were taken

Soult's fighting men were thus reduced to thirty-five thousand, of which fifteen thousand under Clausel and Reille were dispirited by defeat, and the whole in a critical situation, seeing that Hill's force, increased to fifteen thousand men by the junction of Morillo and Campbell, was in their front at Eguaros, and thirty thousand were on their rear in the valley of Lanz; for Picton, finding no enemies in the valley of Zubiri, had joined Cole on the heights.

Wellington had sent some Spaniards to Marcalain when he first heard of Hill's action, yet he was not then aware of the true state of affairs on that side, and his operations were founded on the notion that Soult was in retreat towards the Bastan. Hence he designed to follow closely and push his own left forward to support Graham on the Bidassoa; but he still underrated D'Erlon's force, and thought La Martiniere's division had originally retreated up the Val de Zubiri to Roncesvalles, instead of crossing the intervening ridge to the Lanz valley; and as Foy's column was numerous, and two divisions had been broken at Sauroren, he judged the force immediately under Soult to be very weak, and made dispositions accordingly. The sixth division and the 13th Light Dragoons were ordered to join Picton, the whole to move upon the Roncesvalles; Cole was called down into the valley of Lanz, and Hill was directed to press Soult, turning his right, yet still directing his own march upon Lanz: the seventh division was to let Hill cross its front, and then march for the pass of Dona Maria. These arrangements show that Wellington expected Soult to rejoin Clausel, and make for the Bastan by the pass of Vellate. But the French marshal was so far advanced he could not return to Lanz; he was between two fires, and could only retreat into the valley of St. Estevan by the pass of Dona Maria; wherefore, calling up Clausel, and giving D'Erlon, whose divisions were in good order, the rear-guard, he commenced his march at midnight towards the pass. Mischief was thickening around him. Graham, on the British left, had twenty thousand men ready to move either against Villatte or into the valley of St. Estevan; and there remained on that side the light division, under Charles Alten, of whose operations it is time to speak.

That general had descended the mountain of Santa Cruz on the evening of the 28th, to gain the great road of Irurzun; but whether by orders from Graham, or in default of orders, the difficulty of communication being extreme in those wild regions, he commenced his movement very late, and darkness falling on his rear brigade while in march, the troops got dispersed in that frightful wilderness of woods and precipices. Many soldiers made faggot torches, waving them as signals, and, so moving, the lights served indeed to assist those who carried them, yet misled and bewildered others who saw them at a distance; for the heights and the ravines were alike studded with these small fires, and the soldiers calling to each other filled the whole region with their clamour. Thus they continued to rove and shout until morning showed the face of the mountain covered with scattered men and animals, who had not gained half a league of ground beyond their starting place, and it was many hours ere they could be collected.

Alten, now for three days separated from the army, sent mounted officers in various directions to obtain tidings, and at six o'clock in the evening renewed his march, but at Areysa halted without suffering fires to be lighted; for he knew nothing of the enemy and was fearful of discovering his situation. At night he moved again, and finally established his bivouacs near Lecumberri early on the 30th, having heard the noise of Hill's battle at Buenza in the course of the day. The light division was thus brought into the immediate system of operations, and had Soult continued his march, after driving back Hill, it would have been in great danger. Now it was a new power thrown into Wellington's hands at a critical moment, for Villatte, contrary to the intelligence received, had not advanced, and Soult was therefore completely isolated: he held indeed no resources save what his ability and courage could supply.

His single line of retreat by Dona Maria was secure only as far as San Estevan, and from that town he could march up the Bidassoa to the Bastan, to regain France by the Col de Maya; or down the same river towards Vera by Sumbilla and Yanzi, from both of which roads branching off to the right led over the mountains to Echallar: yet he might be intercepted on either side. The Col de Maya way was good, that down the Bidassoa was a long and terrible defile, so contracted about the bridges of Yanzi and Sumbilla that a few men only could march abreast. This then he had to dread. First, that Wellington by the pass of Vellate would reach the Bastan before him, and block the Maya passes. Second, that Graham would occupy the rocks of Yanzi and cut him off from Echallar. Then, confined to a narrow mountain-way leading from San Estevan to Zagaramurdi, and far too rugged for wounded men and baggage, he would be followed by Hill, and perhaps headed at Urdax by Wellington.

In this state, the first object being to get through Dona Maria, he commenced his retreat in the night of the 30th, while Wellington, still ignorant of the real state of affairs, halted in the valley of Lanz to let Hill pass his front and enter the Bastan. But early on the 31st, Soult's real strength became known, and the seventh division was directed to aid Hill, while Wellington marched himself through the pass of Vellate, and sent Alten orders to cut in upon the French, intercepting their march where he could. Longa, who was with Graham, had instructions to seize the defiles at Yanzi, and aid the light division to block that way, while Graham was to hold all his corps in readiness for the same object.

COMBAT OF DONA MARIA.

General Hill overtook the French rear-guard early on the 31st, just as the seventh division appeared on his right, and the enemy could only gain the summit of the Dona Maria pass under the fire of his guns; there however they turned, and throwing out skirmishers made strong battle. General Stewart, leading the attack and now for the third time engaged with D' Erlon's troops, was again badly wounded and his first brigade was repulsed; yet Pringle renewed the attack with the second brigade, and broke the enemy's right; the seventh division did the same for the left, and some prisoners were taken: a thick fog prevented further pursuit, and the loss of the French was unknown, but that of the allies was four hundred.

The seventh division remained on the mountain. Hill, following his orders, moved by a short rugged way between Dona Maria and Vellate over the Great Spine to join Wellington, who had during this combat entered the Bastan. Meanwhile General Byng, previously pushed forward, had captured at Elisondo a large convoy of provisions and ammunition left there by D'Erlon, had made several hundred prisoners after a sharp skirmish, and seized the pass of Maya. Wellington then occupied the hills through which the road from San Estevan led to the Bastan, and full of hope he was to strike a terrible blow; for Soult, after passing Dona Maria, had halted in San Estevan, although from his scouts he knew the convoy had been taken by Byng. He was in a deep valley, and four divisions were behind the crest of the mountains overlooking his post; the seventh division was on the summit of the Dona Maria pass; the light division and Graham's Spaniards were marching to block the valley at Vera and Echallar; Byng was at Maya, and Hill was moving by Almandoz just behind Wellington; a few hours gained and the French must surrender or disperse !

Strict orders were given to prevent the lighting of fires, the straggling of soldiers, or any other indication of the presence of troops, and the English commander placed himself on some rocks at a culminant point, from whence he could observe every movement. Soult seemed tranquil, and when four of his *"gens d'armes"* were seen to ride up the valley in a careless manner some staff-officers proposed to cut them off. Wellington, whose object was to hide his own presence, forbade this; but the next moment three marauding English soldiers entering the valley, were seen and carried off by the French patrol; half an hour afterwards their drums beat to arms and the columns began to move out of San Estevan towards Sumbilla. Thus the disobedience of three plundering knaves, unworthy of the name of soldiers, deprived one consummate commander of the most splendid success, and saved another from the most terrible disaster.*

Soult walked from his prison, yet his chains still hung upon him. The way was narrow, the multitude great, wounded men borne on their comrades' shoulders filed in long procession with the baggage, Clausel's troops, forming the rear-guard, were therefore still near San

* The facts as here stated were supplied to me by the Duke of Wellington.

Estevan the next morning; and scarcely had they marched a league when Cole's skirmishers and the Spaniards, thronging; along the heights on their flank, opened a fire on them, to which the reply could be made: the soldiers and baggage soon got mixed in disorder, numbers fled up the hills, and the energy of Soult, whose personal exertions were conspicuous, could scarcely prevent a general dispersion. Prisoners and baggage were now taken at every step, and the boldest were dismayed; worse would have awaited them, if Wellington had been on other points well seconded by his subordinate generals.

Instead of taking the first road leading, from Sumbilla to Echallar, the head of the French column passed onward towards that leading from the bridge near Yanzi; the valley narrowed to a mere cleft in the rocks as they advanced, the Bidassoa was on their left, and there was a tributary torrent to cross, the bridge being defended by a battalion of Spanish Caçadores from Vera. The head of the column was by this time as much disordered as the rear, and had the Caçadores been reinforced, only those French near Sumbilla, who could take the road from that place to Echallar, would have escaped; but the Spanish general Longa kept aloof, D'Erlon won the defile, and Reille's divisions were following, when a new enemy appeared.

The light division had been directed to head the French at San Estevan or Sumbilla. The order was received on the evening of the 31st, and General Alten, threading the defiles of Zubieta and descending the deep valley of Lerins, reached Elgoriaga about mid-day on the 1st of August, having then marched twenty four miles. He was little more than a league from Estevan, was about the same distance from Sumbilla, and the movement of the French along the Bidassoa was immediately discovered. Instead of moving direct on Sumbilla he turned to his left, clambered up the great mountain of Santa Cruz and made for the bridge of Yanzi. The weather was very sultry, the mountain steep and hard to overcome, many men fell and died convulsed and frothing at the mouth, others whose spirit and strength had never before been quelled, leaned on their muskets and muttered in sullen tones that they yielded for the first time. However, towards evening, after marching, nineteen consecutive hours, and over forty miles of mountain roads, the head of the exhausted column reached the edge of a precipice near the bridge of Yanzi. Below it, within pistol-shot, Reille's divisions were seen hurrying forward along the horrid defile in which they were pent up, a fire of musketry commenced, and the scene which followed is thus described by an eye-witness.*

"We overlooked the enemy at stone's throw, and from the summit of a tremendous precipice. The river separated us, but the French were wedged in a narrow road with inaccessible rocks on one side and the river on the other. Confusion impossible to describe followed, the wounded were thrown down in the rush and trampled upon, the cavalry drew their swords and endeavoured to charge up the pass of Echallar, but the infantry beat them back, and several, horses and all, were precipitated into the river; some fired vertically at us, the wounded called out for quarter, while others pointed to them, supported as they were on branches of trees, on which were suspended great coats clotted with gore, and blood-stained sheets taken from different habitations to aid the sufferers."

On these miserable supplicants brave men could not fire, and so piteous was the spectacle that it was with averted or doubtful aim they shot at the others, although the latter rapidly plied their muskets in passing, and some in their veteran hardihood even dashed across the bridge of Yanzi to make a counter-attack. It was a soldier-like but vain effort, the night found the British in possession of the bridge; and though the great body of the enemy escaped by the mountain path to Echallar, the baggage was cut off and with many prisoners fell into the hands of the light troops which were still hanging on the rear in pursuit from San Estevan.

That day the French losses were great, yet Wellington was justly discontented with the result. Neither Longa nor Alten had fulfilled their missions. The former should have stopped D'Erlon; the latter should have passed the bridge of Yanzi and struck a great blow: it was for that his soldiers had made such a prodigious exertion.

In the night Soult rallied his divisions about Echallar,

---

* Memoirs of Captain, now Lieut.- Colonel Cooke, Gentleman-at-Arms.

and on the morning of the 2nd occupied the Puerto of that name. His left was on the rocks of Zagaramurdi, his right on the Ivantelly mountain, communicating with Villatte, who held certain ridges between the Ivantelly and the head of the great Rhune mountain. Clausel's three divisions, reduced to six thousand men, were on a strong hill between the Puerto and town of Echallar. This position was momentarily adopted by Soult to make Wellington discover his final object, but that general would not suffer the affront. He had the fourth, seventh, and light divisions in hand, and resolved to fall upon Clausel, whose position was dangerously advanced.

COMBATS OF ECHALLAR AND IVANTELLY.

From Yanzi the light division marched to the heights of Santa Barbara, which were connected with the Ivantelly, thus turning Clausel's position and menacing Soult's right, while the fourth division moved to attack his front, and the seventh menaced his left; these attacks were to be simultaneous, but General Barnes led his brigade of the seventh division against Clausel's strong post before the fourth and light divisions were seen or felt. A vehement fight ensued, yet neither the steepness of the mountain, nor the overshadowing multitude of the enemy, clustering above in support of their skirmishers, could arrest the assailants, and the astonishing spectacle was presented of fifteen hundred men, driving by sheer valour and force of arms six thousand good troops from ground so rugged, the numbers might have been reversed and the defence made good without much merit. Incalculable is the preponderance of moral power in war ! These were the Frenchmen who had assailed the terrible rocks above Sauloren with a force and energy that all the valour of the hardiest British veterans scarcely sufficed to repel; yet now, five days only having elapsed, although posted so strongly, they did not sustain the shock of one-fourth of their own numbers ! And at this very time, eighty British soldiers, the comrades and equals of those who achieved this wonderful exploit, having wandered to plunder, surrendered to some French peasants, who as Lord Wellington truly observed, *" they would under other circumstances have eat up! "*

What gross ignorance of human nature then do those writers display, who assert, that the use of brute force is the highest qualification of a general !

Clausel fell back fighting, to a strong ridge beyond the pass of Echallar, having his right covered by the Ivantelly mountain, which was strongly occupied. Meanwhile the light division ascended the broad heights of Santa Barbara, and halted until the operations of the fourth and seventh divisions rendered it advisable to attack the Ivantelly, which lifted its sugar-loaf head on their right rising as it were out of the Santa Barbara heights, and shutting them off from the ridges through which the troops beaten at Echallar were now retiring. Evening was coming on, a thick mist capped the crowning rocks, where a strong, French regiment was ensconced, and the division, besides its terrible march the previous day, had been for two days without sustenance. Weak and fainting, the soldiers were leaning on their arms when the advancing fire at Echallar imported an attack on the Ivantelly, and Andrew Barnard led five companies of riflemen up the mountain. Four companies of the 43rd followed in support, the misty cloud descended lower, the riflemen were soon lost to the view, and the sharp clang of their weapons, heard in distinct reply to the more sonorous rolling musketry of the French, told what work was going on. For some time the echoes rendered it doubtful how the action went, but the companies of the 43rd could find no trace of an enemy save the killed and wounded: Barnard had fought his way unaided, and without a check to the summit, where his dark-clothed swarthy veterans raised their victorious shout on the highest peak, just as the coming night showed the long ridges of the mountains beyond, sparkling, with the last musket-flashes from Clausel's troops retiring in disorder from Echallar.

This day cost the British four hundred men, and Wellington himself narrowly escaped the enemy's hands. He had taken towards Echallar half a company of the 43rd as an escort, and placed a sergeant, named Blood, with a party to watch in front while he examined his maps. A French detachment endeavoured to cut the party off, and their troops, rushing on at speed, would infallibly have fallen unawares upon Wellington, if Blood, leaping down the precipitous rocks, had not given him warning: as it was, they arrived in time to send a volley after him while galloping away.

Now, after nine days of continual movement during which ten serious actions had been fought, the operations ceased. Of the allies, including the Spaniards, seven thousand three hundred officers and soldiers had been killed, wounded, or taken, and many were dispersed from fatigue or to plunder. On the French side the loss was terrible, and the disorder rendered the official returns inaccurate. Wellington called it twelve thousand, but hearing the French officers admitted more, raised his estimate to fifteen thousand. The engineer *Belmas,* his Journals of Sieges compiled from official documents, sets down above thirteen thousand. Soult in his official correspondence at the time, gave fifteen hundred for Maya, four hundred for Roncesvalles, two hundred on the 27th, eighteen hundred the 28th, after which he spoke no more of losses by battle. There remain therefore to be added, the combats of Linzoain, the battles of Sauroren and Buenza on the 30th, the combats on the 31st, 1st and 2nd: finally, four thousand unwounded prisoners. Let this suffice. It is not needful to sound the stream of blood in all its horrid depths.

BOOK XII.

Catalonia—Combat of Ordal—Renewed Siege of San Sebastian—
Storm of San Sebastian—Battles on the Bidassoa—
Combat of San Marcial—Combat of Vera.

CATALONIA.

While Wellington was thus victorious in Navarre, Lord W. Bentinck, having reorganized Murray's army at Alicant, was pushing the war in Catalonia; for to that province Suchet retired after the battle of Vittoria, relinquishing Valencia and Aragon, though he knew Clausel was at Zaragoza. But in every way his determination to act independently, however injurious it might prove to the emperor's interest, was apparent. Had he joined Clausel, forty-five thousand men, well based on fortresses, would have menaced Wellington's right flank when Soult took the command: neither Sebastian nor Pampeluna could then have been invested, and Soult's recent defeats would have been spared.

Lord William Bentinck had command of the Spanish armies as well as his own, and Lord Wellington had planned a cautious scheme for renewed operations, with reference to his own position in the Pyrenees: but Lord William, whose thoughts were running, on Sicily and an invasion of Italy, pushed headlong into Catalonia, and though a brave and able man he did not meet with much success. Having passed the Ebro late in July, leaving the fortress of Tortoza behind him, he on the 30th sat down before Tarragona with his own and Del Parque's armies.

Up to this time the Spaniards, giving copious but false information to Lord William, and none to Suchet, had induced a series of errors on both sides. The Englishman thinking his adversary weak had pressed forwards rashly; the Frenchman, deeming the other's boldness the result of strength, thought himself weak, and awaited reinforcements from Upper Catalonia. Suchet first recognised his own superior force, and advanced on the 16th of August to attack with thirty thousand men; and then Lord William, also discovering the true state of affairs, refused the battle he had provoked and retired. He had indeed equal numbers, yet of a quality not to be put in competition with his opponents.

During the retreat, his brother, Lord Frederick, being on the left, defeated the French hussars with a loss of fifty men, and it was said either General Habert or Harispe was taken but escaped in the confusion. This checked the enemy, and in the mountains above Tortoza the allies halted. Suchet would not assail them there, but he destroyed the works of Tarragona and took a permanent position behind the Llobregat, thus giving up the fertile Campo de Tarragona allowing the allies to invest Tortoza, and isolating himself entirely from the operations in Navarre, where he might have decided the war. Seeing this timidity, Lord William again moved forward, but again misled by false information, detached Del Parque's army by the way of Tudela to Navarre: meanwhile going himself beyond Tarragona to Villa Franca, he placed Colonel Adam with twelve hundred men ten miles in advance, at the strong pass of Ordal.

In this position, having lost Del Parque's army, and left Whittingham's Spanish division in the rear for the sake of subsistence, Lord William was exposed to a formidable attack from Suchet, who had more than thirty thousand men on the Llobregat, a few miles off. But he could only be approached on two lines—one in front, from Molino del Rey, by the royal road; the other on his left by Martorel and San Sadurni. The first he blocked with Adam's corps, at Ordal, which he now reinforced with three battalions and a squadron of Spanish cavalry; the second, a rugged and difficult way, he guarded by two Catalan corps under Eroles and Manso, reinforced with a Calabrese battalion: there was indeed a third line on his right by Avionet, but it was little better than a goat-path.

He had designed to push his main body close to Ordal on the evening of the 12th, yet from some slight cause, and in war slight causes often determine the fate of nations, he delayed it until next day. Meanwhile he viewed the country in front of that defile without discovering an enemy, his confidential emissaries assured him the

French were not going to advance, and he so expressed himself to Adam on his return. A report of a contrary tendency was made by Colonel Reeves of the 27th, on the authority of a Spanish woman who had before proved her accuracy and ability as a spy, but she was now disbelieved: this incredulity was unfortunate. Suchet thus braved, and his communication with Lerida threatened by Manso on the side of Martorel, was in person actually marching to attack Ordal, and Decaen and Maurice Mathieu were turning the left by San Sadurni.

COMBAT OF ORDAL.

The heights occupied by Adam rose gradually from a magnificent bridge, by which the main road was carried over a deep impracticable ravine. The second battalion of the 27th British Regiment was on the right, some Germans and Swiss with six guns defended a dilapidated fort commanding the main road; the Spaniards were in the centre; the Anglo-Calabrese on the left; a British squadron of cavalry in reserve. A bright moonlight facilitated the movements of the French, three daring scouts sent in advance discovered the state of affairs, and a little before midnight, the leading, column under General Mesclop passed the bridge without let or hindrance, mounted the heights with a rapid pace and driving back the picquets gave the first alarm. The first effort was against the 27th, the Germans and Spanish battalions were then assailed in succession as the French masses got free of the bridge, but the Calabrese were too far on the left to take a share in the action. The combat was fierce and obstinate. Harispe, commanding the French, constantly outflanked the right of the allies, and at the same time pressed their centre, where the Spaniards fought gallantly. Adam was wounded early, Reeves succeeded him, and seeing his flank turned and his men falling fast, in short, finding himself engaged with a whole army on a position of which Adam had lost the key by neglecting the bridge, resolved to retreat. He first ordered the guns to fall back, but seeking to cover tho movement by charging a column of the enemy, which was pressing forward on the high-road, he also fell severely wounded, and there was no recognised commander on the spot to succeed him. Then the affair became confused. For though the order to retreat was given, the Spaniards continued to fight desperately, the 27th thought it shame to abandon them, and as the Germans and Swiss still held the old fort the guns came back. The action was thus continucd with great fury, and Colonel Carey, bringing his Calabrese into line from the left, menaced the right flank of the French. He was too late. The Spaniards, overwhelmed in the centre, were by that time broken, the right was completely turned, the old fort was lost, the enemy's skirmishers got into the rear, and at three o'clock the allies dispersed, the most part in flight: the Spanish cavalry were then overthrown on the main road by the French hussars, and four guns were taken in the tumult.

Captain Waldron with the 27th, reduced to eighty men, being joined by Captain Muller with about the same number of Germans and Swiss, broke through small parties of the enemy and effected a retreat in good order by the hills on each side of the road. Colonel Carey endeavoured to gain the road of Sadurni on the left, but meeting with Decaen's people on that side retraced his steps, crossed the field of battle in the rear of Suchet's columns and made for Villa Nueva de Sitjes, where he finally embarked without loss, save a few stragglers. The overthrow was complete, and the prisoners were at first very numerous, yet darkness enabled many to escape, and two thousand men took refuge with Manso and Eroles.

Suchet, continuing his career, closed about nine o'clock on Lord W. Bentinck, who retired skirmishing behind Villa Franca. He was there assailed by the French horsemen, some of which fell on his rearguard while others edged to their right to secure the communication with Decaen; the latter was looked for by both parties with great anxiety, but he had been delayed by the resistance of Manso and Eroles in the rugged country between Martorel and Sadurni. Suchet's cavalry however, continued to infest the rear of the retreating army until it reached a deep baranco, where, the passage being dangerous and the French horsemen importunate, that brave and honest soldier, Lord Frederick Bentinck, charged their right, and fighting hand to hand with the enemy's general Myers, wounded him and overthrew his squadron. They rallied indeed upon their dragoons and endeavoured to turn the flank, but were stopped by the fire of two guns; and meanwhile the French cuirassiers on the left, while pressing the Brunswick hussars and menacing the infantry, were roughly checked by the fire of the 10th Regiment. This cavalry action was vigorous, and the allies lost more than ninety men, but the baranco was safely passed, and about three o'clock the pursuit ceased. The Catalans meanwhile had retreated towards Igulada and the Anglo-Sicilians retired to Tarragona.

Lord William Bentinck then returned to Sicily, leaving the command to Sir William Clinton. He had committed errors, but the loss at Ordal was due to the folly of Colonel Adam, and whoever relies on his capacity in peace or war will be disappointed.

RENEWED SEIGE OF SAN SEBASTIAN.

After the combats of Echallar and Ivantelly Soult resumed his former defensive positions, that is to say, from the mouth of the Bidassoa up its right bank to Vera, and from thence by the lower ranges of the Pyrenees to St. Jean Pied de Port. Lord Wellington also reoccupied his old positions on the main spine, and on the advanced counter ridges, which gave him the command of the Bastan and the valley of San Estevan. Many causes had concurred to deter him from pushing his success, and though this termination was, perhaps, scarcely defensible on high military principles, the difficulties were so great that he contented himself with renewing the siege of San Sebastian, the blockade of which had been always maintained.

On the 8th of August the attack there was renewed by sinking a shaft and driving a gallery to countermine the enemy, who was supposed to be working under the cask redoubt; but water rose to the height of twelve feet, the work was discontinued, and the siege itself was vexatiously delayed by the negligence of the English government in providing guns and stores, and by the astounding insulting refusal of the Admiralty to supply the necessary naval aid. To use Lord Wellington's expression, *"Since Great Britain had been a naval power, a British army had never before been left in such a situation at a most important moment."*

During this forced inactivity the garrison received supplies and reinforcements by sea, repaired the damaged works, raised new defences, filled the magazines, and put sixty-seven pieces of artillery in a condition to play. Eight hundred and fifty men had been killed and wounded since the commencement of the siege; but more than two thousand six hundred good soldiers, still under arms, celebrated the emperor's birthday, by crowning the castle with a splendid illumination—encircling, it with a fiery legend to his honour in characters so large as to be distinctly read by the besiegers.

On the 19th of August, a battering train demanded by Wellington three months before, did arrive from England, and in the night of the 22nd fifteen heavy pieces w ere placed in battery. A second battering train came on the 23rd, augmenting the number of pieces to a hundred and seventeen; but with characteristic official negligence, this enormous armament brought shot and shells for only one day's consumption !

On the 24th the Chofre batteries were enlarged, and two batteries were begun on the heights of Bartolomeo, designed to breach the faces of the horn-work of St. John and the end of the high curtain, which rose in gradation one above another in the same line of shot. The approaches on the isthmus were pushed forward by the sap, but the old trenches were still imperfect, and at daylight on the 25th a sally from the horn-work swept the left of the parallel, injured the sap, and made some prisoners.

On the 26th fifty-seven pieces opened with a general salvo, and continued to play with astounding, noise and rapidity until evening. The firing, from the Chofres destroyed the revetment of the demi-bastion of St. John, and nearly ruined the towers at the old breach, together with the wall connecting them; but from the isthmus, the batteries only injured the horn-work, and Wellington, who was present at this attack, ordered a new one of six guns to be constructed amongst some ruined houses on the right of the parallel, and only three hundred yards from the main front: two shafts were also sunk for driving galleries to protect this battery against the enemy's mines.

In the morning of the 27th the boats of the squadron, carrying a hundred soldiers, put off to attack the island of Santa Carla, and landed with some difficulty under a heavy fire, yet took the island with a loss of twenty-eight men and officers, eighteen being seamen.

In the night of the 27th the French sallied against the new battery on the isthmus, but on the edge of the trenches the 9th Regiment met and checked them with the bayonet.

At daybreak the besiegers' fire was extremely heavy, and the shrapnel shells were supposed to be destructive; the practice was however very uncertain, the shells frequently flew amongst the guards in the parallel, and one struck the field-officer of the day. To meet sallies the trenches were furnished with banquettes and parapets; yet the work was slow, because the Spanish authorities of Guipuscoa neglected to provide carts to convey materials from the woods, and this hard labour was performed by the Portuguese soldiers.

Lord Wellington again visited the works on the 28th, and in the night the advanced battery, which at the desire of the chief engineer Fletcher had been constructed for only four guns, was armed and opened the 29th; an accident kept back one gun, the enemy's fire dismounted another, and thus only two instead of six guns, as Wellington had designed, smote St. John and the end of the high curtain. The general firing however damaged the castle and the town-works, their guns were nearly silenced, and as sixty-three pieces, of which twenty-nine threw shells or spherical case-shot, were now in play from the Chofres, the superiority of the besiegers was established.

At this time the Urumea was discovered to be fordable by Captain Alexander Macdonald of the artillery, who had voluntarily waded across in the night, passed close under the works to the breach and returned. Hence, as a few minutes would suffice to bring the enemy into the Chofre batteries, to save the guns from being spiked their vents were covered with iron plates fastened by chains; and this was also done at the advanced battery on the isthmus. The materials for a battery to take the defences of the Monte Orgullo in reverse were now sent to the island of Santa Clara, and some pieces on the Chofres were turned against the retaining wall of the hornwork, in the hope of shaking down any mines there without destroying the wall itself, which offered cover for the troops advancing to the assault.

On the isthmus the trenches were wide and good, the sap was pushed to the demi-bastion of the horn-work, and the sea-wall, supporting the high road into the town, which had cramped the formation of the columns in the first assault, was broken through, giving access to the strand and shortening, the way to the breaches. In this state a false attack was ordered in the night to make the enemy spring his mines, a desperate service, executed by Lieutenant Mac-Adam. The order was sudden, no volunteers were demanded, no rewards offered, no means of excitement resorted to; yet such is the inherent bravery of British soldiers, that seventeen men of the Royals, the nearest at hand, immediately leaped forth ready and willing to encounter what seemed certain death. With a rapid pace, all the breaching batteries playing hotly at the time, they reached the foot of the breach unperceived and rushed up in extended order shouting; and firing, but the French musketry laid the whole party low with exception of their commander.

On the 30th, the sea flank of the place being opened from the half-bastion of St. John to the most distant of the old breaches, five hundred feet, the Chofre batteries were turned against the castle and defences of Monte Orgullo, while the advanced battery on the isthmus demolished, in conjunction with the fire from the Chofres, the face of St. John and the end of the high curtain above it. The whole of that quarter was now in ruins, for the San Bartolomeo batteries had broken the demi-bastion of the horn-work and cut away the palisades. Then Wellington, again coming to the siege, resolved to make a lodgement on the breach, and ordered an assault for the next day at eleven o'clock, when the ebb of tide would leave full space between the horn-work and the water.

The galleries on the isthmus had now been pushed close up to the sea wall, and three mines were formed, with the double object of opening an easy way for the troops to reach the strand, and rendering useless any subterranean defensive works of the enemy. At two o'clock in the morning they were sprung and opened three wide passages, which were immediately connected, and a traverse, six feet high was run across the mouth of the main trench on the left, to screen the opening from the grape-shot of the castle. Everything was then ready for the assault, but ere that terrible event is told the French state of defence must be made known.

General Graham had been before the place fifty-two days, during thirty of which the attack was suspended. All that time the garrison had laboured incessantly, and though the heavy fire of the besiegers since the 26th appeared to have ruined the defences of the enormous breach in the sea flank, it was not so. A perpendicular fall behind of more than twenty feet barred progress, and beyond that, amongst the ruins of the burned houses, was a strong counter wall fifteen feet high, loopholed for musketry and extending in a parallel direction with the breaches, which were also cut off from the sound part of the rampart by traverses at the extremities. The only really practicable road into the town was by the narrow end of the high curtain above the half bastion of St. John.

In front of the loopholed wall, about the middle of the great breach, stood the tower of Los Hornos, still capable of some defence, and beneath it a mine was charged with twelve hundred weight of powder. The streets were all trenched and furnished with traverses to cover a retreat to Monte Orgullo; and before the main breach could be even reached a lodgement was to be effected in the horn-work; or, as in the former assault, the advance made under a flanking fire of musketry for two hundred yards, the first step being close to the sea wall at a salient angle, where two mines charged with eight hundred pounds of powder were prepared to overwhelm the advancing columns. To support this system of retrenchments and mines there was still one sixteen-pounder at St. Elmo, flanking the left of the breaches on the river face; a twelve and an eightpounder in the casemates of the cavalier, to sweep the land face of St. John; many guns from the Monte Orgullo, also especially those at the Mirador, could play on the advancing columns, and there was a four-pounder hidden on the horn-work to open during the assault. Neither the resolution of the governor nor the courage of the garrison was abated, but the overwhelming fire had reduced the fighting men, and Rey, who had only two hundred and fifty in reserve, demanded of Soult whether his brave garrison should be exposed to another assault. " *The army would endeavour to succour him,*" was the reply, and he abided his fate.

This assault, before the defences were ruined, was obviously a repetition of the former fatal error; and the same generals who had before publicly disapproved of the operations now more freely dealt out censures, which, not illfounded, were most ill-timed, because doubts descend from the commanders to the soldiers. Lord Wellington thought the fifth division had been thus discouraged, and incensed at the cause, demanded fifty volunteers from each of the fifteen regiments composing the first, fourth, and light divisions, " *men who could show other troops how to mount a breach.*" That was the phrase employed, and seven hundred and fifty gallant soldiers instantly marched to San Sebastian in answer to the appeal. Colonel Cooke and Major Robertson led the Guards and Germans of the first division; Major Rose commanded the men of the fourth division; Colonel Hunt, an officer who had already won his promotion at former assaults, led the fierce rugged veterans of the light division, yet there were good officers and brave soldiers in the fifth division.

At first a simple lodgement on the great breach was designed, and the volunteers and one brigade of the fifth division only were to be employed; but in a council held at night, the engineer Smith maintained that the orders were misunderstood, as no lodgement could be formed unless the high curtain was gained; General Oswald was of the same opinion; wherefore the remainder of the fifth division was brought to the trenches, and General Bradford, having offered the services of his Portuguese brigade, had a discretion to ford the Urumeà from the Chofres and assail the farthest breach.

General Leith, commanding the fifth division, directed the attack from the isthmus, and being offended at the arrival of the volunteers would not suffer them to lead the assault; some he spread along the trenches to keep down the fire of the horn-work, the remainder he kept in reserve with Hay's British and Sprye's Portugese brigades. Robinson's brigade was to assault in two columns, one at the old breach between the towers, the other at St. John and the end of the high curtain. The small breach was left for Bradford, and some large boats filled with troops were to menace the back of Monte Orgullo from the ocean: Graham overlooked all the operations from the Chofres.

STORMING OF SAN SEBASTIAN.

The morning of the 31st broke heavily, and as a thick fog hid every object the batteries could not open until eight o'clock, but from that hour a constant shower of heavy missiles poured upon the besieged until eleven: then Robinson's brigade got out of the trenches, passed through the openings in the sea-wall and was launched against the breaches. While this column was gathering on the strand, near the salient angle of the horn-work, twelve men under a sergeant, whose heroic death has not sufficed to preserve his name, running violently forward, leaped on the covered way to cut the sausage of the enemy's mines, and the French fired the train prematurely; the sergeant and his brave followers were destroyed, and the high sea-wall was thrown with a dreadful crash upon the head of the advancing column, but not more than forty men were crushed and the rush was scarcely checked. The forlorn hope had previously passed beyond the play of the mine, speeding along the strand amidst a shower of grape and shells, the leader, Lieutenant Macguire of the 4th Regiment, conspicuous for his long white plume, his fine figure, and his swiftness, bounding far ahead of his men in all the pride of youthful strength and courage, but at the foot of the great breach he fell dead, and the stormers swept like a dark surge over his body: many died with him and the trickling, of wounded men to the rear was incessant.

A broad strand had been left by the retreating tide, and the sun had dried the rocks, yet they still broke the ranks and the main breach was two hundred yards off; the French also, seeing the first mass of assailants pass the horn-work without attacking, crowded to the river face and poured their musketry into the flank of the second column as it rushed along a few yards below them: yet still running forward the British returned this fire without slackening their speed. Then the batteries of the Monte Orgullo and the St. Elmo sent showers of shot and shells down on them, the two pieces on the cavalier swept the breach in St. John, and the four-pounder in the horn-work, being suddenly mounted on the broken bastion, poured grape-shot into their rear.

Although scourged thus with fire, and their array broken by shot and by the rocks, the stormers reached the great breach and the head of the first column mounted; but the unexpected gulf beyond could only be passed at a few places where meagre parcels of the burned houses were still attached to the rampart, and the deadly clatter of the French muskets from the loop-holed wall beyond soon strewed the narrow crest of the ruins with dead. In vain the following multitude, covering the ascent, sought an entrance at every part; to advance was impossible and the mass slowly sunk downwards, yet remained stubborn and immoveable on the lower part. There they were covered from the musketry in front, yet from several isolated points, especially the tower of Los Hornos under which the great mine was placed, the French still struck them with small arms, and the artillery from Monte Orgullo poured shells and grape without intermission. Meanwhile at the St. John affairs were worse. To reach the top of the high curtain was quite practicable, and the effort to force a way there being strenuous and constant, the slaughter was in proportion; for the traverse on the flank was defended by French grenadiers who would not yield, the two guns on the cavalier swept the front face, and the four-pounder and the musketry from the horn-work swept the river face. In the midst of this destruction some sappers and a working party attached to the assaulting columns endeavoured to form a lodgement; but no artificial materials had been provided, and most of the labourers were killed before they could raise cover.

During this time the British batteries kept up a constant counter-fire, which killed many French, and the reserve brigades of the 5th division gradually fed the attack until the left wing of the 9th Regiment only remained in the trenches. The volunteers who had been with difficulty restrained in the parallel, calling out to know, " *why they had been brought there if they were not to lead the assault,*"—these fierce and terrible men, whose presence had given such offence to Leith that he would have kept them altogether from the assault, being now perforce let loose, went like a whirlwind to the breaches and swarmed up the face of the ruins; but on the crest the stream of fire struck and they came down like a falling wall; crowd after crowd were seen to mount, to totter, to sink, and when the smoke floated away the summit bore no living man.

Graham, standing, on the nearest of the Chofre batteries, beheld this frightful destruction with a stern resolution to win at any cost, and he was a man to have put himself at the head of the last company and died sword in hand rather than sustain a second defeat: but neither his confidence nor his resources were yet exhausted. He directed a new attack on the horn-work, and concentrating the fire of fifty heavy pieces upon the high curtain sent his shot over the heads of the troops gathered at the foot of the breach; a fearful stream of missiles, which pouring along the upper surface of the high curtain broke down the traverses, shattering all things, and strewing the rampart with the mangled limbs of the defenders. When this flight of bullets first swept over the heads of the soldiers a cry arose from some inexperienced people, *"to retire because the batteries were firing on the stormers ;"* but the veterans of the light division, being at that point, were not to be so disturbed, and in the very heat and fury of the cannonade effected a solid lodgement in some house ruins actually within the rampart, on the right of the great breach.

For half an hour the horrid tempest smote upon the works and the houses behind, and then suddenly ceased, when the clatter of French muskets was again heard, showing that the assailants were still in activity. At the same time the 13th Portuguese Regiment under Major Snodgrass, followed by a detachment of the 24th under Colonel Macbean, entered the river from the Chofres. The ford was deep, the water rose above the waist, and when the soldiers reached the middle of the stream, two hundred yards wide, a shower of grape struck the column with terrible havoc, yet the survivors closed and moved on; a second discharge tore the ranks from front to rear; still the regiment moved on, and amidst a confused fire of musketry from the ramparts, and artillery from

St. Elmo, the castle, and the Mirador, landed and rushed against the third breach, while Macbean's men reinforced the great breach. The fighting then again became fierce and obstinate at all the breaches; yet the French musketry rolled with deadly effect, the heaps of slain increased, and once more the great mass of stormers sunk to the foot of the ruins unable to win: the living sheltered themselves as they could, and the dead and wounded lay so thickly that hardly could it be judged whether the hurt or unhurt were most numerous.

It was now evident the assault must fail unless some accident intervened; for the tide was rising, the reserves all engaged, and no greater effort could be expected from men whose passionate courage had been already pushed to the verge of madness. Fortune intervened. A number of powder barrels, live shells, and combustible materials accumulated behind the traverses caught fire, a bright consuming flame wrapped the high curtain, a succession of explosions followed, hundreds of the French grenadiers were destroyed; the rest were thrown into confusion, and while the ramparts were still involved with suffocating eddies of smoke the British soldiers broke in at the first traverse. The French, bewildered by this terrible disaster, yielded for a moment, yet soon rallied, and a close desperate struggle took place along the summit of the high curtain, but the fury of the stormers, whose numbers increased every moment, could not be stemmed; the colours on the cavalier were torn away by Lieutenant Gethin of the 11th Regiment; the horn-work, the land front below the curtain, and the loop-holed wall behind the great breach, all were abandoned, and then the light division soldiers, already established in the ruins on the French left, penetrated into the streets; and at the same moment the Portuguese at the small breach, mixed with British who had wandered to that point seeking for an entrance, burst in on their side.

Five hours this dreadful battle had lasted at the walls, and now the stream of war went pouring into the town; yet the undaunted governor still disputed the victory at his barricades, although several hundreds of men had been cut off in the horn-work, and his garrison was so reduced that even to retreat behind the line of defence separating the town from Monte Orgullo was difficult : however the troops, flying from the horn-work on the harbour flank, broke through a body of the British near the fortified convent of Santa Teresa, and that post was still retained by the French within the town. It was thought Monte Orgullo might have been then carried if a commander of rank to direct the troops had been at hand; but, as in the first assault, whether from wounds or accident no general entered the place until long after the breach had been won, the battalion officers were embarrassed for want of orders, and a thunder-storm, coming down the mountains with unbounded fury just as the place was carried, added to the confusion of the fight—the opportunity was lost.

This storm seemed to be a signal from hell for the perpetration of villany which would have shamed the most ferocious barbarians of antiquity. At Ciudad Rodrigo intoxication and plunder had been the principal objects; at Badajos lust and murder were joined to rapine and drunkenness; at San Sebastian, the direst, the most revolting cruelty was added to the catalogue of crimes: one atrocity, of which a girl of seventeen was the victim, staggers the mind by its enormous, incredible, indescribable barbarity. Some order was at first maintained, but the resolution to throw off discipline was quickly made manifest. A British staff-officer was pursued with a volley of small arms and escaped with difficulty from men who mistook him for a provost-marshal; a Portuguese adjutant, striving to prevent some ruffianism, was put to death in the market-place, not with sudden violence but deliberately. Many officers exerted themselves to preserve order, many men were well conducted, yet the rapine and violence commenced by villains soon spread, the campfollowers crowded into the place, and the disorder continued until fire, following the steps of the plunderer, put an end to his ferocity by destroying the whole town.

Three generals, Leith, Oswald, and Robinson, had been hurt in the trenches; Sir Richard Fletcher, a brave man, was killed; Colonel Burgoyne, next in command of the engineers, was wounded. The carnage at the breaches was appalling. Nearly half the volunteers were struck down, the fifth division suffered in the same proportion, and the whole loss since the renewal of the siege exceeded two thousand five hundred men and officers.

Amongst the last may be mentioned Lieutenant John O'Connel of the 43rd, in blood nearly related to the celebrated turbulent agitator. He was gentle, amiable, and modest, and brave as man could be, and having previously been in several storming parties here again sought in such dangerous service the promotion he had earned before without receiving—he found death.

Monte Orgullo was now to be attacked. Steep and difficult to assail it was, and just below the castle four batteries connected with masonry were stretched across its face; from their extremities, also, ramps protected by redans led to the convent of Santa Teresa, the most salient part of the defence. Towards the harbour and behind the mountain were sea batteries, and if all these works had been of good construction and defended by fresh troops the siege would have been difficult; but the garrison was shattered by the recent assault, most of the engineers were killed, the governor wounded, five hundred men sick or hurt, and the soldiers fit for duty, only thirteen hundred, had four hundred prisoners to guard. The castle was small, the bomb-proofs filled with ammunition and provisions, and but ten guns were left for service, three being on the sea line. There was little water, and the soldiers had to lie on the naked rock, exposed to fire, or only covered by asperities of ground; they were however still resolute to fight, and received nightly, by sea, supplies of ammunition in small quantities.

Lord Wellington arrived the day after the assault, and judging regular approaches up the naked rock impracticable, doubting also the power of vertical fire, he resolved to breach the remaining line of defence and then storm the Orgullo. Meanwhile from the Santa Teresa convent, which was actually in the town, the French killed many men; and when, after several days, it was assaulted, they set the lower parts on fire and retired by a communication from the roof to a ramp on the hill behind. All this time the flames were licking, up the houses, and the Orgullo was overwhelmed with vertical fire.

On the 3rd of September the governor was summoned, he was unshaken, and the vertical fire was continued day and night, the British prisoners suffering, as well as the enemy; for the officer in the castle, irritated by the misery of the garrison, cruelly refused to let the unfortunate captives make trenches to cover themselves. The French however complain, that their wounded and sick men, placed in an empty magazine with a black flag flying, were fired upon, although the English prisoners, in their uniforms, were posted around to strengthen the claim of humanity.

New breaching batteries were now commenced and armed with guns, brought from the Chofres at low water across the Urumea, at first in the night, but the difficulty of labouring in the water during darkness finally induced the artillery officers to transport them in daylight under the enemy's batteries, which did not however fire. In the town labour was impeded by the flaming houses, but near the foot of the Orgullo the ruins furnished shelter for musketeers to gall the garrison, and the Santa Clara Island battery was actively worked by the seamen. With the besieged ammunition was scarce, and the horrible vertical fire, contrary to Lord Wellington's expectation, subdued their energy; yet the action was prolonged until the 8th of September, when fifty-nine heavy battering, pieces opened at once from the island, the isthmus, the horn-work and the Chofres. In two hours the Mirador and Queen's battery were broken, the French fire extinguished, and the hill furrowed in a frightful manner; the bread-ovens were destroyed, a magazine exploded, and the castle, small and crowded with men, was overlaid with the descending shells. Then proudly bending to fate the governor surrendered. On the 9th this brave man and his heroic garrison, reduced to one-third of their original number, and leaving five hundred wounded behind, marched out with the honours of war. The siege thus terminated, after sixty-three days' open trenches, and just as the tempestuous season, then beginning to vex the coast, would have rendered a continuance of the sea blockade impossible.

The excesses committed in the storming of San Sebastian caused great indignation in Spain and justly; but they were used by the Spanish government to create a hatred of the British army, and, horrible as were the facts, it is certain the atrocities were the work of a few. Writers have not been wanting however to excuse them on the insulting ground, that no soldiers can be restrained after storming a town and British soldiers least of all, because they are brutish and insensible to honour ! Shame on such calumnies ! What makes the British soldier fight as no other soldier ever fights? His pay! Soldiers of all nations receive pay. At the period of this assault, a sergeant of the 28th, named Ball, being sent with a party to the coast from Roncesvalles to make purchases for his officers, placed two thousand dollars entrusted to him with a commissary, secured his receipt and persuaded his party to join in the storm. He survived, reclaimed the money, made his purchases, and returned to his regiment. And these are the men, these the spirits who are called too brutish to work upon except by fear ! It is to fear they are most insensible !

BATTLES ON THE BIDASSOA.

While Sebastian was being stormed Soult fought a battle with the covering force, not willingly, nor with much hope of success; but being averse to let it fall without another effort, he thought a bold demeanour would best hide his real weakness. Guided however by the progress of the siege, which he knew through his sea communication, he awaited the last moment of action, striving meanwhile to improve his resources and revive public confidence. Of his dispersed soldiers eight thousand had rejoined, and he was promised a reinforcement of thirty thousand conscripts; but these last were yet to be enrolled, and neither the progress of the siege nor the panic along the frontier, which recurred with increased violence after the late battles, would suffer him to wait.

He knew his enemy's superior strength in positions, number and military confidence, yet expected, as his former effort had interrupted the siege, another would produce a like effect; and he hoped, by repeating the disturbance, as long as he could by sea reinforce and supply the garrison, to lender the siege a wasting operation. To renew the movement against Pampeluna was most advantageous, but it required fifty thousand infantry for attack, twenty thousand for observation on the Lower Bidassoa, and he had not so many. His supplies also were uncertain, the loss, of all the military carriages at Vittolia was still felt, the resources of the country were reluctantly yielded by the people, and to act on the side of St. Jean Pied de Port was therefore impracticable.

To attack the allies' centre was unpromising. Two mountain-chains were to be forced before the movement could seriously affect Wellington, and as the ways were impracticable for guns success would not give any decisive result. To attack the left of the allies by the great road of Irun remained. He could there employ forty-five thousand infantry, but the positions were of perilous strength. The Upper Bidassoa was in Wellington's power, because the Light division, occupying Vera and the heights of Santa Barbara on the right bank, commanded all the bridges. The Lower Bidassoa, flowing from Vera with a bend to the left, separated the hostile armies, and against that line, of nine miles, the attack was necessarily directed. From the broken bridge of Behobia, in front of Irun, to the sea, the river, broad and tidal, offered no apparent passage; from the fords of Biriatu up to those of Vera, three miles, there was only the one passage of Andarlassa, two miles below Vera, and there steep craggy mountain-ridges without roads lining the river forbade great operations. Thus the points of attack were restricted to Vera itself and the fords between Biriatu and Behobia.

To gain Oyarzun, a small town eight miles beyond the Bidassoa and close to Passages, was Soult's object, and a royal road led directly to it by a broad valley between the Pena de Haya and Jaizquibel mountains; but the Pena de Haya, called also the four-crowned mountain, filled all the space between Vera, Lesaca, Irun and Oyarzun, and its staring head, bound with a rocky diadem, was impassable: from the bridges of Vera and Lesaca, however, roads, one of them not absolutely impracticable for guns, passed over its enormous flanks to Irun on one side, to Oyarzun on the other, falling into the royal road at both places. Soult therefore proposed to drive the light division from Santa Barbara, and use the bridges of Lesaca and Vera to force a passage over the Pena de Haya on his own right of its summit, pushing the heads of columns towards Oyarzun and the Upper Urumea, while Reille and Villatte, passing, the Bidassoa at Biriatu, forced their way by the royal road.

Soon he changed this plan, and with great caution and subtilty brought his left from St. Jean Pied de Port to his right, masking the movement by his cavalry, and thus formed two columns of attack on the Lower Bidassoa. One under Clausel, of twenty thousand men with twenty pieces of artillery, was concentrated in the woods behind the Commissari and Bayonette mountains above Vera. The other under Reille, eighteen thousand strong, was placed on the Lower Bidassoa, having Foy's division and some light cavalry in the rear ready to augment it to twenty-five thousand. Thirty-six pieces of artillery and two bridge equipages were disposed near Urogne, on the royal road, all being secreted behind the lower ridge of the mountains near Biriatu.

Soult's first design was to attack at daybreak on the 30th, but his preparations being incomplete he deferred it until the 31st, taking rigorous precautions to prevent intelligence passing over to the allies; Wellington's emissaries had, however, told him in the night of the 29th that the French were in movement, and the augmentation of troops in front of Irun was observed in the morning of the 30th. In the evening the bridge equipage and the artillery were discovered on the royal road, and thus warned he prepared for battle with little anxiety; for a fresh brigade of English foot-guards, most of the marauders and men wounded at Vittoria, and three regiments from England, forming a new brigade under Lord Aylmer, had recently joined.

His extreme left was on the Jaizquibel, a narrow mountain-ridge seventeen hundred feet high, running along the coast and abutting at one end on the Passages harbour, at the other on the navigable mouth of the Bidassoa. Offering no mark for attack, it was only guarded by some Spaniards; but the small fort of Figueras, commanding the entrance of the river at its foot, was garrisoned by seamen from the naval squadron, and Fuenterabia, a walled place, also at its base, was occupied.

The low ground between Fuenterabia and Irun was defended by large field redoubts, connecting the Jaizquibel with some heights covering the royal road to Oyarzun.

On the right of Irun, between Biriatu and the burned bridge of Behobia, a sudden bend in the river presented the convex to the French, who thus commanded the fords; but beyond these fords was a stiff and lofty ridge, called San Marcial, terminating one of the great flanks of the Pena de Haya. The water flowed round the left of this ridge, confining the road from the Behobia bridge to Irun, one mile, to the narrow space between the channel and the foot of the height; Irun itself, defended by a field-work, blocked this way; and hence the French, after passing the river, had to win San Marcial before they could use the great road; but six thousand Spaniards occupied that strong ridge, which was strengthened by abbattis and temporary field-works.

Behind Irun the first British division was posted under General Howard, and Lord Aylmer's brigade supported the left of the Spaniards.

San Marcial, receding from the river on the right, was exposed to an enemy passing above Biriatu; but Longa's Spaniards, drawn off from those slopes of the Pena de Haya descending towards Vera, were posted on those descending towards Biriatu, where they supported the right of the Spaniards on San Marcial.

Eighteen thousand fighting men were thus in position, and as the fourth division was still disposable, a Portuguese brigade was detached from it to replace Longa near Vera, and cover the roads from that place over the flanks of the Pena de Haya. The British brigades of that division were stationed up the mountain, near the foundry of San Antonio, commanding the intersection of the roads coming from Vera and Lesaca, and furnishing a reserve to the Portuguese brigade, to Longa, and to San Marcial—tying all together. The Portuguese brigade being however too weak to guard the enormous slopes near Vera, Inglis's brigade was drawn from Echallar to reinforce it; yet the flanks of the Pena de Haya were so rough and vast the troops seemed sprinkled rather than posted.

In the night of the 30th Soult placed his guns, and gave his orders. Reille was to storm San Marcial, to leave a strong reserve there to meet troops coming from Vera or descending the Pena de Haya, and with the rest of his force drive the allies from ridge to ridge, until he gained the slope of the mountain which descends upon Oyarzun. when the royal road was thus opened, Foy's infantry, with the cavalry and artillery in one column, were to cross by bridges to be laid during the fight.

To aid Reille's progress and provide for a general concentration at Oyarzun, Clausel was to make a simultaneous attack from Vera; not as first designed, by driving the allies from Santa Barbara, but, leaving one division and his guns to keep the light division in check, to cross the river by fords just below the town of Vera and assail the Portuguese brigade and Inglis, forcing his way upwards to the forge of Antonio, from whence he was to fall down again on the rear of San Marcial, or move on Oyarzun.

COMBAT OF SAN MARCIAL.

At daylight on the 31st, Reille forded the Bidassoa above Biriatu with two divisions and two pieces of artillery, to seize a detached ridge just under San Marcial. Leaving there one brigade as a reserve, he detached another to attack the Spanish left, while in person he assailed their right. The side of the mountain was covered with brushwood and very steep, the French troops preserved no order, the supports and skirmishers got mixed in one mass, and the charging Spaniards drove them headlong down.

During this action two bridges were thrown below the fords, by which Villatte's reserve crossed and renewed the fight; one of his brigades reached the chapel San Marcial above, and the left of the Spanish line was shaken; but then the 85th, from Lord Aylmer's brigade, advanced to support, and at that moment Wellington rode up with all his staff. He exhorted the Spaniards, and they, with a noble instinct which never abandons the poor people of any country, acknowledged real greatness without reference to nation; for, shouting in reply they dashed their adversaries down with so much violence that many were driven into the river, and some of the French pontoon boats coming to the succour were overloaded and sunk. It was several hours before the broken and confused masses could be rallied, or the bridges, which were broken up to let the boats save the drowning men, be replaced. When that was effected, Soult sent the whole of Villatte's reserve over the river, called up Foy, and prepared a better attack: with greater hope of success, also, because Clausel was now making good way up the Pena de Haya.

COMBAT OF VERA.

Clausel had descended the Bayonette and Commissari mountains at daybreak in a thick fog, but at seven o'clock the weather cleared, and three heavy columns were seen by the troops on Santa Barbara making for the fords below Vera. A fourth column and the guns remained stationary on the mountains, the artillery opening now and then upon Vera, from which the picquets of the light division were recalled, with the exception of one post in a fortified house commanding the bridge. At eight o'clock the French passed the fords, covered by a fire of artillery, but the first shells thrown fell into the midst of their own ranks, and the British troops on Santa Barbara cheered their battery with a derisive shout. Their march was however sure, and their light troops, without knapsacks, soon commenced battle with the Portuguese brigade, forcing it to retire up the mountain. Inglis fed his line of skirmishers until the whole of his brigade was engaged, but Clausel menaced his left flank from the lowest ford, and the French skirmishers still forced their way upwards in front until the contending masses disappeared fighting amidst the asperities of the Pena de la Haya. The British lost two hundred and seventy men and twenty-two officers, and were driven up to the fourth division at the foundry of San Antonio.

This fight, from the great height and asperity of the mountain, occupied many hours, and it was past two o'clock before even the head of Clausel's column reached Antonio. Meanwhile, his reserve in front of Santa Barbara made no movement, and as Wellington had directed the light division to aid Inglis, a wing of the 43rd, three companies of riflemen and three weak Spanish battalions, drawn from Echallar, crossed the Bidassoa by the Lesaca bridge and marched towards some lower slopes on the right of Inglis. This covered a knot of minor communications coming from Lesaca and Vera, and the remainder of Kempt's brigade occupied Lesaca itself. Thus the chain of connection and defence between Santa Barbara and the positions of the fourth division on the Pena de la Haya was completed.

Clausel seeing these movements, thought the allies at Echallar and Santa Barbara were only awaiting to take him in flank and rear by the bridges of Vera and Lesaca, wherefore he abated his battle and informed Soult of his views, and his opinion was well-founded. Wellington was not a general to have half his army paralyzed by D'Erlon's divisions in the centre, and had on the 30th, when Soult first assembled in front of San Marcial, ordered attacks to be made upon D'Erlon from Echallar, Zagaramurdi and Maya; Hill also had been directed to show the heads of columns towards St. Jean Pied de Port; and on the 31st, when the force and direction of Clausel's columns were known, the seventh division was called to Lesaca. Following these orders, Giron's Spaniards skirmished on the 30th with the advanced posts in front of Sarre, and next day the whole line was assailed. Two Portuguese brigades drove the French from their camp behind Urdax: and burned it, but Abbe who commanded there, collecting all his force on an intrenched position made strong battle and repulsed the attack. Thus five combats besides the assault on Sebastian were fought in one day at different points of the general line, and D'Erlon who had lost three or four hundred men, seeing a fresh column coming from Maya, as if to turn his left, judged that a great movement against Bayonne was in progress and sent notice to Soult. He was mistaken. Wellington only sought by these demonstrations to disturb the French plan of attack, and the seventh division marched towards Lesaca.

D'Erlon's despatch reached Soult at the same time that Clausel's report arrived. All his arrangements for a final attack on San Marcial were then completed, but these reports and the ominous cannonade at San Sebastian, plainly heard during the morning, induced him to abandon this project and prepare to receive a general battle on the Nivelle. In this view he sent Foy's infantry and six troops of dragoons to the heights of Serres, behind the Nivelle, as a support to D'Erlon, and directed Clausel to repass the Bidassoa in the night, to leave a division on the Bayonette mountain and join Foy at Serres.

Reille's troops were not recalled from San Marcial and the battle went on sharply; for the Spaniards continually detached men from the crest to drive the French from the lower ridges into the river until about four o'clock, when, their hardihood abating, they desired to be relieved; but Wellington, careful of their glory, and seeing the French attacks were exhausted, refused to relieve or aid them. It would not be just to measure their valour by this fact; the English general blushed while he called upon them to fight; knowing they had been previously famished by their vile government, and that there were no hospitals to receive, no care for them when wounded. The battle was however arrested by a tempest, which commenced about three o'clock and raged for several hours with wonderful violence, tearing huge branches from the trees, and whirling them through the air like feathers on the howling winds, while the thinnest streams swelling into torrents dashed down the mountains, rolling innumerable stones along with a frightful clatter. Amidst this turmoil and under cover of night the French re-crossed the river at San Marcial.

Clausel's retreat was more unhappy. The order to retire reached him when the storm had put an end to all fighting, and he repassed the fords in person before dark at the head of two brigades, ordering General Vandermaesen to follow with the remainder of the troops. Expecting no difficulty, he neglected to seize the bridge of Vera and the fortified house covering it, occupying himself with suggesting new projects to Soult. Meanwhile Vandermaesen's situation became desperate. Many of his soldiers were drowned by the rising waters, and finally, unable to effect a passage at the fords, he marched up the stream to seize the bridge of Vera, which Clausel should have done before. His advanced guard surprised a corporal's picquet and rushed over, but was driven back by a rifle company posted in the fortified house. This happened at three o'clock in the morning, and the riflemen defended the passage until daylight, when a second company and some Portuguese Caçadores came to their aid. But then the French reserve left at Vera, seeing how matters stood, opened a fire of guns against the house from a high rock just above, and their skirmishers approached it on the right bank, while Vandermaesen plied his musketry from the left bank: the two rifle captains and many men fell under this cross fire and the passage was forced; but Vandermaesen, urging the attack in person, was killed, and more than two hundred of his soldiers were hurt.

Meanwhile Soult, who was preparing a new attack on San Marcial, got Rey's report of the assault on San Sebastian, and also heard that Hill was moving; on the side of St. Jean Pied de Port. San Sebastian was lost, an attempt to carry off the garrison of the castle would cost five or six thousand men, and the whole army would be endangered amongst the terrible asperities of the crowned mountain; for Wellington could now throw his right and centre, thirty-five thousand men, upon the French left during the action, and would be nearer to Bayonne than their right when the battle was beyond the Lower Bidassoa. Three thousand six hundred men had been lost, one general had been killed, four wounded; a fresh attempt would be very dangerous, and serious losses might cause an immediate invasion of France. Reflecting on these things, he resolved to adopt defensive measures at once, for which his vast knowledge of war, his foresight, his talent for methodical arrangement, and his firmness of character, peculiarly fitted him. Twelve battles or combats in seven weeks he had delivered to regain the offensive, unsuccessfully; yet willing still to strive, he called on Suchet to aid him, and demanded fresh orders from the emperor; but Suchet helped him not, and Napoleon's answer indicated at once his own difficulties and his reliance upon the Duke of Dalmatia's capacity and fidelity. "*I have given you my confidence and can add neither to your means nor to your instructions.*"

In this straggling battle the loss of the allies had been one thousand Anglo-Portuguese and sixteen hundred Spaniards: hence the cost of men on the day, including the assault, exceeded five thousand; but the battle in no manner disturbed the siege; the French army was powerless against such strong positions.

BOOK XIII.

English Passage of the Bidassoa and Second Combat of Vera—The Passage of the Lower Bidassoa—Second Combat of Vera—Battle of the Nivelle; Characters of Colonel Lloyd and Lieutenant Freer.

ENGLISH PASSAGE OF THE BIDASSOA AND SECOND COMBAT OF VERA.

The fall of San Sebastian gave Lord Wellington a new port, and let loose a considerable body of troops; Austria had joined the allies in Germany; the English cabinet had promised the continental sovereigns that France should be immediately invaded; the English newspaper editors were actively deceiving the people of all countries by their dictatorial absurd projects and assumptions; the Bourbon partizans were conspiring, and the Duke of Berri desired to join the British army, pretending that twenty thousand Frenchmen were armed and organized to receive him. All was exultation and extravagance, but Wellington, despising such inflated hopes and promises, exposed the absurdity of the newspapers, and checked similar folly in higher places, by observing, " *that if he hed done all that was expected he should have been before that period in the moon.*"

Far from designing to invade France, he felt his own position insecure while Suchet was master of Catalonia: and he was only prevented from transferring the war to that province by the disasters Napoleon now experienced in Germany, rendering it impossible to reinforce Soult. However, pressed by the ministers and the allied sovereigns, he so far bent his military judgement to political pressure, as to undertake the establishing his army in a menacing position on French ground; and in that view matured an offensive movement as daring as any undertaken during the whole war. But to comprehend all the audacious grandeur of this operation, the relative positions of the hostile armies must be glanced at.

Soult's base and place of arms was Bayonne, from whence roads spread out to the Pyrenees like a fan. Two only were great causeways. One, on the French left hand, run to St. Jean Pied de Port; the other, on their right, run along the sea-coast through St. Jean de Luz to Irun. Between these points, a distance of nearly forty miles, the space was filled transversely by a double range of mountain ridges nearly parallel to each other, on which the armies were posted; not in a continuous line, for there were no direct lateral communications, but as the passes and inaccessible peaks governed the dispositions. Thus on the French left, at St. Jean Pied de Port, Foy occupied with fifteen thousand men an entrenched camp in front of that fortress, and was opposed by Hill's right wing, which was planted at the head of the Val Carlos, in the Roncesvalles and Alduides; but Foy could only communicate by a circuitous road, leading across the Nive river at Cambo, with the French centre, entrenched, under D'Erlon, at Ain-hoa and Urdax, opposite the Maya passes, and menacing the Bastan, where Hill's left was posted.

At Urdax the Nivelle river bisected the French positions and then, turning to the left, run to St. Jean de Luz. The line of their right centre, beyond that river, was under Clausel, and thrown forward to Vera, along another batch of mountainous ridges, which, touching on the Bidassoa, lined its right bank to the bridge of Behobia near Irun.

From Clausel's right to the mouth of the Bidassoa, Soult's right wing, under Reille, guarded the French territory.

Clausel's ground comprised the Great La Rhune mountain, two thousand seven hundred feet high, whose bleak rocky head over-looked everything around, and from whose flanks the positions of Sarre shot out on the French left, and on their right the Commissari Bayonette, and Mandale ridge—the two first overhanging Vera, the last lining the Bidassoa down to San Marcial and Irun.

Opposed to Clausel Wellington held, first the Atchiola mountain on the left of Maya, then the Echallar ridges as far as the Ivantelly mountain facing Sarre, and the Santa Barbara ridge abutting on the Bidassoa at Vera, facing the Bayonette and Commissari. On the left bank of the Bidassoa he occupied the flanks of the Pena de Haya to

San Marcial, from whence his redoubts, as before noticed run along the river to the Jaizquibel.

Soult had commenced a chain of entrenched camps and redoubts along his whole line, and in the low country, from the end of the Mandale to the sea, was constructing a double chain of entrenched positions and camps bearing many names and to be noticed in the narrative. These works were approaching completion when Wellington resolved to seize the Great La Rhune with its dependents on both flanks, at the same time forcing the passage of the Lower Bidassoa in face of Soult's entrenchments. Thus he would establish his left in the French territory, from Sarre to the sea, and bring within his own lines the Rhune, the Commissari, and Bayonette mountains, which would give him a salient menacing point of impregnable strength towards France, and shorten his lateral communication on both flanks of those mountains. It would also give entire command of a road running up the Bidassoa from Irun to Vera, and secure the port of Fuenterabia, which, though bad in winter, was desirable for a general whose supplies came from the ocean, and who with scanty means of transport had to sustain the perverse negligence always, and often the hostility of the Spanish authorities.

He had designed to force the passage in the middle of September before the French works were advanced, but his pontoons were delayed by a negligence of orders; the weather then became bad, and the attempt, which depended upon the state of the tides and fords, was of necessity deferred to the 7th of October.

Great subtlety was to be combined with wonderful boldness, for the Bidassoa was broad and tidal below Irun, and the ridges lining it above that point rough and terrible to assail; both water and mountain line were strengthened with works, incomplete indeed, but already of strength in defence; the river was also to be passed and the positions beyond carried between tides, or the troops would be swallowed by the returning flood. Hence to mislead Soult, to support the blockade of Pampeluna, and to ascertain Foy's true position and strength at St. Jean Pied de Port, which menaced anew that blockade, Wellington brought up Del Parque's army from Tudela to Pampeluna, transferred

the Andalusians at the latter place to Giron at Echallar, and directed
Mina to gather his irregulars around the Roncesvalles: then repairing
himself to that quarter on the 1st of October, he surprised a French
post on the Ayrola rock, cut off a scouting party in the Val de
Baygorry, and swept away two thousand sheep.

These movements awakened Soult's jealousy. He expected an
invasion of France without being able to ascertain from what quarter,
and at first, deceived by false information that Cole had reinforced
Hill, thought Mina's troops and the Andalusians were used to mask
an attack by the Val de Baygorry. The arrival of the light cavalry in
the Bastan, Wellington's presence at Roncesvalles, and the loss of the
Ayrola post, seemed to confirm this; but he knew that pontoons were
at Oyarzun, and the deserters, very numerous at this time, said the real
object was the Great Rhune. On the other hand, a French commissary,
taken at San Sebastian and exchanged after remaining twelve days at
Wellington's head quarters, assured him nothing there indicated a
serious attack. This weighed much, because the negligence about the
pontoons, and the wet weather, had caused a delay contradictory to
the reports of the spies and deserters. It was also beyond calculation
that Wellington, merely to please the allied sovereigns in Germany,
should thereby seek to establish his left wing in France, when the most
obvious line for a permanent invasion was by his right and centre, and
there was no apparent cause for deferring his operations.

The cause of the procrastination, namely, the state of the tides and
fords on the Lower Bidassoa, was necessarily impenetrable, and
Soult finally inclined to think the only design was to secure the
blockade of Pampeluna by menacing the French. and impeding their
entrenchments which were now becoming strong. Nevertheless, as
all the deserters and spies came with the same story, he recommended
increased vigilance along the whole line; yet so little did he anticipate
the real project, that on the 6th he reviewed D'Erlon's divisions at
Ainhoa and remained that night at Espelette, doubting if any attack
was intended, and having no fear for his right. But Wellington could
not diminish his troops on the side of Roncesvalles, lest a force should
unite at St. Jean Pied de Port to raise the blockade of Pampeluna;

and at Maya, Hill was already menacing Soult between the Nive and the Nivelle: it was therefore only with his left wing and left centre, and against the French right, that he could act while Pampeluna held out.

Early in October a reinforcement of twelve hundred British soldiers arrived from England. Mina was then on the right of Hill, who was thus enabled to call Campbell's Portuguese from the Alduides, and replace at Maya the third division. which, shifting to its left, then occupied the heights of Zagaramurdi and enabled the seventh division to relieve Giron's Andalusians in the Puerto de Echallar.

These dispositions were made with a view to the attack of the Great Rhune and its dependents, for which Wellington assembled the fourth and light divisions on Santa Barbara, Giron's Spaniards being on their right, and Longa's on their left. The sixth division, supported by the third, was at Zagaramurdi to make a demonstration against D'Erlon's advanced posts. Thus, without weakening his line between Roncesvalles and Echallar, he could assail the Rhune mountain and its dependents with twenty thousand men, and had still twenty-four thousand disposable for the passage of the lower Bidassoa.

It has been before said that between the Andarlasa ford, below Vera, and the fords of Biriatu, a distance of three miles, there were neither roads nor fords nor bridges. The French, trusting to this difficulty of approach and to their entrenchments on the craggy slopes of the Mandale, had collected their troops principally where the Bildox or green mountain, and the entrenched camp of Biriatu overlooked the fords, and against them Wellington directed Freyre's Spaniards from San Marcial.

Between Biriatu and the sea the advanced points of defence were the mountain of *Louis XIV*, a ridge called the *Caffe Republicain*, and the town of Andaya; behind which the *Calvaire d' Urogne*, the *Croix des Bouquets,* and the camp of the *Sans Culottes,* served as rallying posts. The first and fifth divisions, and the unattached brigades of Wilson and Lord Aylmer, in all fifteen thousand men, were destined to assault these works; and the Spanish fishermen had secretly indicated three fords practicable at low water between the

bridge of Behobia and the sea. Wellington therefore, with an astonishing hardihood, designed to pass his columns at the old known fords
above and these secret fords below bridge, though the tides rose
sixteen feet, leaving at the ebb open heavy sands not less than half a
mile broad ! The left bank of the river also was completely exposed
to observation from the enemy's hills, which, though low in comparison of the mountains above the bridge, were strong ridges of defence;
but relying on his previous measures the English general disdained
these dangers, and his anticipations were not belied by the result. For
the unlikelihood that, having a better line of operations, he would
force such a river as the Bidassoa at its mouth, entirely deceived
Soult, whose lieutenants were also very negligent. Of Reille's two
divisions, one under Boyer was dispersed, labouring on the entrenched camp of Urogne far from the river; Villatte's reserve was at
Ascain and Serres; and five thousand men of Maucune's division,
though on the first line, were unexpectant of an attack. The works on
the Mandale were finished, those at Biriatu in a forward state, but
from the latter to the sea all were imperfect.

THE PASSAGE OF THE LOWER BIDASSOA.

On the 6th the night set in heavily. A sullen thunderstorm,
gathering about the craggy summit of the Pena de Maya, came slowly
down its flanks, and towards morning, rolling over the Bidassoa, fell
in its greatest violence upon the French positions. During this turmoil
Wellington, whose pontoons and artillery were close up to Irun,
disposed a number of guns and howitzers along the crest of San
Marcial, and his columns secretly attained their stations along the
banks of the river. The Spaniards, one brigade of Guards, and
Wilson's Portuguese, stretching from the Biriatu fords to the broken
bridge of Behobia, were ensconced behind the lower ridge of San
Marcial, which had been seized by the French in the attack of the 31st;
another brigade of Guards and the Germans were concealed near
Irun, close to a ford, below bridge, called the Great Jonco; the fifth
division were covered by a river embankment opposite Andaya;
Sprye's Portuguese and Lord Aylmer's brigade were posted in the
ditch of Fuenterabia.

All the tents were left standing in the camps, and the enemy, seeing no change on the morning of the 7th, were unsuspicious; but at seven o'clock, the fifth division and Aylmer's brigade, emerging from their concealment took the sands in two columns. The left one moved against the French camp of the Sans Culottes, the other against the ridge of Andaya, but no shot was fired until they passed the low water channel, when an English rocket was sent up from the steeple of Fuenterabia as a signal. Then the artillery opened from San Marcial, the troops near Irun, covered by the fire of a battery, made for the Jonco, and the passage above the bridge also commenced.

From the crest of San Marcial seven columns could now be seen at once, attacking on a line of five miles; those above bridge plunging at once into the fiery contest, those below, appearing in the distance like huge serpents sullenly winding over the heavy sands. The Germans missed the Jonco ford and got into deep water, yet quickly recovered the true line, and the French, completely surprised, permitted even the brigades of the fifth division to gain the right bank and form their lines before a hostile musket flashed. The cannonade from San Marcial was heard by Soult at Espelette, and at the same time the sixth division made a false attack on D'Erlon's positions; the Portuguese brigade under Colonel Douglas, was however pushed too far and got beaten with the loss of a hundred and fifty men.

Soult now comprehending the true state of affairs hurried to his right, but his camps on the Bidassoa were lost before he arrived. For when the British artillery first opened, Maucune's troops assembled at their different posts, and the French guns opened from the Louis XIV. and Caffe Republicain; then the alarm spread, and Boyer marched from Urogne to support Maucune, without waiting for the junction of his working parties; but his brigades moved separately as they could collect, and before the first came into action, Sprye's Portuguese, forming the extreme left of the allies, were menacing the camp of the Sans Culottes: thither therefore one of Boyer's regiments was ordered, while the others advanced by the royal road towards the Croix des Bouquets. Andaya, guarded only by a picquet, was meanwhile abandoned, and Reille, thinking the camp of the Sans

Culottes would be lost before Boyer's men could reach it, sent a battalion there from the centre; he thus weakened the chief point; for the British brigades of the fifth division were now bearing from Andaya towards the Croix des Bouquets under a fire of guns and musketry.

The first division had passed the river, one column above bridge, preceded by Wilson's Portuguese, the other below, preceded by the German light troops, who with the aid of the artillery on San Marcial won the Caffe Republicain and the mountain of Louis XIV., driving the French to the Croix des Bouquets. This last was the key of the position, and towards it guns and troops were now hastening from both sides, but the Germans were there brought to a check, for the heights were strong and Boyer's leading battalions close at hand; at that moment however, Colonel Cameron, coming up with the 9th Regiment, passed through the German skirmishers and vehemently ascended the first height, whereupon the French opened their ranks to let their guns retire, and then retreated at full speed to a second ridge, somewhat lower, but only to be approached on a narrow front. Cameron as quickly threw his men into a single column and bore against this new position under a concentrated fire, yet his violent course did not seem to dismay the French until within ten yards when the furious shout and charge of the 9th appalled them and the ridges of the Croix des Bouquets were won as far as the royal road. Cameron lost many men and officers, and during the fight the French artillery and scattered troops, coming from different points and rallying on Boyer's battalions, had gathered on other ridges close at hand.

The entrenched camp above Biriatu had been at first well defended in front, but the Spanish right wing being opposed only by a single battalion, soon won the Mandale mountain whereupon the French fell back from the camp to the Calvaire d'Urogne. Then Reille, beaten at the Croix des Bouquets and having both his flanks turned, the left by the Spaniards, the right along the sea-coast, retreated in great disorder through the village of Urogne. The British skirmishers entered that place in pursuit, but were immediately beaten out again by the second brigade of Boyer's division; for Soult had now arrived with part of Villatte's reserve and many guns, and by his presence restored order just as retreat was degenerating into flight.

Reille lost eight guns and four hundred men; the allies only six hundred men, of which half were Spaniards, so easy had the skill of the English general rendered this stupendous operation. But if Soult, penetrating Wellington's design, had met the allies with the sixteen thousand troops of that quarter, instead of the five thousand actually engaged, the passage could scarcely have been forced; and a simple check would have been tantamount to a terrible disaster, because in two hours the returning tide would have come with a swallowing flood upon the rear.

SECOND COMBAT OF VERA .

Equally unprepared and unsuccessful were the French on the side of Vera, although the struggle there proved more fierce and constant. Before daybreak Giron descended with his Spaniards from the Ivantelly rocks, and Alten with the light division from Santa Barbara; the first to the gorge of the pass leading from Vera to Sarre, the last to the town of Vera, where he was joined by half of Longa's force. One brigade, consisting of the 43rd, 17th Portuguese Regiment, and two battalions of British riflemen, were in columns on the right of Vera; the other brigade under Colonel Colborne, consisting of the 52nd, two battalions of Caçadores, and a third battalion of British riflemen, were on the left of that town: half of Longa's division was between these brigades, the other half, after crossing the ford of Salinas, drew up on Colborne's left. The whole of the narrow vale of Vera was thus filled with troops ready to ascend the mountains; and General Cole, displaying his force to advantage on the heights of Santa Barbara, presented a formidable reserve.

Taupin's division guarded the enormous positions in front. His right was on the Bayonette, from whence a single slope descended to a small plain, two parts down the mountain. From this platform three distinct tongues shot into the valley below, each defended by an advanced post; the platform itself was secured by a star redoubt, behind which, about half-way up the single slope, there was a second retrenchment with abbatis. Another large redoubt and an unfinished breast-work on the superior crest completed the defence.

The Commissari, a continuation of the Bayonette, towards the Great Rhune, had in front a profound gulf thickly wooded and filled with skirmishers; and between this gulf and another of the same nature, run the main road from Vera over the Puerto, piercing the centre of the French position. Ascending with short abrupt turns, this road was blocked at every uncovered point with abbatis and small retrenchments, each obstacle being commanded at half musket shot by small detachments placed on all the projecting parts overlooking the ascent. A regiment, entrenched above on the Puerto itself, connected the troops on the crest of the Bayonette and Commissari with those on a saddle-ridge, which joined those mountains with the Great Rhune, and was to be assailed by Giron.

Between Alten's right and Giron's left was an isolated advanced ridge called by the soldiers the *Boar's Back*, the summit of which, half a mile long and rounded at each end, was occupied by four French companies. This huge cavalier, thrown as it were into the gulf on the allies' right of the road, covered the Puerto and the saddle-ridge; and though of mean height in comparison of the towering ranges behind, was yet so lofty, that a few warning-shots, fired from the summit by the enemy, only reached the allies at its base with that slow singing sound which marks the dying force of a musket-ball. It was essential to take this Boar's back before the general attack commenced, and five companies of riflemen, supported by the 17th Portuguese, assailed it at the Vera end, while a battalion of Giron's Spaniards, preceded by a company of the 43rd, attacked it on the other. Meanwhile the French were in confusion.

Clausel knew by a spy in the night that the Bayonette was to be assaulted, and in the morning had heard from Conroux who was at Sarre, that Giron's camps were abandoned although the tents of the seventh division were still standing; at the same time musketry was heard on the side of Urdax, a cannonade on the side of Irun; then came Taupin's report that the vale of Vera was filled with troops, and to this last quarter Clausel hurried. On his left the Spaniards had then driven Conroux's outposts from the gorge leading to Sarre, and a detachment was creeping up towards the unguarded head of the Great Rhune; wherefore, ordering four regiments of Conroux's division to occupy the summit, the front, and the flanks, of that mountain, he placed a reserve of two other regiments behind it, hoping thus to secure possession and support Taupin: but that general's fate had been already decided by Alten.

Soon after seven o'clock a few cannon-shot from some mountain-guns, of which each side had a battery, were followed by the Spanish musketry on the right, and the next moment the Boar's back was simultaneously assailed at both ends. The riflemen on the Vera side ascended to a small pine-wood two-thirds up and there rested, but soon resumed their movement and with a scornful gallantry swept the French off the top, disdaining to use their rifles, save a few shots down the reverse side to show they were masters of the ridge. This had been the signal for the general attack. The Portuguese followed the victorious sharp-shooters; the 43rd, preceded by their own skirmishers and the remainder of the riflemen of the right wing, plunged into the rugged pass; Longa entered the gloomy wood of the ravine on their left; and beyond Longa, Colborne's brigade, moving by narrow paths, assailed the Bayonette. The 52nd took the middle tongue, the Caçadores and riflemen the two outermost, all bearing with a concentric movement against the star redoubt on the platform above. Longa's second brigade should have flanked the left of this attack with a wide skirting movement; but neither he nor his starved soldiers knew much of such warfare, and therefore quietly followed the riflemen in reserve.

Soon the open slopes were covered with men and with fire, and a confused sound of mingled shouts and musketry filled the deep hollows, from whence the white smoke came curling up from their gloomy recesses. The French, compared with their assailants, seemed few and scattered on the mountain side, and Kempt's brigade fought its way without a check through all the retrenchments on the main pass, the skirmishers spreading wider as the depth of the ravines on each side lessened and melted into the higher ridges. When half-way up an open platform gave a clear view over the Bayonette slopes, and all eyes were turned that way. Longa's right brigade, fighting in the gulf between, seemed labouring and over-matched; but beyond it, on the broad open space in front of the star-fort, Colborne's Caçadores and riflemen were seen to come out in small bodies from a forest which covered the three tongues of land up to the edge of the platform. Their fire was sharp, their pace rapid, and in a few moments they closed upon the redoubt in a mass; the 52nd were not then in sight, and the French, thinking from the dark clothing all were Portuguese, rushed in close order out of the entrenchment; they were numerous and very sudden, the rifle as a weapon is overmatched by the musket and bayonet, and this rough charge sent the scattered assailants back over the rocky edge of the descent. With shrill cries the French followed, but just then the 52nd soldiers appeared on the platform and raising their shout rushed forward; their red uniform and full career startled the hitherto adventurous French, they stopped short, wavered, turned, and fled to their entrenchment. The 52nd, following hard, entered the works with them, and then the riflemen and Caçadores, who had meanwhile rallied, passed it on both flanks; for a few moments everything was hidden by a dense volume of smoke, but again the British shout pealed high and the whole mass emerged on the other side, the French, now the fewer, flying, the others pursuing, until the second entrenchment, half-way up the parent slope, enabled the retreating troops to make another stand.

The exulting and approving cheers of Kempt's brigade then echoed along the mountain-side, and with renewed vigour the men continued to scale the craggy mountain, fighting their toilsome way to the top of the Puerto. Meanwhile Colborne. after having carried the second entrenchment above the star-fort, was brought to a check by the works on the crest of the mountain, from whence the French not only plied his troops with musketry at a great advantage but rolled huge stones down the steep. These works were well lined with men and strengthened by a large redoubt on the right, yet the defenders faltered, for their left flank was turned by Kempt, and the effects of Wellington's general combinations were then felt in another quarter.

Freyre's Spaniards, after carrying the Mandale mountain, had pushed to a road leading from the Bayonette to St. Jean de Luz, which was the line of retreat for Taupin's right wing. The Spaniards got there first, and Taupin, being thus cut off on that side, had to file his right under fire along the crest of the Bayonette to reach the Puerto de Vera road, where he joined his centre, but, so doing, lost a mountain battery and three hundred men. These last were captured by Colborne in a remarkable manner. Accompanied by one of his staff and half-a-dozen riflemen, he crossed their march unexpectedly, and with his usual cool intrepidity ordered them to lay down their arms; an order which they, thinking themselves entirely cut off, obeyed. During these events, the French skirmishers in the deep ravine between the two lines of attack, being feebly pushed by Longa's troops, retreated slowly, and getting amongst some rocks from whence there was no escape also surrendered to Kempt. Taupin's right and centre being then completely beaten fled down the side of the mountain, closely pursued until they rallied upon Villatte's reserve, which was in order of battle on a ridge extending across the gorge of Olette, between Urogne and Ascain. The Bayonette, Commissari, and Puerto de Vera, were thus won after five hours' incessant fighting, and toiling, up their craggy sides. Nevertheless the battle was still maintained by the French troops on the summit of the Rhune.

Giron, after driving Conroux's advanced post from the gorge leading from Vera to Sarre, had pushed a battalion towards the head of the Great Rhune, and placed a reserve in the gorge to cover his rear from any counter-attack. When his left wing was free to move by the capture of the *Boar's back*, he fought his way up abreast with the British line until near the saddle-ridge, a little to the right of the Puerto; but there his men were arrested by a strong line of abbatis, from behind which two French regiments poured a heavy fire. An adventurer named Downie, then a Spanish general, exhorted them and they kept their ranks, yet did not advance; but there happened to be present an officer of the 43rd Regiment, named Havelock,* who

---

* Colonel Havelock, since killed in the Punjaub at the head of the 14th Dragoons.

being attached to Alten's staff had been sent to ascertain Giron's progress. His fiery temper could not brook the check. He took off his hat, called upon the Spaniards, and putting spurs to his horse at one bound cleared the abbatis and went headlong among the enemy. Then the soldiers, shouting for "*El chico blanco,*"— "*the fair boy,*" so they called him, for he was very young and had light hair,—with one shock broke through at the very moment the French centre was flying under the fire of Kempt's skirmishers from the Puerto on the left.

The two defeated regiments retired by their left to the flanks of the Rhune, and thus Clausel had eight regiments concentrated on this great mountain. Two occupied the highest rocks called the Hermitage; four were on the flanks, which descended towards Ascain on one hand and Sarre on the other; the remaining two occupied a lower parallel mountain behind called the Small Rhune. Giron's right wing first dislodged a small body from a detached pile of crags about musket-shot below the summit of the Great Rhune, and then assailed the bald staring rocks of the Hermitage itself, endeavouring at the same time to turn it on the right. At both points the attempts were defeated with loss; the Hermitage was impregnable: the French rolled down stones large enough to sweep away a whole column at once, and the Spaniards resorted to a distant musketry which lasted until night.

In this fight Taupin lost two generals, four hundred men killed and wounded, and five hundred prisoners. The loss of the allies was nearly a thousand, of which half were Spaniards, and the success was not complete; for while the French kept possession of the summit of the Rhune the allies' new position was insecure.

Wellington, observing that the left   flank of the mountain descending towards Sarre was less inaccessible, concentrated the Spaniards next day on that side for a combined attack against the mountain itself, and against the camp of Sarre. At three o'clock in the afternoon the rocks which studded the lower parts of the Rhune slope were assailed by the Spaniards, and detachments of the seventh division descended from the Puerto de Echallar upon the fort of San Barbe and other outworks covering the French camp of Sarre. The Andalusians easily won the rocks and an entrenched height

commanding the camp; for Clausel, alarmed by some slight demonstrations of the sixth division in rear of his left, thought he should be
cut off from his great camp, and very suddenly abandoned, not only
the slope of the mountain but all his advanced works in the basin
below, including the fort of San Barbe. His troops were thus concentrated on the height behind Sarre, still holding with their right the
smaller Rhune, but the consequences of his error were soon apparent.
Wellington established a strong body of Spaniards close to the
Hermitage, and the two French regiments there, seeing the lower
slopes and San Barbe given up, imagined they also would be cut off,
and without orders abandoned their impregnable post in the night.
Next morning some of the seventh division rashly pushed into the
village of Sarre, but were quickly repulsed and would have lost the
camp and works taken the day before if the Spaniards had not
succoured them.

The whole loss on the three days' fighting was fourteen hundred
French and sixteen hundred of the allies; but many of the wounded
were not brought in until the third day after the action, and others
perished miserably where they fell, it being impossible to discover
them in those vast solitudes. Some men also descended to the French
villages, got drunk, and were taken; nor was the number small of
those who plundered in defiance of Lord Wellington's proclama-
tions. He arrested and sent several officers to England, observing in
his order of the day, that if he had five times as many men he could
not venture to invade France unless marauding was prevented. It is
remarkable likewise, that the French troops on the same day acted
towards their own countrymen in the same manner, and Soult also
checked the mischief with a terrible hand, causing a captain of some
reputation to be shot as an example for having suffered his men to
plunder a house in Sarre.

With exception of the slight checks sustained at Sarre and Ainhoa,
the course of these operations had been eminently successful, and the
bravery of troops who assailed and carried such stupendous positions
must be admired. To them the unfinished state of the French works
was not visible. Day after day, for more than a month, entrenchment
had risen over entrenchment, covering the slopes of mountains

scarcely accessible from their natural steepness and asperity. These could be seen, but the growing strength of the works, the height of the mountains, the broad river with its heavy sands and its mighty rushing tide, all were despised by those brave soldiers; and while they attacked with such confident valour, the French fought in defence of their dizzy steeps with far less fierceness than when, striving against insurmountable obstacles, they attempted to storm the lofty rocks of Sauroren. Continual defeat had lowered their spirit. Yet the feeble defence on this occasion may be traced to another cause. It was a general's, not a soldier's battle. Wellington had with overmastering combinations overwhelmed every point. Taupin's and Maucune's divisions, each less than five thousand strong, were separately assailed, the first by eighteen, the second by fifteen thousand men; and at neither point were Reille and Clausel able to bring their reserves into action before the positions were won.

Soult complained that his lieutenants were unprepared, although repeatedly told an attack was to be expected; and though they heard the noise of the guns and pontoons about Irun on the night of the 5th, and again on the night of the 6th. The passage of the river had, he said, commenced only at seven o'clock, long after daylight; the enemy's masses were clearly seen forming on the banks, and there was full time for Boyer's division to arrive before the Croix des Bouquets was lost; yet the battle was fought in disorder with less than five thousand men, instead of ten thousand in good order and supported by Villatte's reserve. To this negligence they also added discouragement. They had so little confidence in the strength of their positions, that if the allies had pushed vigorously forward before his own arrival, they would have entered St. Jean de Luz and forced the French army back upon the Nive and Adour. This was true, but such a stroke did not comport with Wellington's system. He could not go beyond the Adour, he doubted whether he could even maintain his army during the winter in the position he had already gained; and he was averse to the experiment, while Pampeluna held out and the war in Germany bore an undecided aspect.

Soult was very apprehensive for some days of another attack; but when he saw Wellington's masses form permanent camps he ordered Foy to recover the fort of San Barbe, which blocked a pass leading from the vale of Vera to Sarre and defended some narrow ground between La Rhune and the Nivelle river. Abandoned without reason by the French, it was only occupied by a Spanish picquet, several battalions being encamped in a wood close behind. Many officers and men quitted their troops to sleep in the fort, and on the night of the 12th three French battalions surprised and escaladed the work; the Spanish troops behind went off in confusion at the first alarm, and two hundred soldiers with fifteen officers were made prisoners. Two Spanish battalions, ashamed of the surprise, made a vigorous effort to recover the fort at daylight, but were repulsed. An attempt was then made with five battalions, but Clausel brought up two guns, and a sharp skirmish took place in the wood which lasted for several hours, the French endeavouring to regain the whole of their old entrenchments, the Spaniards to recover the fort. Neither succeeded. San Barbe remained with the French, who lost two hundred men, while the Spaniards lost five hundred. Soon after this action a French sloop of war run from St. Jean de Luz, but three English brigs cut her off, and the crew after exchanging a few distant shots set her on fire and escaped in boats to the Adour.

Head-quarters were now fixed in Vera, and the allied army was organized in three grand divisions. The right, having Mina's and Morillo's battalions attached to it, was commanded by General Hill, and extended from Roncesvalles to the Bastan. The centre, occupying Maya, the Echallar, Rhune and Bayonette mountains, was given to Marshal Beresford. The left, extending from the Mandale mountain to the sea, was under Sir John Hope. This officer succeeded Graham, who had returned to England. Commanding in chief at Coruna after Sir John Moore's death, he was superior in rank to Lord Wellington during the early part of the Peninsular war; but when the latter obtained the baton of field-marshal at Vittoria, Hope, with a patriotism and modesty worthy of the pupil of Abercrombie, the friend and comrade of Moore, offered to serve as second in command, and Wellington joyfully accepted him, saying—*"He was the ablest officer in the army."*

BATTLE OF THE NIVELLE.

After the passage of the Bidassoa, Soult was assiduous to complete an immense chain of intrenchments, some thirty miles long, which he had previously commenced The space between the sea and the upper Nivelle, an opening of sixteen miles, was defended by double lines, and the lower part of that river, sweeping behind the second of them, formed a third line, having the intrenched camp of Serres on its right bank the upper river separated D'Erlon's from Clausel's positions, but was crossed by the bridge of Amotz; the left of D'Erlon rested on the rough Mondarain mountains, which closed that flank, abutting on the Nive.

Beyond the Nive, Foy was called down that river towards the bridge of Cambo, which was fortified in rear of D'Erlon's left, and from thence Soult had traced a second chain of intrenched camps, on a shorter line behind the Nivelle, by San Pe, to join his camp at Serres thus placed, Foy had the power of reinforcing D'Erlon or menacing the right of the allies according to events.

Reille still commanded on the right in the low ground covering St Jean de Luz.

Lord Wellington could scarcely feed his troops; those on the right, at Roncesvalles, went two days without provisions, being blocked up by snow; and the rest of the army, with the exception of the first division, was lying out on the crests of high mountains very much exposed This made them indeed incredibly hardy and eager to pour down on the fertile French plains below; but notwithstanding his recent bold operation, their general looked to a retreat into Spain and a removal of the war to Catalonia; for his position was scarcely tenable from political and other difficulties, all of which he had foreseen and foretold when the foolish importunity of the English Government urged him to enter France And if Soult, who was continually, though vainly urging Suchet to co-operate with him, had persuaded that marshal to act with vigour the allies must have retreated to the Ebro Suchet however could not stir, and the war in Germany having taken a favourable turn Wellington eventually resolved to force the French lines.

For this object, when Pampeluna surrendered, early in November, Hill's right was moved from Roncesvalles to the Bastan with a view to the battle, and Mina took its place on the mountains; but then the Spanish general Freyre suddenly declared that he was unable to subsist and must withdraw a part of his troops. This was a disgraceful trick to obtain provisions from the English, and it was successful, for the projected attack could not be made without his aid. Forty thousand rations of flour, with a formal intimation that if he did not co-operate the whole army must retire again into Spain, contented him for the moment; but it was declared the supply given would only suffice for two days, although there were less than ten thousand soldiers in the field !

Heavy rain again delayed the attack, but on the 10th of November, ninety thousand combatants, seventy-four thousand being Anglo-Portuguese, descended to battle, and with them ninety-five pieces of artillery, all of which were with inconceivable vigour thrown into action: four thousand five hundred cavalry and some Spaniards remaining in reserve near Pampeluna. The French had been augmented by a levy of conscripts, many of whom however deserted to the interior, and the fighting men did not exceed seventy-nine thousand, including the garrisons. Six thousand were cavalry, and as Foy's operations were extraneous, scarcely sixty thousand infantry and artillery were actually in line.

On Soult's side each lieutenant-general had a special position to defend. The left of D'Erlon's first line, resting on the fortified rocks of Mondarain, could not be turned; his right was on the Nivelle, and the whole, strongly intrenched, was occupied by one of Abbe's and one of D'Armagnac's brigades. The second line, on a broad ridge several miles behind, was occupied by the remaining brigades of those divisions, and its left did not extend beyond the centre of the first line; but the light reached to the bridge of Amotz where the Nivelle, flowing in a slanting direction, gave greater space. Three great redoubts were in a row on this ridge, and a fourth had been commenced close to the bridge.

On the light of D'Erlon s second line, that is to say beyond the bridge of Amotz, Clausel's position extended to Ascain, along a strong range of heights fortified with many redoubts, trenches, and abbatis; and as the Nivelle, after passing Amotz, swept in a curve completely round this range to Ascain, both flanks rested alike upon that river,—the bridges of Amotz and Ascain being close on the right and left, and a retreat open by the bridges of San Pe and Harastaguia in rear of the centre. Two of Clausel's divisions, reinforced by one of D'Erlon's under General Maransin, were there posted. In front of the left were the redoubts of San Barbe and Grenada, covering the village and ridge of Sarre. In front of the right was the smaller Rhune, which was fortified and occupied by a brigade of Maransin's division: a new redoubt with abbatis was also commenced to cover the approaches to the bridge of Amotz.

On the right of this line, beyond the bridge of Ascain, Daricau's division of Clausel's corps, and the Italian brigade of San Pol, drawn from Villatte's reserve, held the intrenched camp of Serres; they thus connected Clausel's position with Villatte's, which crossed the gorges of Olette and Jollimont. Reille's position, strongly fortified on the lower ground and partially covered by inundations, was nearly impregnable.

Soult's weakest point was between the Rhune mountains and the Nivelle, where the space, gradually narrowing as it approached the bridge of Amotz, was the most open and the least fortified. The Nivelle, being fordable above this bridge, did not hamper the allies' movements, and a powerful force acting in that direction could therefore pass by D'Erlon's first line, and break between the right of his second line and Clausel's left; it was thus Wellington framed his battle; for seeing the French right could not be forced, he decided to hold it in check while he broke their centre and pushed down the Nivelle to San Pe.

In this view, Hill, leaving four of Mina's battalions to face the rocks of Mondarain, moved in the night by the passes of the Puerto de Maya to fall on D'Erlon.

On Hill's left, Beresford was to send the third division against the unfinished redoubts and intrenchments covering the bridge of Amotz, thus turning D'Erlon's right while it was attacked in front by Hill.

On the left of the third division, the seventh, descending from the Echallar pass, was to storm the Grenada redoubt, pass Sarre, and assail Clausel abreast with the third division.

On the left of the seventh, the fourth division, assembling on the lower slopes of the greater Rhune, was to descend upon San Barbe, and then, moving through Sarre also, to assail Clausel abreast with the seventh division.

On the left of the fourth division, Giron's Spaniards, gathered higher up the flank of the great Rhune, were to move abreast with the others, leaving Sarre on their right. They were to drive the enemy from the lower slopes of the smaller Rhune, and then join the attack on Clausel's main position. In this way Hill's and Beresford's corps, forming a mass of more than forty thousand infantry, were to be thrust on both sides of the bridge of Amotz, between Clausel and D'Erlon.

Charles Alten with the light division and Longa's Spaniards, together eight thousand, was likewise to attack Clausel's line on the left of Giron, while Freyre's Gallicians approached the bridge of Ascain to prevent reinforcements coming from the camp of Serres. But ere Alten could assail Clausel's right the smaller Rhune which covered it was to be taken. This outwork was a hog's-back ridge, rising abruptly out of table-land opposite the greater Rhune and inaccessible along its front, which was precipitous and from fifty to two hundred feet high; on the enemy's left the rocks gradually decreased, descending by a long slope to the valley of Sarre, and, two-thirds down, the 34th French Regiment was placed, with an outpost at some isolated crags between the two Rhunes. On the enemy's right the hog's back sunk by degrees into an open platform, but was covered at its termination by a marsh scarcely passable. The attacking troops had therefore first to move against the perpendicular rocks in front, and then to file, under fire, between the marsh and lower rocks to gain an accessible point from whence to fight their way along the narrow ridge of the hog's-back; the bristles of the latter being huge perpendicular crags built up with loose stones into small forts or castles which communicated by narrow foot-ways, and rose one above another until the culminant point was attained.

Beyond this ridge an extensive table-land was bounded

by a deep ravine, one narrow space on the right of the marsh excepted, where the enemy had a traverse of loose stones running perendicularly from behind the hog's-back and ending in a star fort. This rampart and fort, and the hog's-back itself, were defended by Barbot's brigade, whose line of retreat was a low neck of land bridging the deep ravine and linking the Rhune to Clausel's main position. A reserve was placed there to sustain the 34th French Regiment on the ,lope of the mountain, and to protect the neck, which was the only approach to the main position in that part: to storm the smaller Rhune was therefore a necessary preliminary to the general battle.

Alten, filing his troops after dark on the 9th, from the Hermitage, the Commissari, and the Puerto de Vera, collected them at midnight on that slope of the greater Rhune which descended towards Ascain. His main body, turning; the marsh by the left, was to assail the stone traverse and lap over the star fort by the ravine beyond; Longa, stretching still farther on the left, was to turn the smaller Rhune altogether; the 43rd Regiment was to assail the hog's-back. The battalion of riflemen and the mountain-guns were left on the greater Rhune, with orders to assail the French 34th and connect Alten's attack with Giron's. All these troops gained their respective stations so secretly the enemy had no suspicion of their presence, although for several hours the columns were lying within half musket-shot of the works: towards morning indeed, five or six guns fired in a hurried manner from the low ground near the sea broke the stillness, yet all remained quiet on the Rhunes: the British troops silently awaited the rising of the sun, when three guns fired from the summit of the Atchubia mountain were to be the signal of attack.

BATTLE OF THE NIVELLE.

With great splendour the day broke, and as the first ray of light played on the summit of the lofty Atchubia the signal guns were fired in rapid succession; then the light division soldiers leaped up, and the French beheld with astonishment the columns rushing onward from the flank of the great Rhune. Running to their works with much tumult, they opened a few pieces, which were answered from the top of the greater Rhune by the mountain-artillery, and two companies of the 43rd were detached to cross the marsh, if possible, and keep down the enemy's fire from the lower part of the hog's-back. The action being thus commenced, the remainder of that regiment advanced against the high rocks, from whence the French shot fast and thickly; but the quick even movement of the line deceived their aim, and the soldiers, running forward very swiftly, turned suddenly between the rocks and the marsh and were immediately joined by the two companies, which had passed that obstacle notwithstanding its depth. Then all together jumped into the lower works, and the men, exhausted by their exertions, for they had run over half a mile of very rough difficult ground with a wonderful speed, remained for a few minutes lying down and panting within half-pistol shot of the first stone castle, from whence came a sharp and biting musketry: when their breath returned they arose and with a stern shout commenced the assault.

As numerous as the assailants were the defenders, and for six weeks they had been labouring on their well contrived castles; but strong and valiant in arms must the soldiers have been who stood in that hour before the veterans of the 43rd. One French grenadier officer only dared to sustain the rush. Standing alone on the high wall of the first castle and flinging large stones with both his hands, a noble figure, he fought to the last and fell, while his men, shrinking on each side, sought safety among the rocks behind. Close and confused then was the fight, man met man at every turn yet with a rattling fire of musketry, sometimes struggling in the intricate narrow paths, sometimes climbing the loose stone walls, the British soldiers won their desperate way, and soon carried a second castle, named by the French the magpie's nest because of a lofty rock within it, on which a few marksmen were perched. From this castle they were driven into a culminant citadel, called the Donjon, larger than the others, and covered by a natural ditch or cleft in the rocks fifteen feet deep.

Here they made a final stand, and the assailants, having, advanced so as to look into the rear of the rampart and star fort on the table-land below, suspended the vehement throng of their attack for a while; partly to gather head for storming the Donjon, partly to fire on the enemy beneath, who were warmly engaged with the two battalions of riflemen, the Portuguese Caçadores, and the 17th Portuguese. This last regiment was to have followed the 43rd, but seeing how rapidly and surely the latter were carrying the rocks, had moved at once against the traverse on the other side of the marsh. The French thus pressed in front, and taught by the fire they were outflanked on the ridge above; seeing the and also turning their extreme right by the deep ravine beyond the star fort, abandoned their works below. Then the 43rd gathering a strong head stormed the Donjon. Some leaped with a shout down the deep cleft in the rock, others turned it by the narrow paths on each flank, and the walls were abandoned at the moment of being scaled. Thus in twenty minutes six hundred old soldiers were hustled out of this labyrinth; yet not so easily but that the victorious regiment lost eleven officers and sixty-seven men.

The whole mountain was now cleared, for the riflemen, dropping almost perpendicularly down from the greater Rhune upon the post of crags, had seized it with small loss yet they were ill seconded by Giron's Spaniards, and hardly handled by the French 34th, which maintained its main post on the slope, and covered the flight of the confused crowd then rushing down from the smaller Rhune towards the neck of land behind there however all rallied and seemed inclined to renew the action, yet, after some hesitation, continued their retreat. This favourable moment for a decisive stroke had been looked for by the commander of the 43rd, but the officer intrusted with the reserve companies of the regiment had thrown them heedlessly into the fight, and rendered it impossible to collect in time a body strong enough to assail such a heavy mass. The contest at the stone rampart and star fort, being shortened by the rapid success on the hog'sback, had not been very severe, but General Kempt, always conspicuous for his valour, was severely wounded nevertheless he did not quit the field, and soon re-formed his brigade on the platform he had so gallantly won Longa, daring the fight, got close to Ascain, in connection with Freyre's troops, and in this state of affairs, the enemy now and then cannonading from a distance, Alten awaited the progress of the army on his right, for the columns there had a long way to march and it was essential to regulate the movements

The signal-guns from the Atchubia which sent the light division against the Rhune, had also sent the fourth and seventh divisions against San Barbe and Grenada, and while eighteen guns, placed in battery against the former, poured streams of shot, the troops advanced with scaling-ladders. The skirmishers soon got in rear of the work, whereupon the French leaping out fled, and then Ross's battery of horse-artillery, galloping to a rising ground in rear of the Grenada fort, drove the enemy from there also. After that the following troops won the village of Sarre and the heights beyond, and advanced to the attack of Clausel's main position.

It was now eight o'clock, and, to the troops posted on the Rhune, a splendid spectacle was presented. On one hand the ships of war, slowly sailing to and fro, were exchanging, shots with the fort of Socoa, while Hope, menacing all the French lines in the low ground, sent the sound of a hundred pieces of artillery bellowing up the rocks. He was answered by nearly as many from the tops of the mountains, amidst the smoke of which the summit of the great Atchubia glittered to the rising sun, while fifty thousand men, rushing down its enormous slopes with ringing shouts, seemed to chase the receding shadows into the deep valley. The plains of France, so long overlooked from the towering crags of the Pyrenees, were to be the prize of battle, and the half-famished soldiers in their fury were breaking through the iron barrier erected by Soult as if it were but a screen of reeds.

The principal action was on a space of seven or eight miles, yet the skirts of battle spread wide, and in no point had the combinations failed. Far on the right Hill by a long and difficult night march had got near the enemy before seven o'clock; opposing then his Spanish troops to Abbe's left wing on the Mondarain rocks, he with the second division brushed back D'Armagnac's brigade from the forge of Urdax and the village of Ainhoa; but he called the sixth division and Hamilton's Portuguese over the Nivelle, to act on the right instead of the left bank, against the bridge of Amotz. Thus three divisions approached D'Erlon's second position in mass, yet the country was very rugged, and it was eleven o'clock before they got within cannon-shot of the French redoubts, each of which contained five hundred men They were placed along the summit of a high ridge thickly clothed with bushes and covered by a ravine; but General Clinton, leading the sixth division on the extreme left, turned this ravine and drove the enemy from the unfinished works covering the bridge, after which, wheeling to the right, he advanced against the nearest redoubt and the garrison abandoned it meanwhile the Portuguese and the second division, passing the ravine, appeared on the right of the sixth, menacing the second and third redoubts, whereupon all were abandoned D'Armagnac then set fire to his hutted camp and retreated to Helbacen de Borda, behind San Pe, pursued by Clinton Abbe's second brigade, forming the French left, though separated by a ravine from D'Armagnac, after some hesitation also retreated towards Cambo, where his first brigade, coming down the Mondarain mountain rejoined him.

It was the progress of the battle on the left of the Nive that rendered D'Erlon's fight on the right bank so feeble; for after the fall of San Barbe and Grenada Conroux endeavoured to defend the village and heights of Sarre, but while the fourth and seventh divisions carried those points, the third division, on their right, pushed rapidly to the bridge of Amotz; presenting in conjunction with the sixth division the narrow end of a wedge now formed by Beresford's and Hill's corps. The French were thus driven from all their unfinished works covering that bridge on both sides of the Nivelle, and Conroux's division, spread from Sarre to Amotz, was broken by superior numbers at every point when he attempted to defend the finished works at the bridge itself, he fell mortally wounded, his troops retired, and the third division, seizing the bridge, established itself on some heights between that structure and a large unfinished work called the redoubts of Louis XIV. All this happened about eleven o'clock, and D'Erlon, fearing to be cut off from San Pe, then gave up his strong position to Hill, as before shown; at the same time the remainder of Conroux's troops fell back in disorder from Sarre, pursued by the fourth and seventh divisions, which were immediately established on the left of the third. The communication between Clausel and D'Erlon was thus cut, the left flank of one and the right flank of the other were broken, and a direct communication between Hill and Beresford was secured by the same blow

Clausel still stood firm with Taupin's and Mansarin's divisions, and the latter having recovered Barbot's brigade from the smaller Rhune, occupied the redoubt of Louis XIV where, supported with eight field-pieces, he attempted to cover the flight of Conroux's troops Ross's horse artillery, the only battery which had surmounted the difficulties of ground after passing Sarre, silenced these guns, and the infantry were then assailed in front by the fourth and seventh divisions, and in flank by the third division The redoubt of Louis XIV was soon stormed and the garrison bayoneted, Conroux's men continued to fly, Maransin's were cast headlong into the ravines behind their position, and that general was taken, but escaped in the confusion Giron also came up now, yet too late, and after having abandoned the riflemen on the lower slopes of the smaller Rhune.

Taupin's division and a large body of conscripts forming Clausel's right, still remained to fight. Their left rested on a large work called the signal redoubt, which had no artillery, yet overlooked the whole position; their right was covered by two redoubts overhanging a ravine which separated them from the camp of Serres; some works in the ravine itself protected their communication by the bridge of Ascain; and behind the signal redoubt, on a ridge crossing the road to San Pe, along which Maransin and Conroux's divisions were flying, there was another work called the redoubt of Harastaguia, where Clausel thought he might still dispute the victory, if his reserve division in the camp of Serres could come to his aid. In this view he drew the 31st French Regiment from Taupin to post it in front of the redoubt of Harastaguia; his object being to rally Maransin's and Conroux's troops and form a new line, the left on Harastaguia, the right on the signal redoubt, into which last he threw six hundred of the 88th Regiment. In this position, having a retreat by the bridge of the Ascain, he resolved to renew the fight, but his plan failed at the moment of conception, because Taupin could not stand before the light division, which was now again in full action.

About half-past nine, Alten, seeing the whole of the columns on his right as far as the eye could reach well engaged with the enemy, had passed the low neck of land in his front, the 52nd Regiment leading with a rapid pace and a very narrow front, under a destructive cannonade and musketry from the intrenchments, which covered the side of the opposite mountain. A road coming from Ascain, by the ravine, led up the position, and as the 52nd pushed their attack along it the French abandoned the intrenchments on each side, and forsook even the crowning works above. This formidable regiment was followed by the remainder of the division, yet Taupin awaited the assault above, being supported by the conscripts in his rear; but at that moment the Spaniards opened a distant skirmishing fire against the works covering the bridge of Ascain on his right, whereupon a panic seized his men, and the 70th Regiment abandoned the two redoubts above, while the conscripts were withdrawn. Clausel ordered Taupin to retake the forts, yet this only added to the disorder; the 70th Regiment, instead of facing about, disbanded entirely and were not reassembled until next day. There remained only four regiments unbroken: one, the 88th, was in the signal redoubt, two with Taupin kept together in the rear of the works on the right, and the 31st covered the fort of Harastaguia, now the only line of retreat.

In this emergency, Clausel, anxious to bring off the 88th Regiment, ordered Taupin to charge on one side of the signal redoubt, intending to do the same himself on the other at the head of the 31st Regiment; but the latter was now vigorously attacked by the Portuguese of the seventh division, and the fourth division was rapidly interposing between that regiment and the redoubt. Moreover Alten, previous to this, had directed the 43rd, preceded by Andrew Barnard's riflemen, to turn, at the distance of musket-shot, the right flank of the redoubt; wherefore Taupin, instead of charging, was himself charged in front by the riflemen, and being menaced at the same time in flank by the fourth division, retreated, closely pursued by Barnard until that intrepid officer fell dangerously wounded. Meanwhile the seventh division broke the French 31st, and the rout became general, the French fled to the different bridges over the Nivelle, and the signal redoubt was left to its fate.

This formidable work barred the way of the light division, yet it was of no value to the defence when the forts on its flanks were abandoned. Colborne approached it in front with the 52nd Regiment, Giron's Spaniards menaced it on Colborne's right, the fourth division was passing to its rear, and Kempt's brigade was turning it on the left. Colborne, whose military judgment was seldom at fault, seeing the work must fall, halted under the brow of the conical hill on which it was situated to save his men; but some of Giron's Spaniards made a vaunting though feeble demonstration of attacking it on his right and were beaten, and at that moment a staff-officer, without warrant, for Alten on the spot assured the Author of this History that he sent no such order, rode up and directed Colborne to advance. It was not a moment for remonstrance. The steepness of the hill covered his men until he reached the flat top, and then the troops made their rush; but then a ditch, thirty feet deep, well fraised and palisaded, stopped them short, and the fire of the enemy stretched the foremost in death. The intrepid Colborne, escaping miraculously, for he was always at the. head on horseback, immediately led the regiment under the brow to another point, where, thinking to take the French unawares, he made another rush, yet with the same result: at three different places did he rise to the surface in this manner, and each time the head of his column was swept away. Then holding out a white handkerchief he summoned the commandant, and showed to him how his work was surrounded, whereupon he yielded, having had only one man killed; but on the British side there fell two hundred soldiers of a regiment never surpassed in arms since arms were first borne by men—victims to the presumptuous folly of a young staff-officer.

During this affair all Clausel's other troops had crossed the Nivelle, Maransin's and Conroux's divisions near San Pe, the 31st Regiment at Harastaguia, Taupin between that place and the bridge of Serres. They were pursued by the third and seventh divisions; and the skirmishers of the former, crossing by Amotz and a bridge above San Pe, entered that place while the French were in the act of passing the river below. Conroux's troops then pushed on to Helbacen de Borda, a fortified position on the road from San Pe to

Bayonne, where they were joined by Taupin, and by D'Erlon with D'Armagnac's division, while Clausel rallied Maransin's men and took post on some heights immediately above San Pe.

Soult was not present at any of these actions. He had hurried on the first alarm from St. .Jean de Luz to Serres with his reserve artillery and spare troops and now menaced Wellington's left flank by Ascain; whereupon the latter halted the fourth and light divisions and Giron's Spaniards, to face Serres until Clinton's division was well advanced on the right of the Nivelle. When he was assured of its progress he crossed the Nivelle with the third and seventh divisions, and drove Maransin from his new position, after a hard struggle in which General Inglis was wounded, and the 51st and 68th Regiments were handled very roughly. This ended the battle in the centre, for darkness was coming on and Clinton's men had been marching or fighting for twenty-four hours: but three divisions were now firmly established in rear of Soult's right, of whose operations it is time to treat.

In front of Reille's intrenchments were two advanced positions, the camp of the Sans Culottes on the right, the Bons Secours in the centre, covering Urogne. The first had been carried early in the morning by the fifth division, which advanced to the inundation covering the heights of Bordegain and Ciboure: the second was also easily taken by the Germans and the Guards, and immediately afterwards the 85th Regiment drove a French battalion out of Urogne. The first division then menaced the camp of Belchena, and the German skirmishers passed a small stream covering that part of the line, yet were driven back by the enemy, whose musketry and cannonade were brisk along the whole front. Meanwhile Freyre, advancing on the right of the first division, opened a battery against a large work covering Ascain, where he was opposed by his own countrymen under Casa Palacio, commanding the remains of Joseph's Spanish guards. This false battle was maintained until nightfall, with equal loss of men, yet great advantage to the allies, because it entirely occupied Reille and Villatte, and prevented their troops in the camp of Serres from passing by the bridge of Ascain to aid Clausel, who was thus overpowered. When that event happened, and Wellington had passed the Nivelle at San Pe, Reille retired to the heights of Bidart on the road to Bayonne. He retired in good order, destroying the bridges.

During the night the allied army halted on the position gained in the centre, but an accidental conflagration catching a wood completely separated their picquets towards Ascain from the main body—spreading far and wide over the heath, it lighted up all the hills, a blazing sign of war to France.

On the 11th the army advanced in order of battle. Hope forded the Nivelle above St. Jean de Luz and marched on Bidart; Beresford moved by the roads leading, upon Arbonne; Hill brought his left forward into communication with Beresford, and with his centre faced Cambo on the Nive. This change of front and the time required to restore the bridges for the artillery, enabled Soult to rally his army upon a third line of fortified camps which he had previously commenced, the right resting on the coast at Bidart, the centre at Helbacen Borda, the left at Ustaritz on the Nive. His front was of eight miles, but the works were only slightly advanced, and dreading a second battle on so wide a field he drew back his centre and left to Arbonne and Arauntz, broke down the bridges on the Nive at Ustaritz, and at two o'clock a slight skirmish, commenced by the allies in the centre, closed the day's proceedings.

Next morning the French retired to the ridge of Beyris, having their right in advance at Anglet and their left in the intrenched camp of Bayonne near Marac. The movement was covered by a dense fog, but when the day cleared Hope took post at Bidart on the left; Beresford then occupied Ahetze, Arbonne, and the hill of San Barbe in the centre, and Hill endeavoured to pass the fords and restore the broken bridges of Ustaritz. He also made a demonstration against the works at Cambo, but heavy rain in the mountains rendered the fords impassable and both points were defended successfully by Foy, whose operations having been distinct from the rest require notice.

D'Erlon, mistrusting the strength of his own position, had in the night of the 9th sent Foy orders to march from Bidaray to Espelette; but the messenger did not arrive in time, and on the morning of the 10th, Foy, following Soult's previous instructions, drove Mina's battalions from the Gorospil mountain; then pressing against the flank of Morillo on Hill's right he forced him also back fighting to the Puerto de Maya. However D'Erlon's battle was at this period receding fast, and Foy fearing to be cut off retired with the loss of a colonel and one hundred and fifty men, having taken a quantity of baggage and a hundred prisoners. Continuing his retreat all night he reached Cambo and Ustaritz on the 11th, and on the 12th defended them against Hill.

Such were the principal circumstances of the batlle of the Nivelle, whereby Soult was driven from a mountain position he had been fortifying for three months. He lost four thousand two hundred and sixty-five men and officers, including twelve or fourteen hundred prisoners, and one general killed. His field-magazines at St. Jean de Luz and Espelette fell into the hands of the victors, and fifty one pieces of artillery were taken; the greater part abandoned in the redoubts of the low country to Hope. The allies had two generals, Kempt and Byng, wounded, and they lost two thousand six hundred and ninety-four men and officers.

In the report of the battle, scant and tardy justice was done to the light division. Acting alone, for Longa's Spaniards scarcely fired a shot, that division, of only four thousand seven hundred men and officers, first carried the smaller Rhune defended by Barbot's brigade, and then beat Taupin's division from the main position, driving superior numbers from the strongest works: numbering less than one-sixth of the whole force employed against Clausel, it had defeated one-third of that general's corps. So doing, it lost many brave men, and of two who fell I will speak.

The first, low in rank, being but a lieutenant, was rich in honour, for he bore many scars and was young of days. He was only nineteen, and had seen more combats and sieges them he could count years. Slight in person, and of such surpassing and delicate beauty that the Spaniards often thought him a girl disguised in man's clothing. he was yet so vigorous, so active, so brave, that the most daring and experienced veterans watched his looks on the field of battle, and would obey his slightest sign in the most difficult situations. His education was incomplete, yet his natural powers were so happy, the keenest and best-furnished intellects shrunk from an encounter of wit, and all his thoughts and aspirations were proud and noble, indicating future greatness if destiny had so willed it. Such was Edward Freer of the 43rd, one of three brothers who all died in the Spanish war. Assailed the night before the battle with that strange anticipation of coming death, so often felt by military men, he was pierced with three balls at the first storming of the Rhune rocks, and the sternest soldiers in the regiment wept even in the middle of the fight when they heard of his fate.

On the same day and at the same hour was killed Colonel Thomas Lloyd. Ee likewise had been a long time in the 43rd. Under him Freer had learned the rudiments of his profession, but promotion had placed Lloyd at the head of the 94th, and leading that regiment he fell. In him were combined mental and bodily powers of no ordinary kind. A graceful symmetry of person combined with Herculean strength, and a frank majestic countenance, indicated a great and commanding character. His military acquirements were extensive both from experience and study, and on his mirth and wit, so well known in the army, it is only necessary to remark, that he used the latter without offence, yet so as to increase his ascendancy over those with whom he held intercourse; for though gentle he was valiant, ambitious, and conscious of fitness for great exploits. He like Freer was prescient of and predicted his own fall, yet with no abatement of courage. When he received the mortal wound, a most painful one, he would not suffer himself to be moved, but remained watching the battle and making observations upon the changes in it until death came, and at the age of thirty, the good, the brave, the generous Lloyd died. Tributes to his merit have been published by Lord Wellington and by one of his own poor soldiers ! by the highest and by the lowest ! To their testimony I add mine: let those who served on equal terms with him say, whether in aught I have exceeded his deserts.

BOOK XIV.

Passage of the Nive—Battles in front of Bayonne—Combat of Arcangues—First Battle of Barrouilhet—Second Battle of Barrouilhet—
Third Combat of Barrouilhet—Battle of St. Pierre—Operations
beyond the Nive.

Soult, having lost the Nivelle, at first designed to leave part of his
force in the entrenched camp of Bayonne, and take a flanking position
behind the Nive, half-way between Bayonne and St. Jean Pied de
Port. With his left on the entrenched mountain of Ursouia, his right
on the heights above Cambo, the double bridge-head of which would
enable him to make offensive movements on the left bank, he hoped
to confine Wellington to the district between that river and the sea,
and render his situation very uneasy during the winter if he did not
retire. He was forced to modify this plan; the Bayonne camp was incomplete; the work on the Ursouia mountain had been neglected,
contrary to his orders; the bridgehead at Cambo was only commenced
on the right bank, and on the left constructed defectively: the river in
dry weather was fordable also at Ustaritz below Cambo, and in many
places above that point. Remaining therefore at Bayonne with six
divisions and Villatte's reserve, he sent D'Erlon with three divisions
to reinforce Foy at Cambo.

But neither D'Erlon's divisions nor Soult's whole army could
have stopped Wellington if other circumstances had permitted him to
follow up his victory. Neither the works of the Bayonne camp nor the
barrier of the Nive could have barred the progress of his fiery host, if
Nature had not opposed her obstacles. The clayey country at the foot
of the Pyrenees was impassable after rain, except by the royal road
near the coast or by that of St. Jean Pied de Port, and both were in the
power of the French. On the bye-roads the infantry sunk to the mid-
leg, the cavalry above the horses' knees, even to the saddle-girths in
some places, and the artillery could not move at all. Rain and fogs on
the 12th had enabled Soult to regain his camp and secure the high road

to St. Jean Pied de Port; his troops then easily recovered their proper posts on the Nive, while Wellington, fixed in the swamps, could only make the ineffectual demonstration at Ustaritz and Cambo, already noticed. On the 16th, uneasy for his right flank, he directed Hill to menace Cambo again, where Foy had orders to preserve the bridge-head on the right-bank in any circumstances, and only abandon the left bank in the event of a general attack; but the officer at the bridge now destroyed in a panic all the works and the bridge itself This was a great loss to Soult, and enabled Wellington to take cantonments.

Bad weather was not the only obstacle to the British operations. During the battle of the 10th Freyre's and Longa's soldiers had pillaged Ascain and murdered several persons; and next day all the Spanish troops committed excesses in various places. On the right, Mina's battalions, who were mutinous, made a plundering and murdering incursion towards Hellette; the Portuguese and British soldiers commenced like outrages, killing two persons in one town, but General Pakenham, arriving at the moment, put the perpetrators to death, nipping this wickedness in the bud at his own risk, for legally he had not that power. He was a man whose generosity, humanity and chivalric spirit, excited the admiration of every honourable person; yet is he the officer who, falling at New Orleans, has been so foully traduced by American writers. Pre-eminently distinguished by his detestation of inhumanity and outrage, he has been with astounding falsehood represented as instigating his troops there to infamous excesses; but from a people holding millions of their fellow-beings in the most horrible slavery, while they prate and vaunt of liberty until men turn with loathing from the sickening folly, what can be expected?

Terrified by these excesses the French fled even from the large towns. Wellington soon dissipated their fears. On the 12th, although expecting a battle, he put to death all the Spanish marauders he could take in the act, and then with many reproaches, and despite of the discontent of their generals, forced the whole to withdraw into their own country. He disarmed the mutinous battalions under Mina, placed Giron's Andalusians in the Bastan under O'Donnel, quartered Freyre's Gallicians between Irun and Ernani, and sent Longa over the Ebro. Morillo's division alone remained with the army. These decisive proceedings, marking the lofty character of the man, proved not less politic than resolute; the people returned, and, finding strict discipline preserved, adopted an amicable intercourse with the invaders. However the loss of such a mass of troops, and the weather, reduced the army for a moment to a state of inactivity, the head-quarters were fixed at St. Jean de Luz and the troops took permanent cantonments.

The left wing extended from Bidart on the sea-coast to the Nive, on an opening of six miles. The right wing, thrown back at right angles, lined the bank of that river for eight miles. In front of Bidart, the broad ridge of Barrouilhet crossing the great coast-road was occupied, the principal post being the mayor's house, which was covered by tanks and pools, between which the road led. The centre of the left wing was on a continuation of this ridge near the village of Arcangues; the right was on the hill of San Barbe, close to Ustaritz on the Nive.

These posts were not established without combats. On the 18th the generals, John Wilson and Vandeleur, were wounded, and next day Beresford, who had seized the small bridge of Urdains at the junction of some roads, was attacked in force, yet maintained the bridge. This acquisition covered the right flank of the troops at Arcangues, but on the 23rd the light division had an action there, very ill managed by the divisional generals, and lost ninety men, of which eighty fell in the 43rd Regiment.

Wellington, having nearly nine thousand cavalry and a hundred guns, fretted on the curb in his contracted position until December, when the weather cleared and he resolved to force the line of the Nive and extend to his right, a resolution which led to sanguinary battles, for Soult's positions were then strong and well chosen. Bayonne, his base, being situated at the confluence of the Nive and the Adour rivers furnished bridges for the passage of both; and though weak in itself, was covered by Vauban's entrenched camp, which was exceedingly strong and not to be lightly attacked. In this camp Soult's right, under Reille, three divisions including Villatte's reserve, touched on the lower Adour, where there was a flotilla. His front was protected by

inundations and a swamp, through which the royal coast road led to
St. Jean de Luz, and along which fortified outposts extended to
Anglet. On his left Clausel's three divisions extended to the Nive,
being partly covered by the swamp, partly by a fortified honse, partly
by an artificial inundation spreading from the small bridge of Urdains
to the Nive; and beyond these defences the country held by the allies
was a deep clay, covered with small farm-houses and woods, very
unfavourable for movement.

On the right of the Nive, Vauban's camp being continued to the
upper Adour under the name of the "Front of Mousserolles," was held
by D'Erlon's four divisions, with posts extending up the right bank
of the Nive; that is to say, D'Armagnac fronted Ustaritz, and Foy was
at Cambo. The communication with the left bank of the Nive was
double; circuitous through Bayonne, direct by a bridge of boats.
Moreover, after the battle of the Nivelle, Soult brought General
Paris's division from St. Jean Pied de Port to Lahoussoa close under
the Ursouia mountain, whence it communicated with Foy's left by the
great road of St. Jean Pied de Port.

The Nive, the Adour, and the Gave de Pau, which falls into the
latter many miles above Bayonne, were all navigable; the first as far
as Ustaritz, the second to Dax:, the third to Peyrehorade, and the
French had magazines at the two latter places; yet they were fed with
difficulty, and to restrain Soult from the country beyond the Nive, to
intercept his communications with St. Jean Pied de Port, to bring a
powerful cavalry into activity and obtain secret intelligence from the
interior, were Wellington's inducements to force a passage over the
Nive. But to place an army on both sides of a navigable river, with
communications bad at all times and subject to entire interruptions
from rain; to do this in face of an army possessing, short communications, good roads, and entrenched camps for retreat, was a delicate
and dangerous operation.

Hope and Alten, having twenty-four thousand combatants and
twelve guns, were ordered to drive back all the French advanced posts
in front of their camp, between the Nive and the sea, on the 9th, and
thus keep Soult in check while Beresford and Hill crossed the Nive—
Beresford at Ustaritz with pontoons, Hill at Cambo and Larressore by
fords.

Both generals were then to repair the bridges at those points with materials prepared beforehand. To cover Hill's movement on the right and protect the valley of the Nive from General Paris, who being at Lahoussoa might have penetrated to the rear of the army during the operations, Morillo's Spaniards were to cross at Itzassu. At this time D'Armagnac was opposite Ustaritz, Foy's division extended from Halzou, in front of Larressore to the fords above Cambo, having the Ursouia mountain between its left and Paris: the rest of D'Erlon's troops occupied some heights in advance of Mousserolles.

PASSAGE OF THE NIVE.

At Ustaritz the double bridge was broken, but an island connecting them was in possession of the British. Beresford laid his pontoons down on the hither side in the night, and, on the morning of the 9th, a beacon lighted on the heights above Cambo gave the signal of action; the passage was soon forced, the second bridge laid, and D'Armagnac driven back; but the swampy nature of the country between the river and the high road by retarding the attack gave him time to retreat. Hill also forced his passage in three columns above and below Cambo with slight resistance, though the fords were so deep that several horsemen were drowned, and the French very strongly posted, especially at Halzou, where a deep strong mill-race had to be crossed as well as the river.

Foy, seeing by the direction of Beresford's fire that his own retreat was endangered, went off hastily with his left, leaving his right wing under General Berlier at Halzou, without orders; hence, when General Pringle attacked the latter from Larressore the sixth division was already on the high road between Foy and Berlier, and though the latter escaped by cross roads he did not rejoin his division until two o'clock in the afternoon. Meanwhile Morillo passed at Itzassu, and Paris retired to Hellette, where he was joined by a regiment of light cavalry from the Bidouse river: Morillo followed, and in one village his troops murdered fifteen peasants, amongst them several women and children.

Hill placed a brigade of infantry at Urcurray to cover the

bridge of Cambo, and to support the cavalry, which he despatched to scour the roads and watch Paris and Pierre Soult. With the rest of his troops he marched against the heights of Mousserolles in front, and was there joined by the sixth division, the third remaining to cover the bridge of Ustaritz.

It was now one o'clock, Soult came from Bayonne, approved of D'Erlon's dispositions, and offered battle. His line crossed the high road, and D'Armagnac's brigade, coming from Ustaritz, was in advance at Villefranque. A heavy cannonade and skirmish ensued along the front, but no general fight took place because the deep roads retarded the rear of Hill's columns; however the Portuguese of the sixth division drove D'Armagac with sharp fighting out of Ville-franque about three o'clock, and a brigade of the second division was established in advance to connect Hill with Beresford.

Three divisions of infantry, wanting the brigade left at Urcurray, now hemmed up for four French divisions; and as the latter, notwith-standing their superiority of numbers, made no advantage of the broken movements caused by the deep roads, the passage of the Nive may be judged a surprise, and Wellington had so far overreached his noble adversary. Yet he had not trusted an uncertain chance. The French masses by falling upon the heads of his columns while the rear was still labouring in the deep roads might have caused disorder; but they could not have driven either Hill or Beresford over the river again, because the third division was close at hand, and a brigade of the seventh could from San Barbe have followed by the bridge of Ustaritz. The greatest danger was, that Paris, reinforced by Pierre Soult's cavalry, should have fallen upon Morillo, or the brigade left at Urcurray in the rear, while Soult, reinforcing D'Erlon with fresh divisions from the other side of the Nive, attacked Hill and Beresford in front: but it was to prevent that, Hope and Alten, whose operations are now to be related, had been ordered to act on the left bank.

Hope, having twelve miles to march from St. Jean de Luz before he copuld reach the French works, put his troops in motion during the night, and about eight o'clock passed between the tanks with his right, while his left descended from the platform of Bidart towards Biaritz. The French outposts retired fighting and Hope, sweeping with a half circle to his right, preceded by the fire of his guns and many skirmishers, faced the entrenched camp about one o'clock. His left rested on the Lower Adour; his centre menaced an advanced work on the ridge of Beyris: his right was in communication with Alten, who had halted about Bussussary and Arcangues until Hope's fiery crescent closed on the French camp; then he also advanced, but with the exception of a slight skirmish at the fortified house met no resistance. Three divisions, some cavalry and the unattached brigades, equal to a fourth division, sufficed therefore to keep six French divisions in check on this side, and when evening closed fell back towards their original positions, yet under heavy rain and with gr eat fatigue to Hope's troops, for even the royal road was knee-deep of mud, and they were twenty four hours under arms. The whole day's fighting cost eight hundred men of a side, the loss of the allies being rather greater on the left of the Nive than on the right.

BATTLES IN FRONT OF BAYONNE.

Wellington's wings were now divided by the Nive, and Soult resolved to fall upon one with all his forces united. The prisoners assured him the third and fourth divisions were both in front of Mousserolles, he was able to assemble troops with greatest facility on the left of the river, and as the allies' front there was most extended, he chose that side for his counter-stroke. In Bayonne itself were eight thousand men, troops of the line and national guards, with which he occupied the entrenched camp of Mousserolles; then placing, ten gun-boats on the Upper Adour, to guard it as high as the confluence of the Gave de Pau, he made D'Erlon file four divisions over the boat-bridge on the Nive, to take post behind Clausel's corps on the other side. He thus concentrated nine divisions of infantry and Villatte's reserve, with a body of cavalry and forty guns, in all sixty thousand combatants, including conscripts, to assail a quarter where the allies, although stronger by one division than he imagined, had yet only thirty thousand infantry with twenty-four guns.

His first design was to pour on to the table-land of Bussussary and Arcangues, and act as circumstances should dictate, and judged so well of his position that he warned the Minister of War to expect good news for the next day: indeed his enemy's situation, though better than he knew of, gave him a right to anticipate success, for on no point was this formidable counter-attack anticipated. Wellington was on the right of the Nive, awaiting daylight to assail the heights where he had last seen the French. Hope's troops, with exception of the Portuguese under General Campbell, who were at Barrouilhet, slept in their cantonments —the first division at St. Jean de Luz six miles from the outposts, the fifth division between that place and Bidart, and all exceedingly fatigued. The light division had orders to retire from Bussussary to Arbonne, four miles; a part had marched before dawn, but Kempt, suspicious of the enemy's movements, delayed the rest until he could see well to his front: he thus saved the position.

The extraordinary difficulty of moving through the country, the numerous inclosures and copses which intercepted the view, the recent easy success on the Nive, and a certain haughty confidence, sure attendant of a long course of victory, had rendered the English general somewhat negligent, and the troops were not prepared for a battle. His general position was, however, strong. Barrouilhet could only be attacked along the royal road on a narrow front between the tanks, where he had directed entrenchments to be made; but there was only one brigade there, and a road, made with difficulty by the engineers, supplied a bad flank communication with the light division. The Barrouilhet ridge was prolonged to the platform of Bussussary, but bulged there too near the enemy to be safely occupied in force, wherefore the ridge of Arcangues, behind it, was the real position of battle on that side.

From the Bussussary platform three tongues of land shot out, and the valleys between them, as well as their slopes, were covered with copse-woods. The left-hand tongue was held by the 52nd Regiment; the central tongue by the picquets of the 43rd, with supporting companies in succession towards an open common, across which the troops had to pass to the church of Arcangues. The third tongue was guarded, partly by the 43rd, partly by riflemen, but the valley there was not occupied. One brigade of the seventh division, covered by the inundation and holding the bridge of Urdains, continued this line of posts to the Nive; the other brigades being behind San Barbe and belonging rather to Ustaritz than to this front: the fourth division was several miles behind the right of the light division.

If Soult had, as he first designed, burst with his whole army upon Bussussary and Arcangues, it would have been impossible for the light division, scattered over difficult ground, to have stopped him for half an hour; and there was no support within several miles, no superior officer to direct the concentration of the different divisions. Wellington had ordered all the line to be entrenched, but the works were commenced on a great scale, and, as is usual when danger does not spur, the soldiers had laboured so carelessly, that a few abbatis, the tracing of some lines and redoubts, and the opening of a road of communication were all the results. The French could thus have gained the broad open hills beyond Arcangues, separated the fourth and seventh from the light division, and cut all off from Hope. Soult, however, in the course of the night, for reasons which have not been stated, changed his project, and at day-break Reille marched with Boyer's and Maucune's divisions, Sparre's cavalry, and from twenty to thirty guns against Hope by the main road on the right. He was followed by Foy and Villatte, but Clausel assembled his troops near the fortified house in front of Bussussary, and one of D'Erlon's divisions approached the bridge of Urdains.

COMBAT OF ARCANGUES.

Heavy rain fell in the night, but the morning broke fair, and at dawn French soldiers were observed close to the most advanced picquet of the 43rd on the left, pushing each other about as if at gambols, yet lining by degrees the nearest ditches; a general officer was also seen behind a farmhouse within pistol-shot, and the heads of columns could be perceived in the rear. Thus warned, some companies were thrown on the right into the basin, to prevent the enemy from penetrating that way to the small common between Bussussary and Arcangues. Kempt's foresight in delaying his march to Arbonne was now manifest, and he immediately placed the reserves of his brigade in the church and mansion-house of Arcangues. Meanwhile the French, breaking forth with loud cries and a rattling musketry, had fallen at a running pace upon the 43rd at the tongue and in the basin, while a cloud of skirmishers, descending on their left, penetrated between them and the 52nd, seeking to turn both. The right tongue was in like manner assailed, and the assault was so strong and rapid, the enemy so numerous, the ground so extensive, that to cross the common and reach the church of Arcangues would have been impossible if serious resistance had been attempted at first. Wherefore, delivering their fire at pistol shot distance, the picquets fell back in succession, with eminent coolness and intelligence. For though they had to run at full speed to gain the common before the enemy, who was constantly outflanking them by the basin; though the ways were so deep and narrow no formation could be preserved; though the fire of the French was thick and close, and their cries vehement in pursuit, the instant the open ground was attained, the crowd of seeming fugitives turned and presented a compact and well formed body, defying and deriding the efforts of their adversaries.

The 52nd, which was half a mile to the left, was but slightly assailed, yet fell back also to the main ridge; for though the ground did not permit Colonel Colborne to see the enemy's strength, the rapid retreat of the 43rd told him the affair was serious. Well did the regiments of the light division understand each other's qualities, and in good time he withdrew to the main position. On the right-hand tongue the troops were not so fortunate; the enemy, moving by the basin, reached the common before them, and about a hundred of the 43rd and riflemen were intercepted. The French were in a hollow road and careless, never doubting that the officer of the 43rd, Ensign Campbell, a youth scarcely eighteen years of age, would surrender; but with a shout he broke into their column sword in hand, and though the struggle was severe and twenty of the 43rd and thirty of the riflemen with their officer remained prisoners, he reached the church with the rest.

D'Armagnac's division of D'Erlon's corps now pushed close up to the bridge of Urdains, and Clausel assembling his three divisions by degrees at Bussussary, opened a sharp fire of musketry. The position was however safe. A mansion-house on the right, covered by abbatis and not easily accessible, was defended by a rifle battalion and the Portuguese. The church and churchyard were occupied by the 43rd, supported with two mountain-guns, their front being covered by a declivity of thick copse wood filled with riflemen, and only to be turned by narrow hollow roads leading on each side to the church. On the left, the 52nd, supported by the remainder of the division, spread as far as the great basin which separated this position from the ridge of Barrouilhet, towards which some small posts were pushed: yet there was still a great interval between Alten and Hope.

As the skirmishing grew hot, Clausel brought up twelve guns with which he threw shot and shells into the churchyard of Arcangues, and four or five hundred infantry made a rush forwards, but a heavy fire from the 43rd sent them back over the ridge where their guns were posted. Yet their cannonade would have been murderous, if this musketry had not made the gunners withdraw their pieces a little behind the ridge, and caused their shot to fly wild and high. Kempt, thinking the distance too great, was at first inclined to stop the fire, but the moment it lulled the French pushed their pieces forwards again, and their shells knocked down eight men in an instant: the muskets then recommenced and the shells again flew high. The village and mansion-house on the right were defended by the riflemen, and the action, hottest where the 52nd fought, continued all day. It was not very severe, yet both French and English writers, misled perhaps by an inaccurate phrase in the public dispatch, have represented it as a desperate attack by which the light division was driven into its entrenchments; whereas the picquets only were forced back, and there were no entrenchments, save those made on the spur of the moment by the soldiers in the churchyard.

FIRST BATTLE OF BARROUILHET.

On that side Reille, having two divisions, drove Campbell's Portuguese from Anglet about nine o'clock, and Sparre's cavalry cut down a great many men. The French infantry then assailed the position of Barrouilhet, but moving along a narrow ridge, confined on each flank by tanks, only two brigades could get into action by the main road, and the rain had rendered all the bye-roads so deep that it was midday before their line of battle was filled. This delay saved the allies, for the attack here also was so unexpected that the first division and Lord Aylmer's brigade were at rest in St. Jean de Luz and Bidart when the action commenced, and the latter did not reach the position before eleven o'clock; the foot-guards did not march until after twelve, and only arrived at three o'clock when the fight was done; all the troops were exceedingly fatigued, only ten guns could be brought into play, and from some negligence part of the infantry were without ammunition.

Robinson's brigade of the fifth division first arrived to support Campbell and fight the battle. The French skirmishers had then spread along the whole valley, while their columns moved by the great road against the mayor's house on the platform of Barrouilhet, where the ground was thick of hedges and coppice-wood. A most confused fight took place. The assailants, cutting ways through the hedges, poured on in smaller or larger bodies as the openings allowed, and were immediately engaged, at some points successfully, at others beaten, and few knew what was going on to the right or left of where they stood. By degrees Reille engaged both his divisions, and some of Villatte's reserve also entered the fight, but then Bradford's Portuguese and Aylmer's brigade arrived on the allies' side, which enabled Greville's brigade of the fifth division, hitherto in reserve, to relieve Robinson's troops who had suffered severely, and he himself was dangerously wounded.

A notable action now happened with the 9th Regiment under Colonel Cameron. Posted on the extreme left of Greville's brigade, there was between it and Bradford's brigade a Portuguese battalion.

opposite the 9th was a coppice-wood possessed by the enemy, whose skirmishers were continually gathering in masses and rushing out as if to assail the regiment, and were as often driven back; but the ground was so broken that nothing could be seen on the flanks, and after some time Cameron, who had received no orders, heard a sudden firing along the main road close to his left. His adjutant, sent to look out, returned quickly to say a French regiment, which must have passed unseen in small bodies between the Portuguese battalion and the 9th, was rapidly filing into line on the rear. The 4th British Regiment was in column at a short distance, and its commander, Colonel Piper, was directed by Cameron to face about and fall on the French regiment; but he took a wrong direction, no firing followed, and the adjutant again hurried to the rear in observation. The 4th Regiment was not to be seen, and the enemy's line was then nearly formed, whereupon Cameron, leaving fifty men to answer the skirmishing fire, which now increased from the copse, faced about and marched against the new enemy, who was about his own strength. The French opened fire, slowly at first, but increasing vehemently as the distance lessened, until the 9th sprung forwards to charge; then the adverse line broke and fled by their flanks in disorder, those who made for their own right brushing the left of Greville's brigade and carrying off an officer of the Royals in their rush: yet the greatest number were made prisoners and Cameron having lost eighty men and officers resumed his old ground.

Reille's divisions were now all repulsed, but Villatte still menaced the right flank, and Foy, taking possession of the narrow ridge connecting Bussussary with the platform of Barrouilhet, threw his skirmishers into the great basin leading to Arbonne and menaced Hope's right flank. It was now two o'clock, and Soult, his columns being then all in hand, gave orders to renew the battle, and his masses were beginning to move, when Clausel reported that a large body of troops, coming from the right of the Nive, was menacing D'Armagnac near Urdains. Unable to account for this, Soult, who saw the Guards and Germans coming up from St. Jean de Luz, and the unattached brigades already in line, suspended his attack, and ordered D'Erlon who had two divisions in reserve, to detach one to the support of D'Almagnac: ere that could be done the night fell.

The troops seen by Clausel were the third, fourth, sixth and seventh divisions, whose movements during the battle it is time to notice. When Wellington discovered that the heights in Hill's front were abandoned, he directed that officer to push parties close up to the front of Mousserolles; but then hearing the cannonade on the left bank of the Nive repaired there. In passing, he made the third and sixth divisions recross that river, and ordered Beresford to lay another bridge of communication lower down the Nive at Villefranque, to shorten the line of movement. When he saw how the battle stood with Hope and Alten, he made the seventh division close in from the hill of San Barbe, placed the third division at Urdains, and brought up Cole's division to an open heathy ridge a mile behind the church of Arcangues, from thence a brigade moved into the basin on the left of Colborne to cover Arbonne, and the whole division was ready to oppose any attempt to penetrate between Hope and Alten. It was these dispositions which checked Clausel and prevented Soult's attack at Barrouilhet.

In this battle two generals and twelve hundred Anglo-Portuguese had been killed and wounded, three hundred made prisoners. The French had one general, Villatte, wounded, and lost two thousand men; and when the action terminated two regiments of Nassau with one of Frankfort came over to the allies. These men were not deserters. Their prince having abandoned Napoleon in Germany sent secret instructions to his troops to do so likewise, and in good time, for Napoleon's orders to disarm them reached Soult the next morning.

SECOND BATTLE OF BARROUILHET.

In the night of the 10th Reille withdrew behind the tanks, while Foy and Villatte moved along the connecting ridge towards Bussussary, to unite with Clausel's left and D'Erlon's reserve; hence on the morning of the 11th the French army, D'Armagnac's division which remained at Urdains excepted, was concentrated, for Soult feared a counter-attack. The French deserters indeed declared that Clausel had formed a body of two thousand choice grenadiers to assault the village and church of Arcangues, yet the day passed there with only a slight skirmish. Not so at Barrouilhet. There was a thick fog, and at ten o'clock Lord Wellington, desirous to ascertain what Soult was doing, directed the 9th Regiment to skirmish beyond the tanks, but not to push the action if the French augmented their force. Cameron did so and the fight was becoming warm, when Colonel Delancy, a staff-officer, rashly directed the 9th to enter the village an error sharply corrected. For the fog cleared up, and Soult, who had twenty-four thousand men at that point, seeing the 9th unsupported, made a counter-attack so strong and sudden that Cameron only saved his regiment with the aid of some Portuguese troops hastily brought up by Hope. The fighting then ceased and Wellington went to the right, leaving Hope with orders to drive back the French picquets and re-establish his own outposts.

Soult, hitherto seemingly undecided, was roused by this second insult. He ordered Daricau's division to attack the right of Barrouilhet in reply, while Boyer's division fell on by the main road between the tanks. The allies, unexpectant of battle, had dispersed to gather fuel, for the time was wet and cold, wherefore the French penetrated in all directions; they outflanked the right, they passed the tanks, seized the outhouses of the mayor's house and occupied the coppice in front of it; and though driven from the outbuildings by the Royals, the tumult was great and the coppice was filled with men of all nations inter-mixed and fighting in a perilous manner. Robinson's brigade was very hardly handled, the officer commanding it was wounded, a squadron of French cavalry again cut down some Portuguese near the wood; and on the right the colonel of the 84th having unwisely entered a hollow road, the French, having the banks, killed him and a great number of his men. However the 9th Regiment, posted on the main road, plied Boyer's flank with fire, the 85th Regiment, came into action, and Hope, conspicuous from his gigantic stature and heroic courage, was seen wherever danger pressed, encouraging the troops at one time he was in the midst of the enemy, his clothes were pierced with bullets and he was severely wounded in the ankle, yet he would not quit the field, and thus by his calm intrepidity restored the battle; the French were beaten from Barrouilhet, but they had recovered their original posts and continued to gall the allies with a fire of shot and shells until the fall of night.

In this fight six hundred men of a side fell, and as the fifth division was very much reduced the first division took its place in the line. Meanwhile Soult sent his cavalry over the Nive to Mousserolles to check the incursions of Hill's horsemen.

THIRD COMBAT OF BARROUILHET.

Rain again fell heavily in the night, and, though the morning broke fair, neither side seemed inclined to recommence hostilities; but the advanced posts being very close to each other at ten o'clock a quarrel arose For Soult observing the fresh regiments of the first division close to his posts, imagined the allies were going to attack him, and reinforced his front; this caused an English battery to fall into a like error, it opened on the advancing troops and in an instant the whole line of posts was engaged. Soult then brought up a number of guns, the firing continued without object for many hours, and four hundred men of a side were killed or wounded, although the great body of the French army remained concentrated and qu iet on the ridge between Barrouilhet and Bussussary.

Wellington, expecting Soult would finally abandon his attack to fall on Hill, had sent Beresford orders to reinforce the latter with the sixth division by the new bridge if necessary; and also with the seventh division by Ustaritz without waiting for further instructions; yet now, seeing Soult's tenacity, he drew the seventh division again towards Arbonne. Beresford had however made a movement towards the Nive, and this, with the march of the seventh and some changes in the position of the fourth division, caused Soult to believe the allies were gathering with a view to attack his centre on the morning of the 13th; and it is remarkable that the deserters, at this early period, told him the Spaniards had re-entered France, although orders to that effect were not, as we shall find, given until the next day. Convinced then that his bolt was shot on that side of the Nive, he left two divisions and Villatte's reserve in the entrenched camp, and marched with the other seven to Mousserolles, intending to fall upon Hill.

That general had pushed his scouting parties far abroad, and when Sparre's horsemen arrived at Mousserolles on the 12th, Pierre Soult advanced from the Bidouze river with all his light cavalry, and being supported by General Paris drove the allies' posts from Hasparen Colonel Vivian, who commanded there, ordered Major Brotherton to charge with the 14th Dragoons across the bridge It was an ill-judged order and the impossibility of succeeding was so manifest, that when Brotherton, noted throughout the army for his daring, galloped forward, only two men and one subaltern, Lieutenant Southwell, passed the narrow bridge with him and they were all taken except one man who was killed. Vivian charged with his whole brigade to rescue them, but in vain and he fell back to Urcurray upon Morillo's Spaniards; Hill then put a British brigade in march to support him on the 12th, yet recalled it at sunset, because he had then discovered Soult's columns passing the Nive by the boat-bridge above Bayonne.

Wellington, feeling the want of numbers, now brought forward a division of Gallicians to St Jean de Luz, and one of Andalusians from the Bastan to Itzassu, and to prevent plunder fed them from the British magazines. The Gallicians were to support Hope, the Andalusians to protect the rear of the army from General Paris and Pierre Soult.

Hill now took a position of battle on a front of two miles.

His left, composed of the 28th, 34th and 39th Regiments under General Pringle, occupied a wooded ridge crowned by the chateau of Villefranque, where it covered the new pontoon bridge of communication, but was separated from the centre by a small stream forming a chain of ponds in a deep marshy valley.

His centre was on both sides of the high road, near the hamlet of St Pierre, on a crescent-shaped height, broken with rocks and close brushwood on the left hand; on the right hand inclosed with high and thick hedges, one of which, at the distance of a hundred yards, covered part of the line and was nearly impassable. Here Barnes's British brigade of the second division were posted, the 71st Regiment being on the left, the 50th in the centre, the 92nd on the right Ash-

worth's Portuguese were posted in advance immediately in front of
St Pierre, with skirmishers occupying a small wood covering their
right. Twelve guns under Ross and Tullock were in the centre,
looking down the great road; and half a mile in rear Lecor's Portuguese and two guns were in reserve.

The right, under Byng, was composed of the 3rd, 57th, 31st, and
66th. The first-named was posted on a height running parallel with the
Adour, called the ridge of Old Moguerre because a village of that
name was on the summit; pushed in advance, this regiment could only
be assailed by crossing a narrow swampy valley, the upper part of
which was held by Byng with the remainder of the brigade, his post
being also covered by a great mill-pond.

One mile in front of St Pierre a range of counter heights were
held by the French, but the basin between was broad, open, and commanded by the fire of the allies. All parts were too heavy and enclosed
for the action of cavalry, and the French infantry could only approach
in force on one narrow front of battle along the high road, until within
cannon-shot, but then two narrow difficult lanes branched off to the
right and left, crossing the swampy valleys on each side, and leading,
the one against the allies' right, where the 3rd Regiment was posted;
the other against their left.

In the night of the 12th rain swelled the Nive and carried away
the bridge of communication; it was soon restored, but for the time
Hill was cut off from the rest of the army; and while seven French
divisions of infantry, furnishing thirty five thousand combatants,
approached him in front, an eighth under General Paris, and the
cavalry of Pierre Soult, menaced him in rear. To meet those in his
front he had only fourteen guns and fourteen thousand men in
position; to check those on his rear but four thousand Spaniards and
Vivian's cavalry at Urcurray.

BATTLE OF ST. PIERRE.

Morning broke with a heavy mist, under cover of which Soult
formed his order of battle D'Erlon, having D'Armagnac's, Abbe's,
and Daricau's divisions of infantry, Sparre's cavalry, and twenty-
two guns, marched in front; Foy and Maransin followed, but the

remainder of the army was in reserve, for the roads would not allow of any other order The mist hung heavily, and the French masses, at one moment quite shrouded in vapour, at another dimly seen or looming sudden and large, and dark, at different points, appeared like thunder-clouds gathering before the storm; but at half-past eight Soult pushed back the British picquets in the centre, the sun burst out, and the sparkling fire of the light troops spread wide in the valley and crept up the hills on either flank, while the bellowing of forty pieces of artillery shook the banks of the Nive and the Adour.

Daricau, marching on the French light, was directed against Pringle D'Armagnac, moving on the left, took Old Moguerre as his point of direction, and sought to force Byng's light Abbe assailed the centre at St Pierre, where General Stewart commanded Hill took his station on a commanding; mount in the rear, from whence he could see the whole battle and direct the movements.

Abbe, a man noted for vigour, pushed his attack with great violence and gained ground so rapidly with his light troops on the left of Ashworth's Portuguese, that Stewart sent the 71st Regiment and two guns from St Pierre to the latter's aid; then the French won the small wood on Ashworth's right, and half of the 50th Regiment was detached to that quarter The wood was thus retaken, and the flanks of Stewart's position secured, but his centre was weakened, the fire of the French artillery was concentrated against it, and Abbe pushed on there with such a power that, despite of the play of musketry on his flanks and a crushing cannonade in his front, he gained the top of the position, and drove back the remainder of Ashworth's Portuguese, together with the other half of the 50th Regiment, which had remained in reserve.

General Barnes now brought the 92nd Regiment from behind St Pierre with so furious a counter-attack that the French skirmishers fell back in disorder on each side, leaving their column to meet the charge, which was so roughly pushed that the French mass wavered and gave way. Abbe immediately replaced it with another, and Soult, redoubling the heavy play of his heavy guns from the heights, sent a battery of horse artillery galloping down into the valley, where it opened fire close to the allies with destructive activity. The cannonade and musketry then rolled like a prolonged peal of thunder, and Abbe's second column, regardless of Ross's guns, though they tore the ranks in a horrible manner, advanced so steadily up the high road, that the 92nd was compelled to take shelter behind St. Pierre. The Portuguese guns, their British commanding officer having fallen wounded, then limbered up to retire, and the French skirmishers reached the thick hedge in front of Ashworth's right.

Barnes, seeing that hard fighting only could save the position, now made the Portuguese guns resume fire, while the wing of the 50th and the Caçadores gallantly held the small wood on the right; but he was soon wounded, the greatest part of his and Stewart's staff were hurt, and the matter seemed desperate. For the light troops, overpowered by numbers, were all driven in, except those in the wood, the artillerymen were falling at the guns, Ashworth's line crumbled rapidly before the musketry and cannonade, the ground was strewed with the dead in front, and the wounded crawling to the rear were many . If the French light troops could then have penetrated through the thick hedge, defeat would have been inevitable. For the column of attack was steadily advancing up the main road, and a second column launched on its right was already victorious, because the colonel of the 71st shamefully withdrew that gallant regiment and abandoned the Portuguese. Pringle was still fighting strongly against Daricau's superior numbers on the hill of Villefranque; but on the extreme right, the colonel of the 3rd regiment also shamefully abandoned his strong post to D'Armagnac, whose leading brigade then rapidly turned Byng's other regiments on that side.

Foy's and Maransin's divisions, hitherto retarded by the deep roads, were now coming into line to support Abbe, and at a moment when the troops opposed to him were deprived of their reserve, because Hill, beholding the retreat of the 3rd and 71st Regiments, descended in haste from his mount, turned the latter back, renewed the fight in person, and bringing one brigade of Lecor's reserve to the same quarter sent the other against D'Armagnac at Old Moguerre. Thus at the decisive moment of the battle the French reserve was augmenting, while that of the allies was thrown as a last resource into action. However the right wing of the 50th and Ashworth's Caçadores never lost the small wood in front, upholding the fight there and towards the high road with unflinching courage: this gave the 92nd Regiment time to reform behind the hamlet of St. Pierre, and its gallant colonel, Cameron, once more led it down the road with colours flying and music playing, resolved to give the shock to whatever stood in the way. At this sight the British skirmishers on the flanks, suddenly changing from retreat to attack, rushed forward and drove those of the enemy back on each side; yet the battle seemed hopeless, for Ashworth was badly wounded, his line was shattered, and Barnes, who had not quitted the field for his former hurt, was now shot through the body.

The 92nd was but a small clump compared with the heavy mass in its front, and the French soldiers seemed willing enough to close with the bayonet, until an officer riding at their head suddenly turned his horse, waved his sword and appeared to order a retreat: then they faced about and retired across the valley to their original position, in good order however, and scarcely pursued by the allies, so exhausted were the victors. This retrograde movement, for there was no panic or disorder, was produced partly by the gallant advance of the 92nd and the returning rush of the skirmishers; partly by the state of affairs immediately on the right of the French column, where the 71st, indignant at their colonel's conduct, had returned to the fight with such fierceness, and were so well aided by Lecor's Portuguese, Hill and Stewart in person leading the attack, that the hitherto victorious French were overthrown there also, at the very moment when the 92nd came with that brave show down the main road. Many men fell and Lecor was wounded, but the double action in the centre being seen from the hill of Villefranque, Daricau's division, already roughly handled by Pringle, also fell back in confusion; while on the extreme right, Buchan's Portuguese, detached by Hill to recover the Moguerre ridge, ascended under flank fire from Soult's guns, and rallied the 3rd Regiment: in happy time, for D'Armagnac's first brigade had passed Byng's flank at the mill-pond and was in rear of his line.

It was now twelve o'clock, and while the fire of the light troops and cannonade in the centre continued, the contending generals restored their respective orders of battle. Soult's right wing had been quite repulsed by Pringle, his left was giving way before Buchan, and the difficult ground forbad his sending immediate succour to either; moreover in the exigency of the moment he had called D'Armagnac's reserve brigade to sustain Abbe's retiring columns. However that brigade, and Foy's and Maransin's divisions, were in hand to renew the fight in the centre, and the allies could not, unsuccoured, have sustained a fresh assault, their ranks being wasted with fire, nearly all the staff killed or wounded, and three generals badly hurt.

In this crisis Hill, seeing Buchan well engaged on Old Moguerre and Byng master of his ground in the valley of the mill-pond, drew the 57th Regiment from the latter place to reinforce his centre; at the same time the bridge of boats having been restored, the sixth division, which had been marching since daybreak, appeared in order of battle on the mount below St. Pierre. It was soon followed by the fourth and third divisions, and two brigades of the seventh division were likewise in march. With the first of these troops came Wellington. He had hurried from Barrouilhet when the first sound of cannon reached him, yet he arrived only to witness the close of the battle—the crisis was past. Hill's day of glory was complete.

Soult, according to the French method, now made another attack, or rather demonstration against the centre to cover his new dispositions, but he was easily repulsed, and at the same moment Buchan drove D'Armagnac headlong off the Moguerre ridge. The French masses continued to maintain a menacing position on the high road, and on a hillock rising between the road and the mill-pond, but were soon dispossessed by Wellington, who sent Byng with two battalions against the hillock, and some troops from the centre against those on the high road. At this last point however the generals and staff had been so cut down, that Colonel Currie, the aide-de-camp, could find no superior officer to deliver the order to and led the troops himself to the attack. Both charges were successful, and two of the light guns, sent down in the early part of the fight by Soult and which had played without ceasing, were taken.

The battle now abated to a skirmish, under cover of which the French endeavoured to carry off their wounded and rally their stragglers, but at two o'clock Wellington commanded a general advance of the whole line. Then the French retreated fighting, and the allies, following close on the side of the Nive, plied them with musketry until dark yet they maintained their line towards the Adour, and Sparre's cavalry passing out that way rejoined Pierre Soult. This last general and Paris had during the day skirmished with Morillo and Vivian's cavalry at Urcurray, until the ill-success at St. Pierre became known, when they retired.

In this bloody action Soult had designed to employ seven divisions of infantry with one brigade of cavalry on the front, and one brigade of infantry with a division of cavalry on the rear; but the state of the roads and the narrow front did not permit more than five divisions to act, and only half of those were seriously engaged. His loss was certainly three thousand, making a total, on the five days' fighting, of six thousand men with two generals, Villatte and Maucomble, wounded. Hill had three generals and fifteen hundred men killed or wounded, and Wellington's loss on the five days' fighting was five thousand, including five hundred prisoners. Five generals, Hope, Robinson, Barnes, Lecor and Ashworth, were wounded.

OPERATIONS BEYOND THE NIVE.

When Soult lost the battle of St. Pierre, he left three divisions on the Mousserolles camp, sent two over the Nive to reinforce Reille, and passing the Adour in the night with Foy's division, extended it up the right bank of that river to the confluence of the Gave de Pau, to protect the navigation, on which his supplies now depended. To intercept those supplies, to cut the French communication with St. Jean Pied de Port, and open a fertile tract of country for the subsistence and action of his powerful cavalry, had been Wellington's object in forcing the passage of the Nive; for Bayonne could not be assailed with success until the army occupying, the entrenched camp in its front was drawn away by want.

Soult was resolved to hold his position around that fortress, and the country beyond the Nive favoured that object, being deep, traversed by many rivers, which flooding with every shower in the mountains furnished in their concentric courses to the Adour barriers not easy to break through without great loss: and to turn them by their sources near the mountains required wide movements, and fine weather to harden the roads. But the winter of 1813 was peculiarly wet. Still Soult's security depended on the weather, and three fine days made him tremble. He was now also dependent on water-carriage for his supplies, his chief magazines being at Dax on the Adour, and Peyrehorade on the Gave de Pau; the latter only twenty-four miles from Bayonne, and both so exposed to sudden incursions that he was compelled to entrench them.

While thus watching clouds and skies for the signal of great operations, the two commanders carried on a minor warfare of posts and surprises. Soult, finding the navigation of the Adour most endangered near Urt, where the river narrowed, sent Foy across to cast a bridge and fortify a head to it; but Wellington, forestalling the attempt, drove him back again, and the supplies were then only brought down at night by stealth or with a guard of gunboats under fire: indeed the French army could not have been thus supplied if the coasting trade from Bordeaux to Bayonne had been interrupted by the English navy, but Wellington's remonstrances on that head were still unheeded by the Admiralty. However Soult was so embarrassed, that leaving Reille with but four divisions in Vauban's camp, he transferred his head-quarters to Peyrehorade, and sent Clausel with two divisions, all the light cavalry and Trielhard's heavy dragoons beyond the Adour to take post on the Bidouze, one of the many rivers descending concentrically from the Pyrenees to the Adour. His advanced posts were then pushed to the Joyeuse and Aran rivers, close to Wellington, who immediately made counter dispositions, and thus the principal fronts of opposition were placed on a line perpendicular to that against Bayonne, which thus became secondary.

This did not prevent the minor warfare for the command of the navigation of the Adour being continued. Hill seized the island of Holriague in the Adour; those of Berens and Broc above it, were taken by Foy, and the allies were momentarily embarrassed by the loss of their boat-bridge on the Nive, which was carried away by a flood. On their extreme right Morillo, having without authority taken two squadrons of the 18th Hussars to aid one of his foraging incursions, abandoned them at a critical moment, whereby their major, Hughes, two captains and a lieutenant were wounded and many men lost. Mina also invaded the valleys of Baygorry, plundering, burning, and murdering men, women, and children; whereupon the people there took arms, and being reinforced with two hundred regulars from St. Jean Pied de Port surprised one of his battalions and pressed the others with vigour. This gave Soult hopes of exciting the Basques to an insurgent warfare; and General Harispe, a Basque by birth and of great reputation, who had been long expected from Suchet's army, now arrived to aid this plan. If Harispe had come in November, Wellington's strict discipline being then unknown, a formidable warfare would have been raised. It was now too late for a general rising, yet his presence, and Mina's incursions, with the licentious conduct of Morillo, had so awakened the warlike propensities of the Baygorry Basques, that Harispe soon made a levy and commenced active operations. To aid him Soult extended and strengthened his own left, and made the light cavalry menace all the outposts, whereupon Wellington, thinking he sought a general battle, resolved to fall on him at once, but was stopped by the sudden swelling of the rivers. When they subsided, he marched to attack Clausel in the centre, and as Soult was there in person a general battle seemed inevitable; but the movements on both sides were founded on mistakes, and the matter ended with a slight skirmish.

Harispe reinforced with Paris's division and Dauture's brigade then drove Mina with loss into the high mountains, surprised Morillo's foragers, and captured some English dragoons. Lord Wellington, fearing this warfare, put forth his authority in a vigorous manner to check the Spanish generals, and a sullen obedience followed, yet the Basque insurrection spread, and he therefore published a manifesto calling on the people to declare for war   or   peace, announcing his intention to burn their villages and put them to death if they continued insurgent—in fine, to treat them as the French generals had treated the insurgents in Spain. This stopped Harispe's efforts, and Soult, who now expected reinforcements and was desirous to resume the offensive with his whole army, ordered him to abandon his Peasant war, to concentrate his regular force and hem in the allies' right. Then Harispe, always daring and active, drove back all Morillo's foragers, and with them a body of English cavalry: at the same time one of Hill's cavalry posts on the left was cut off in retaliation for a French post which had been surprised by the sixth division, with circumstances entirely opposed to good feeling and to the generous habits long established between the light division and the French soldiers, of which the following are fine illustrations.

On the 9th of December, the 43rd was assembled within twenty yards of a French out-sentry, yet he continued his beat for an hour without concern, relying so confidently on the customary system as to place his knapsack on the ground. When the order to advance was given, one of the British soldiers told him to go away and helped him to replace his pack before the firing commmenced. Next morning the French in like manner warned a 43rd sentry to retire. At another time Lord Wellington, desirous to gain the top of a hill occupied by the enemy near Bayonne, ordered his escort of riflemen to drive the French away, and seeing the soldiers stealing up too close, as he thought, called out to fire, but with a loud voice one of those veterans replied, No Firing ! Holding up the butt of his rifle towards the French, he tapped it in a peculiar way, and at the private signal, which meaned, *We must have the hill for a short time,* the French, who could not maintain yet would not have relinquished it without a fight if they had been fired upon, quietly retired: yet this signal would never have been made if the post had been one capable of a permanent defence, so well did those veterans understand war and its proprieties.

Soult's conscripts were now deserting fast, and the inclemency of the weather filled his hospitals, while Wellington's bronzed soldiers, impassive to fatigue, patient to endure, fierce in execution, were free from serious maladies, ready and able to plant their colours wherever their general listed.

The country was however a vast quagmire; neither provisions nor orders could be conveyed to the different quarters; a Portuguese brigade was several days without food from the swelling of the rivulets, which stopped the commissariat mules. At the sea-side the troops were better off, yet with a horrible counterpoise; for on that iron-bound coast, storms and shipwrecks were so frequent, that scarcely a day passed without some vessel, sometimes many together, being seen embarked and drifting towards the reefs, which shoot out like needles for several miles. Once in that situation there was no human help ! A faint cry might be heard at intervals, but the tall ship floated solemnly onwards until the first rock arrested her, when a roaring surge would dash her to pieces and the shore was strewed with broken timbers and dead bodies. January was thus passed by the allies, but February saw Wellington break into France, the successful invader of that mighty country.

BOOK XV.

Passages of the Gaves and the Adour—Passage of the Gaves—Combat of Garris—Passage of the Adour—Passage of the Gaves continued Battle of Orthes—Combat of Aire.

PASSAGES OF THE GAVES AND THE ADOUR.

While the armies remained inactive, political difficulties accumulated on both sides in a strange manner. What those difficulties were and their causes must be sought for in the original History: this work treats only of battles. Yet their gravity will be understood when it is said, that Soult, surrounded with traitors and lukewarm friends, had his army again so reduced by drafts that he proposed to Napoleon, then driven from Germany and striving hard to defend France on the east, no longer to contend with Wellington in regular warfare, but to scatter his forces as great partizan corps in opposition to the invasion. On the other hand, Wellington seriously warned his Government that he looked to San Sebastian as a post where he should soon have to fight for an embarkation against the united French and Spanish armies ! In fine that the war could no longer be continued. Suddenly however his position was ameliorated by a change in the Spanish councils, by the approach of fine weather, and the simultaneous receipt of a large sum in gold, which enabled him again to employ the Spaniards in France with less danger of their plundering the country. He had sent before him the fame of a just discipline and wise consideration for the people, and there was indeed nothing he dreaded more than the insurgent warfare projected by Soult. Harispe's Basques had done him more mischief than the French army, the terrible menace of destroying their villages and killing all the male population, by which he stopped their warfare, marked his apprehensions, and he neglected no means of conciliation.

He permitted the local authorities to carry on the internal government, to take their salaries and raise the necessary taxes, and by opening the ports he drew a large commerce to support his army; he established many channels for intelligence, political and military, and would have extended his policy further if the English ministers had not abruptly and ignorantly interfered with his proceedings. Finally, foreseeing that his gold, being in foreign coin, would create embarrassment, he adopted an expedient which he had before practised in India; for knowing that in a British army a wonderful variety of vocations, good and bad, may be found, he secretly caused false coiners and die-sinkers to be sought for amongst the soldiers, and they, when assured no ill was designed for them, very readily acknowledged their peculiar talents. With these men he secretly coined gold Napoleons, marking them with a private stamp and carefully preserving their just fineness and weight, to enable the French government, when peace should be established, to call them in again. He thus avoided all the difficulties of exchange, and removed a fruitful source of quarrels between the troops and shopkeepers, the latter being always fastidious in taking and desirous of abating the real worth of strange coin; while the former attribute to fraud any declination from the value at which they receive their money. This sudden increase of current coin tended also to diminish the pressure necessarily attendant upon troubled times.

Nor was his provident sagacity less eminent in military than in administrative and political operations. During the bad weather he had formed large magazines at the ports, examined the course of the Adour, and carefully meditated on his plans. To penetrate France and rally a great Bourbon party under the protection of his army was the system he desired to follow; and though the last depended on the proceedings of the allied sovereigns, his own military operations would not clash, because to drive the French from Bayonne and blockade or besiege it were the first steps in either case.

That fortress and its citadel, comprising in their circuit the confluence of the Nive and the Adour, could not be safely invested with less than three times the number necessary to resist the garrison at any one point; and hence the whole must be so numerous as seriously to weaken the forces operating towards the interior. How and where to cross the Adour for the investment was also a subject of solicitude. It was a great river with a strong current, and well guarded by troops and gun-boats above Bayonne; still greater was it below the town, and there the ebb-tide run seven miles an hour; there also, gun-boats, a sloop of war, and armed merchant-vessels could be employed to interrupt the passage. To collect boats enough to bridge the stream above or below Bayonne, and the carriage of them, an immense operation in itself, would inevitably give notice of the design, unless the French army were first driven away; and even then the garrison of Bayonne, fifteen thousand men, might baffle the attempt. Nevertheless in the face of these difficulties he resolved to pass, his preparations being proportionate to the greatness of the design.

Many reasons concurred to make him throw his bridge below and not above Bayonne, and in that view he had collected at St. Jean de Luz forty large sailing-boats of from fifteen to thirty tons' burthen, called *chasse-marees*, as if for the commissariat service; but he had them secretly loaded with materials for his bridge, designing with naval aid to run up the Adour to a certain point, upon which the troops and artillery were to move; then with hawsers, and rafts made of pontoons, he designed to throw over a covering body, trusting that the greatness and danger of the attempt would lull suspicion. No obstacles deterred him. All the French trading vessels in the Adour had in January secretly offered to come out upon licenses and serve his commissariat; but he was compelled to forego that advantage by the silly meddling of the English ministers, which added greatly to the difficulty of his enterprise, inasmuch as it forced him, instead of receiving these men as friends and coadjutors, to prepare means for burning their vessels.

Soult was not less active in defensive measures. He had fortified all the main passes of the rivers on the great roads leading against his left; yet the diminution of his force in January had compelled him to withdraw his outposts from Anglet, which enabled Wellington to examine the whole course of the Adour below Bayonne and arrange for the passage with more facility. Soult then, in pursuance of Napoleon's system of warfare, which always prescribed a recourse to moral force to cover physical weakness, concentrated his left wing against the allies' right beyond the Nive, and renewed that harassing, partizan warfare already noticed, endeavouring to throw his adversary entirely upon the defensive.

He knew however he could not thus check the allies long; and judging Wellington would aim at Bordeaux and the line of the Garonne, while his own line of retreat must ultimately be in a parallel direction with the Pyrenees, he tried to organize in time a defensive system. In this view he sent Daricau, a native of the Landes, to prepare an insurgent levy in that wilderness, and directed Maransin to the High Pyrenees to extend the insurrection of the mountaineers, already commenced in the Lower Pyrenees by Harispe.

At Bordeaux there was a small reserve, which he urged the Minister of War to increase with conscripts from the interior, and he sent artillery men there, ordering various dispositions: but there was no public spirit awakened and treason was rife in that city.

On the side of the Lower Pyrenees he improved the works of Navarrens, and designed an entrenched camp; the castle of Lourdes in the High Pyrenees was already defensible, and he gave orders to fortify the castle of Pau, thus providing supporting points for a retreat. At Mauleon he put on foot partizan corps, and had hopes of forming a reserve of seven or eight thousand national guards, gens d'armes and artillerymen at Tarbes. Dax, containing his principal depots, was being fortified, and the communication with it maintained across the rivers by bridges, with bridge-heads at Port de Lannes, Hastingues, Peyrehorade, and Sauveterre; but in the beginning of February floods carried away that at Port de Lannes, and the communication between Bayonne and the left of the army was thus interrupted until he established a flying bridge.

Such was his situation when Wellington retook the offensive, with one hundred and twenty thousand infantry and fifteen thousand cavalry, as Soult supposed; for he knew not of the political and financial difficulties which had reduced the English general's power and prevented the junction of the reinforcements expected. His emissaries told him that Clinton's Catalonian force was broken up, and the British part in march to join Wellington; that the garrisons of Carthagena, Cadiz and Ceuta were at hand, and reinforcements were coming from England and Portugal. This made him conclude there was no intention of pressing the war in Catalonia, and that all would be united to march against him; wherefore with more earnestness than before he urged that Suchet should be ordered to join him, that their united forces might form a dike against the torrent which threatened to overwhelm the south of France. The real power opposed to him was however much below these calculations. Twenty thousand British and Portuguese had been promised by their governments, but did not arrive; Clinton's army was still in Catalonia; the regular Spanish forces available, and that only partially on account of their licentious conduct, did not exceed thirty thousand; the Anglo-Portuguese were but seventy thousand, with ninety five pieces of artillery.

Soult, exclusive of his garrisons and detachments at Bordeaux and in the High Pyrenees, exclusive also of the conscripts of the second levy which were now beginning to arrive, had only thirty-five thousand soldiers of all arms, three thousand being cavalry, with forty pieces of artillery. But Bayonne alone, without reference to St. Jean Pied de Port and Navarrens, occupied twenty-eight thousand of the allies; and by this and other drains Wellington's superiority was so reduced, that his penetrating into France, that France which had made all Europe tremble at her arms, must be viewed as a surprising example of courage and fine conduct, military and political.

PASSAGE OF THE GAVES.

In the second week of February the weather set in with a strong frost, and the English general advanced, precisely at the moment when General Paris had marched with a convoy from Navarrens to make a last effort for the relief of Jaca in Spain, where a French garrison still remained. But clothing for the troops, which had been long negligently delayed in   England, arrived at that moment also, and the regiments, wanting the means of carriage, had to march for it to the coast. The first design was therefore restricted to turning the French left by the sources of the rivers with Hill's corps, marching by the roots of the Pyrenees; Beresford meanwhile keeping the centre in check upon the lower parts of the same rivers, in hope that Soult's attention would thus be attracted while the passage of the Adour was being made below Bayonne. It would seem also, that uncertain if he should be able to force the passage of the tributary rivers with his right, Wellington intended, if his bridge was happily thrown, to push his main operations in that quarter, turning the Gaves by the right bank of the Adour: a fine conception by which his superiority of numbers would have best availed him to seize Dax and the Port de Landes, and cut Soult off from Bordeaux.

Events frustrated this plan. On the 14th Hill, having twenty thousand combatants and sixteen guns, marched in two columns; one to drive Clausel's posts beyond the Joyeuse, another by the great road of St. Jean Pied de Port against Harispe. This last body had the Ursouia mountain on its right, while beyond it Morillo marched against the same point. Harispe, who had only three brigades, principally conscripts, retired skirmishing in the direction of St. Palais. The line of the Joyeuse was thus turned by the allies, the direct communication with St. Jean Pied de Port was out, that place was invested by Mina's battalions, and on the 15th Hill, leaving a regiment to observe the road of St. Jean, marched upon Garris, pushing back Harispe's rearguard.

Soult knew of the intended operations on the 12th, but hearing the allies had collected boats and constructed a fresh battery near Urt on the Upper Adour, and that the pontoons had reached Urcurray, thought Wellington's design was to turn his left with Hill's corps, to press him on the Bidouze with Beresford's, and keep Bayonne in check with the Spaniards, while Hope crossed the Adour *above* that fortress. Wherefore, when Hill's movement commenced, he resolved to dispute the passage of the Bidouze, and the two Gaves of Mauleon and Oleron in succession. He had already four divisions on the Bidouze, and he recalled Paris to post him between St. Palais and St. Jean Pied de Port in observation of Mina, whom he supposed to be stronger than he was.

COMBAT OF GARRIS.

Harispe, having Paris under his orders, and supported by Pierre Soult with a brigade of light cavalry, now covered the road from St. Jean with his left, the upper line of the Bidouze with his right; from thence Villatte, Taupin and Foy were extended to its confluence with the Adour. Hill moved against Harispe. The latter had just occupied in advance of the Bidouze a ridge called the Garris mountain, which stretched to St. Palais, when his rear-guard came plunging into a deep ravine in his front, closely followed by the light troops of the second division. Upon the parallel counter-ridge thus gained, General Hill immediately established himself, and though the evening was beginning to close his skirmishers descended into the ravine, while two guns played over it upon four thousand men, arrayed on the opposite mountain by Harispe. In this state of affairs Wellington arrived. He was anxious to turn the line of the Bidouze before Soult could strengthen himself there, and seeing the communication with General Paris, by St. Palais, was not well maintained, sent Morillo along the ridge towards that place; then menacing Harispe's centre with Le Cor's Portuguese division, he directed Pringle's brigade to attack, saying with concise energy *"The hill must be taken before dark."*

This expression caught the fancy of the soldiers, and was repeated by Colonel O'Callaghan, as he and Pringle placed themselves at the head of the 39th, which, followed by the 28th, immediately rushed with loud and prolonged shouts into the ravine. Pringle fell wounded, and most of the mounted officers had their horses killed; but the troops, covered by the thick wood, gained the summit of the Garris mountain, on the right of the enemy, who thinking from the shouting that a larger force was coming retreated. The 39th then wheeled to their right, intending to sweep the summit, when the French, discovering their error, came back at a charging pace and receiving a volley without flinching tried the bayonet. O'Callaghan, distinguished for strength and courage, had two strokes from that weapon, but repaid them with fatal power in each instance, and the French, nearly all conscripts, were beaten off. Twice however they came back, and fought until the fire of the 28th was beginning to be felt, when Harispe, seeing the remainder of the second division ready to support the attack, Le Cor advancing against his centre, Morillo in march towards St. Palais, retreated to that town, and calling in Paris broke down the bridges over the Bidouze. He lost altogether five hundred men, two hundred being taken, and would hardly have escaped if Morillo had not been slow. The allies lost one hundred and sixty, most of them in the bayonet contest.

During these operations Picton, marching on Hill's left, menaced Villatte; but Beresford, though his scouting parties, on the left of Picton, approached the Bidouze, facing Taupin and Foy, remained on the Joyeuse, as the pivot upon which Wellington's right was to sweep round the French positions. Foy however had observed the movement of two other divisions, pointing as he thought towards the French left, and his reports to that effect reached Soult at the moment the latter received notice that St. Jean Pied de Port was invested. Thinking then that Wellington would not attempt to pass the Adour above Bayonne, but win his way to that river by constantly turning the French left, he made new dispositions.

His line on the Bidouze was strong, yet too extended, and he resolved to abandon that and the Mauleon for the Gave d'Oleron, placing his right at Peyrehorade, his left at Navarrens. Villatte therefore took post at Sauveterre on the Oleron where the bridge had a well-fortified head; from thence Taupin lined the right bank to the confluence of the Gave de Pan, which Foy guarded from Peyrehorade to its confluence with the Adour, his front being prolonged by D'Erlon towards Dax. One brigade of cavalry was in reserve at Sauveterre and the head-quarters went to Orthes. But the magazines of ammunition were at Bayonne, Navarrens, and Dax; and Soult, seeing his communications with all those places likely to be intercepted before he could remove his stores, wrote to the minister of war to form new depots.

On the 16th Wellington repaired the broken bridges of St.

Palais, and after a skirmish Hill crossed the Bidouze, but the day was spent in the operation. Meanwhile the centre divisions passed the Joyeuse.

The 17th Hill advanced towards the Mauleon, while Picton, on his left, made for the heights of Somberraute, both corps converging upon General Paris, who, in defence of the Mauleon Gave, attempted to destroy the bridge of Arriveriete. Lord Wellington was too quick. The 92nd regiment, covered by the fire of some guns, passed at a ford above, and beating two French battalions from the village secured the passage. The troops halted there, having marched only five miles, and though Paris relinquished the Gave he did not retire until the morning of the 18th. The allies then seized the main road between Sauveterre and Navarrens on the left bank of the Oleron Gave, while Harispe, Villatte, and Paris, supported by a brigade of cavalry, concentrated at Sauveterre; Taupin was lower down on their right; Foy on the right of Taupin; D'Erlon on the left of the Adour, above its confluence with the Gave de Pau.

Soult, thrown from the commencement of the operations entirely upon the defensive, was now at a loss to discover his adversary's object. In this uncertainty, sending Pierre Soult with a cavalry brigade and two battalions of infantry to act between Oleron and Pau and communicate with the partisan corps forming at Mauleon, he decided to hold the Gaves as long as he could; and, when they were forced, concentrate his army at Orthes and fall upon the first of the converging columns that approached. He had considered every likely movement, as he thought, and his conjectures had indeed embraced every plan of operation possible, except the one contemplated by his adversary, namely, the stupendous bridge over the Adour *below* Bayonne. That was now to be done, and Wellington designed to superintend the casting of it in person; hence, when he had established his right strongly beyond the Mauleon and Bidouze rivers and knew his pontoons were well advanced, he returned rapidly to St. Jean de Luz. Everything there depending on man was ready, but the weather was boisterous with snow for two days, and Wellington, fearful of letting Soult strengthen himself on the Gave of Oleron, returned on the 21st to Garris, deciding to press his operations on that side in person and leave Hope and Admiral Penrose to throw the bridge.

PASSAGE OF THE ADOUR.

Hope had twenty-eight thousand men and twenty pieces of artillery, and in the night of the 22nd the first division, with six eighteen-pounders and a rocket battery, cautiously filed towards the river; the road was deep and one of the guns falling into a ditch delayed the march, yet at daybreak the whole reached some sand-downs which lined the river bank. The French picquets were then driven into the intrenched camp, the pontoon train and field-artillery came down opposite the village of Boucaut, and the eighteen poun-ders were placed in battery on the bank. The light troops, meanwhile, closed to the edge of the marsh covering Vauban's camp; and from Arcangues and Urdains the enemy's attention was attracted by false attacks, which were prolonged beyond the Nive by the fifth division.

The gun-boats and chasse-marees should have reached the mouth of the Adour at the time the troops reached the bank; but the wind was contrary and none were seen. Hope, whose firmness no untoward event could ever shake, then resolved to try the passage with the army alone; the French flotilla opened fire on his columns, but his artillery and rockets retorted so fiercely that three of the gun-boats were destroyed, and the sloop so hardly handled that about one o'clock the whole took refuge higher up the river. Sixty men of the guards were then rowed in pontoons across the mouth of the river in the face of a French picquet, which, seemingly bewildered, retired without firing. A raft was formed with the remainder of the pontoons, a hawser was stretched across, and Colonel Stopford passed with six hundred of the guards, the 60th Regiment, and some rockets: yet slowly and at slack water, for the tide ran strongly and the waters were wide.

General Thouvenot, deceived by spies and prisoners, thought the light division was with Hope as well as the first division, and that fifteen thousand men had been embarked at St. Jean de Luz to land between Cape Breton and the Adour; he feared therefore to send a strong force to any distance; and when he heard of Stopford's detachment on the right bank, detached only two battalions under Macomble to gain information, because a pine-forest and the bending of the river prevented him from obtaining a view from Bayonne. Macomble menaced Stopford, but the latter, flanked by the field artillery on the other bank, received him with a discharge of rockets; projectiles which, like the elephants in ancient warfare, often turn upon their own side: this time, amenable to their directors, they smote the French column and it fled amazed with a loss of thirty wounded. It is however obvious that if Thouvenot had kept strong guards with a field-battery on the right bank of the Adour, Hope could not have passed his troops in pontoons, no vessels could have crossed the bar, and to disembark troops between the river and Cape Breton must have been attempted. This error was fatal to the French. The British remained unmolested until twelve o'clock on the 24th, and then the long expected flotilla was seen under a press of sail making with a strong breeze for the mouth of the river.

To enter the Adour is, from the flatness of the coast, never an easy task; it was now most difficult; the high winds of the preceding days had raised a great sea, and the enemy had removed one of the guiding flag-staves by which the navigation was ordinarily directed. In front of the flotilla came the boats of the men of war, and the naval captain, O'Reilly, ran his craft, a chosen Spanish vessel, first into the midst of the breakers, which rolling in a frightful manner over the bar dashed her on to the beach. That brave officer, stretched senseless on the shore, would have perished with all his crew but for the ready succour of the soldiers; some were drowned, but the remainder with an intrepid spirit launched their boat again to aid the passage.

O'Reilly had been followed successfully by Lieutenant Debenham in a six-oared cutter, but the tide was then falling, and the remainder of the boats, the impossibility of passing until high water being evident, drew off and a pilot was landed to direct the line of navigation by concerted signals. When the flood again came, the crews being promised rewards in proportion to their successful daring, the whole flotilla approached in close order; with it however came black clouds and a driving gale which sent along the whole coast a rough tumbling sea, dashing and foaming without an interval of dark water to mark the entrance of the river. The men-of-war's boats first drew near this terrible surge, and Mr. Bloye of the Lyra, having the chief pilot with him, heroically led into it, but in an instant his barge was ingulfed and he and all with him were drowned. The following vessels seeing the Lyra's boat thus swallowed swerved in their course, and shooting up to the right and left kept hovering undecided on the edge of the tormented waters. Suddenly Lieutenant Cheyne of the Woodlark pulled ahead, and striking the right line with courage and fortune combined, safely passed the bar. The wind then lulled, the waves as if conquered abated somewhat of their rage, and the chasse-marees, manned with Spanish seamen, but having an engineer officer with a party of sappers in each who compelled them to follow the men-of-war's boats, came plunging one after another through the huge breakers and reached the point designed for the bridge. Thus was achieved this perilous and glorious exploit. Not without more loss. Captain Elliot of the Martial, with his crew and the crews of three transports' boats, perished close to the shore in despite of the most violent efforts made by the troops to save them; three other vessels, cast on the beach, lost part of their crews; and one large chasse-maree, full of men, after passing the line of surf safely, was overtaken by a swift bellying wave which broke on her deck and dashed her to pieces.

Eight thousand men were now on the right bank. They remained in the sand-hills for the night, and next morning, sweeping in a half-circle round the citadel and its entrenchments, placed their left on the Adour above the fortress, their right on the same river below; the water however made such a bend that their front was little more than two miles wide, and for the most part covered by a marshy ravine. This nice operation was effected without opposition, because the Vauban camps, menaced by the troops on the other side of the Adour, were so extensive that Thouvenot's force was scarcely sufficient to maintain them. The bridge was then constructed three miles below Bayonne, at a place where the river was contracted to eight hundred feet by strong retaining walls, built with the view of sweeping away the bar by increasing the force of the current. Bridge and boom were the joint conception of Colonel Sturgeon and Major Todd of the Staff corps; but the execution was confided entirely to the latter, who, with a mind less brilliant than Sturgeon's, yet more indefatigable, very ably and usefully served his country throughout this war.

Twenty-six chasse-marees, moored head and stern at distances of forty feet, were first bound together with ropes; two thick cables were then carried loosely across their decks, the ends, cast over the walls on each bank, being strained and fastened in various modes to the sands. They were sufficiently slack to meet the spring-tides, which rose fourteen feet, and planks were tied upon them without any supporting beams. The boom, moored with anchors above and below, was a double line of masts connected with chains and cables, so as to form a succession of squares, in the design, if a vessel broke through the outside, that it should by the shock turn round in the square and get entangled with the floating wrecks of the line it had broken. Gun-boats, with aiding batteries on the banks, were then stationed to protect the boom, and to keep off fire-vessels, row-boats were furnished with grappling irons. The whole was by the united labour of seamen and soldiers finished on the 26th, and, contrary to the general opinion on such matters, Major Todd assured the Author of this History that he found the soldiers, with minds quickened by the wider range of knowledge attendant on their service, more ready of resource, and their efforts under a regular discipline of more avail, with less loss of time, than the irregular activity of the seamen. But fortune, the errors of the enemy, the matchless skill and daring of the British seamen, and the discipline and intrepidity of the British soldiers, combined by the genius of Wellington, were all necessary to the success of this stupendous undertaking, which must always rank amongst the prodigies of war.

When the bridge was finished Hope contracted the line of investment, a difficult operation, for the position of the French outside the citadel was exceedingly strong. The flanks were protected by ravines, the sides of which were covered with fortified villas, the front being on a ridge, crowned by the village and church of St. Etienne, both dominant, strongly entrenched, and under the fire of the citadel. Three converging columns, covered by skirmishers, were employed, and the wings attained the edges of the ravines at either side, their flanks resting on the Adour above and below; but a very vigorous action happened in the centre. The German and a brigade of guards were to attack simultaneously, the guards on the left, the light German troops on the right, their heavy infantry in the centre; some accident retarded the wings, and St. Etienne being first attacked the citadel guns opened and the skirmishing fire was heavy; yet the Germans stormed church and village, forced the entrenched line of houses, and took a gun, which however they could not carry off under the fire of the citadel. The action then ceased for a time, but the people of Bayonne were in such consternation that Thouvenot to re-assure them sallied at the head of the troops, charged the Germans twice, and fought well; he was however wounded and finally lost a gun and the position of St. Etienne: the British loss was however not less than five hundred men and officers.

PASSAGE OF THE GAVES CONTINUED.

While Hope passed the Adour, Wellington pushed his operations on the Gaves with great vigour. Six divisions of infantry and two brigades of cavalry were concentrated on the Gave d'Oleron, between Sauveterre and Navarrens. Beresford lined the Bidouze to its confluence with the Adour, and the 23rd drove Foy from his works on the lower parts of the Oleron Gave, into the bridge-head at Peyrehorade. Soult's right and centre were thus held in check, and the rest of his army was at Orthes and Sauveterre.

On the 24th Wellington advanced to force the Gave d'Oleron. During the previous days his movements had again deceived Soult, who thought the light division was with Hope, and imagined the first division was with Beresford; he did not expect however to hold the Gave, and looked to a final concentration at Orthes.

On the 24th also, Morillo, reinforced with a detachment of cavalry, moved towards Navarrens, where rough ground concealed his real force while his scouters beat back the French outposts; then a battalion menaced the fords of the Gave at Doguen, with a view to draw the attention of the garrison from the ford of Ville Nave, three miles below, where Wellington designed really to pass. For that object a great concentric movement was now in progress. Favoured by the hilly nature of the country, which concealed all the columns, the sixth division moved towards the ford of Montfort, three miles below that of Ville Nave, while a battalion of the second division menaced the ford of Barraute below Montfort. Picton marched against the bridge-head of Sauveterre, with orders to make a feint of forcing the passage there. Vivian's hussars, coming up from Beresford's right, threatened other fords upon Picton's left, and Beresford, keeping Foy in check at Peyrehorade with the seventh division, sent the fourth above the confluence of the waters to seek a fit place to throw a bridge. Thus the French front was menaced on a line of twenty-five miles, but the great force was above Sauveterre.

The first operations were not happily executed. Some of the columns missed the fords, and Picton, opening a cannonade at Sauveterre, made four companies of Keane's brigade and some cavalry pass the Gave in the vicinity of the bridge; but they were driven back with a loss of ninety men and officers, of whom some were drowned and thirty made prisoners: the diversion was however complete and the general operations successful. Soult on the first alarm drew Harispe from Sauveterre, placing him on the road to Orthes where a range of hills parallel to the Gave of Oleron separates it from the Gave of Pau; only a division of infantry and Berton's cavalry then remained at Sauveterre, and Villatte, alarmed by Picton's demonstrations, abandoned his works on the left bank and destroyed the bridge. Meanwhile the sixth division passed without opposition at Montfort above Sauveterre, and the main body, meeting at the ford of Ville Nave with only a small cavalry picquet, crossed with no more loss than two men drowned: a happy circumstance, for the waters were deep and rapid, the cold intense, and the ford so narrow the passage was not completed before dark. To have forced it in face of an enemy would have been exceedingly difficult; and it is remarkable that Soult, who was with Harispe only five miles from

Monfort and seven from Ville Nave, should not have sent that general down to oppose either passage.

On the 25th at daylight, Wellington pushed the French rear-guard into the suburb of Orthes, which masked the bridge there, and the Portuguese of the light division lost twenty-five men in the skirmish. The second, sixth, and light divisions, Hamilton's Portuguese, five regiments of cavalry, and three batteries, were now massed in front of Orthes; the third division and a brigade of cavalry were in front of the broken bridge of Berenx five miles lower down the Gave; the fourth and seventh divisions, with Vivian's cavalry were in front of Peyrehorade, from whence Foy retired to Orthes.

On the morning of the 26th, Beresford, finding Foy had abandoned Peyrehorade, passed the Gave, partly by a pontoon bridge, partly by a ford where the current ran so strong that a column was like to have been carried away bodily; but he had previously detached the 18th Hussars to find another ford higher up, which was effected under the guidance of a miller, and the hussars gaining the high road to Orthes drove some French cavalry through Puyoo. There they rallied on their reserves and beat back the foremost of the pursuers; yet they would not await the shock of the main body, now reinforced by Vivian's brigade and commanded by Beresford in person. In this affair Major Sewell, an officer of the staff, who had frequently manifested his personal prowess, being without a sword, pulled a large stake from a hedge and with that weapon overthrew two hussars in succession, only ceasing to fight when a third cut his club in twain. Beresford now threw out a detachment on his left to intercept the enemy's communication with Dax, and Wellington sent Lord Edward Somerset's cavalry with the third division across the Gave, by some fords. below the broken bridge of Berenx. Then directing Beresford to take a position for the night on some heights near the village of Baights, he proceeded to throw a pontoon bridge at Berenx; and thus after a circuitous march of more than fifty miles with his right wing, and the passage of five Gaves, he had again united it with his centre and secured a direct communication with Hope.

The bridge of Orthes, an ancient and beautiful structure,

could not be easily forced. Composed of irregular arches, it had a tower in the centre, the gateway of which was built up, and the principal arch in front of the tower was mined, the houses on both sides contributing to the defence. The river immediately above and below the bridge was deep, and full of needle-rocks; but above the town the water, spreading wide, with flat bank presented the means of crossing. Wellington's first design was to pass there with Hill's troops and the light division, but when he heard Beresford had crossed the Gave below, he suddenly threw his bridge at Berenx. This operation was covered by Beresford, while Soult's attention was diverted by a continual skirmish at the suburbs of Orthes; by the appearance of Hill's columns above the town; and by Wellington's taking cognizance of the position near the bridge so openly as to draw a cannonade. The latter thought that when Soult knew Beresford and Picton were over the Gave he would not await a battle, and the emissaries reported that he was already in retreat; a circumstance to be borne in mind, because next day's operation required success to justify it.

Hope's happy passage of the Adour now became known and he was instructed to establish a line of communication to the port of Lannes, where a permanent bridge was to be formed with boats brought up from Urt; a direct intercourse was thus secured; yet Wellington felt he was going beyond his strength if Suchet should send reinforcements to Soult; wherefore he called up Freyre's Spaniards, who were to cross the Adour below Bayonne and join him by the port of Lannes. O'Donnel's Andalusians and the Prince of Anglona's troops were also directed to be in readiness to enter France. These orders were given with great reluctance. The feeble resistance made by the French in the difficult country already passed, left him without much uneasiness as to the power of Soult's army in the field, but his disquietude was extreme about the danger of an insurgent warfare.

" *Maintain the strictest discipline, without that we are lost,*" was his expression to Freyre; and he issued a proclamation authorizing the people of the districts he had overrun to arm themselves for the preservation of order under the direction of their mayors. He invited them to arrest all straggling soldiers and followers of the army soldiers and followers of the army, all plunderers and evil doers, and convey them to head-quarters with proof of their crimes, promising to punish the culpable and pay for all damages. At the same time he confirmed all the local authorities who chose to retain their offices: on the sole condition of having no political or military intercourse with the countries still possessed by the French army. Nor was his proclamation a dead letter. In the night of the 25th the inhabitants of a village, near the road leading from Sauveterre to Orthes, shot one English soldier dead and wounded a second who had come with others to plunder. Wellington caused the wounded man to be hung as an example, and also forced an English colonel to quit the army for suffering his soldiers to destroy the municipal archives of a small town.

Soult had no thought of retreating. His army was concentrated, and every bridge except that at Orthes, the ancient masonry of which resisted his mines, was destroyed. One regiment of cavalry was on his right, watching the fords as far as Peyrehorade; three others, with two battalions of infantry, under Pierre Soult, watched those between Orthes and Pau. Two regiments of cavalry remained with the army, and the design was to fall upon the first column which should cross the Gave. But the officer at Puyoo, who had suffered Vivian's hussars to pass on the 26th without opposition, made no report of the event, which enabled Beresford to complete his movement unmolested, instead of being assailed by t wo-thirds of the French army. It was not until three o'clock in the evening that Soult knew of his being over the Gave, although he was then close on the flank of the French army, his scouters being on the Dax road in its rear: and at the same time the sixth and light divisions were seen descending from the heights beyond the river pointing towards Berenx.

In this crisis the French marshal hesitated whether to fall upon Beresford and Picton while the latter was still passing the river, or take a defensive position. Finally, judging he had not time to form an attack, he decided upon the latter, and under cover of a skirmish, hastily threw his army on a new line across the road from Peyreho-rade. His right extended to the heights of San Boes, along which ran the road from Orthes to Dax; and the line was prolonged on the left to Castetarbe, a village close to the Gave. Having thus opposed a temporary front to Beresford, he made dispositions to receive battle next morning, bringing Villatte's infantry and Pierre Soult's cavalry from the other side of Orthes through that town: it was this movement that led Wellington's emissaries to say he was retiring.

Soult's position was on a ridge of hills, partly wooded, partly naked.

In the centre was an open rounded hill, from whence long narrow tongues shot out towards the high-road of Peyrehorade on the left; on the right by St. Boes, towards the church of Baights; the whole presented a concave front covered with a marshy ravine, which was crossed by two shorter necks coming from the round hill in the centre.

The road from Orthes to Dax passed behind the line to the village of St. Boes; and behind the centre a succession of undulating bare heathy hills trended for several miles to the rear.

Behind the right the country was low and deep; but Orthes, receding from the river up the slope of a steep hill, was behind the left wing.

Reille, having Taupin's, Roguet's, and Paris's divisions under him, commanded on the right, holding the ground from St. Boes to the centre.

D'Erlon, commanding Foy's and D'Armagnac's divisions, was on Reille's left, extending along a ridge towards the road of Peyrehorade—the second being in reserve. Villatte's division and the cavalry were posted above the village of Rontun, on open heathy hills, from whence they overlooked the low country beyond St. Boes, and furnished a reserve to both D'Erlon and Reille.

Harispe, whose troops as well as Villatte's were under Clausel's orders, occupied Orthes and the bridge, having a regiment near the ford of Souars above the town. Thus the French army extended from St. Boes to Orthes, but the great mass was disposed towards the centre. Twelve guns were attached to Harispe, twelve were upon the round hill in the centre, sweeping the ground beyond St. Boes, sixteen were in reserve on the Dax road.

At daybreak on the 27th, the sixth and light divisions, having passed the Gave near Berenx, by a pontoon bridge thrown in the night, wound up a narrow way between high rocks to the great road of Peyrehorade, and the third division, with Lord Edward Somerset's cavalry, were already established there, having skirmishers pushed forwards to the edge of the wooded height occupied by D' Erlon's left. Beresford, having the fourth and seventh divisions and Vivian's cavalry, then gained the ridge of St. Boes and approached the Dax road beyond. Hill, with his own British and Le Cor's Portuguese division, menaced the bridge of Orthes, and the ford of Souars from the left bank. Between Beresford and Picton, a mile and a half, there were no troops; but half-way, in front of the French centre, was a Roman camp crowning an isolated peering hill nearly as lofty as the centre of Soult's position.

On this camp, now covered with vineyards, but then open and grassy, with a few trees, Wellington stopped for an hour to examine the enemy's order of battle; his two divisions were then coming up from the river, yet so hemmed in by rocks that only a few men could march abreast, and their point of union with the third division was little more than cannon-shot from the French left. It was a critical moment, and Picton did not conceal his disquietude; but Wellington, imperturbable, continued his observations without seeming to notice his dangerous position. When the troops reached the main road he reinforced Picton with the sixth, and drew the light division by cross roads behind the Roman camp, thus connecting his wings and forming a central reserve; because from that point byeways led, on the left to the church of Baights and the Dax road; on the right to the Peyrehorade road; and two others led by the low necks across the marsh to the French position.

This marsh, the open hill, where Soult's guns and reserves were gathered, and the narrow tongues on either side, combined to forbid a front attack, and the flanks were scarcely more promising. The ridge occupied by the French left sunk indeed to a gentle undulation in crossing the Peyrehorade road; yet to push there between D'Erlon and Orthes would have been useless, because that town was strongly occupied by Harispe, and covered by an ancient wall. To turn the St. Boes flank the troops must have descended into the low marshy country beyond the Dax road, where the heathy hills trending backwards from the centre of the French position would have enabled Soult to oppose a new front, at right angles to his actual position; the whole of the allied army must then have made a circuitous flank movement within gun-shot, through a difficult country, or Beresford's left must have been dangerously extended and the whole line weakened. Nor could the movement be hidden, because the hills, although only moderately high, were abrupt on that side, affording a full view of the low country, and Soult's cavalry detachments were in observation on every brow.

It only remained to assail the French flanks along the narrow ridges, making the principal effort at St. Boes, and overlapping the French right to seize the road to St. Sever, while Hill passed the Gave at Souars and cut off the road to Pau, thus enclosing the beaten army in Orthes. This was no slight affair. On Picton's side it was easy to obtain a footing on the flank ridge near the high road; but beyond that the ground rose rapidly, and the French were gathered thickly with a narrow front and plenty of guns. On Beresford's side they could only be assailed along the summit of the St. Boes ridge, advancing from the high church of Baights and the Dax road; but the village of St. Boes was strongly occupied, the ground immediately behind it strangled to a narrow pass; and sixteen guns on the Dax road, placed behind the centre of Soult's line and well covered from counter-fire, were ready to crush any column emerging from the gorge of St. Boes.

BATTLE OF ORTHES.

From daybreak there had been a slight skirmish, with occasional cannon-shots on the allies' right, and the French cavalry at times pushed parties forward on each flank; but at nine o'clock Wellington commenced the real attack. The third and sixth divisions won without difficulty the lower part of the ridges occupied by Foy, and endeavoured to extend their left towards the French centre with a sharp fire of musketry; yet the main battle was on the other flank. There Cole, keeping Anson's brigade of the fourth division in reserve, had assailed St. Boes with Ross's British brigade and Vasconcellos' Portuguese, his object being to get on to the open ground beyond. Fierce and slaughtering was the struggle; five times breaking through the scattered houses did Ross carry his battle into the wider space beyond; but ever as his troops emerged the French guns from the centre hill smote them in front, and the reserved battery on the Dax road swept through them with grape from flank to flank; while Taupin's supporting masses, rushing forward with a wasting fire and lapping the flanks with skirmishers, which poured along the ravines on either hand, forced the shattered columns back into the village. It was in vain that with desperate valour the allies broke time after time through the narrow way and strived to spread a front beyond: Ross fell dangerously wounded, and Taupin's troops, thickly clustered and well supported, defied every effort. Nor was Soult less happy on the other side. From the narrowness of the ground the third and sixth divisions could only engage a few men at once, no progress was made; one small detachment, which Picton extended to his left, attempting to gain the smaller tongue jutting out from the central hill, was very suddenly charged as it neared the summit, by Foy, and driven down again in confusion, losing several prisoners.

When the combat had continued with unabated fury on the side of St. Boes for three hours, Wellington sent a caçadore regiment of the light division from the Roman camp to protect the right flank of Ross's brigade against the French skirmishers; this was of no avail, for the Portuguese already there under Vasconcellos being unable to sustain the violence of the enemy, had given way in disorder, and the French pouring on, the British troops retreated through St. Boes with difficulty. This happened at the moment when the detachment on Picton's left was repulsed, victory seemed to declare for the French, and Soult, conspicuous on his central hill, the knot of all his combinations, seeing his enemies thus broken and thrown backwards on each side, put all his reserves in movement to complete the success. It is said that in the exultation of the moment he smote his thigh, exclaiming, ~'At last I have him." And it was no vain glorious speech, the crisis seemed to justify the exultation.

There was however a small black cloud rising just beneath, unheeded by the French commander amidst the thundering din and tumult that now shook the field of battle, but which soon burst with irresistible violence.

Wellington, seeing St. Boes was inexpugnable, had suddenly changed his plan of battle. Supporting Ross with Anson's brigade, which had not hitherto been engaged, he backed both with the seventh division and Vivian's cavalry, thus establishing a very heavy body towards the Dax road. Then he ordered the third and sixth divisions to be thrown in mass upon the French left, and at the same time sent the 52nd Regiment down from the Roman camp, with instructions to cross the marsh in front, mount the French position, and assail the flank and rear of the troops engaged with the fourth division at St. Boes. Colonel Colborne, so often distinguished, immediately led this regiment across the marsh under a skirmishing fire, the men sinking at every step above the knees, in some places to the middle; yet still pressing forwards with that stern resolution and order to be expected from the veterans of the light division, soldiers who had never yet met their match in the field, they soon obtained footing on firm land, and ascended the heights in line at the moment when Taupin, on the French right, was pushing vigorously through St. Boes; and when Foy and D'Armagnac, hitherto more than masters of their positions, were being assailed on the left by the third and sixth divisions.

With a mighty shout and a rolling fire the 52nd soldiers dashed forwards between Foy and Taupin, beating down a French battalion in their course and throwing everything before them into disorder. General Bechaud was killed, Foy was dangerously wounded, and his troops, discouraged by his fall and by this sudden storm from a quarter where no enemy was expected, for the march of the 52nd had been hardly perceived save by the skirmishers, got into confusion, and the disorder spreading to Reille's wing, he also was forced to fall back and take a new position. The narrow pass behind St. Boes was thus opened, and Wellington, seizing the critical moment, thrust the fourth and seventh divisions, Vivian's cavalry, and two batteries of artillery through, and spread a front beyond. Victory was thus secured. For the third and sixth divisions on the other flank had won D'Armagnac's position and established a battery of guns on a knoll, from whence the bullets ploughed through the French masses from one flank to another; and though a squadron of French chasseurs, coming suddenly at a hard gallop down the main road of Orthes, charged these guns and rode over some of the sixth division which had advanced too far, their brave career was too madly pushed, they got entangled in a hollow way and nearly all destroyed. The third and seventh divisions then advanced and the wings of the army were united.

Soult now concentrated his forces on the heathy hills beyond the Dax road, and with Taupin's, Roguet's, Paris's, and D'Armagnac's divisions made strong battle to cover the rallying of Foy's disordered men. But his foes were not all in front. Hill, having twelve thousand combatants, received orders, when Wellington changed his plan of attack, to force the passage of the Gave, partly to prevent Harispe from falling upon the flank of the sixth division, partly in hope of a successful issue: and so it happened. Unable to force the bridge, he forded the river above, at Souars, drove back the troops there, seized the heights, cut off the French from the road to Pau, and turned the town of Orthes. He thus menaced Soult's only line of retreat by Salespice, on the road to St. Sever, at the moment the junction of the allies' wings was effected on the French position. Clausel, so pressed, made Harispe abandon Orthes and close towards Villatte on the heights above Rontun, leaving however some conscript battalions on a rising point near the road of St. Sever called the Motte de Turenne, while in person he endeavoured to check Hill with two cavalry regiments and a brigade of infantry.

Soult, seeing that Hill's passage at Souars rendered the whole position untenable, now gave orders for a general retreat. This was a perilous matter. The heathy hills upon which he was now fighting, furnished for a short distance a succession of parallel positions favourable for defence, but then resolved themselves into a low ridge running to the rear on a line parallel with the road to St. Sever; and on the opposite side of that road, at cannon-shot distance, was a corresponding ridge along which Hill, judging by the firing how matters went, was now rapidly advancing. Five miles off was the *Luy de Bearn*, and four miles further on the *Luy de France*, two rivers deep and with difficult banks. Beyond them the Lutz, the Gabas, and the Adour crossed the line; and though once beyond the wooden bridge of Sault de Navailles on the *Luy de Bearn,* these streams would necessarily cover the retreat, it seemed impossible to carry off by one road and one bridge a defeated army still closely engaged in front. Soult did so however. For Paris sustained the fight on his right until Foy and Taupin's troops rallied, and when the impetuous assault of the 52nd and a rush of the fourth and seventh divisions, drove Paris back, D'Armagnac interposed to cover him until the union of the allies' wings was completed: then both retired, covered by Villatte. In this manner the French yielded step by step and without confusion, and the allies advanced with an incessant deafening musketry and cannonade, yet losing many men, especially on the right where the third division were very strongly opposed. As the danger of being cut off at Salespice by Hill became imminent, the retrograde movements were more hurried and confused, and Hill seeing this quickened his pace. At last both sides began to run violently, and so many men broke from the French ranks, making across the fields towards the fords, and there was such a rush by the rest to gain the bridge of Sault de Navailles, that the whole country was covered with scattered bands, amongst which General Cotton poured Lord Edward Somerset's hussars, first breaking through a covering body opposed to him by Harispe. In this charge two or three hundred men were sabred, and two thousand threw down their arms in an inclosed field; yet from some mismanagement the greatest part, recovering their weapons, escaped, and the pursuit ceased at the Luy of Bearn.

Apparently the French army was now entirely dispersed, yet it was not so. Soult passed the Luy of Bearn and destroyed the bridge with the loss of only six guns and less than four thousand men killed, wounded, and prisoners. Many thousands of conscripts however threw away their arms, and one month afterwards the stragglers still amounted to three thousand. Nor would the passage of the Luy have been effected so happily, if Wellington had not been struck by a musket ball just above the thigh, which caused him to ride with difficulty. The loss of the allies was two thousand three hundred, of which fifty, with three officers, were taken; among the wounded were Wellington, General Walker, General Ross, and the Duke of Richmond, then Lord March; this last had served on the head-quarter staff during the whole war without a hurt, but being made a captain in the 52nd, like a good soldier joined his regiment the night before the battle, and was shot through the chest a few hours afterwards; thus learning by experience the difference between the labours and dangers of staff and regimental officers, which are generally in the inverse ratio to their promotions.

General Berton, who had been between Pau and Orthes during the battle, was cut off by Hill's movement; but skirting that general's march he retreated by Mant and Samadet with his cavalry, picking up two battalions of conscripts on the road. Meanwhile Soult, having no position to rally upon, continued his retreat in the night to St. Sever, breaking down all the bridges behind him. Wellington pursued at daylight in three columns, one in the centre by the main road, the others on the right and left. At St. Sever he hoped to find the French still in confusion, but they had crossed the river, the bridge was broken, and the allied army halted. The result of the battle was however soon made known far and wide, and Daricau, who with a few hundred soldiers was endeavouring to form an insurgent levy at Dax, immediately destroyed part of the stores, removed the rest to Mont Marsan, and retreated through the Landes to Langon on the Garonne.

From St. Sever, which offered no position, Soult turned short to his own right, moving upon Barcelona up the Adour. He left D'Erlon however with two divisions of infantry, some cavalry and four guns, at Caceres on the right bank, sent Clausel into Aire on the opposite side of the river, abandoned his magazines at Mont Marsan, and opened the direct road to Bordeaux; but with his right he commanded another road by Roquefort to that city, while his left protected at Aire the magazines and artillery parc at that place, and covered the road to Pau. This movement made it difficult to judge what line he meant to adopt.

Wellington passed the Adour at St. Sever, and sent the light division and some cavalry to seize the magazines at Mont Marsan; at the same time he pushed a column towards Caceres, where a cannonade and charge of cavalry had place, and a few persons were hurt on both sides. Next day, when Hill had reached the Adour between St. Sever and Aire, D'Erlon was driven back skirmishing to Barcelona on the other bank. It was then evident that Soult had abandoned Bordeaux; yet the pursuit could not be pushed vigorously, because every bridge was broken; and a violent storm on the evening of the 1st, filling the smaller rivers and torrents, carried away the pontoon bridges and cut off all the supplies: the bulk of the army therefore halted on the right bank of the Adour until the bridges could be repaired.

Hill, who was on the left bank, had meanwhile marched to seize the magazines at Aire. Moving in two columns he reached that place on the 2nd at three o'clock, and having two divisions of infantry, a brigade of cavalry, and a battery of horse-artillery, expected no serious opposition. Clausel was however there in order of battle with Villatte's and Harispe's divisions, and some guns. Occupying a steep ridge, which was high and wooded on the right where it overlooked the river, but merging on the left into a wide table-land, over which the great road led to Pau, his position was strong, yet insecure. It could be readily outflanked on the left by the table-land, and was uneasy for retreat on the right, because the ridge was narrow and the ravine behind very rugged, with a mill-stream at the bottom; moreover a branch of the Adour flowing behind Aire cut it off from Barcelona, and behind the left wing was the greater Lees, a river with steep banks and only one bridge.

COMBAT OF AIRE.

Hill attacked without hesitation. General Stewart with two British brigades fell on the French right, a Portuguese brigade assailed their centre, and the other brigades followed in columns of march; but the action was sudden, the Portuguese were pushed forward in a slovenly manner by General Da Costa, a man of no ability, and the French under Harispe met them, on the flat summit, with so rough a charge that they gave way in flight while the rear of the allies' column was still in march. The fight was thus like to be lost, when Stewart, having easily won the heights on the French right, where Villatte, fearing to be enclosed, made but a feeble resistance, immediately detached Barnes with the 50th and 92nd Regiments to the aid of the Portuguese, and the vehement assault of these troops turned the stream of battle; the French were broken in turn and thrown back on their reserves. Yet they rallied and renewed the action with great courage, fighting obstinately until Byng's British brigade came up; then Harispe was driven towards the river Lees, and Villatte quite through the town of Aire into the space between the two branches of the Adour behind.

Reille, who was at Barcelona when the action began, now brought up a division to support Villatte, and the combat was continued until night at that point, while Harispe passed the Lees and broke the bridge. The French lost many men. Two generals, Dauture and Gasquet, were wounded, a colonel of engineers was killed, a hundred prisoners were taken, many of Harispe's conscripts threw away their arms and fled to their homes, and the magazines fell into the conqueror's hands. The British lost one hundred and fifty men, General Barnes was wounded, Colonel Hood killed. The Portuguese loss was never officially stated, it could not nave been less than the British, and the vigour of the action showed that the enemy's courage was not abated by the battle of Orthes. His retreat was now made up the Adour by both banks, but he was not followed, because new combinations were opening on both sides.

BOOK XVI.

Garonne—Adour—Combat of Vic Bigorre—Death and Character of
Colonel Sturgeon; surprising Feat of Captain Light—Combat of Tarbes—
Operations on the Garonne—Major Hughes; Battle of Toulouse
—Sally from Bayonne.

GARONNE.

Very perilous was Soult's state after the battle of Orthes. Losses in
actions, desertion of conscripts, and the dispersion of the old soldiers,
had reduced his army; all his magazines were taken; his officers were
discontented; he was ill seconded by the civil authorities, and a strong
Bourbon party was actively exciting the people to insurrection. He
was, however, a man formed by nature to struggle with difficulties,
and always appeared greatest in desperate circumstances. Retreating
towards the foot of the Pyrenees, he took a position covering Tarbes,
and commanding the great road from Pau to Toulouse; there he
reorganized his army, called in all the detachments made before the
battle, put the national guards and gens d'armes of the Pyrenees in
activity, and directed the commanders of districts behind him to
collect all the old soldiers they could, and send them to the army.
Then, to counteract the machinations of the Bourbonists, he issued a
proclamation remarkable for its power, and evincing the sternest
resolution, which was not belied by his acts, though his difficulties
hourly increased.

But Wellington also was embarrassed. The weather had stopped
his pursuit when vigorous action would have been decisive; Soult
had rallied on a new line of retreat with strong defensive positions;
the allied army, weakened by every step in advance, would, if
it followed the French, have to move between the Garonne and
the Pyrenees, exposing both its flanks and its rear to all the power
which the French government could command. It was, therefore,
neccssary to find a counterpoise by increasing his own force and

strengthening the Bourbonists. He had long been promised twenty thousand additional men from England and Portugal, but the governments of both countries failed in their engagements. He had heard and believed that Suchet had detached ten thousand men to join Soult, and he had, as before shown, called up Freyre's Gallicians through the Landes, because there was less temptation for plunder there, and he had provided them entirely from the English magazines and military chest; yet their entrance into France was instantly marked by outrages which began to dispose the people to listen to Soult's proclamation, and an insurrection was to be feared. Inactive, however, he could not remain, and while awaiting the junction of the Spaniards he detached Beresford with twelve thousand men against Bordeaux, remaining with only twenty-six thousand in position to observe Soult, who could from Tarbes move by Roquefort, and gain Bordeaux before Beresford. That general entered the city on the 12th; and the mayor, Lynch, eager to betray his sovereign, very quickly tore his own scarf of honour off to meet the invaders with a welcome. The Duke of Angouleme then arrived, the Bourbonists took the ascendant, and Beresford returned to the army with the fourth division and Vivian's cavalry, leaving Lord Dalhousie behind with the seventh division and three squadrons.

Then the Napoleonists, recovering from their first stupor, bestirred themselves. A partizan officer cut off fifty men sent by Lord Dalhousie over the Garonne; the peasants of the Landes formed bands and burned the houses of gentlemen who had assumed the white colours; forces of ,various descriptions were being assembled beyond the Garonne, and General Decaen was sent by the emperor to organize and command them. General Beurman also, who had been detached by Suchet with six thousand men to aid Lyons, was now directed to descend the Garonne towards Bordeaux, where a counter-insurrection was being prepared. But then the English fleet under Admiral Penrose entered the Garonne, sweeping it of French vessels of war, and ruining the batteries on the banks; whereupon Lord Dalhousie crossed the river, and, meeting with General L'Huillier at Etauliers, took three hundred prisoners, the French flying at the first onset. Better troops were, however, gathering in that quarter, and the British force would have been eventually in danger, if Napoleon, the man of mightiest capacity for good known to history since the days of Alexander the Great, had not been just then overthrown to make room for despots; who, with minds enlarged only to cruelty, avarice, dissoluteness, and treachery, were secretly intent to defraud their people of the just government they demanded as the compensation for serving ungrateful masters.

While Beresford was detached, Soult and Wellington remained in observation, each thinking the other stronger than himself; for the English general, hearing of Beurman's march, believed his troops had joined Soult, and the latter, not knowing of Beresford's march until the 13th, concluded Wellington had still those twelve thousand men. The numbers on each side were, however, nearly equal. Three thousand French stragglers had been collected, but were kept back by the generals of the military districts, and Soult had therefore in line, exclusive of conscripts without arms, only twenty-eight thousand sabres and bayonets, with thirty-eight pieces of artillery. Wellington had twenty-seven thousand sabres and bayonets, with forty-two guns; having, besides, pushed detachments to Pau, to Roquefort, into the Landes, and towards the Upper Garonne.

Two great roads led to Toulouse; one on the English left from Aire by Auch; the other on their right from Pau by Tarbes; Soult commanded both, and Wellington thought he would take that of Auch; wherefore he desired Beresford to lean towards it in returning from Bordeaux; but Soult had arranged for the other line, and was only prevented from retaking the offensive, on the 9th or 10th, by the loss of his magazines, which forced him to organize a system of requisition first for subsistence. Meanwhile his equality of force passed away; for on the 13th, the day on which he heard of Beresford's absence, Freyre came up with eight thousand Spanish infantry, and next day Ponsonby's heavy cavalry arrived. Wellington was then the strongest, yet awaited Beresford's arrival, and was uneasy about his own situation. He dreaded the junction of Suchet's twenty thousand veterans; the English ministers, instead of troops, had sent ridiculous projects. The French army in his front, having recovered its stragglers, and being reinforced by conscripts, was now reorganized in six divisions, under Daricau, Maransin, Villatte, D'Armagnac, Taupin, and Harispe. General Paris's troops, hitherto acting as an unattached body, were thus absorbed; the cavalry, composed of Berton's and Vial's brigades, was commanded by Pierre Soult, and seven thousand conscript infantry under Travot formed a reserve. Again, therefore, driven by necessity, Wellington called Giron's Andalusians and Del Parque's troops also into France, although Freyre's soldiers had by their outrages already created wide-spread consternation.

The head-quarters had been fixed at Aire, with the army on each side of the Adour, all the bridges being restored, and some small bands which had appeared upon the left flank and rear were dispersed by the cavalry; Soult was, however, organizing an extensive system of partizans towards the mountains, waiting only for money to give it activity. Meanwhile, though the main bodies were a long day's march asunder, the regular cavalry had frequent encounters, and both generals claimed the superiority. In this desultory warfare, on the night of the 7th, Soult sent a strong detachment to Pau to arrest some nobles who had assembled to welcome the Duke of Angouleme; but General Fane got there first with a brigade of infantry and two regiments of cavalry, and the stroke failed; the French, however, returning by another road, made prisoners of an officer and four or five English dragoons. A second French detachment, penetrating between Pau and Aire, carried off a post of correspondence; and two days after, when Fane had quitted Pau, a French officer with only four hussars captured there thirty-four Portuguese, with their commander and ten loaded mules.

It was these excursions which gave Soult a knowledge of Beresford's march, and he resolved to attack the allies, thinking to strike a good blow on the 13th, by throwing his army offensively upon the high tabular land between Pau and Aire; the country was open for all arms, yet the movement produced only a few skirmishes. Pierre Soult pushed back Fane's cavalry posts on the English right with the loss of two officers and a few men wounded; on the left, Berton, having two regiments, sought to pass a difficult muddy ford, but the head of his column was overthrown by Sir John Campbell with a squadron of the 4th Portuguese cavalry. The latter were however too few to bar the passage, and Berton, getting a regiment over higher up, charged the retiring troops in a narrow way, killed several, and took some prisoners, amongst them Bernardo de Sa, since well known as Count of Bandeira.

Wellington, imagining the arrival of Suchet's troops had caused Soult's boldness, made only defensive dispositions, and on the 14th Pierre Soult again drove back Fane's horsemen; at first with some loss, yet finally was himself driven clear off the Pau road. Both generals, acting under false information, were afraid to strike, each thought his adversary stronger than he really was; but Soult, who was in a tangled country, now hearing that Bordeaux had fallen, first took alarm, and retreated in the night of the 16th. Pierre Soult then again got on to the Pau road, and detached a hundred chosen troopers under Captain Dania to molest the communication with Orthes. By a forced march that partizan reached Hagetnau at nightfall, surprised six officers and eight medical men with their baggage, made a number of other prisoners, and returned on the evening of the 18th. This enterprise, so far in the rear, was supposed to be an insurgent exploit; wherefore Wellington seized the authorities at Hagetnau, and again declared he would hang all the peasants caught in arms, and burn their villages.

Soult's offensive operations had now terminated. He sent his conscripts to Toulouse and prepared for a rapid retreat on that place. His recent operations had been commenced too late, he should have moved the 10th or 11th, when there were not more than twenty-two thousand men in his front. Wellington's passive state, which had been too much prolonged, was also at an end; all his reinforcements and detachments were either up or close at hand, and he could now put in motion forty thousand bayonets, six thousand sabres and sixty pieces of artillery.

On the evening of the 17th the hussars went up the valley of the Adour, closely supported by the light division, and, half a march behind, by the fourth division coming from Bordeaux.

The 18th, the hussars, the light and the fourth division, advanced towards Plaissance; and Hill's troops, on the right, marched against Conchez, keeping a detachment on the Pau road in observation of Pierre Soult's cavalry; the centre, under Wellington, moved by the high road leading from Aire to Toulouse. The French right was thus turned by the valley of the Adour, while Hill, with a sharp skirmish in which eighty British and Germans were killed or wounded, drove back their outposts upon Lembege.

Soult retired during the night to a strong ridge behind a small river with rugged banks, called the Laiza, his right, under D'Erlon, was extended towards Vic Bigorre, on the great road of Tarbes, and Berton's cavalry took post in column, covering Vic Bigorre, where the road was lined on each side by deep and wide ditches. In this situation, being pressed by Bock's cavalry, Berton suddenly charged, and took an officer and some men, yet finally he was beaten and retreated. Soult, thinking a flanking column only was in the valley of the Adour, moved to fall upon it with his whole army. But he recognised the skill of his opponent when he found the whole of the allies' centre had also been thrown on to the Tarbes road, and was close to Vic Bigorre; while the light division, beyond the Adour, was getting in rear of it by Rabastans, upon which place the hussars had driven a body of French cavalry. Berton's horsemen then passed in retreat, the danger of being cut off from Tarbes was imminent, and Soult in alarm ordered Berton to join the cavalry at Rabastans, and cover that road to Tarbes, while D'Erlon checked the allies at Vic Bigorre on the main road, and enabled him personally to hasten with Clausel's and Reille's divisions to Tarbes by a circuitous way.

D'Erlon, not comprehending the crisis, moved slowly with his baggage in front, and, having the river Lechez to cross, rode on before his troops, expecting to find Berton at Vic Bigorre; but he met the German cavalry there, and had only time to place Daricau's division, now under Paris, amongst some vineyards, when hither came Picton to the support of the cavalry, and fell upon him.

COMBAT OF VIC BIGORRE.

The French left flank was secured by the Lechez river; the right, extended towards the Adour river, was exposed to the German cavalry, while the front was attacked by Picton. The action commenced about two o'clock, and Paris was driven back in disorder; but then D'Armagnac entered the line, and, spreading to the Adour, renewed the fight, which lasted until D'Erlon, after losing many men, and seeing his right turned beyond the Adour by the light division and the hussars, fell back behind Vic Bigorre, and took post for the night. This action was vigorous. Two hundred and fifty Anglo-Portuguese fell, and amongst them died Colonel Henry Sturgeon. Skilled to excellence in almost every branch of war, and possessing a variety of other accomplishments, he used his gifts so gently for himself, so usefully for the service, that envy offered no bar to admiration, and the whole army felt painfully mortified that his merits were passed unnoticed in the public despatches.

Soult's march was through a deep sandy plain, very harassing, and it would have been dangerous if Wellington had sent Hill's strong cavalry in pursuit; but the country was unfavourable for quick observation, and the French covered their movements with rearguards whose real numbers it was difficult to ascertain. One of these bodies was posted on a hill, the end of which abutted on the high road, the slope being clothed with trees, and well lined by skirmishers. Lord Wellington desired to know what force thus barred his way, yet all the exploring attempts were stopped by the enemy's fire. Captain William Light, distinguished by the variety of his attainments, an artist, musician, mechanist, seaman, and soldier, then made the trial. He rode forward as if he would force his way through the French skirmishers, but in the wood dropped his reins and leaned back as if badly wounded; his horse appeared to canter wildly along the front of the enemy's light troops, and they, thinking him mortally hurt, ceased their fire, and took no further notice. He thus passed unobserved through the wood to the other side of the hill, where there were no skirmishers, and, ascending to the open summit above, put spurs to his horse, and, galloping along the French main line, counted their regiments as he passed. His sudden appearance, his blue undress, his daring confidence, and his speed, made the French doubt if he was an enemy, and a few shots only were discharged, while he, dashing down the opposite declivity, broke from the rear through the very skirmishers whose fire he had at first essayed in front, reached the spot where Wellington stood, and told him there were but five battalions on the hill.

Soult now felt that a rapid retreat upon Toulouse was inevitable, yet, determined to dispute every position offering the least advantage, he was on the morning of the 20th again in order of battle on the heights of Oleac, three miles behind Tarbes, which he still covered with Harispe's and Villatte's divisions, both under Clausel. The plain of Tarbes, apparently open, was yet full of deep ditches which forbad the action of horsemen; wherefore he sent his brother with five regiments of cavalry to his right flank in observation of the route to Auch, fearing Wellington would by that line intercept his retreat to Toulouse.

At daybreak Hill moved with the right along the high road; the centre, under Wellington, composed of the light division and hussars, Ponsonby's heavy cavalry, the sixth division and Freyre's Spaniards, marched by the road from Rabastens; Cole, having the left, was making forced marches with the fourth division and Vivian's cavalry, and throwing out detachments to watch Pierre Soult.

COMBAT OF TARBES.

Wellington's column was separated by a branch of the Adour from Hill's, and when he approached Tarbes the light division and the hussars attacked Harispe's division on the heights of Orleix; Clinton, making a flank movement to his left through the village of Dours with the sixth division, then opened a cannonade against Harispe's right, and endeavoured to get between that general and Soult's position at Oleac; Hill, moving by the other bank of the river, assailed the town and bridge of Tarbes, which were defended by Villatte. These operations were designed to envelop and crush Clausel's troops, which seemed easy, because there appeared only a fine plain fit for the action of cavalry between them and Soult. The latter, however, having sent his baggage and incumbrances off during the night, saw the movement without alarm, being better acquainted with the difficult nature of the plain behind, in which he had been forced to make roads to enable Harispe to retreat upon Oleac without passing through Tarbes. Nevertheless there was danger: for while Hill menaced Tarbes, the light division, supported with cavalry and guns, fell upon Orleix, and Clinton with a brisk cannonade penetrated between Harispe and Pierre Soult, cutting the latter off from the army.

The action commenced at twelve o'clock. Hill's artillery thundered on the right, Clinton's answered it on the left, and Alten threw the light division in mass upon the centre, where Harispe's left brigade, posted on a strong hill, was suddenly assailed by the three rifle battalions. There the fight was short, yet wonderfully fierce and violent; for the French, probably thinking their opponents Portuguese on account of their green dress, charged with great hardiness, and being encountered by men not accustomed to yield, the fight was muzzle to muzzle, and very difficult it was to judge at first who should win. At last the French gave way, and Harispe, his centre being thus suddenly overthrown, retired rapidly over the plain by Soult's roads before Clinton could get into his rear; then also Hill forced the passage of the Adour at Tarbes, and Villatte retreated along the highroad to Tournay, yet under a continued cannonade. The flat country was now covered with confused masses of pursuers and pursued, all moving precipitately and with an eager musketry, the French guns replying as they could to the allies' artillery; the situation of the retreating troops seemed desperate; but, as Soult had foreseen, the British cavalry could not act, and Clausel extricating his divisions with great ability gained the main position, where four fresh divisions were drawn up in order of battle and immediately opened all their batteries on the allies. The pursuit was thus checked, and before Wellington could make arrangements for a new attack darkness came on, wherefore he halted on the banks of the Larret and Larros rivers. The loss of the French is unknown, that of the allies did not exceed one hundred and twenty, of whom twelve officers and eighty men were of the rifle battalions.

During the night Soult retreated in two columns, one by the main road, the other on the left of it, guided by fires lighted on different hills as points of direction. Next day he reached St. Gaudens with D'Erlon's and Reille's corps, while Clausel, who had retreated across the fields, halted at Monrejean, and was there rejoined by Pierre Soult's cavalry. This march of more than thirty miles was made with a view to gain Tulouse in the most rapid manner; for Soult having now seen Wellington's infantry and his five thousand horsemen, and hearing from his brother that the fourth division and Vivian's cavalry were on his right, feared they would cut him off from Toulouse—his great depot, the knot of all his future combinations, and the only position where he could hope to make a successful stand with his small army.

The allies pursued in three columns, but their marches were short. However, at St. Gaudens four squadrons of French cavalry were overtaken and overthrown by two squadrons of the 13th dragoons; they galloped in disorder through St. Gaudens, yet rallied on the other side and were again broken and pursued for two miles, many being sabred and above a hundred taken prisoners. In this action the veteran Major Dogherty of the 13th was seen charging between his two sons at the head of the leading ,squadron.

On the 23rd Hill was at St. Gaudens, Beresford at Puymauren, Wellington at Boulogne.

The 24th Hill was in St. Martory, Beresford in Lombez, Wellington at Isle en Dodon.

The 25th Hill entered Caceres, Beresford reached St. Foy, and Wellington was at Samatan.

On the 26th Beresford, marching in order of battle by his left, his cavalry skirmishing to the right, took post on the Auch road behind the Aussonnelle stream, facing the French army, which was on the Touch covering Toulouse. The allies thus took seven days to march what Soult had done in four; but the two armies being thus again brought together in opposition with a common resolution to fight, it is fitting to show how the generals framed their combinations.

OPERATIONS ON THE GARONNE.

Soult, a native of these parts, had chosen Toulouse as a strategic post, because that ancient capital of the south, having fifty thousand inhabitants, commanded the principal passage of the Garonne, was the centre of a great number of roads on both sides of that river, and the chief military arsenal of the south of France. There he could most easily feed his troops, assemble, arm, and discipline the conscripts, control and urge the civil authorities with more power, and counteract the machinations of the discontented it also gave him command of various lines of operations. He could retire upon Suchet by Carcassonne, or towards Lyons by Alby. He could go behind the Tarn and defend successively that river and the Lot, or even retreat upon Decaen's army near Bordeaux, and thus draw the allies down the right bank of the Garonne as he had before drawn them up the left bank; assured that Wellington must follow him, and with weakened forces, as it would be necessary to leave troops in observation of Suchet.

Thus reasoning, he placed a separate body of troops recently assembled by General Loverdo from the interior, at Montauban, with orders to construct a bridge-head on the left of the Tarn. This secured the passage of that river, a point of assembly for detachments observing the Garonne below Toulouse, and the command of several great roads. But to hold Toulouse was a great political object. It was the last point connecting him at once with Suchet and Decaen; while he held it, the latter general and the partizans organized in the mountains about Lourdes could act, each on their own side, against Wellington's long lines of communication. At Toulouse Suchet could aid him, either with his whole force, or by a detachment to the Upper Garonne, where General Lafitte had collected seven or eight hundred national guards and other troops: Suchet, however, though strongly urged, treated this proposition, as he had done those before made, with contempt.

Toulouse was not less valuable as a position of battle.

The Garonne, flowing along the allies' right, presented the concave of a deep loop, at the bottom of which was bridge masked by the suburb of St. Cyprien; this last, originally protected by an ancient brick wall three feet thick and flanked by massive towers, was now strengthened by Soult with a line of exterior entrenchments.

Beyond the river was the city, inclosed by an old wall flanked with towers, and so thick as to hold twenty-four pound guns.

The great canal of Languedoc, which joined the Garonne a few miles below the town, was generally within point-blank shot of this wall, covering it on the north and east, as the Garonne and St. Cyprien did on the west.

Eastward, two suburbs, St. Stephen and Guillermerie, lying on both sides of this canal, were entrenched and protected by the hills of Sacarin and Cambon, which were also entrenched, and flanked the approaches to the canal above and below the suburbs.

Eight hundred yards beyond these hills a high ridge called Mont Rave ran nearly parallel with the canal, its outer slope was exceedingly rugged, and overlooked a marshy plain, through which the Ers river flowed.

South of the town was a plain, but there the suburb of St. Michel furnished another outwork; and some distance beyond it a range of heights, called the Pech David, commenced, trending westward up the Garonne in a nearly parallel direction.

Such being Soult's position, he calculated, that as Wellington could not force the passage by the suburb of St. Cyprien without an enormous sacrifice of men, he must seek to turn the flanks above or below Toulouse, leaving a force to blockade St. Cyprien lest the French should issue thence against his communications. If he passed the Garonne above Toulouse, and above its confluence with the Arriege, he would have to cross the latter river also, which could only be effected at Cintegabelle, one march higher up. He would then have to come down the right bank, through a country at that time impracticable for guns, from rain. If he passed the Garonne below the confluence of the Arriege, his movements would be overlooked from the Pech David, and the heads of his columns attacked; if that failed, Toulouse and the Mont Rave remained as a position of battle, from whence there was a secure retreat upon Montauban.

For these reasons the passage above Toulouse could lead to no decisive result: but a passage below was a different matter. Wellington would then cut the army off from Montauban and attack Toulouse from the northern and eastern quarters; and the French, losing the battle, could only retreat by Carcassonne to unite with Suchet in Roussillon; where with their backs to the mountains and the allies between them and France they would starve. Convinced therefore that the attack would be on that side, Soult lined the Garonne with his cavalry as far as the confluence of the Tarn, and called up some troops, recently collected at Agen under General Despeaux, to line the Tarn itself, his design being to attack the allies if they crossed between that river and the Garonne rather than lose his communication with Montauban.

Wellington having suffered the French to gain three days' march in the retreat from Tarbes had little choice of operations. He could not halt until the Andalusians and Del Parque's troops joined him, without giving Soult time to strengthen his defence; nor without appearing fearful of the French people, which would have been very dangerous. Still less could he wait for the fall of Bayonne. He had taken the offensive, and the invasion of France being begun could not be relinquished. Leading an army victorious and superior in numbers, his business was to fight; and as he could not force St. Cyprien, he had to pass the Garonne above or below Toulouse.

A passage below was undoubtedly the prudent course; but Wellington, observing that, when across, the south side of the city would be most open to attack, resolved to cast his bridge at Portet, six miles above Toulouse; designing to throw his right wing suddenly into the open country between the Garonne and the canal of Languedoc, while with his centre and left he assailed the suburb of St. Cyprien.* Hence, at eight o'clock in the evening of the 27th, one of Hill's brigades approached the river, some men were ferried over and the bridge was commenced; but the river being measured was too wide for the pontoons, there were no trestles, and that project was necessarily abandoned.

* This plan and the reasons for it are taken from MS. notes written by the Duke of Wellington in reply to my inquiries.

Had it been effected, some great advantage would have been gained; for Soult only knew of the attempt two days later, and then by emissaries, not by scouts. Wellington persisted. Collecting a great body of infantry about Portet, he began by driving the French horsemen from the Touch river, which was in his front, for his army lined the bank of the Garonne above Toulouse, and did not face St. Cyprien. In this operation a single squadron of the 18th Hussars, under Major Hughes, being inconsiderately pushed by Colonel Vivian across the bridge of St. Martin de la Touch, suddenly came upon a regiment of French cavalry. The rashness of the act, as often happens in war, proved the safety of the British; for the enemy, thinking a strong support must be at hand, discharged their carbines and retreated at a canter; Hughes followed, the speed of both parties increased; and as the road did not admit egress by the sides, this great body of horsemen was pushed headlong by a few men under the batteries of St. Cyprien.

Soult's attention being thus attracted below Toulouse, a bridge was laid near Pensaguel, two miles above the confluence of the Arriege, and Hill passed the Garonne with thirteen thousand sabres and bayonets, eighteen guns, and a rocket brigade. His advanced guard then pushed on rapidly by the great road to seize the bridge of Cintegabelle fifteen miles up the Arriege; and to secure a ferry-boat known to be at Vinergue. The main body followed with intent to pass the Arriege at Cintegabelle, and so come down the right bank to attack Toulouse on the south, while Wellington assailed St. Cyprien. This march was to have been made privily in the night of the 30th, but the pontoon bridge was not finished until five in the morning of the 31st; Soult thus got notice in time to observe the strength of the column, and ascertain that the great body of the army was still in front of St. Cyprien. Knowing what swamps were to be passed, and having the suburbs of St. Michel and St. Etienne now in a state of defence, he thought the operation only a feint to draw off a part of his army from Toulouse while St. Cyprien was assaulted or the Garonne passed below the city; wherefore, keeping his infantry in hand, he merely sent cavalry up the Arriege in observation, and directed Lafitte, who had some regular horsemen and national guards higher up, to hang upon Hill's skirts and pretend to be the van of Suchet's army. He was, however, disquieted, because the allies' baggage, to avoid encumbering the march, had been sent higher up the Garonne, to cross at Carbonne, and was by the scouts reported as a second column increasing Hill's force to eighteen thousand men.

While in this uncertainty, Soult first heard of the measurement of the river made at Portet in the night of the 27th, and that many guns were still there; hence, as he could not know why the bridge was not thrown, he concluded the intent was to cross there also when Hill should descend the Arriege. To meet this danger, he gave Clausel orders to fall upon the head of the allies with four divisions if they should attempt the passage before Hill came down; resolving in the contrary case to fight in the suburbs of Toulouse and on the Mont Rave, because the positions on the right of the Arriege were all favourable to the assailants. He was, however, soon relieved from anxiety. Hill passed the Arriege at Cintegabelle and sent his cavalry forward; but his artillery were unable to follow in that deep country, and as success and safety alike depended on rapidity, he returned and recrossed the Garonne in the night, keeping, a flying bridge and a small guard of infantry and cavalry on the right bank: he was followed by Lafitte's horsemen, who picked up a few stragglers and mules, but no other event occurred, and Soult was well pleased that his adversary had thus lost three or four important days.

Being now sure the next attempt would be below Toulouse, he changed his design of marching down the Garonne to fight between that river and the Tarn; and as his works for the city and suburbs were nearly complete, he concluded to hold Toulouse in any circumstances, and set his whole army and all the labouring population to entrench the Mont Rave, beyond the canal, thinking thus to bear the shock of battle, come on which side it would. Fortune favoured him. The Garonne continued so full and rapid that Wellington remained inactive before St. Cyprien until the evening of the 3rd, when, forced to adopt the lower passage, and the flood having abated, the pontoons were carried in the night to Grenade, fifteen miles below Toulouse. The bridge was then well thrown, and thirty guns placed in battery on the left bank to protect it. The third, fourth, and sixth divisions, with three brigades of cavalry, the whole under Beresford, immediately passed; and the horsemen being pushed to the front and flanks captured a large herd of bullocks destined for the French. But again the Garonne flooded high, the light division and the Spaniards were unable to follow, the bridge got damaged and was taken up.

Soult soon heard by his cavalry scouts of this passage, but not of the force across, and as Morillo's Spaniards, whom he mistook for Freyre's, were then in front of St. Cyprien, he thought Hill had moved also to Grenade, and that the greatest part of the allied army was over the Garonne. Wherefore, observing Beresford with cavalry, he continued to work at his field of battle, his resolution to fight for Toulouse being confirmed by hearing that the allied sovereigns had entered Paris.

On the 8th the water subsided again, and the bridge was once more laid; Freyre's Spaniards and the Portuguese artillery then crossed, and Wellington in person advanced within five miles of Toulouse. Marching up both banks of the Ers, his columns were separated by that river, which was impassable without pontoons, and it was essential to secure one of the stone bridges. Hence, when his left approached the heights of Kirie Eleison, on the great road of Alby, Vivian's horsemen first drove Berton's cavalry up the right of the Ers towards the bridge of Bordes; then the 18th Hussars descended towards that of Croix d'Orade, where after some skirmishing a French regiment suddenly appeared in front of the bridge. The opposite bank of the river was as instantly lined with dismounted carbineers, and the two parties stood facing each other, hesitating to begin, until the approach of some British infantry, when both sounded a charge at the same moment; but the English horses were so quick the French were in an instant jammed up on the bridge, and their front ranks sabred, while the rear went off in disorder. They had many killed or wounded, lost above a hundred prisoners, and were pursued through the village of Croix d'Orade, yet rallied beyond on the rest of their brigade and advanced again; whereupon the hussars recrossed the bridge, which was now defended by the British infantry. The communication between the allied columns was thus secured. The credit of this brilliant action was erroneously given to Colonel Vivian in the despatch. That officer was wounded by a carbine shot previous to the charge at the bridge, and the attack was conducted by Major Hughes.

Wellington having, from the heights of Kirie Eleison, examined the French general's position, decided to attack on the 9th; and, to shorten his communications with Hill, had his bridge on the Garonne relaid higher up at Seilh, where the light division were to cross at daybreak; but the pontoons were not relaid until late in the day, and he, extremely incensed at the failure, was forced to defer his battle until the 10th.

Soult had now by means of his fortresses, his battles, the sudden change of his line of operations after Orthes, his rapid retreat from Tarbes, and his clear judgment in fixing upon Toulouse as his next point of resistance, reduced the strength of his adversary to an equality with his own. He had gained seventeen days for preparation, and had compelled Wellington to fight on ground naturally adapted for defence and well fortified; where one-third of his force was separated by a great river from the rest; where he could derive no advantage from his numerous cavalry, and was overmatched in artillery. Covering three sides of Toulouse the French position was indeed very strong. The left was at St. Cyprien on the west; the centre at the canal on the north; the right at Mont Rave on the east; the reserve of conscripts manned the ramparts of Toulouse, and the urban guards within the town aided the transport of artillery and ammunition to different posts.

Hill was in front of St. Cyprien, and he could only communicate with the main body by the pontoon bridge at Seilh, a circuit of ten or twelve miles. Wellington was advancing from the north, but being still intent to assail on the south, where Soult was weakest in defence, he examined the country on the left of the Ers, designing under cover of that river to make a flank march and gain the open ground which he had formerly vainly endeavoured to reach by passing at Portet and Pinsaguel. Again he was baffled by the deep country, which he could not master so as to pass the Ers by force in the upper part; and all the bridges there, with the exception of Croix d'Orade, were mined or destroyed. There was no choice then but to attack the north and east fronts. The first, open and flat, and easily approached by the great roads of Montauban and Alby, was yet impregnable in defence; because the canal, the bridges over which were strongly defended by works, was under the fire of the ramparts of Toulouse, and for the most part within musket-shot. Wherefore, as at St. Cyprien, a fortress, not a position, was opposed, and the assault was necessarily confined to the Mont Rave or eastern front.

Naturally strong and rugged, that ridge was covered by the Ers river, and presented two distinct platforms, Calvinet and St. Sypiere. Between them, where the ground dipped a little, two routes called the Lavaur and Caraman roads led to Toulouse, passing the canal at the Guillemerie and St. Etienne suburbs.

The Calvinet platform was fortified on the left with two large redoubts, having open entrenchments in front. On the right were two other large forts, called the Colombette and Tower of Augustines. St. Sypiere had also two redoubts, one on the extreme right called St. Sypiere, the other without a name near the road of Caraman.

The whole occupation was two miles long, and to attack the front it was necessary to cross the Ers under fire, advancing over ground naturally marshy and now almost impassable from artificial inundations to the assault of the ridge and its works. If the assailants should force a way between the two platforms, they would, while their flanks were battered by the redoubts above, come in succession upon new works, at Cambon and Sacarin; upon the suburbs of Guillemerie and Etienne; upon the canal; and finally upon the ramparts of the town. But the Ers could not be passed except at Croix d'Orade, and Wellington was reduced to a flank march under fire, between that river and Mont Rave, until he could gain ground to present a front to the latter and storm it; after which the canal was to be crossed above ere the army could be established on the south of Toulouse. To impose that march had been Soult's object, and his army was disposed in the following order to render it disastrous.

Reille defended St. Cyprien with Taupin's and Maransin's divisions.

Daricau's division lined the canal on the north from its junction with the Garonne to the road of Alby, defending the bridge-head of Jumeaux, the convent of the Minimes, and the Matabiau bridge.

Harispe's division held the Mont Rave, his right being at St. Sypiere, his centre at the Colombette, about which Vial's horsemen were also collected; his left looked down the road of Alby, having in front a detached eminence within cannon-shot, called the Hill of Pugade, occupied by St. Pol's brigade.

Soult's remaining divisions were in columns behind the Mont Rave.

This order of battle formed an angle, each side about two miles long, the apex towards the Alby road being covered by the Pugade hill.

Wellington made the following dispositions of attack for the 10th. Hill to menace St. Cyprien, augmenting or abating his efforts according to the progress of the main battle. The third and light divisions and Freyre's Spaniards to move against the northern front; the two first, supported by Bock's cavalry, were to menace the line of canal defended by Daricau—Picton at the bridge of Jumeaux and the Minimes; Alten to connect him with Freyre, who, reinforced with the Portuguese artillery, was to carry the hill of Pugade, and then halt to cover Beresford's column. This last, composed of the fourth and sixth divisions with three batteries, was to move round the left of the Pugade, and along the low ground between the Mont Rave and the Ers, until the rear should pass the road of Lavaur in the centre, when it was to wheel into line and attack the platform of St. Sypiere. Freyre was then to assail that of Calvinet, and Ponsonby's dragoons were to connect that general's left with Beresford's column. Meanwhile Lord Edward Somerset's hussars and Vivian's cavalry were to ascend both banks of the Ers in observation of Berton's cavalry; because the latter could by the bridges of Bordes and Montaudran pass from the right to the left bank, destroy the bridges, and fall on the head of Beresford's troops.

BATTLE OF TOULOUSE.

On the 10th of April, at two o'clock in the morning, the light division passed the Garonne by the bridge at Seilh, and at six the army moved to the attack. Picton and Alten on the right, drove the French posts behind the works covering the bridges on the canal. Freyre, marching along the Alby road, was cannonaded by St. Pol until he passed a small stream, when the French general, following his instructions, retired to the works on the Calvinet platform: the Spaniards were thus established on the Pugade, opposite the apex of the French position, which the Portuguese guns cannonaded heavily.

Beresford, preceded by the hussars, marched from Croix d'Orade in three columns abreast, masked by the Pugade until he entered the marshy ground; but he left his guns behind, fearing to engage them in that deep and difficult country. Beyond the Ers, on his left, Vivian's cavalry, now under Colonel Arentschildt, drove Berton's horsemen back over the bridge of Bordes, which the French general destroyed with difficulty. The German hussars then gained the bridge of Montaudran higher up, though defended by a detachment sent there by Berton, who remained in position near the bridge of Bordes, looking down the left of the Ers.

During these operations Freyre, who had demanded leave to lead the battle at Calvinet, from error or impatience assailed while Beresford was still in march, and his Spaniards, nine thousand strong, advanced in two lines and a reserve with great resolution, throwing forward their flanks so as to embrace the hill. The French musketry and great guns thinned their ranks at every step, but closing upon the centre they mounted the ascent under a formidable fire, which increased in violence until their right wing, raked also from the bridge of Matabiau, became unable to endure the torment, and the leading ranks madly jumped for shelter into a hollow road, twenty-five feet, deep, covering this part of the French entrenchments; the left wing and the second line ran back in disorder, the Cantabrian fusiliers, under Colonel Leon de Sicilia, alone maintaining their ground under cover of a bank which protected them. Then the French came leaping out of their works with loud cries, and lining the edge of the hollow road, poured an incessant stream of shot upon the helpless crowds in the gulf below, while a battery from the Matabiau, constructed to rake the hollow, sent its bullets from flank to flank, hissing through the quivering mass of flesh and bones.

The Spanish generals rallied their troops and led them back again to the brink of the fatal hollow; but the frightful carnage below, with the unmitigated fire in front, filled them with horror: again they fled, and again the French bounding from their trenches pursued, while several battalions sallying from the Matabiau and Calvinet also followed them. The country was now covered with fugitives, and the pursuers' numbers and vehemence increased, until Wellington pushed forward with Ponsonby's cavalry and the reserve artillery, while a brigade of the light division, wheeling to its left, menaced the flank of the French, who then returned to the Calvinet.

More than fifteen hundred Spaniards had been killed or wounded, and their defeat was not the only misfortune Picton, regardless of his orders, which, his temper on such occasions being known, were especially given both verbally and in writing, had turned his false attack into a real one against the bridge of Jumeaux; but the enemy, fighting from a work too high to be forced without ladders, and approachable only on open ground, repulsed him with a loss of four hundred men and officers; amongst the latter Colonel Forbes of the 45th was killed, and General Brisbane was wounded. Thus from the hill of Pugade to the Garonne the French had vindicated their position, the allies had suffered enormously; and beyond the Garonne, although Hill forced the exterior line of entrenchments, the inner line, more contracted and strongly fortified, could not be stormed. The musketry now subsided for a time, yet a prodigious cannonade was kept up along the whole of the French line; and by the allies, from St. Cyprien to where the artillery left by Beresford was, in concert with the guns on the Pugade, pouring shot incessantly against the Calvinet platform injudiciously it has been said by Beresford's guns, because the ammunition, thus used for a secondary object, was afterwards wanted when a vital advantage might have been gained.

In this state the victory depended on Beresford's attack, and, from Picton's error, Wellington had no reserves to enforce the decision; for the light division and the heavy cavalry only remained in hand, and were necessarily retained to cover the rallying of the Spaniards, and protect the artillery employed to keep the enemy in check. The crisis therefore approached with all happy promise to the French. The repulse of Picton, the dispersion of the Spaniards, and the strength of St. Cyprien, enabled Soult to draw Taupin's whole division first, and then one of Maransin's brigades, from that quarter, to reinforce his battle on Mont Rave; thus three divisions and the cavalry, in all fifteen thousand combatants, were disposable for a counter-attack. With this mass he might have fallen upon Beresford, whose force, originally less than thirteen thousand bayonets, was cruelly reduced, as it made slow way for two miles through ground deep and tangled with watercourses: sometimes moving in mass, sometimes filing under the French musketry, always under fire of their guns without one to reply, the length of the column augmented at every step, and frequent halts were necessary to close up.

Between the river and the heights the ground became narrower, and more miry as the troops advanced, Berton's cavalry was ahead, an impassable river was on the left, and three French divisions supported by artillery and horsemen overshadowed the right flank! Meanwhile Soult, eyeing this terrible march, had carried Taupin's division to the platform of St. Sypiere, supporting it with one of D'Armagnac's brigades, and now, after a short hortative, ordered Taupin to fall on, while a regiment of Vial's cavalry descended the Lavaur road to intercept retreat, and Berton's horsemen assailed the flank from the bridge of Bordes. But this was not half the force which might have been employed. Taupin's artillery, retarded in its march, was still in the streets of Toulouse, and that general, instead of attacking frankly, waited until Beresford had completed his flank march and formed his lines at the foot of the heights. Then the French infantry poured down the hill, but some well directed rockets, whose noise and dreadful aspect were unknown before, dismayed his soldiers; whereupon the British skirmishers running forwards plied them with a biting fire, Lambert's brigade of the sixth division, aided by Anson's and some provisional battalions of the fourth division, followed with a terrible shout, and the French fled to the upper ground. Vial's horsemen, trotting down the Lavaur road, had meanwhile charged the right flank, but Beresford's second and third lines being thrown into squares repulsed them; and on the other flank Cole had been so sudden in his advance that Berton's cavalry had no opportunity to charge. Lambert killed Taupin, wounded a general of brigade, and without a check won the summit of the platform; his skirmishers even pursued down the reverse slope, while Cole, meeting with less resistance, had still more rapidly gained the height at his side: so complete was the rout that the two redoubts were abandoned from panic, and the French sought shelter in Sacarin and Cambon.

Soult, astonished at this weakness in troops from whom he had expected so much, and who had but just before given him assurances of their resolution and confidence, was now in fear that Beresford would seize the bridge of the Demoiselles on the canal, and so gain the south side of Toulouse. Wherefore, covering the flight as he could with Vial's cavalry, he hastily led D'Armagnac's other brigade to Sacarin, checked the British skirmishers there, and rallied the fugitives; Taupin's guns arrived from the town at the same moment, and the mischief being thus stayed, a part of Travot's conscripts moved to the bridge of the Demoiselles. This new order of battle required fresh dispositions for attack, but the indomitable courage of the British soldiers had decided the first great crisis of the fight, and was still buoyant. Lambert's brigade wheeled to its right across the platform, menacing the French left flank on the Calvinet platform, while Pack's Scotch brigade and Douglas's Portuguese, composing the second and third lines of the sixth division, formed on his right, to march against the Colombette redoubts. Then also Arentschildt's cavalry came down from the bridge of Montaudran on the Ers river, round the south end of the Mont Rave, where in conjunction with the skirmishers of the fourth division it again menaced the bridge of the Demoiselles.

Entirely changed now was the aspect and form of the battle. The French, thrown entirely on the defensive, occupied three sides of a square. Their right, extending from Sacarin to the Calvinet platform, was closely menaced by Lambert, solidly established on the St. Sypiere; the redoubts of Colombette and Augustines were menaced by Pack and Douglas, and the left, thrown back to the Matabiau, awaited a renewed attack: the whole position was very strong, not exceeding a thousand yards on each side, with the angles defended by formidable works. The canal and the city furnished a refuge, while the Matabiau on one side, Sacarin and Cambon on the other, insured retreat.

In this contracted space were concentrated Vial's cavalry, Villatte's division, one brigade of Maransin's, another of D'Armagnac's, and the whole of Harispe s division, except the regiment driven from the Sypiere redoubt. The victory was therefore still to be contended for, and with apparently inadequate means; for on the right Picton was paralyzed by Daricau, the Spaniards not to be depended upon, and there remained only the heavy cavalry and light division; which Wellington could not thrust into action under pain of being without a reserve in the event of a repulse. The final stroke therefore was still to be made on the left, and with a small force, seeing Lambert's brigade, and Cole's division, were necessarily employed to keep in check the French at the bridge of the Demoiselles, at Cambon and Sacarin, where Clausel seemed disposed to retake the offensive.

At half-past two o'clock Beresford renewed the action with the brigades of Pack and Douglas. Ensconced in the Lavaur road on Lambert's right, they had been hitherto protected from the fire of the French redoubts; but now scrambling up the steep banks of the road, under a wasting fire of cannon and musketry, they carried all the French breastworks—the Colombette and Augustine redoubts being taken by the 42nd and 79th Regiments. It was a surprising action when the loose attack imposed by the ground is considered; and the French, although they yielded to the first thronging rush of the British, came back with a reflux, their cannonade was incessant, their reserves strong, and the struggle became terrible. Harispe, under whom the French seemed always to fight with extraordinary vigour, surrounded the redoubts with a surging multitude, broke into the Colombette, killed or wounded four-fifths of the

42nd, and retook the Augustine also; but then the 11th and 91st Regiments came up and the French again abandoned those works: yet so many of the allies had fallen that they appeared only as a thin line of skirmishers.

Some British cavalry, riding up from the low ground, now attempted to charge, but were stopped by a deep hollow road, into which several troopers fell and there perished. Meanwhile the combat about the redoubts continued, yet the French, though most numerous, never could retake the Platform; and when Harispe and General Baurot had fallen dangerously wounded, drew off by their right to Sacarin, and by their left towards the Matabiau.

During this contest the Spaniards had again attacked the Calvinet platform from Pugade hill, but were again put to flight; the French thus remained masters of their entrenchments in that quarter, and Beresford halted to reform his battle and receive his artillery, which came to him with great difficulty, and little ammunition from the heavy cannonade it had previously furnished. However, Soult, seeing the Spaniards, supported by the light division, had rallied a fourth time; that Picton again menaced the bridge of Jumeaux and the Minime convent; and that Beresford, master of three-fourths of Mont Rave, was, now ready to advance along the summit, relinquished the Calvinet platform entirely, and withdrew about five o'clock behind the canal, still holding Sacarin and Cambon. Wellington was then master of the Mont Rave, and so ended the battle of Toulouse, in which the French had five generals and about three thousand men killed or wounded, and they lost a gun. The allies lost four generals and more than four thousand six hundred men and officers, two thousand being Spaniards. A lamentable spilling of blood, and useless, for before this period Napoleon had abdicated the throne of France, and a provisional government was constituted at Paris.

During the night Soult replaced the ammunition expended in the action, reorganized and augmented his field artillery from the arsenal of Toulouse, and made dispositions for fighting the next morning behind the canal. Looking however to a final retreat, he wrote to Suchet to inform him of the result of the contest, and proposed a combined plan of operations illustrative of the firmness and pertinacity of his temper. " March," said he, " with the whole of your forces by Quillan upon Carcassonne. I will meet you there with my army, we can then retake the initiatory movement, transfer the seat of war to the Upper Garonne, and holding on by the mountains compel the enemy to recall his troops from Bordeaux, which will enable Decaen to recover that city and make a diversion in our favour."

On the morning of the 11th he was again ready but Wellington was not. The French position, within musketshot of the city walls, was still inexpugnable on the northern and eastern fronts; the conquest of Mont Rave was only a preliminary step to the passage of the canal, and throwing of the army on the south side of the town; a great matter, requiring fresh dispositions,and provision of ammunition only to be obtained from the parc on the other side of the Garonne. Hence, to accelerate the preparations, to ascertain Hill's state, and give him further instructions, Wellington repaired on the 11th by Seilh to St. Cyprien; but the day was spent before the arrangements for the passage of the canal could be completed, and the attack was therefore deferred until daylight.

Meanwhile the light cavalry were sent up the canal, to interrupt the communications with Suchet and menace Soult's retreat on Carcassonne. Their appearance on the heights above Baziege, together with the preparations in front, taught Soult he would soon be shut up in Toulouse instead of fighting; wherefore, leaving eight pieces of heavy artillery, two generals, Harispe being one, and sixteen hundred men whose wounds were severe, to the humanity of the conquerors, he filed out of the city with surprising order and ability, made a forced march of twenty-two miles, cut the bridges over the canal and the Upper Ers, and the 12th established his army at Villefranche. Hill followed, and at Baziege the light cavalry beat the French with the loss of twenty-five men, cutting off a like number of gens d'armes on the side of Revel.

Now Wellington entered Toulouse in triumph, the white flag was displayed, and, as at Bordeaux, a great crowd of persons adopted the Bourbon colours; but the mayor, faithful to his sovereign, retired with the French army; and the British general, true to his honest line of policy, again warned the Bourbonists that their revolutionary movement must be at their own risk. In the afternoon however two officers, the English colonel, Cooke, and the French colonel, St. Simon, arrived from Paris, charged to make known to the armies the abdication of Napoleon. They had been detained near Blois by the officiousness of the police attending the court of the Empress Louisa, and the blood of eight thousand brave men had overflowed the Mont Rave in consequence: nor did their arrival immediately put a stop to the war. When St. Simon, in pursuance of his mission, reached Soult's quarters on the 13th, that marshal, not without just cause, demurred to his authority, and proposed to suspend hostilities until authentic information could be obtained from the ministers of the emperor; then sending all his incumbrances by the canal to Carcassonne, he took a position of observation at Castelnaudary and awaited the progress of events. Wellington refused to accede to his proposal, and as General Loverdo, commanding at Montauban, had acknowledged the authority of the provincial government, he thought Soult designed to make a civil war, and therefore marched against him. The 17th the outposts were on the point of engaging, when the Duke of Dalmatia, having then received official information from the chief of the emperor's staff, notified his adhesion to the new state of affairs in France; with this honourable distinction, that he had faithfully sustained the cause of his great monarch until the very last moment.*

Lord Wellington immediately transmitted the intelligence to the troops at Bayonne. Too late. Misfortune and suffering had there fallen upon one of the brightest soldiers of the British army.

SALLY FROM BAYONNE.

During the progress of the main army in the interior, General Hope had conducted the investment of Bayonne with

---

* Soult has been foully and falsely accused of fighting at Toulouse, knowing that the war was over, and the slander was repeated by Lord Aberdeen in the House of Lords, when the Marshal was minister in France. The Duke of Wellington, with a generous warmth, instantly rose and truly declared that Soult did not know, and it was impossible he could know, of the Emperor's abdication when he fought the battle.

all the unremitting vigilance that difficult operation required. He had gathered gabions and fascines and platforms, and was ready to attack the citadel, when rumours of the events at Paris reached him, yet indirectly and without any official character to warrant a formal communication to the garrison: he made them known indeed at the outposts, but to such irregular communications, which might be intended to deceive, the governor naturally paid little attention. At this time the fortified posts at St. Etienne were held by a brigade of the fifth division; from thence to the extreme right the Guards had charge of the line, one company being in St. Etienne itself; Hinuber's German brigade was encamped as a support to the left; the remainder of the first division was in the rear.

In this state, about one o'clock in the morning of the 14th, a deserter gave General Hay, who commanded the outposts that night, an exact account of a projected sally; the general could not speak French, and sent him to Hinuber, who interpreted the man's story to Hay, put his own troops under arms, and transmitted the intelligence to Hope. It would appear that Hay, perhaps disbelieving the man's story, took no additional precautions, and it is probable neither the German brigade nor the reserves of the Guards would have been under arms but for Hinuber. However, at three o'clock, the French, commencing with a false attack on the left of the Adour as a blind, poured suddenly out of the citadel to the number of three thousand combatants; they surprised the picquets, and with loud shouts, breaking through the chain of posts at various points, carried with one rush the church and the village of St. Etienne, with exception of a fortified house defended by Captain Forster of the 38th. Masters of every other part, and overbearing all before them, they drove picquets and supports in heaps along the Peyrehorade road, killed General Hay, took Colonel Townsend of the Guards prisoner, divided the wings of the investing troops, and, passing in rear of the right, threw the whole line into confusion. Then it was that Hinuber, having his Germans in hand, moved up to Etienne, rallied some of the fifth division, and being joined by a battalion of Bradford's Portuguese, bravely gave the counter-stroke to the enemy and regained the village and church.

On the right the combat was still more disastrous. Neither picquets nor reserves could sustain the fury of the assault, and the battle was most confused and terrible; for on both sides the troops, broken into small bodies by the inclosures, and unable to recover their order, came dashing together in the darkness, fighting often with the bayonet;—and sometimes friends encountered, sometimes foes—all was tumult and horror. The guns of the citadel, vaguely guided by the flashes of the musketry, sent their shot and shells booming at random through the lines of fight, while some gun-boats, dropping down the river, opened their fire upon the flank of the supporting columns, which being put in motion by Hope on the first alarm were now coming up. One hundred pieces of artillery were thus in full play at once, the shells set fire to the fascine depots, and to several houses, the flames from which cast a horrid glare over the striving masses.

Amidst this confusion General Hope suddenly disappeared, none knew how or wherefore at the time. Afterwards it became known, that having brought up the reserves, he had pushed for St. Etienne by a hollow road behind the line of picquets; but the French were on both banks; he endeavoured to return, was wounded, and his horse, a large one, as was necessary to sustain the gigantic warrior, having received eight bullets fell on his leg. His staff had escaped from the defile, yet two of them, Captain Herries and Mr. Moore, nephew to Sir John Moore, returning, endeavoured to draw him from beneath the horse, but were both dangerously wounded and carried off with Hope, who was again badly hurt in the foot by an English bullet.

Light now beginning to break enabled the allies to act with more unity. The Germans were in possession of St. Etienne, the reserve brigades of the foot Guards, rallied in mass by General Howard, suddenly raised their shout, and running in upon the French drove them back to their works with such slaughter, that their own writers admit a loss of one general and more than nine hundred men. On the British side General Hay was killed, Stopford wounded, and the whole loss was eight hundred and thirty men and officers, of which more than two hundred, with the commander-in-chief, were taken. Captain Forster's firm defence of the fortified house first, and next the ready gallantry with which Hinuber's Germans retook St. Etienne, had staved off a very terrible disaster.

A few days after this piteous event the convention made with Soult became known and hostilities ceased.

All the French troops in the south were then reorganized in one body under Suchet, but so little inclined to acquiesce in the revolution, that Prince Polignac, acting for the duke of Angouleme, applied to the British commissary-general Kennedy, for a sum of money to quiet them.

The Portuguese soldiers returned to Portugal; the Spaniards to Spain; their generals, it is said, being inclined to declare for the Cortes against the king, but they were diverted from it by the influence of Lord Wellington.

The British infantry embarked at Bordeaux, some for America, some for England; the cavalry, marching through France, took shipping at Boulogne. Thus the war terminated, and with it all remembrance of the veterans' services.

Yet those veterans had won nineteen pitched battles and innumerable combats; had made or sustained ten sieges and taken four great fortresses; had twice expelled the French from Portugal, once from Spain; had penetrated France, and killed, wounded, or captured two hundred thousand enemies—leaving of their own number forty thousand dead, whose bones whiten the plains and mountains of the Peninsula.

THE END.

PRINTED BY HARLEQUIN PRESS
OBAN. ARGYLL